German Political Thought and the Discourse of Platonism

"This book is a genuine *tour de force*. Paul Bishop reads the tradition of German political thought through the prism of the allegory of the cave in Plato's Republic. His aim is not merely to re-contextualise and re-interpret, but to reveal the continued relevance of the history of ideas to our own time. In a series of penetrating interpretations ranging from Plato and Aristotle via Rousseau, Kant, Hegel, Marx, and Nietzsche to Heidegger, Adorno, and Habermas, he addresses the central challenges of modernity—such as the relation between the individual and society, the promises and pitfalls of economic development, and the role of the state. This is an original and engaging way into the intricacies of German thought. Supremely erudite yet invariably accessible, the book works on two levels: undergraduate students will be able to use it as a general introduction, while scholars will benefit from its interpretative subtleties and historical insights. *German Political Thought and the Discourse of Platonism* is one of the most fascinating philosophical studies I have read in a long time."

—Henk de Berg *is Professor of German at the University of Sheffield, UK, and co-editor of* Modern German Thought from Kant to Habermas *(2012)*

"Paul Bishop offers a stunning revision of political thinking via Plato and his continued presence in German philosophy. Plato's Cave is the famous allegory that depicts humans as doomed to remain prisoners deluded by shadows on the cave wall when their only hope of freedom is to focus on the mystical fire itself. In a powerful analysis of foundational dialogues with Plato from Aristotle and Rousseau to moderns such as Nietzsche, Marx, the Frankfurt School and Habermas, Bishop offers a compelling argument about the nature of politics in the twenty-first century. Do we build societies based upon the revolutionary potential of individual consciousness or must we provide an Ideal model after the example of Plato? Digging for the Platonic heart of the German philosophical heritage, *German Political Thought and the Discourse of Platonism* plots new routes into who we are and how we got here. This book is a must for political scientists, German scholars, philosophers and all who seek positive visions for a viable global future."

—Susan Rowland *is Chair of the Engaged Humanities and the Creative Life M.A. at Pacifica Graduate Institute, USA. Her recent book is* Remembering Dionysus *(2017)*

"Paul Bishop's new book takes us on an absorbing journey through the history of German political thought. Bishop's central premise is that the discourse of Platonism provides a gateway to understanding the connections between thinkers ranging from Kant to Habermas. With clarity and concision, Bishop brings the reader to a deeper comprehension of the German engagement with Platonism. This book will appeal to anyone interested in the continuity of German thought and its observations on fundamental questions regarding human interaction with the world."

—James M. Skidmore *is Associate Professor of German Studies and Director of the Waterloo Centre for German Studies at the University of Waterloo, Canada*

Paul Bishop

German Political Thought and the Discourse of Platonism

Finding the Way Out of the Cave

palgrave
macmillan

Paul Bishop
School of Modern Languages and Cultures
University of Glasgow
Glasgow, UK

ISBN 978-3-030-04509-8   ISBN 978-3-030-04510-4   (eBook)
https://doi.org/10.1007/978-3-030-04510-4

Library of Congress Control Number: 2018962021

Cover image: © Plato's Cave 122cm × 183cm Oil on Canvas by Lalita Hamill

This Palgrave Macmillan imprint is published by the registered company Springer Nature Switzerland AG
The registered company address is: Gewerbestrasse 11, 6330 Cham, Switzerland

Those who do not move do not notice their chains. ~
(Rosa Luxemburg, attrib.)

*It is easier to perceive error than to find truth, for the former
lies on the surface and is easily seen, while the latter lies
in the depth, where few are willing to search for it.* ~
(Johann Wolfgang von Goethe, MuR, §166)

*The more people chant about their freedom and now free they are,
The more loudly I hear their chains rattling.* ~
(George Orwell, attrib.)

Preface

In the centre of Glasgow it is a short distance from Central Station to the River Clyde and the several bridges that span it for the use of traffic, for trains, or for pedestrians. Glasgow Bridge (or Jamaica Street Bridge) was built between 1895 and 1899, replacing an earlier seven-arched bridge that had been built in classical style by Thomas Telford in 1833 (itself a replacement for a yet earlier bridge built in 1772) but had subsequently proved to be too narrow and too shallow. From Glasgow Bridge one can see the remains of another bridge, since disappeared: the first Caledonian Railway Bridge, built between 1876 and 1878. This wrought iron bridge carried four tracks, supported on giant cast iron cylinders sunk to the bedrock—all filled with concrete, and extended above the riverbed with great pillars of Dalbeattie granite.[1] These massive pillars, now redundant, bear the following inscriptions in Greek and English:

ΤΑ ΓΑΡ ΔΗ ΜΕΓΑΛΑ
ΠΑΝΤΑ ΕΠΙΣΦΑΛΗ ΚΑΙ ΤΟ
ΛΕΓΟΜΕΝΟΝ ΤΑ ΚΑΛΑ
ΤΩΙ ΟΝΤΙ ΧΑΛΕΠΑ

ALL GREATNESS
STANDS FIRM IN
THE STORM

It is tempting to read these inscriptions as a typical Neoclassical Victorian statement of confidence in the industrial future of Glasgow, but in fact these inscriptions are much more recent. In 1990, the artist Ian Hamilton Finlay won a commission from a project organised by Television South West Arts entitled *New Works for Different Places: TWSA Four Cities Project* (the cities in question being Derry, Glasgow, Newcastle, and Plymouth). Ian Hamilton Finlay's design for a work of public art in Glasgow involved inscribing the words now found on these pillars, but what does the quotation mean?

The phrase is, in fact, a quotation from book 6 of Plato's *Republic*, based on the translation into German made by the German philosopher, Martin Heidegger (1889–1976). It can be found in the concluding paragraphs of his Rectoral Address, made in 1933 to the University of Freiburg, and it is a problematic translation in what is widely regarded as a controversial speech. Leaving aside (for now) the controversy surrounding Heidegger's address, the original Greek, τὰ γὰρ δὴ μεγάλα πάντα ἐπισφαλῆ, καὶ τὸ λεγόμενον τὰ καλὰ τῷ ὄντι χαλεπά, could also be translated as "for all great things are precarious, and, as the proverb truly says, 'fine things are hard.'" In some respects, the English version seems (as Lairich Rig has pointed out) directly contrary to the meaning of Plato's statement, for the English translation says that great things endure, while the Greek text says that great things are hard to achieve, emphasizing instead their instability and their impermanence (ἐπισφαλής: "prone to fall, unstable, precarious"; Liddell & Scott, 9 edn.]).

Few people crossing the bridge seem to notice the quotations (although maybe the members of the short-lived Glasgow rock band, Midnight Lion, did; see their 2011 song, "All Greatness Stands Firm"). Yet these inscriptions, as recent as they are, serve as a reminder of the persistence of Platonic thought which, like the pair of granite pillars, stands strong—even if it is not regarded, like the pillars, as any longer fulfilling a useful function. Although this is not a book about Glasgow, but about German Political Thought, Ian Hamilton Findlay's choice for his inscription of a quotation from Plato, following the translation made by Heidegger, provides us with a suitable symbol for the surprising presence of the *Republic* in the hustle and bustle of a great city as, in the background, the trains trundle noisily over the second Caledonian Railway Bridge into and out of Central Station; and maybe it might prompt us to ponder the truth or otherwise of Plato's assertion—however one chooses to translate it.

While the central theme of this volume may at first sight appear obscure, or even quirky, this book has been written in the conviction that it is neither of these things (however inadequate its treatment in the following pages may be) but in fact of major significance. For we live in a time when the focus on all things German—the enduring successfulness of the German economy, the role of German economic policy in determining the fate of the euro zone, the German response to the refugee crisis—keeps growing by the day. On 25 July 2014 the magazine *Newsweek* placed on its title cover the following slogan: "Spot a problem. Analyse it. Solve it. Welcome to the German Century," while inside Rose Jacobs wrote a story entitled "On Top of the World: This Could Be the Start of a Century of German Success."[2] In an article published in the *Financial Times* on 20 June 2015, Simon Kuper argued that "we need German thinking."[3] And on 24 September 2015 *Time* magazine named Angela Merkel not just "Person of the Year" but also "Chancellor of the Free World." Even those who criticize Germany recognize its importance; witness the cover of the *New Statesman* of 25 June 2012 which depicted Merkel as a Terminator and described her as "Europe's most dangerous leader."[4] Since the election of President Trump, Merkel has come to be seen—despite domestic political problems—as more important than ever.

At the same time, this significance of the Germans is not something to be taken for granted: as became clear when putting together a book proposal for this title. According to one commissioning editor for a major university press, the subject of German Political Thought was going to be "too niche" for her list. Evidently, I disagree with this conclusion. To borrow a phrase from one of the articles mentioned above, we need to understand German thinking (which does not exclude us from understanding how other people, such as the French, also think...).[5] And a point of entry into the tradition of German Political Thought is one that is by no means foreign to us, for it can be found in the discourse of Platonism.

After all, there has long been a culture of engagement with the discourse of Platonism in the English-speaking world,[6] even if this engagement has, in more recent times, become attenuated. In the middle of the seventeeth century, a group of philosophers and theologians, known as the Cambridge Platonists because of their connections with the University of Cambridge, revived interest in the philosophical discourse of Platonism.[7] Among the Cambridge Platonists were such figures as Ralph Cudworth (1617–1688), the author of a study originally planned in three volumes, entitled *The True Intellectual System of the Universe* (1678; 3 vols, 1845),[8] and Henry More (1614–1687), the author of (among many other works) a *Manual of Ethics* (1666), the *Divine Dialogues* (1668), and a *Manual of Metaphysics* (1671). Other members of this group of thinkers were Benjamin Whichcote (1609–1683), John Smith (1618–1652), Peter Sterry (1613–1672), Nathaniel Culverwell (1619–1651), John Worthington (1618–1671), as well as Viscountess (Anne) Conway (1631–1679), George Rust (d. 1670), and John Norris (1657–1711).

In the eighteenth century, the London-born scholar Thomas Taylor (1758–1835) undertook an extensive programme of translating Platonic and Neoplatonic works. Taylor composed for himself the following motto: "No servile scribe am I, nor e'er shall be, / My sire is Mind, whose sons are always free," and his epitaph (again, written by himself) expresses the resilience of attitude with which he went to his grave: "Health, strength, and ease, and manhood's active age, / Freely I gave to Plato's sacred page. / With Truth's pure joys, with Fame my days were crown'd / Tho' Fortune adverse on my labours frown'd." As these lines hint, Taylor's life, personally as professionally, was not an easy one; yet, although he was mocked in his day and excluded from the academic establishment, and although the accuracy of his work has been questioned (but also defended), he proved to be instrumental in cultivating and nurturing an interest in the discourse of Platonism among such British writers as William Blake (1757–1827), Percy Bysshe

Shelley (1792–1822), and William Wordsworth (1770–1850),[9] as well as among such American Transcendentalist thinkers as Ralph Waldo Emerson (1803–1882), Amos Bronson Alcott (1799–1888), and G.R.S. Mead (1863–1933), that last of whom was to become the secretary to Helena Blavatsky (1831–1891), the founder of the Theosophical Society. Taylor was, in the phrase (borrowed from Empedocles) that has been applied to him, "an exile from the orb of light,"[10] but he helped carry the light of Platonism into the modern world.

Over and above the specific Platonic context of Idealism, the nineteenth century saw the establishment of a philosophical movement known as British Idealism, whose influence lasted into the twentieth century. Among the figures in the first generation of this movement were T.H. Green (1836–1882), F.H. Bradley (1846–1924), and Bernard Bosanquet (1848–1923), while a second wave of thinkers including J.M.E. McTaggart (1866–1925), H.H. Joachim (1868–1938), John Henry Muirhead (1855–1940), and R.G. Collingwood (1889–1943) carried it forward. Its last exponent was the philosopher Geoffrey Reginald Gilchrist Mure (1893–1979), whose career included serving as Warden of Merton College and as Pro-Vice Chancellor of the University of Oxford.[11]

There is a specifically Scottish (and even Glaswegian) dimension to this revival of interest in Idealism.[12] This dimension is embodied in such figures as Edward Caird (1835–1908), who held the Chair of Moral Philosophy at Glasgow, Alfred Edward Taylor (1869–1945), who held chairs in Moral Philosophy at the University of St. Andrews (1908–1024) and then at the University of Edinburgh (1924–1941), and James Hutchison Stirling (1820–1909), the author of a major work on Hegelian philosophy called *The Secret of Hegel* (1865), a book whose "rather terse translations of the *Logic*, with commentary in the style of [Thomas] Carlyle," made it "almost as impenetrable as Hegel himself."[13] So it would be wrong to think of the Idealist tradition as having died away in the course of time and having nothing to say to us today: the work of Terry Pinkard has helped clarify "the legacy of Idealism" for modern philosophy,[14] and a volume co-written by Jeremy Dunham, Iain Hamilton Grant, and Sean Watson argues persuasively for the Idealism as "a rich and untapped resource for contemporary philosophical arguments and concepts."[15]

As this title of James Hutchison Stirling's book—*The Secret of Hegel*—suggests, British Idealism was more influenced by German Idealism in general and Hegel in particular than it was by the discourse of Platonism.[16] Yet rather than examining the links between German and British Idealism, this study aims to uncover another tradition within German Thought itself—the discourse of Platonism. By this, I do not mean Platonism in the strict sense that it acquired specific German forms (as will be analysed by the contributions to the Brill Companion volume being assembled by Alan Kim),[17] and could thus be described as "German Platonism." Rather, we are using the discourse of Platonism to refer to a leitmotif that can serve as an Ariadne's thread through a complex labyrinth of political-theoretical texts, mainly (although, as we shall see, not entirely exclusively) written in German.

This book has arisen from a course offered to undergraduate students, and it seeks to offer the conclusions, arrived at while teaching it, to a wider audience. It does so, out of a sense there we still need to engage with both traditions: with the discourse of Platonism and with the problem of how—in terms of the famous allegory in book 7 of the *Republic*—we are to find our way out of the cave; and with the tradition of German Political Thought as a whole. The response of my students to this basic proposition has encouraged me to write this book as a summary of what, in our lectures and seminars, we have discovered together.

When going through the course approval process to introduce the course, its aim and outcomes were sent for comment to an external academic consultant. To my surprise, this senior academic suggested that there would be no use to students of business in studying the figures now discussed in this book: among whom are Marx, the Frankfurt School, and Habermas. Can it really be the case that these figures have nothing to say to us? (Now it is true that, outside the arts and humanities seminar room, Marx has largely been regarded as having an ever decreasing explanatory value. Yet in May 2013, the former Greek Finance Minister Yanis Varoufakis, in his address to the 6th Subversive Festival in Zagreb, explained why he believes Marx must "remain central to our analysis of capitalism," even if he insisted "we should remain 'erratic' in our Marxism.")[18] Later on, the same academic consultant also queried the use of the term "the good life," apparently without realizing that this term, originally associated with Aristotle, has remained a philosophical constant for centuries—indeed, millennia.[19] Have we, even or precisely at the highest levels of our educational system, become deaf to one of the key ideals of ancient Greek philosophy as well as to the insights of German Political Thought alike?

So while the idea of intellectual continuity has fallen out of fashion in the rush to embrace postmodernism, the notion of a persistence of discourse offers a way in which to reappraise a tradition which brings together some of the most fascinating philosophical and political theoretical texts ever written. How to approach them remains a challenge for the reader in the twenty-first century, coming to them as she or he will with all the distractions of the (social) media–driven (post)modern world. Yet given the importance of Germany for our current time, in a century which—if *Newsweek* is right—will belong to Germany, then it is not an idle exercise to try and understand the intellectual tradition of political thought that emanates from this country. To understand the Germans, we need to begin with the Greeks—and we shall have to mention the French (or, at least, the Swiss) as well ....

The choice of texts discussed in this volume has been hugely influenced by the selection made by the German philosopher Norbert Hoerster in a collection which became a classic of its kind, an anthology of political philosophical texts extracted from works by Plato, Aristotle, Cicero, Augustine, and Thomas Aquinas; by Machiavelli, Hobbes, and Locke; by Hume, Montesquieu, Rousseau, and Kant; by Hegel, Marx & Engels, and J.S. Mill.[20] Hoerster (b. 1937) taught philosophy of law and social philosophy at the University of Mainz, holding the Chair of Law and Social Philosophy until his retirement in 1998. Although he has become perhaps best known for his controversial views on bioethics and his strong defence of humanism, Hoerster became a name familiar to many German students of philosophy, and in this collection he achieved a powerful pedagogical tool that deserves to be better known in the English-speaking world.

In short, this study is an exercise in exploring a tradition. It should be noted how this notion of tradition is being used—*not* in the sense of a set of views that are (to use an expression deployed by Neil Kinnock in his leader's speech at the Labour conference in Bournemouth, 1985) "pickled" into "a rigid dogma, a code,"[21] but rather in the sense that "tradition" has been defined by Peter Kingsley—as "indicating something neither rigid nor fixed but fluid and accommodating," as "a kind of receptacle allowing for the pooling and absorbing of individual resources, so that new contributions transform the old until they are transformed in turn."[22]

Although I cannot match the scope of George Klosko's magisterial survey of political theory,[23] or the deftness of analysis offered by Grahame Lock in his audio course on Western political theory,[24] I nevertheless hope that readers might become interested in or even intrigued by the persistence in Western thought of the discourse of Platonism and consider for themselves what it might mean to find a way out of the cave.

Glasgow, UK   Paul Bishop

Notes

1. For information regarding the remains of the first Caledonian Railway Bridge and Ian Hamilton Finlay's inscriptions, I am indebted to the following sources: Elizabeth Williamson, Anne Riches, and Malcolm Higgs, *Glasgow* [*The Buildings of Scotland*] (London: Penguin, 1990), 622–623; Lairich Rig, "All Greatness Stands Firm in the Storm," available online http://www.geograph.org.uk/photo/1658814, accessed 19.4.2017; *Public Monuments & Sculpture Association*, National Recording Project, "All Greatness Stands Firm in the Storm," available online http://www.pmsa.org.uk/pmsa-database/2309/, accessed 19.4.2017; Sea Kayaking with seakyakphoto.com, available online http://seakayakphoto.blogspot.co.uk/2010/12/all-greatness-stands-firm-in-storm.html, accessed 19.4.2017.
2. Rose Jacob, "On Top of the World: This Could Be the Start of a Century of German Success," *Newsweek*, 25 July 2014.
3. Simon Kuper, "Why We Need German Thinking," *Financial Times*, Weekend Supplement: Life & Arts, 2.
4. Mehdi Hasan, "Angela Merkel's Mania for Austerity Is Destroying Europe," *New Statesman*, 25 June 2012.
5. Sudhir Hazareesingh, *How the French Think: An Affectionate Portrait of an Intellectual People* (London: Allen Lane, 2015).

6. John H. Muirhead, *The Platonic Tradition in Anglo-Saxon Philosophy: Studies in the History of Idealism in England and America* (London and New York: Allen & Unwin and Macmillan, 1931).

7. C.A. Patrides (ed.), *The Cambridge Platonists* (Cambridge: Cambridge University Press, 1980).

8. Ralph Cudworth, *The True Intellectual System of the Universe: Wherein All the Reason and Philosophy of Atheism Is Confuted, and Its Impossibility Demonstrated, with a Treatise Concerning Eternal and Immutable Morality*, 3 vols (London: Thomas Tegg, 1845).

9. For further discussion, see Anna Baldwin and Sarah Hutton (eds), *Platonism and the English Imagination* (Cambridge: Cambridge University Press, 2005).

10. See "Synopsis of the Pagan Creed," §20, in "On the Theology of the Greeks" [1820], in Thomas Taylor (trans.), *Collected Writings on the Gods and the World* [Thomas Taylor Series, vol. 4] (Sturminster Newton, Dorset: Prometheus Trust, 2006), 185–213 (211); originally §21 in "The Creed of the Platonic Philosophers," in "The Life and Works of Thomas Taylor, the Platonist (Concluded)," in *The Platonist* 1, nos. 11 and 12 (December 1881–January 1882), 179–187 (184–186, esp. 186).

11. See David Boucher (ed.), *The British Idealists* (Cambridge: Cambridge University Press, 1997).

12. See David Boucher (ed.), *The Scottish Idealists: Selected Philosophical Writings* (Exeter and Charlottesville, VA: Imprint Academic, 2004).

13. David Boucher, "The Scottish Contribution to British Idealism and the Reception of Hegel," in Gordon Graham (ed.), *Scottish Philosophy in the Nineteenth and Twentieth Centuries* (Oxford: Oxford University Press, 2015), 154–181 (p. 163). See James Hutchison Stirling, *The Secret of Hegel: Being the Hegelian System in Origin, Principle, Form and Matter* (London: Longman, Green, Longman, Roberts, & Green, 1865).

14. Terry Pinkard, *German Philosophy 1760–1860: The Legacy of Idealism* (Cambridge: Cambridge University Press, 2002).

15. Jeremy Dunham, Iain Hamilton Grant, Sean Watson, *Idealism: The History of a Philosophy* [2011] (Abingdon and New York: Routledge, 2014).

16. For an introduction to the thinking of German Idealism, see Rüdiger Bubner, *German Idealist Philosophy* (Harmondsworth: Penguin, 1997);

translated from Rüdiger Bubner, *Deutscher Idealismus* [*Geschichte der Philosophie in Text und Darstellung*, vol. 6] (Stuttgart: Reclam, 1978). And for further discussion, see Karl Ameriks (ed.), *The Cambridge Companion to German Idealism* (Cambridge and New York: Cambridge University Press, 2000); Matthew C. Altman, *The Palgrave Handbook of German Idealism* (Houndmills, Basingstoke, and New York: Palgrave Macmillan, 2014).

17. Alan Kim (ed.), *Brill's Companion to German Platonism* (Leiden and Boston: Brill, forthcoming).

18. Yanis Varoufakis, "Confessions of an Erratic Marxist in the Midst of a Repugnant European Crisis," available online https://yanisvaroufakis. eu/2013/12/10/confessions-of-an-erratic-marxist-in-the-midst-of-a-re-pugnant-european-crisis/, accessed 02.08.2016.

19. See William B. Irvine, *A Guide to the Good Life: The Ancient Art of Stoic Joy* (Oxford and New York: Oxford University Press, 2009); Bettany Hughes, *The Hemlock Cup: Socrates, Athens and the Search for the Good Life* (London: Jonathan Cape, 2010); John Cottingham, *Philosophy and the Good Life: Reason and the Passions in Greek, Cartesian and Psychoanalytic Ethics* (Cambridge: Cambridge University Press, 1998).

20. Norbert Hoerster (ed.), *Klassische Texte der Staatsphilosophie* [1947] (Munich: dtv, 2011).

21. Neil Kinnock, Labour Party Conference Speech, 11 October 1985. A commentary on this speech, published on the British Political Speech website, notes that parts of Kinnock's speech, such as its remark about "the grotesque chaos of a Labour council—a Labour council—hiring taxis to scuttle round a city handing out redundancy notices to its own workers," exemplifies Aristotle's principle in his *Rhetoric*, book 3, that metaphor can set something "more intimately before our eyes" (1405b; Aristotle, *Complete Works*, ed. Jonathan Barnes, 2 vols (Princeton, NJ: Princeton University Press, 1984), vol. 2, p. 2241). For an example of a static approach to the notion of tradition, see T.J. Reed, *Thomas Mann: The Uses of Tradition* (Oxford: Clarendon Press, 1974).

22. Peter Kingsley, *Ancient Philosophy, Mystery, and Magic: Empedocles and Pythagorean Tradition* (Oxford: Clarendon Press, 1995), 160.

23. George Klosko, *History of Political Theory: An Introduction*, vol. 1, *Ancient and Medieval*, vol. 2, *Modern*, 2nd edn (Oxford: Oxford University Press, 2012–2013).

24. Grahame Lock, *Political Philosophy: An Audio Course on Western Political Theory* (Gouderak: Home Academy, 2016).

Acknowledgements

I should like to acknowledge the help and support received when writing this book from the students who participated in the course on German Political Thought in the autumn semester of 2014 and in subsequent years; from the feedback and suggestions for extension and improvement of the original proposal of this book given by two anonymous reviewers for Palgrave Macmillan; from the Commissioning Editor at Palgrave Macmillan, Esme Chapman, and her Editorial Assistant, Chloe Fitzsimmons; and from Assistant Editor at Palgrave Macmillan, Beth Farrow. And, as always, from Helen Bridge, without whom I would not know that the political is also the personal.

A Note on Gender Inclusive Language

Throughout this book I have, where possible, used gender inclusive language; where translations used do not use gender inclusive language, the reader is invited to update the term "man" and associated pronouns and possessives to include women, men, and transgender individuals, however they identify.

Contents

List of Figures

1

What Is Politics?

Before we embark on our exploration of the tradition of German Political Thought, we should ask ourselves a fundamental question: what *is* politics? In conversation, we use the term very loosely: it can refer to party politics ("do I vote Labour or Conservative? SNP or Ukip?"), to global issues ("who will be the next President of America?"), or closer to home (and often more insidiously) to what is going on at work—"office politics" ("who moved my cheese?"). Yet the origin of the term is far more circumscribed and precise.[1]

For the word "politics" derives from the ancient Greek word *polites*, meaning "a citizen of the *polis*," that is, of the city state. Those matters which were of concern to all citizens of a city and which, as a result, required a communal decision in order to resolve them, were called *ta politika*. Correspondingly, the conduct of the process whereby communal decisions were arrived at was called *politike techne*. In other words, politics originally had a precise, limited meaning: the conduct of politics took place in public, it was a privilege of all free citizens (and so, not of slaves) to participate in it, and it concerned itself exclusively with matters of public interest.

© The Author(s) 2019
P. Bishop, *German Political Thought and the Discourse of Platonism*,
https://doi.org/10.1007/978-3-030-04510-4_1

In the intervening centuries—indeed, millennia—the sphere of politics has broadened, as the public sphere itself has expanded and become more diverse. Alongside the spheres of economics (the world of business and commerce) and of society (the world of family, friends, neighbours, and fellow citizens), the sphere of politics has expanded and become increasingly entangled with those other spheres. (Can politicians create jobs? How much money should private financial concerns give to political parties? Then again, what is the private and what is the public sphere? Is it a purely private matter if a man hits or psychologically abuses his wife? Or she him?) As a result, the clear division found in antiquity between private and public, between economics and politics, has blurred to the point of almost disappearing completely.

We should also examine the origin of another word we shall be using: "theory." For the political thought we shall be examining in this volume could also be described as "Political Theory," a major division of academic activity, particularly in universities in the United States. Again, the original meaning of the word "theory" is perhaps slightly different from what we might expect, especially given the disdain displayed toward theory rather than practice ("that question is purely theoretical") or the virtual hijacking of the term by literary theory (an approach to textual analysis that has broadened into cultural studies and often refers to itself simply as "Theory"). For the term derives from the Greek word *theoria*, meaning "sight" or "vision." Essentially a contemplative act or activity, it refers to a kind of mental (or even spiritual) contemplation as opposed to practical actions (that is, *praxis*). Today, we use the term "theory" more broadly to refer to any systematic, scientific attempt to develop a coherent explanation about an aspect of reality; whether the goal of this attempt is to *explain*, or to *control*, that reality, remains an open question. In the case of Plato especially, however, it is helpful to recall this primary meaning of theory.

We can turn to two twentieth-century thinkers in the German tradition for further explanation as to what politics involves. To use a term found in the work of the German Neo-Kantian philosopher Ernst Cassirer (1874–1945), we could describe politics as a reflection of the fact that humankind is an *animal symbolicum*, i.e., a "symbolic animal."[2] In the sense that Cassirer uses this term, he means that human beings, unlike other animals, inhabit a universe that is symbolic: that is to say, we inhabit a system that goes beyond the immediate present and physical contingency to develop a historical perspective, an ability to plan for the future and—ultimately—a sense of self. Writing in the 1940s, Cassirer—a German Jew who found himself in exile in the USA—was well aware of the problems of the contemporary politics of his age, which he discusses in *The Myth of the State* (1946).[3] Nevertheless, there is good reason to extend the list of different kinds of symbolic form with which Cassirer provides us in his philosophical masterpiece, the *Philosophy of Symbolic Forms* (1923–1929)—language, myth, and knowledge (or scientific cognition)—and in his *Essay on Man* (1944)—myth and religion, language, history, and science—by adding "politics," for it conforms exactly to the sense Cassirer gives to the term "symbolic form." In 1921 Cassirer defined "symbolic form" as follows: "Under a 'symbolic form' should be understood every energy of mind [*Energie des Geistes*] through which a mental content of meaning [*geistiger Bedeutungsgehalt*] is connected to a concrete, sensory sign [*konkretes sinnliches Zeichen*] and made to adhere internally to it."[4] Or as Cassirer put it in *Language and Myth* (1946): symbols are not "mere figures which refer to some given reality by means of suggestion and allegorical renderings" but "forces, each of which produces and posits a world of its own," and thus "the special symbolic forms"—such as myth, art, language, and science—"are not imitations, but *organs* of reality, since it is solely by their agency that anything real becomes an object for intellectual apprehension, and such is made visible to us."[5] And understood in this sense, it is possible to talk about law as a symbolic form and to locate the heart of Cassirer's thinking in the politics of the just individual.[6] In the sense that Cassirer and others use the term, we could think of "politics" as a symbolic form as well.

At the same time, the German sociologist Max Weber (1864–1920) provides us with some more concrete definitions of the political. In a famous lecture, the second of a series given to a students' political union in Munich in 1919 (during the German November Revolution in the wake of the country's defeat in the First World War), Weber defined for his audience what he understood by "Politics as Vocation":

What do we understand by politics? The concept is extremely broad and comprises any kind of *independent* leadership in action. One speaks of the currency policy of the banks, of the discounting policy of the Reichsbank, of the strike policy of a trade union; one may speak of the educational policy of a municipality or a township, of the policy of the president of a voluntary association, and, finally, even of the policy of a prudent wife who seeks to guide her husband. Tonight, our reflections are, of course, not based upon such a broad concept. We wish to understand by politics only the leadership, or the influencing of the leadership, of a *political* association, hence today, of a *state*.[7]

For Weber, the question of politics inevitably involves the question of power, including its expression as physical force (and, in this sense, as "violence"):

"Every state is founded on force," said Trotsky at Brest-Litovsk.[8] That is indeed right. If no social institutions existed which knew the use of violence, then the concept of "state" would be eliminated, and a condition would emerge that could be designated as "anarchy," in the specific sense of this word. Of course, force is certainly not the normal or the only means of the state — nobody says that — but force is a means specific to the state. Today the relation between the state and violence is an especially intimate one. In the past, the most varied institutions — beginning with the sib[9] — have known the use of physical force as quite normal. Today, however, we have to say that a state is a human community that (successfully) claims the *monopoly of the legitimate use of physical force* within a given territory. Note that "territory" is one of the characteristics of the state. Specifically, at the present time, the right to use physical force is ascribed to other institutions or to individuals only to the extent to which the state permits it. The state is considered the sole source of the "right" to use violence. Hence, "politics" for us means striving to share power or striving to influence the distribution of power, either among states or among groups within a state.

This corresponds essentially to ordinary usage. When a question is said to be a "political" question, when a cabinet minister or an official is said to be a "political" official, or when a decision is said to be "politically" determined, what is always meant is that interests in the distribution, maintenance, or transfer of power are decisive for answering the questions and determining the decision or the official's sphere of activity. He who is active in politics strives for power either as a means in serving other aims, ideal or egoistic, or as "power for power's sake," that is, in order to enjoy the prestige-feeling that power gives.[10]

Now this definition of politics in terms of *power* stands at variance with other definitions given by thinkers, both within and outside the German tradition. For Plato, the question of politics as he examines it in the *Republic* is essentially a question about the nature of justice. For Aristotle, the question of politics is how a political community can become a community with ethical integrity, one that embodies the aim of achieving the "good life." Or for the English philosopher John Locke (1632–1704), the power of the state is limited by the inherent rights of those human beings whose protection and security the state is meant to serve and guarantee.

The diversity of the principles underlying political thought can be illustrated by comparing two major documents that embody a set of political principles. First of all, think of the American Declaration of Independence, composed by Thomas Jefferson and published in 1776:

We hold these Truths to be self-evident, that all Men are created equal, that they are endowed by their Creator with certain unalienable Rights, that among these are Life, Liberty and the pursuit of Happiness — That to secure these Rights, Governments are instituted among Men, deriving their just Powers from the Consent of the Governed, that whenever any Form of Government becomes destructive of these Ends, it is the Right of the People to alter or to abolish it, and to institute new Government, laying its foundation on such Principles, and organizing its Powers in such Form, as to them shall seem most likely to effect their Safety and Happiness.[11]

While the founding text of American independence, this declaration also reflects the ideals and values of the European Enlightenment, not least its emphasis, along with "life" and "liberty," on "happiness" (or, at any rate, the "pursuit" of it). As a statement it is bold, self-confident; indeed, almost utopian.

By contrast, a second foundational political text, the "Basic Law" (or *Grundgesetz*) of the Constitution of the Federal Republic of Germany, strikes a very different note. At the outset of its 146 (!) articles, stand the following two sober statements:

1. Human dignity shall be inviolable. To respect and protect it shall be the duty of all state authority.
2. The German people therefore acknowledge inviolable and inalienable human rights as the basis of every community, of peace and of justice in the world.[12]

All too palpably, the bald statement of these noble principles reminds us, by the mere fact that they need saying at all, that the tradition of political thought had, in the twentieth century, led to appalling bloodshed and loss of life. At the same time, the document goes on to consider all kinds of details not mentioned in the American Declaration: how the federal budget is to be managed, for instance, or transport and telecommunications, or (in the post-unification updated version) the status of Berlin as the capital of the Federal Republic of Germany.

Equally, these two political documents also serve to remind us of two different ways of regarding politics. On the one hand, one can think of politics as about how to lead or to influence the government of a state. In any political system, this involves the question of the relationship between the people and its leadership; in some systems, between the masses and their leader. On the other, one can think of politics as a system that is trying to lead us, the people, to that seemingly most elusive of goals, peace. But how do we get there, if universal peace—a subject about which, in 1795, Immanuel Kant (1724–1804) could naively and unblushingly write an essay—[13] is indeed our goal?

In this respect, it is helpful to distinguish, as Dolf Sternberger (1907–1989) did, between three different kinds of political outlook, each associated with a particular thinker.[14] First, there is the "daimonological" approach, associated with the Italian Renaissance political theorist, Machiavelli. Even the name "Machiavelli," with its implications of skulduggery, deception, and deceit—which are, if one reads him carefully, unwarranted and unfair—tells us all we need to know about this view of politics. It regards politics as essentially about power, and especially the struggle for power; it sees human beings as pitted against each other in a relentless battle. Or, in the words of Francis Urquhart from the British TV series *House of Cards*: "Deeper than honour, deeper than pride, deeper than lust, deeper than love is the getting of it all. The seizing and the holding on. The jaw is locked, biting into power and hanging on. Biting and hanging on …".

Second, there as an approach that Sternberger calls "eschatological," in reference to the theological concept of the "last days" or the "end of the world." This approach is associated with St Augustine, whose treatise *The City of God* underpinned the medieval political outlook. According to this view, politics as the path to the attainment of perfect peace and justice necessarily involves a theological dimension, implying that while in *this* world, they might not (and, thanks to its fallen nature, probably will not) ever be attained, they *will* be—in the next world. On this account, politics can only take us so far on our journey; there is a promise of a "happy end," but not (in a literal sense) in our life time.

Third and finally, there is the "politological" approach. The model political thinker for this approach is Aristotle, who conceives of politics in eminently pragmatic terms. On this account, politics represents an attempt undertaken by free, equal, and rational citizens to reach a rational and peaceful agreement on their differences or on decisions to be taken. Today, this approach is associated with such thinkers as John Rawls (1921–2002) and Jürgen Habermas (b. 1929).

In short, Sternberger identifies three different kinds of answer to the question of the identity of the political. It is about power (the "daimonological" approach), or about salvation (the "eschatalological" approach), or about achieving consensus (the "politological" approach). But if there are different kinds of politics, there are different kinds of Political Theory too.

Indeed, there must inevitably be different kinds of Political Theory, because that Theory itself exists, not in a vacuum, but in a real, socio-political context. After all, there must be a reciprocal relationship between three different elements: (1) theoretical reflection, or the attempt, rationally and discursively, to understand what is happening; (2) what is actually happening, that is to say, political practice itself; and

(3) the developments in society which are driven by that reflection and that practice. If anything characterizes politics, it is its dynamic nature, and this dynamic takes place between theory, practice, and societal change, each of these three terms interacting with the other two.

Yet it is also the case that another approach to Political Theory sees its task in even more fundamental terms. On this account, the task of Political Theory is essentially to bring transparency to what is happening in the political sphere. In other words, it should investigate beyond (or beneath) the "tip of the iceberg," i.e., the "visible" themes, slogans, and headlines of the political world, in order to "uncover" the "hidden" structures or themes that inform them. While committed to bringing transparency, this approach risks turning into conspiracy theory, or an esoteric account of political developments of the kind one can find in interminable YouTube videos …

Perhaps the most important distinction to grasp when thinking about Political Theory is the difference between normative and empirical approaches. Both when considering older, historical examples of Political Theory as well as modern or contemporary ones, it is useful to ask oneself: is this Theory normative, i.e., concerning itself with questions about what *should be*, or empirical, i.e., concerning itself with questions about what *is*? Is it trying to articulate how people *should* behave in the political sphere, or is it trying to describe what they actually *do*? In the case of Aristotle or John Rawls, for instance, we are dealing with political theories that describe a norm or an ideal, how people *should* behave if they wish to be just. By contrast, in the work of Machiavelli or Max Weber, we are dealing with political theories that attempt to describe how, in their view, the political sphere actually *does* operate. (And if the political sphere is a dirty business, then—well, this will be reflected in the corresponding political theory.)

As we shall see, the question of whether a political thinker is taking a normative or an empirical approach is crucial to understanding the ambitions of the thinkers discussed in this volume. It underpins all subsequent attempts to classify political theory in terms of norms, principles, and concepts (such as theories of well-being, justice, or human rights; the notion of freedom, the concept of property, the problem of war and the goal of peace, as well as a theory of utopia); or in terms of the institutions and organisations of the state (the origins of the state, its different organs and means of expression, constitutional and legal theory, various aspects of what one could call political anthropology, not to mention the tricky question of the relationship between the citizen and the state); or in terms of a theory of democracy (the notion of the sovereignty of the people, the advantage and disadvantages of democracy as a political system, and criticism of it). As we shall see, democracy is by no means the favoured system among the political thinkers introduced in this volume, yet as one of its staunchest defenders, Winston Churchill, once said:

> Many forms of Government have been tried and will be tried in this world of sin and woe. No one pretends that democracy is perfect or all-wise. Indeed, it has been said that democracy is the worst form of Government except all those other forms that have been tried from time to time.[15]

Finally, one should remember that political thought has a curious habit leading one both into the real world and out of it again: into the smoke-filled backrooms where deals are made or debating chambers where passionate speeches are declaimed, but also into a consideration of the relationship between the self and the world.

At the conclusion of his essay entitled "'Objectivity' in Social Science and Social Policy," Weber wrote:

> All research in the cultural sciences in an age of specialization, once it is oriented towards a given subject matter through particular settings of problems and has established its methodological principles, will consider the analysis of the data as an end in itself. It will discontinue assessing the value of the individual facts in terms of their relationships to ultimate value ideas. Indeed, it will lose its awareness of its ultimate rootedness in the value-ideas in general. And it is well that should be so. But there comes a moment when the atmosphere changes. The significance of the unreflectively utilized viewpoints becomes uncertain and the road is lost in the twilight. The light of the great cultural problems moves on. Then science too prepares to change its standpoint and its thinking apparatus and to view the streams of events from the heights of thought.

It follows those stars which alone are able to give meaning and direction to its labors:

The newborn impulse fires my mind,
I hasten on, his beams eternal drinking,
The Day before me and the Night behind,
Above me Heaven unfurled, the floor of waves beneath me.
(Faust: Act I, Scene II)[16]

These magnificent lines from Goethe's *Faust*, with which Weber concludes his essay, come from the scene in Part One in which Faust, out walking with his assistant, Wagner, on Easter Day, sees the setting sun, and is fascinated by its rich hues. As we shall see, the image of the sun plays an important role in Plato's *Republic*, one of the key texts governing the argument of this analytical survey of German Political Thought in relation to the discourse of Platonism.

In the course of our discussion of the German tradition in political thought, we shall focus on the following five main themes:

- the relation between the individual and society
- the primacy of the economic
- our engagement with the material world
- the notion of the contract
- the function of the state

Using these five ideas as "benchmarks" for the thinkers discussed in the pages that follow will help illustrate both the specificities of the thought of each individual thinker as well as the common thread of concerns which, albeit in different ways and in varying degrees, runs through all of them. And the common thread which runs through them is the discourse of Platonism, centered on the famous allegory of the cave in Plato's *Republic*.

For the significance of Plato to recent and contemporary political thinking can only be described as massive. In the twentieth century, the political thought of Plato underwent a remarkable revival; if, indeed, it can ever be said to have truly died out. As we shall see, the translation of Plato from Greek into German was played an important role in the project of German Romanticism—or at least in the Romanticism of Friedrich Schlegel (1772–1829) and Friedrich Schleiermacher (1768–1834), as well as in the critical philosophy of Kant. As Alan Kim has shown, Plato and his notion of form served as important reference points for twentieth-century German philosophers, especially Paul Natorp (1854–1924) and Martin Heidegger (1889–1976).[17] Major works on Plato also appeared by such classical philologists as Paul Friedländer (1882–1968) and the celebrated classicist, Ulrich von Wilamowitz-Moellendorff (1848–1931).[18]

The first half of the twentieth century also saw new translations of Plato being made: of Plato's political writings by the social economist Wilhelm Andreae (1888–1962) in four volumes in 1925, covering the *Republic* (the text and commentary, vols. 1 and 2), *The Statesman* (vol. 3), and other political writings and letters (vol. 4)[19]; and by the economist Edgar Salin (1892–1974) in four volumes published in 1945 (the *Apology*, the *Crito*, and the *Phaedo*), in 1946 (the *Theaetetus*), in 1950 (the *Euthyphron*, the *Laches*, the *Charmides*, and the *Lysis*), and in 1952 (the *Symposium* and the *Phaedrus*).[20] Yet the reception of Plato in Germany in the twentieth century was by no means restricted to such professional academic figures, be they philosophers or classicists. For Plato played a significant role in the political and cultural thinking of the electric range of thinkers centred on the idiosyncratic figure of the Symbolist poet, Stefan George (1868–1933).[21]

Various members of what was known as the *George-Kreis* (or "George Circle") wrote studies of Plato; so many that, already in 1929, a study was published by Franz Josef Brecht (1899–1982) under the title *Platon und der George-Kreis*.[22] Survey articles of the early twentieth-century German interest in Plato were published by the psychiatrist and philosopher Kurt Hildebrandt (1881–1966) (see his "Plato for the Present" [1910][23] and "The New Image of Plato: Comments on Recent Literature" [1930/1931]),[24] who was a member of the Circle, and works by Circle members were considered sufficiently important to be treated by Hans-Georg Gadamer (1900–2002) alongside works by Friedländer (see above), Reinhardt (see below), and Werner Jaeger (1888–1961), a Plato scholar who went on to write the multivolume study, *Paideia:*

The Ideals of Greek Culture (1933–1937).[25] Among the writers and intellectuals of the George Circle who wrote on Plato, the following are the most important.

To begin with, a short study was published, in the publishing house of the journal edited by George called *Blätter für die Kunst*, by Heinrich Friedemann (1888–1915) under the title *Plato: His Form* (1914).[26] Friedemann, a teacher, had sent the manuscript of his study to one of George's collaborators, Friedrich Gundelfinger (known as Friedrich Gundolf) (1880–1931), in the summer of 1914, before being killed in action in the First World War in Masuria, a region then part of East Prussia and now in northern Poland.[27] Friedemann's work was greatly admired by George who, in conversation with Berthold Vallentin (1877–1933), declared that all subsequent books were based on Friedemann's and that consequently this book was "the most important."[28]

After the First World War, Edgar Salin published his *Habilitation* on the subject of Plato, entitled *Plato and the Greek Utopia* (1921).[29] Salin's study had very little to do with economics, and in some respects very little to do with intellectual history, using images and symbols (the sphere, the disc, and the surface; the temple, the ear of corn, and the grape) as the main vehicle for its argumentation. (In discussing interest rates, for instance, Salin claimed that "paying interest belongs, wherever it occurs, to linear or multidimensional time—in any strictly cyclical conception of time there is no place for it.")[30] A year later, Kurt Hildebrandt published his *Nietzsche's Contest with Socrates and Plato* (1922),[31] its title alluding to Nietzsche's earlier essay, "Homer's Contest" (1872). In 1927 and 1928, two major studies appeared, one by the economist Kurt Singer (1886–1962) entitled *Plato the Founder* (1927),[32] and the other by the classical philologist Julius Stenzel (1883–1935) entitled *Plato the Educator* (1928).[33] Although each book had a different emphasis—Singer presenting Plato as someone concerned "not with knowledge of the world nor escape from the world," but as "the shaping of a life of beauty" (p. 159), and Stenzel offering an intellectual portrait of Plato in a series, "The Great Educators," which included volumes on Pestalozzi (vol. 3), Rousseau (vol. 5), Fichte (vol. 11), and Herder, Schiller, and Goethe (vols. 9 and 10)—both were orientated around Plato's own account of his ambition as a Founder and an Educator as set out in his Seventh Letter (325e–326a).

In 1933, Kurt Hildebrandt—at the time, clinical director of a civic mental hospital in Berlin-Lichtenberg but soon to replace (in 1934) Julius Stenzel as the Chair of Philosophy at the Christian-Albrechts-Universität in Kiel—published *Plato: The Struggle of Spirit for Power* (1933).[34] Like other works by members of the George-Circle published by Bondi, this book bore a swastika signet on its cover and title page. Now the swastika had been used by the Circle long before its identification with National Socialism, but since Hildebrandt had joined the Party in the spring of 1933, its use signified the author's allegiance to Germany's new political rulers. (In fact, Hildebrandt's embrace of Nazi race theory and his intellectual trajectory in general become clear in the titles of such works as *Norm, Decadence, Decay in Relation to the Individual, the Race, the State* (1934; 1939). After the Second World War, his article "The Idea of War in Goethe, Hölderlin, Nietzsche" (1941) was banned in the Soviet Occupation Zone,[35] while the GDR banned his study of *Norm, Decadance, Decay.*) Lest the impression arise that the entire work of the Circle was compromised by the likes of Hildebrandt, it is worth recalling that the work one might describe as the final one in the Circle's reception of Plato was *Plato: Pictures and Testimonies* (1935) by the industrialist and journalist Robert Boehringer (1884–1974).[36] This work featured a series of new photographs of heads of Plato, together with archaeological descriptions of these busts. While the political views of the George-Circle undoubtedly underwent major shifts,[37] this is true of Plato reception in Germany in general.

For as the case of Kurt Hildebrandt makes clear, however, the reception of Plato in Germany in the twentieth century is, for obvious reasons, inseparable from political developments in this period. Thus the rise to power of National Socialism forms, in varying degrees, the background to some readings of Plato (and, indeed, of classical culture in general).[38] Even before the National Socialists took power, Plato was being mobilized for the purposes of eugenics and racial theory by, for instance, Hans F.K. Günther (1891–1968), the author of *Plato as a Protector of Life* (1928).[39] The passages in the *Republic* where Plato discusses selective breeding to produce a ruling class (see Book 5)

could all-too-easily be instrumentalized to promote Nazi eugen-
ics.[40] The extent of the appropriation of Plato for use in service of the
National Socialist cause is clear from an article such as "Plato as the
Educator of the German Individual" by Adolf Rusch (1883–1955),
a secondary-school teacher at the Mommsen-Gymnasium in Berlin-
Grunewald.[41] Aside from the disastrous misinterpretation of Plato
in the 1930s and 1940s in Germany, the influence of the discourse of
Platonism goes far deeper—as the present study will argue.

Significantly, the discussion of Platonism in the Anglo-Saxon
world in the twentieth century was shaped by German intellectuals
as well, especially those who had fled or chose to stay away from Nazi
Germany.[42] Arguably the most important of these is the American
political philosopher Leo Strauss (1899–1973), one of the leading figures in the Chicago School of political philosophy and one of the
most influential conservative political thinkers of the twentieth century. Strauss foregrounded the distinction between "exoteric" (or public) and "esoteric" (or secret) teaching, arguing in *Persecution and the
Art of Writing* (1952) that such philosophical figures as Maimonides,
Al-Farabi and pre-eminently (but by no means exclusively) Plato, write
in a disguised way, hiding their message within multiple layers of meaning and reference.[43] In *The City and the State* (1964), Strauss engaged
with Plato's *Republic* (as well as Aristotle's *Politics* and Thucydides's
Peloponnesian War) in a way that suggested not only early Greek
thought's political, but ultimately its religious, significance. "For what
is 'first for us'[44] is not the philosophic understanding of the city but
that understanding which is inherent in the city as such, in the pre-
philosophic city, according to which the city sees itself as subject and
subservient to the divine in the ordinary understanding of the divine
or looks up to it," Strauss remarks, before concluding that "[o]nly
by beginning at this point will we be open to the full impact of the
all-important question which is coeval with philosophy although the
philosophers do not frequently pronounce it — the question *quid sit
deus*," in other words, *what does God mean?*[45] In recent years, Strauss
has been hailed (or attacked) as the intellectual godfather of the
US-administration of George W. Bush, especially in respect of its policy toward Iraq and the decision taken in 2003 to invade that country.

(In particular, Paul Wolfowitz and Richard Perle have been mentioned in connection with a Straussian influence on the Bush administration.) Needless to say, the evidence for this connection is slim, yet it is telling that any connection of the kind has been made at all.[46]

Strauss disagreed strongly with the interpretations of Plato, especially the *Republic*, offered by Martin Heidegger (see Chapter 8) as well as by Karl Popper (1902–1994), a British political philosopher who had been born in Vienna. In *The Open Society and Its Enemies* (1945), Popper held Plato—and the tradition arising from him, especially Hegel and Marx—to be ultimately responsible for the rise of totalitarianism in the twentieth century.[47] Across its two volumes, *The Spell of Plato* and *The High Tide of Prophecy: Hegel, Marx, and the Aftermath*, Popper developed a critique, not just of Plato, but of historicism (the view according to which history unfolds according to universal laws), as well as a defence of liberal democracy, i.e., the "open society." In its turn, Popper's work sparked a vigorous debate, and the work inspired praise and furious criticism alike.[48] In 1993, the Hungarian-born business magnate George Soros founded the Open Society Foundations (OSF) to promote the legacy of Popper in the form of financial support for projects supporting public health, public education, and social justice initiatives (without, or so its critics argue, challenging the existing social order).

A different approach to the "openness" of the "open society" was taken by the American academic Allan Bloom (1930–1992). For as Bloom put it in *The Closing of the American Mind* (1987), the "openness" of relativism can be seen as leading, paradoxically, to a great "closing."[49] Bloom examined contemporary American rock music, personal (and especially erotic) relationships, and above all American education; viewing them from a Platonic (and Nietzschean) perspective, he contrasted them unfavourably with the rigour and discipline of a Platonic training of the mind and body. What did Plato mean to show, he asked, by "the image of the cave in the *Republic*" and by "representing us as prisoners in it"? Bloom's answer was that "a culture is a cave," and Plato "did not suggest going around to other cultures as a solution to the limitations of the cave" (38). Indeed, Bloom argued that "the very term Enlightenment is connected with Plato's most powerful image about the relation between thinker and society, the cave" (264). Access to this Platonic tradition is facilitated by Bloom's excellent translation and interpretative essay on the *Republic*, published in 1968.[50]

So if, on the one hand, some (pre-eminently Popper) have tried to argue that Plato's authoritarian outlook leads directly to totalitarianism, others (such as John Wild in *Plato's Theory of Man* [1946] and *Plato's Modern Enemies and the Theory of Natural Law* [1953], or Leo Strauss in *What Is Political Philosophy? and Other Studies* [1959]) offer an entirely different view: namely, that totalitarianism is precisely a product of modern philosophy's revolt against the tradition of classical philosophy, represented by Plato. For, insofar as modern philosophy encourages relativism, materialism, historicism, and positivism, all these things "eventually provide totalitarianism with a good springboard."[51] The fact that, in the homily at the pre-conclave Mass before he was elected pope, Joseph Ratzinger/Benedict XVI used the combative phrase about "a dictatorship of relativism," shows that, in the twenty-first century, this issue is one that is not going away.[52] More recently, in the wake of the British referendum on the UK's membership of the EU and the election in the US of President Trump, the adjective "post-truth" has been used to describe the state of political culture in the Western world.

Finally, it is worth mentioning that a highly specific form of late twentieth-century Platonic revival has been taking place, albeit outside the academic-philosophical mainstream. In the UK, the Prometheus Trust was founded in 1986 to promote, in its own words, "the advancement of [...] a comprehensive and liberal education for the development of self-determined, rational, integral and versatile individuals." The name of the Trust is an allusion to a passage in Pausanias's *Description of Greece* (book 1, §30), which records that "in the [Platonic] Academy is an altar to Prometheus and from it they run to the city carrying burning torches."[53] A core part of the Trust's work consisted in bringing out a complete edition of the published translations of Thomas Taylor (1758–1835), the so-called "English Platonist," publishing a series of Late Platonic texts, and organising annual conferences and other events. Ten years earlier, on the West Coast of the USA the Noetic Society was founded in 1976 by Pierre Grimes, who had studied for his doctorate at the University of Pacifica's American Academy of Asian Studies, become a Lecturer in Comparative Philosophy at the Institute of Integral Studies, and gone on to teach philosophy for many years at Goldenwest College. From 1986, as Director of the Philosophical Midwifery Program at the Academy for Philosophical Midwifery, Grimes sought to revive the tradition of "Socratic midwifery" and, from 1995 to 1999, he regularly gave lectures at the Philosophical Research Society in Los Angeles, CA, on the subject of Wisdom Literature in the Platonic Tradition.[54] If Grimes's approach to Plato as a form of yoga strikes one as far-fetched, one might remember that Leo Strauss saw us, the moderns, as dwelling in a second (artificial) cave beneath the first (natural) cave; regarded revelation as the source of this "cave beneath the cave"; and implied that Christianity, through its confusion of philosophy and revelation (as well as much else), was a cave beneath the cave beneath the cave.[55] In *Persecution and the Art of Writing*, Strauss extended Plato's cave metaphor in the *Republic* in a new and startling way:

> People may become so frightened of the ascent to the light of the sun, and so desirous of making that ascent utterly impossible to any of their descendants, that they dig a deep pit beneath the cave in which they were born, and withdraw into that pit. If one of the descendants desired to ascend to the light of the sun, he would first have to try to reach the level of the natural cave, and he would have to invent new and and most artificial tools unknown and unnecessary to those who dwelt in the natural cave. He would be a fool, he would never see the light of the sun, he would lose the last vestige of the memory of the sun, if he perversely thought that by inventing his new tools he had progressed beyond the ancestral cave-dwellers.[56]

Before we have even begun our examination of the discourse of Platonism in relation to German Political Thought, a terrible kind of *mise en abîme* has opened up, the prospect of an infinite number of caves, each further away from the idea of the Good that, as we shall see, animates Plato's conception of politics. Can we ever get of the cave? And, if we did, then—recalling the injunction made by Socrates to Glaucon (*Republic*, 519 c–d and 520 b–c)—would we ever be able to find the way back…?

So where or how are we to locate Plato: as a political thinker? as a metaphysical philosopher? or as a spiritual guru? While the emphasis of this present volume is firmly on Plato's contribution to political theory (and, specifically, the tradition of German Political Thought), one of the most fascinating aspects of his reception in the German-speaking world has been the way in which the door has been kept open to all of these and many other possibilities, raising in turn a fundamental political question: does social change begin with society as a whole or with the individual? From the top, down—or from the bottom, up? And if, as Plato argues in the *Republic*, to understand justice in the city we must compare it to justice in the individual soul (cf. *Republic*, 369 a–b),[57] what does this tell us about politics and about the city? And what does it tell us about the soul?

Notes

1. For further discussion, which shapes and informs the discussion of this chapter, see Christian Schwaabe, *Politische Theorie 1: Von Platon bis Locke*, 2nd edn (Paderborn: Fink, 2010), esp. 9–20; *Politische Theorie 2: Von Rousseau bis Rawls*, 3rd edn (Paderborn: Fink, 2013); see also Peri Roberts and Peter Sutch, *An Introduction to Political Thought: A Conceptual Toolkit*, 2nd edn (Edinburgh: Edinburgh University Press, 2012). For useful collections of primary texts in relation to political theory, see Michael Rosen and Jonathan Wolff, *Political Thought* (Oxford: Oxford University Press, 1999); Hans Maier and Horst Denzer (eds), *Klassiker des politischen Denkens*, vol. 1, *Von Plato bis Hobbes*, and vol. 2, *Von Locke bis Max Weber*, 3rd edn (Munich: Beck, 2007); Steven M. Cahn, *Political Philosophy: The Essential Texts* (New York and Oxford: Oxford University Press, 2015).
2. Ernst Cassirer, *An Essay on Man: An Introduction to the Philosophy of Culture* [1944] (New Haven and London: Yale University Press, 1972), 25–26.
3. Ernst Cassirer, *The Myth of the State* [1946] (New Haven and London: Yale University Press, 1974).
4. Ernst Cassirer, "Der Begriff der symbolischen Form im Aufbau der Geisteswissenschaften," in *Vorträge der Bibliothek Warburg*, 1921/1922;

reprinted in *Wesen und Wirkung des Symbolbegriffs* [1956] (Darmstadt: Wissenschaftliche Buchgesellschaft, 1969), 169–200 (175); translated in John Michael Krois, *Cassirer: Symbolic Forms and History* (New Haven and London: Yale University Press, 1987), 50.

5. Ernst Cassirer, *Language and Myth* [1946], trans. Susanne K. Langer (New York: Dover, 1953), 8.

6. Deniz Coskun, *Law as Symbolic Form: Ernst Cassirer and the Anthropocentric View of Law* (Dordrecht: Springer, 2007); Bertrand Vergely, *Cassirer: La Politique du juste* (Paris: Michalon, 1998).

7. Weber, "Politics as Vocation," in *From Max Weber: Essays in Sociology*, eds and trans. H.H. Gerth and C. Wright Mills (New York: Oxford University Press, 1946; revised edn, London and New York: Routledge, 2009), 77–128 (77).

8. The Treaty of Brest-Litovsk was signed on 3 March 1918 between the Bolshevik government of Soviet Russia and the so-called Central Powers (Germany, Austria-Hungary, Bulgaria, and Ottoman Empire), ceding Poland, the Baltic States, and Belarus to Germany and ending Russia' involvement in the First World War. As the People's Commissar for Foreign Affairs, Leon Trotsky (1879–1940) negotiated this peace treaty, regarded as unfavourable to Russia.

9. The sib is an anthropological term referring to a kinship group (cf. Middle and modern High German *Sippe*, deriving from Old English *sibb* and Old High German *sibbia*), as the OED explains.

10. Weber, "Politics as Vocation," 78.

11. "The Declaration of Independence" [1776], in *The Declaration of Independence & The Constitution of the United States* (New York: Bantam, 1998), 53–54.

12. *Basic Law for the Federal Republic of Germany* [1949], Article 1, clauses 1 and 2.

13. Kant, "Perpetual Peace: A Philosophical Sketch" [1795], in Hans Reiss (ed.) and H.B. Nisbet (trans.) *Political Writings* (Cambridge and New York: Cambridge University Press, 1970), 93–130.

14. Dolf Sternberger, *Drei Wurzeln der Politik*, 2 vols (Frankfurt am Main: Insel, 1978). For a visual representation of this approach, see Andreas Vierecke, Bernd Mayerhofer, and Franz Kohut, *dtv-Atlas Politik*, illus. Werner Wildermuth, 2nd edn (Munich: dtv, 2011), 10–11.

15. Winston Churchill, speech in the House of Commons (11 November 1947); in Winston S. Churchill, *His Complete Speeches, 1897–1963*, ed.

Robert Rhodes James, 8 vols (London: Chelsea House; Bowker, 1974), vol. 7, 7566. As Churchill went on to declare, "there is a broad feeling in our country that the people should rule, continuously rule, and that public opinion, expressed by all constitutional means, should shape, guide, and control the actions of Ministers who are their servants and not their masters."

16. Max Weber, "'Objectivity' in Social Science and Social Policy," in *On the Methodology of the Social Sciences*, ed. and trans. Edward A. Shils and Henry A. Finch (Glencoe, IL, 1949), 50–112 (112); cf. Weber, *Gesammelte Aufsätze zur Wissenschaftslehre* (Tübingen: Mohr (Siebeck), 1988), 146–214 (214).

17. Alan Kim, *Plato in Germany: Kant—Natorp—Heidegger* (Sankt Augustin: Academia-Verlag, 2010).

18. Paul Friedländer, *Platon*, vol. 1, *Eidos, Paideia, Dialogos*; vol. 2, *Die Platonischen Schriften* (Berlin: de Gruyter, 1928–1930; 3rd edn in 3 volumes, 1975) (volume 1 is available in English as Paul Friedländer, *Plato: An Introduction*, trans. Hans Meyerhoff (London: Routledge, 1958)); Ulrich von Wilamowitz-Moellendorff, *Platon*, vol. 1, *Leben und Werke*; vol. 2, *Beilagen und Textkritik* (Berlin: Weidmann, 1919; 2nd edn, 1920; 3rd edn, *Platon: Sein Leben und seine Werke*, rev. Bruno Snell, 1948).

19. Platon, *Staatsschriften*, ed. and trans. Wilhelm Andreae, 4 vols (Jena: Fischer, 1925) (vol. 1, *Der Staat: Vorwort, Text und Übersetzung*; vol. 2, *Der Staat: Einleitung und Erläuterungen*; vol. 3, *Der Staatsmann*; vol. 4, *Staatsschrifte/Briefe*).

20. Platon, *Apologie; Kriton; Phaidon*, trans. Edgar Salin (Basel: Schwabe, 1945); Platon, *Theaitet*, trans. Edgar Salin (Basel: Schwabe, 1946); Platon, *Euthyphron; Laches; Charmides; Lysis*, trans. Edgar Salin (Basel: Schwabe, 1950); Platon, *Gastmahl; Phaidros* (Basel: Schwabe, 1952).

21. For further discussion, see Stefan Rebenich, "'Dass ein strahl von Hellas auf uns fiel': Platon im George-Kreis," *George-Jahrbuch* 7 (2008–2009), 115–141; Melissa S. Lane, "The Platonic Politics of the George Circle: A Reconsideration," in Melissa S. Lane and Martin A. Ruehl (eds), *A Poet's Reich: Politics and Culture in the George Circle* (Rochester, NY: Camden House, 2011), 133–163. For discussion of the influence of Plato in relation to his biography and in relation to his subsequent reception, see Thomas Karlauf, *Stefan George: Die Entdeckung des Charisma* (Munich: Pantheon, 2008), 401–405; Ulrich Raulff, *Kreis*

ohne Meister: Stefan Georges Nachleben (Munich: dtv, 2012), 130–140 and Chapter 6, "Die platonische Provinz," 428–496.

22. Franz Josef Brecht, *Platon und der George-Kreis* (Leipzig: Dieterich, 1929).

23. Kurt Hildebrandt, "Plato für die Gegenwart," *Die Grenzboten* 69, no. 2 (1910), 449–455. In 1927, Werner Jaeger published an essay entitled "Plato's Role in the Construction of Greek Education"; see "Platos Stellung im Aufbau der griechischen Bildung," in Werner Jaeger, *Humanistische Reden und Vorträge*, 2nd edn (Berlin: de Gruyter, 1960), 117–157. See also Werner Jaeger, *Paideia: The Ideals of Greek Culture* [1933–1947], trans. Gilbert Highet [1939–1943], 3 vols (New York and Oxford: Oxford University Press, 1965–1986).

24. Kurt Hildebrandt, "Das neue Platon-Bild: Bemerkungen zur neueren Literatur," *Blätter für die deutsche Philosophe* 4 (1930/1931), 190–202.

25. Hans-Georg Gadamer, "Die neue Platoforschung" [1933], *Logos* 22 (1933), 63–79; reprinted in *Gesammelte Werke*, vol. 5, *Griechische Philosophie I* (Tübingen: Mohr (Siebeck), 1985), 212–229.

26. Heinrich Friedemann, *Platon: Seine Gestalt* (Berlin: Blätter für die Kunst, 1914).

27. *»Jüdisch, römisch, deutsch zugleich…«: Karl Wolfskehl: Briefwechsel aus Italien 1933–1938*, ed. Cornelia Blasberg (Hamburg: Luchterhand, 1993), 324.

28. Berthold Vallentin, *Gespräche mit Stefan George 1902–1931* (Amsterdam: Castrum Peregrini, 1967), 94. According to George, "the entire new engagement with Plato is influenced by this book and this book itself has only become possible because there has been the experience of the Platonic form in our time" (94). The starting-point of this conversation had been the publication by yet another writer on Plato, Karl Reinhardt's *Platons Mythen* (Bonn: Cohen, 1927). Reinhardt (1886–1958) was one of the leading Hellenists of the time, and was based for most of his career at the University of Frankfurt.

29. Edgar Salin, *Platon und die griechische Utopie* (Munich and Leipzig: Duncker & Humblot, 1921).

30. Salin, *Platon und die griechische Utopie*, 153. For an overview of the relationship between economists and the George Circle, see Korinna Schönhart, *Wissen und Visionen: Theorie und Politik der Ökonomen im Stefan George-Kreis* (Berlin: Akademie-Verlag, 2009).

31. Kurt Hildebrandt, *Nietzsches Wettkampf mit Sokrates und Plato* (Dresden: Sibyllen-Verlag, 1922).

32. Kurt Singer, *Platon der Gründer* (Munich: Beck, 1927). Singer's interest in Plato goes back to 1920, when he had published a lecture entitled "Plato and Greek Culture"; see Kurt Singer, *Platon und das Griechentum: Ein Vortrag* (Heidlberg: Weiss, 1920).

33. Julius Stenzel, *Platon der Erzieher* (Leipzig: Meiner, 1928).

34. Kurt Hildebrandt, *Platon: Der Kampf des Geistes um die Macht* (Berlin: Bondi, 1933).

35. Kurt Hildebrandt, "Die Idee des Krieges bei Goethe—Hölderlin—Nietzsche," in August Faust (ed.), *Das Bild des Krieges im deutschen Denken*, 2 vols (Stuttgart and Berlin: Kohlhammer, 1941), vol. 1, 371–409.

36. Robert Boehringer, *Platon: Bildnisse und Nachweise* (Breslau: Hirt, 1935); revised as *Homer, Platon* (Düsseldorf and Munich: Küpper, 1974), and *Der Genius des Abendlandes*, 3rd edn (Düsseldorf and Munich: Küpper, 1972).

37. See Kurt Weigand, "Von Nietzsche zu Platon: Wandlungen in der politischen Ethik des George-Kreises," in Eckhard Heftrich, Paul Gerhard Klussmann, and Hans Joachim Schrimpf (eds), *Stefan George-Kolloquium* (Cologne: Wienand, 1971), 67–99.

38. See Teresa Orozco, "Die Platon-Rezeption in Deutschland um 1933," in Ilse Korotin (ed.), *"Die besten Geister der Nation": Philosophie und Nationalsozialismus* (Vienna: Pictus, 1994), 141–185; Andrea D'Onofrio, "Die Antike im Spiegel der Blut-und-Boden Ideologie: Odal und die Deutung des Klassischen Altertums im Dritten Reich," *Storia della Storiografia* 42 (2002), 74–102.

39. Hans F.J. Günther, *Platon als Hüter des Lebens: Platons Zucht- und Erziehungsgedanken und deren Bedeutung für die Gegenwart* (Munich: Lehmanns, 1928; 2nd edn, 1936; 3rd edn, Pähl: von Bebenburg, 1966).

40. For further discussion, see François-Xavier Ajavon, "L'étrange et inquiétant Platon de Hans F.K. Günther: Un exemple d'appropriation idéologique de la pensée grecque," *Laval théologique et philosophique* 62, no. 2 (2006), 267–284; David J. Galton, "Greek Theories on Eugenics," *Journal of Medical Ethics* 24 (1998), 263–267.

41. Adolf Rusch, "Plato als Erzieher zum deutschen Menschen," in *Humanistische Bildung im nationalsozialistischen Staate* (Leipzig and Berlin: Teubner, 1933), 44–49.

42. For an overview, see Kyriakos N. Demetriou, "A 'Legend' in Crisis: The Debate over Plato's Politics, 1930–1960," *Polis* 19, nos. 1–2 (2002), 61–91.

43. George Klosko, "The 'Straussian' Interpretation of Plato's *Republic*," *History of Political Thought* 7, no. 2 (Summer 1986), 275–293.

44. For the notion of "first for us," see Strauss's earlier remarks in this work: "[…] [T]he things which are 'first in themselves' are somehow 'first for us'; the things which are 'first in themselves' are in a manner, but necessarily, revealed in men's opinions," and "[t]he highest opinions, the authoritative opinions, are the pronouncements of the law," which "makes manifest the just and noble things and […] speaks authoritatively about the highest things, the gods who dwell in heaven" (Strauss, *The City and Man* (Chicago and London: University of Chicago Press, 1964), 19–20).

45. Strauss, *The City and Man*, 241.

46. For further discussion, see Heinrich Meier, *Carl Schmitt, Leo Strauss und "Der Begriff des Politischen": Zu einem Dialog unter Abwesenden*, 3rd edn (Stuttgart: Metzler, 2013); *Das theologisch-politische Problem: Zum Thema von Leo Strauss* (Stuttgart: Metzler; Poeschel, 2003). Neil G. Robertson, "Platonism in High Places: Leo Strauss, George W. Bush and the Response to 9/11," in Michael Meckler, *Classical Antiquity and the Politics of America: From George Washington to George W. Bush* (Waco, TX: Baylor University Press, 2006), 153–174.

47. Karl R. Popper, *The Open Society and Its Enemies*, vol. 1, *The Spell of Plato*, vol. 2, *The High Tide of Prophecy: Hegel, Marx, and the Aftermath* (London: Routledge, 1945).

48. See Renford Bambrough (ed.), *Plato, Popper and Politics: Some Contributions to a Modern Controversy* (Cambridge, New York: Heffer; Barnes & Noble, 1967).

49. Allan Bloom, *The Closing of the American Mind* [1987] (New York: Simon & Schuster, 1988), 42–43.

50. Allan Bloom, *The Republic of Plato: Translated with Notes and an Interpretive Essay* [1968] (New York: Basic Books, 1991).

51. Takeshi Sasaki, "Plato and *Politeia* in Twentieth-Century Politics," *Études platoniciennes* 9 (2012), 147–160 (158). See John D. Wild, *Plato's Theory of Man: An Introduction to the Realistic Philosophy of Culture* (Cambridge, MA: Harvard University Press, 1946); *Plato's Modern Enemies and the Theory of Natural Law* (Chicago: University of Chicago Press, 1953); Leo Strauss, *What Is Political Philosophy? and Other Studies* [1959] (Chicago: University of Chicago Press, 2001).

52. Mass "Pro Eligendo Romano Pontifice": Homily of his Eminence, Joseph Ratzinger, Dean of the College of Cardinals, Vatican Basilica, Monday 18 April 2005: "We are building a dictatorship of relativism that does not recognize anything as definitive and whose ultimate goal consists solely of one's own ego and desires." Available online http://www.vatican.va./gpll/documents/homily-pro-eligendo-pontif-ice_20050418_en.html. Consulted 29.12.2016.

53. Pausanias, *Description of Greece*, Books I–II, trans. W.H.S. Jones (Cambridge, MA; London: Harvard University Press, 1918), 167.

54. See Pierre Grimes and Regina L. Uliana, *Philosophical Midwifery: A New Paradigm for Understanding Human Problems with Its Validation* (Costa Mesa, CA: Hyparxis, 1998), esp. Part One, 1–22. For further discussion, see M.F. Burnyeat, "Socratic Midwifery, Platonic Inspiration," *Bulletin of the Institute of Classical Studies* 24 (1977), 7–16; Julius Tomin, "Socratic Midwifery," *The Classical Quarterly* [NS] 37, no. 1, 1987, 97–102; Radcliffe G. Edmonds III, "Socrates the Beautiful: Role Reversal and Midwifery in Plato's *Symposium*," *Transactions of the American Philological Association* 130 (2000), 261–285; Paul Stern, *Knowledge and Politics in Plato's "Theaetetus"* (Cambridge: Cambridge University Press, 2007), Chapter 3, "Socratic Midwifery," 32–81.

55. For further discussion of the motif of the cave in the thought of Leo Strauss, see David Janssens, *Between Jerusalem and Athens: Philosophy, Prophecy, and Politics in Leo Strauss's Early Thought* (Albany, NY: State University of New York Press, 2008), Chapter 3, "The Second Cave," 77–108.

56. Leo Strauss, *Persecution and the Art of Writing* [1952] (Chicago and London: University of Chicago Press, 1988), 155–156.

57. "Justice, which is the subject of our enquiry, is, as you know, sometimes spoken of as the virtue of an individual, and sometimes as the virtue of a state. […] And is not a state larger than an individual? […] Then in the larger the quantity of justice is likely to be larger and more easily discernible. I propose therefore that we enquire into the nature of justice and injustice, first as they appear in the state, and secondly in the individual, proceeding from the greater to the lesser and comparing them. […] And if we imagine the state in process of creation, we shall see the justice and injustice of the state in process of creation also" (Plato, *Republic*, 368a–369b, trans. Jowett).

2

Plato and the Cave

Our story begins with Plato (427–347 BCE), but we need to contextualize him chronologically (in time) and geographically (in space). The origins of the Western philosophical tradition are to be found in southern Europe and in western Asia, in areas now called Italy, Greece, and Turkey. (Some historians have argued that the tradition begins even further south—in Egypt, and hence in Africa.)[1] Within the timeframe of 600–300 BCE, an astonishing explosion of thought took place. Now our modern chronology, previously using the terms "Before Christ" and "Anno Domini" and now, more politically correctly (or ideologically neutrally), "Before Common Era" and "Common Era", orientates itself around the year zero, that is, the symbolic date of the birth of Jesus Christ. (In fact, some scholars reckon it would be more accurate to date his birth at around 6–4 BCE.) But it is conventional to divide ancient Greek thought into two periods, using the figure of Socrates (470/469–399 BCE) as a turning-point and referring to the earlier period as "pre-Socratic."[2]

Associated with such towns in western Asia and southern Europe as Miletus (home to Thales), Samos (Pythagoras), Ephesus (Heraclitus), Elea (Parmenides), and Agrigento (Empedocles), these thinkers were

© The Author(s) 2019
P. Bishop, *German Political Thought and the Discourse of Platonism*,
https://doi.org/10.1007/978-3-030-04510-4_2

extensively edited and studied by German scholars in the nineteenth and twentieth centuries; Hermann Diels (1848–1922) and Walther Kranz (1884–1960) produced a comprehensive edition of the fragmentary remains of the pre-Socratics' surviving works, introducing a reference system still used today to cite these texts, and such philosophers as Nietzsche and Heidegger discussed their thought in detail.[3] Karl Marx wrote his doctoral dissertation on the theory of nature found in two later thinkers (one pre-Socratic, one post-Socratic) from the atomist tradition, Democritus and Epicurus,[4] and Karl Popper (1902–1994) argued for a return to the pre-Socratic tradition in his presidential address to the Aristotelian Society in London in 1958, entitled "Back to the Pre-Socratics."[5]

It is hard to say much about Socrates, for he left no writings and we know him only by reputation.[6] We know him from the drama of a contemporary playwright, Aristophanes, who presented him as a figure of fun; from his pupil, Xenophon, who has left us with an account of his defence of Socrates in court (see below); and from the extensive writings of another of his pupils, Plato, who in numerous dialogues shows us Socrates in discussion and debate with his contemporaries, including some notable thinkers of the time.

Of these thinkers, some of them belonged to a notable tradition within pre-Socratic philosophy, which Plato saw it as his duty, drawing on the thought of Socrates, to combat: Sophism. Now the tradition of Sophism is often presented in a negative light, not least because of its reputation in the dialogues of Plato; more recently, such commentators as the Scottish classical scholar W.K.C. Guthrie (1906–1981) and the French popular philosopher Michel Onfray (b. 1959) have attempted to restore its reputation and, in one way or another, to rehabilitate it.[7]

The tradition of Sophism is associated with such thinkers as Protagoras of Abdera and Gorgias of Leontinoi, both of whom lend their names to the titles of dialogues by Plato (evidently, the *Protagoras* and the *Gorgias*).[8] Two ideas characterize the thought of this school: first, a far-reaching *scepticism* about the possibility of reaching certainty in any question of epistemology or morals. In short, one might describe Sophism as an early instance of *relativism*, a school of thought which a recent Pope, Benedict XVI, castigated for exerting a "tyranny" over the modern world. If Benedict is right, then—in this specific sense—Sophism is alive and well. Its second characteristic is equally widespread in the modern world: its emphasis on the primacy of rhetoric; or, to use more modern terms, its belief in the importance of "communication," "marketing," or "public relations." To Gorgias the following view is attributed, that "whoever can speak has the masses in his power," and David Hoffmann explains the choice of Gorgias for one of Plato's dialogues as follows:

> Gorgias, after whom the dialogue was named, was an eminent personage from the city of Leontini on the island of Sicily, a teacher of the art of rhetoric or political speech (prominent speakers in assembly were called *rhetores*). Gorgias' speaking style combined hypnotic rhyme and rhythm with a powerful kind of situational logic and antithesis. It so impressed Periclean Athens and the rest of the Greek world that he was able to build a solid gold statue of himself at Delphi with the money he earned in instruction fees […], a feat that is well beyond the means of most speech instructors today. Although Gorgias himself has only a relatively minor role in the conversation, the dialogue as a whole investigates the relationship between Gorgias' style of political rhetoric and justice.[9]

Indeed, in the fragments that remain of his *Encomium on Helen*, Gorgias attributes the following power to rhetoric:

> Speech is a great power, which achieves the most divine works by means of the smallest and least visible form; for it can even put a stop to fear, remove grief, create joy, and increase pity. […]
> That Persuasion, when added to speech, can also make any impression it wishes on the soul, can be shown, firstly, from the arguments of the meteorologists, who by removing one opinion and implanting another, cause what is incredible and invisible to appear before the eyes of the mind; secondly, from legal contests, in which a speech can sway and persuade a crowd, by the skill of its composition, not by the truth of its statements; thirdly, from the philosophical debates, in which quickness of thought is shown easily altering opinion.
> The power of speech over the constitution of the soul can be compared with the effect of drugs on the bodily state: just as drugs by driving out different humours from the body can put an end either to the disease or

to life, so with speech: different words can induce grief, pleasure or fear; or again, by means of a harmful kind of persuasion, words can drug and bewitch the soul.[10]

Given the importance (and, indeed, power) of "corporate communications" and "marketing strategies," particularly in the field of politics, in our modern world, Plato's combat against Sophism acquires a fresh relevance today.

In particular, the followers of the Sophist tradition developed a theory of law or a theory of justice, disagreement with which lies at the heart of Plato's major political treatise, *The Republic* (in Greek, *Politeia*). (Other political works by Plato include *The Statesman* and his late work, *The Laws*, which for reasons of space we cannot consider in detail here.) For instance, is the law a tool of society's strongest members, as Thrasymachus argues? Or is it, as Callicles declares (in the *Gorgias*), a tool of its weaker members? Or is the law a means for reciprocal protection among *all* the members of society, as Protagoras contends? Answering these questions lies at the heart of *The Republic*, which sets out to answer the question, "What is justice?", and ends up achieving so much more. As Benjamin Jowett (1817–1893), the influential translator of Plato and Thucydides (whose translation of *The Republic* is cited here), put it, no other dialogue of Plato "has the same largeness of view and the same perfection of style; no other shows an equal knowledge of the world, or contains more of those thoughts which are new as well as old, and not of one age only but of all."[11]

From the outset it should be noted that, as we saw in the previous chapter, Plato's *Republic* can be, and has been, interpreted in a variety of ways, from both left-wing and right-wing political perspectives in varying degrees of extremity. In the twentieth century, the figure of Plato became a subject of intense debate and interest, not only from National Socialists but also from members of the circle around the poet Stefan George (1868–1933); some have argued, incorrectly in my view, that these two groups are essentially aligned in their outlook … In addition, the text has also been read in an "esoteric" way by such commentators as Leo Strauss (1899–1973) and Allan Bloom (1930–1992), and as a kind of blueprint for the "spiritual" development of the individual.

The core of Plato's approach to politics, which is inseparable from his approach to the larger issues of ontology (how things are) and epistemology (how we can know about things), is his allegory of the cave, itself to be found, significantly enough, in his *Republic*. (Plato's dialogues can be conveniently divided into three categories, depending on their date of composition: the early dialogues, such as the *Gorgias*, the *Protagoras*, and the first book of the *Republic*; then the "transitional" dialogues, to which books 2–10 of the *Republic* belong; and finally the late dialogues, among which are *The Statesman* and *The Laws*. In several respects, then, the *Republic* and the allegory found in its book 7 are central to Plato's thought.)

Allegory of the Cave

The Republic opens with Socrates relating how, on the previous day, he had "gone down" with his friend Glaucon, son of Ariston (and Plato's older brother), to the Piraeus, the port of Athens, to pay his devotions to the goddess (i.e., the Thracian deity, Bendis) (327a) (Fig. 2.1). The ensuing discussion with Cephalus, Polemarchus, and Thrasymachus about the definition of justice (book 1) leads to further discussion with Glaucon and Adeimantus (another brother) about the origin and nature of justice, prompting Socrates (in book 2) to set up a comparison between justice in the city and justice in the individual soul, in order to discern what justice is:

> Justice, which is the subject of our enquiry, is, as you know, sometimes spoken of as the virtue of an individual, and sometimes as the virtue of a state. [...] And is not a state larger than an individual? [...] Then in the larger the quantity of justice is likely to be larger and more easily discernible. I propose therefore that we enquire into the nature of justice and injustice, first as they appear in the state, and secondly in the individual, proceeding from the greater to the lesser and comparing them. [...] And if we imagine the state in process of creation, we shall see the justice and injustice of the state in process of creation also.
>
> (*Republic*, 368a–369b)

Allegorical level	Object of knowledge	Kind of knowledge
shadowy reflections	images	*eikasía*
artificial objects	living beings, objects	*pístis*
[the fire in the cave]		[the sun]
reflections of natural objects	mathematical objects	*diánoia*
natural objects	the Ideas	*nóēsis*
[the sun]		[the Idea of the Good]

Fig. 2.1 The allegory of the cave

The ensuing debate leads in book 7 to the famous allegory of the cave, which can be divided into four stages. The first stage (514a–515c) tells the story of a group of human beings in a subterranean cave:

I said, let me show in a figure how far our nature is enlightened or unenlightened: — Behold! human beings living in a underground den, which has a mouth open towards the light and reaching all along the den; here they have been from their childhood, and have their legs and necks chained so that they cannot move, and can only see before them, being prevented by the chains from turning round their heads. Above and behind them a fire is blazing at a distance, and between the fire and the prisoners there is a raised way; and you will see, if you look, a low wall built along the way, like the screen which marionette players have in front of them, over which they show the puppets. [...] And do you see, I said, men passing along the wall carrying all sorts of vessels, and statues and figures of animals made of wood and stone and various materials, which appear over the wall? Some of them are talking, others silent [...] and they see only their own shadows, or the shadows of one another, which the fire throws on the opposite wall of the cave. [...] To them, I said, the truth would be literally nothing but the shadows of the images.

(*Republic*, 514a–515c)

In the second stage, Socrates narrates how one of these human beings is liberated within the cave (515c–e):

And now look again, and see what will naturally follow if the prisoners are released and disabused of their error. At first, when any of them is liberated and compelled suddenly to stand up and turn his neck round and walk and look towards the light, he will suffer sharp pains; the glare will distress him, and he will be unable to see the realities of which in his former state he had seen the shadows; and then conceive some one saying to him, that what he saw before was an illusion, but that now, when he is approaching nearer to being and his eye is turned towards more real existence, he has a clearer vision, — what will be his reply? And you may further imagine that his instructor is pointing to the objects as they pass and requiring him to name them, — will he not be perplexed? Will he not fancy that the shadows which he formerly saw are truer than the objects which are now shown to him? [...] And if he is compelled to look straight at the light, will he not have a pain in his eyes which will make him turn away to take and take in the objects of vision which he can see, and which he will conceive to be in reality clearer than the things which are now being shown to him?

(*Republic*, 515c–e)

In the third stage, the liberation of this human being continues and, exiting the cave, he accedes to the light (515e–516c)[12]:

And suppose once more, that he is reluctantly dragged up a steep and rugged ascent, and held fast until he's forced into the presence of the sun himself, is he not likely to be pained and irritated? When he approaches the light his eyes will be dazzled, and he will not be able to see anything at all of what are now called realities. [...] He will require to grow accustomed to the sight of the upper world. And first he will see the shadows best, next the reflections of men and other objects in the water, and then the objects themselves; then he will gaze upon the light of the moon and the stars and the spangled heaven; and he will see the sky and the stars by night better than the sun or the light of the sun by day. [...] Last of all he will be able to see the sun, and not mere reflections of him in the water, but he will see him in his own proper place, and not in another; and he will contemplate him as he is. He will then proceed to argue that this is he who gives the season and the years, and is the guardian of all that is in the visible world, and in a certain way the cause of all things which he and his fellows have been accustomed to behold. And when he remembered his old habitation, and the wisdom of the den and his fellow-prisoners, do you not suppose that he would felicitate himself on the change, and pity them? [...] And if they were in the habit of conferring honours among themselves on those who were quickest to observe the passing shadows and to remark which of them went before, and which followed after, and which were together; and who were therefore best able to draw conclusions as to the future, do you think that he would care for such honours and glories, or envy the possessors of them? Would he not say with Homer,

> Better to be the poor servant of a poor master, and to endure anything, rather than think as they do and live after their manner?[13]

(*Republic*, 515e–516c)

Finally, a fourth stage follows, for the prisoner, thus liberated, must look back and attempt to return back down into the cave (516c–517b). The goal of this final stage is to attempt the liberation of those who remain in the cave, but it brings with it a great risk for the one who returns:

Imagine once more, I said, such an one coming suddenly out of the sun to be replaced in his old situation; would he not be certain to have his eyes full of darkness? [...] And if there were a contest, and he had to compete in measuring the shadows with the prisoners who had never moved out of the den, while his sight was still weak, and before his eyes had become steady (and the time which would be needed to acquire this new habit of sight might be very considerable) would he not be ridiculous? Men would say of him that up he went and down he came without his eyes; and that it was better not even to think of ascending; and if any one tried to loose another and lead him up to the light, let them only catch the offender, and they would put him to death. [...] This entire allegory, I said, you may now append, dear Glaucon, to the previous argument; the prison-house is the world of sight, the light of the fire is the sun, and you will not misapprehend me if you interpret the journey upwards to be the ascent of the soul into the intellectual world according to my poor belief, which, at your desire, I have expressed whether rightly or wrongly God knows. But, whether true or false, my opinion is that in the world of knowledge the Idea of good appears last of all, and is seen only with an effort; and, when seen, is also inferred to be the universal author of all things beautiful and right, parent of light and of the lord of light in this visible world, and the immediate source of reason and truth in the intellectual; and that this is the power upon which he who would act rationally, either in public or private life must have his eye fixed.

(*Republic*, 516c–517b)

The allegory of the cave is one of the most fundamental texts in the tradition of Western thought, and it can be interpreted in a number of ways; here, we shall examine just three:

- educational
- epistemological/metaphysical/ontological
- political

First, as educational. According to Plato himself, education provides "the greatest safeguard" against tyranny (*Republic*, 416b), and education is "the one great — or, rather than great, sufficient — thing" that will guide citizens, for "sound rearing and education, when they are preserved, produce good natures" (423e and 424a). Correspondingly, R.G. Tanner (1970) and Peter Losin (1996) have argued that the allegory of the cave is a critique of the shortcomings of Greek education and an attempt to propose an alternative.[14] Elsewhere in the *Republic* Plato sets out this alternative, outlining in book 7 a programme for the rulers of the city-state consisting of arithmetic, geometry, solid geometry, astronomy, harmony, and dialectic. The purpose of this education is to offer a training in the knowledge of Ideas. Arithmetic is something that is "apt to draw men toward being" (523a), geometry "makes it easier to make out the *Idea* of the good" (526e), and dialectic is the process by means of which "a man tries by discussion — by means of argument without the use of any of the senses — to attain to each thing that itself *is* and doesn't give up before he grasps by intellection itself that which is good itself" (532a).

Second, as epistemological/metaphysical/ontological. Underlying this critique of education and informing it is a view that is at once epistemological (i.e., concerned with *how* we know), metaphysical (i.e., concerned with *what* we know), and indeed ontological (i.e., concerned with the *how* and the *what* of our knowledge). On this account, the allegory of the cave is related to two other allegories in book 6—the image of the sun and the image of the divided line (see below)—,[15] and to Plato's belief in the *reality of the Ideas*, according to which "what provides the truth to the things known and gives power to the one who knows, is the *Idea* of the good" (508e): "And, as the cause of the knowledge and truth, you can understand it to be a thing known; but, as fair as these two are — knowledge and truth — if you believe that it is something different from them and still fairer than they, your belief will be right" (508e).

Third, as political. As well as addressing itself to the problems of education and to the questions of epistemology, metaphysics, and ontology, the allegory of the cave admits of a political dimension as well. After all, the human beings in the cave are being held as prisoners, and the shadows on the wall of the cave are described as "the shadows of the just" (517d). The prisoners are said to have been in the cave "from childhood with their legs and necks in bonds" (514a). So these prisoners are specifically described as being bound in chains, and it is significant that Socrates later speaks of the tyrant as being "bound in such a prison," that is, as having "a nature full of many fears and loves of all kinds" (579b). Moreover, we note that the prisoners do not realize that they are prisoners. Indeed, they set up among themselves as system for distributing "honours, praises, and prizes for the man who is sharpest at making out the things that go by," whereas Socrates suggests that he would, in the words of Homer, "want very much 'to be on the soil, a serf to another man, to a portionless man' [*Odyssey*, book 11, ll. 489–490], and to undergo anything whatsoever rather than to opine those things and live that way" (516d). Hence on one level it is in the prisoners' interest to maintain the status quo, and so anyone who returns from the upper level becomes "the source for laughter," and if the prisoners were "somehow able to get their hands on and kill the the man who attempts to release and lead up," then they would indeed kill him (517a).

What, then, are these chains? David Lay Williams interprets them as "created by those manipulating the system in the form of ideology,"[16] and it is from these ideological chains that we must be freed. Indeed, the allegory of the cave is positively saturated with political and revolutionary vocabulary: it talks about "prisoners," "chains," turning around (i.e., revolution), exiting the cave (i.e., liberation), and returning to the prisoners to set them free in turn.

In another part of the *Republic*, Socrates explains this allegory in relation to the image of a divided line (509d–511e).[17] Imagine, he says, a line divided into two uneven segments, giving us a longer segment and a shorter segment. Then, he says, subdivide these segments again in the same proportion, giving us a total of four segments in all in ever decreasing length. This line, Socrates suggests, provides us with a matrix for classifying the kind or degrees of knowledge illustrated figuratively in the allegory of the cave. The prisoners sees the shadows of objects projected on the wall: this is the realm of images, called the domain of opinion or *eikasia*. Next, we have the realm of objects, seen only by the prisoners if they turn their heads round: this realm of objects is the domain of belief or *pistis*. In other words, Plato is distinguishing between our perceptions of objects and objects themselves. But we are still within the cave: audaciously, Plato proposes to duplicate this division, only not in the realm of objects and perceptions, but in the realm of the ideal.

In other words, we have to go beyond the knowledge of things and objects and acquire a more abstract kind of understanding, which Plato associates with mathematics: he calls this domain "reflection" or *dianoia*. But we can, he says, go yet further, and acquire a kind of intuitive knowledge he calls "insight" or *noësis*: this is the realm of the Platonic Ideas, a realm of pure intellectual forms. Corresponding to these different sorts of objects of knowledge are two fundamentally different kind of knowing: what the fire is to the realm of the cave ("objective" knowledge) the sun is to the outside realm ("ideal" knowledge). If the fire is the light that enables us to see the world, then the sun represents what Plato calls the Idea of the Good (507b–509c), which enables us to see the realm of the Ideas (and, on Neoplatonic readings, actually brings into everything into being). Hence the keystone in the architecture of Plato's argument in the allegory of the cave is the Idea of the Good (Fig. 2.2).

And here lies the link between the allegory of the cave and Plato's political thought. For his ontology and his epistemology feed into his political views, which do not make full sense without them. The allegory itself provides us with a clue to its political implications. After all, the people in the cave are prisoners; they are sitting there **in chains**, and whether or not they know they are prisoners is irrelevant: they may **think they are free**, but they **are not**. These individuals are prisoners who have to be **liberated**; they have to undertake, literally, a **revolution** by turning their heads around from the wall of the cave to the fire. Then, when they understand their predicament, they are able to escape from the cave and enter into the free realm of the Ideas; if anyone succeeds in doing this, he or she must not remain outside, but must go back into the cave in order to liberate the others. Here, Plato is politically astute: for he realizes that it is in the interest of some of the prisoners to retain the status quo, and of those who, despite or because of their existing condition, are concerned with their "honours and glories," he says: "If any one tried to loose another and lead him up to the light, let them only catch the offender, and they would put him to death." (As indeed, Socrates himself was put to death by the Athenians…)[18]

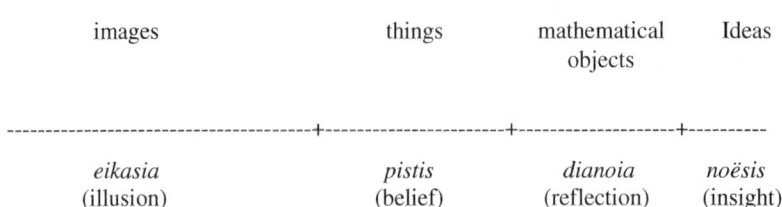

Fig. 2.2 Diagram of the divided line

Bearing in mind the implications of the allegory of the cave, let us turn to consider Plato's political thought in further detail. The extracts included here come from the *Republic*, then the *Gorgias*, and then back to the *Republic* for Plato's conclusion about the role of the philosopher in the political life of the state.

Now the central question of the *Republic* is this: is it always better to be just than unjust? (If we look around us, we can that this question has lost none of its urgency.) In this first extract, Thrasymachus argues that justice (*dikaion*) has been established by the strong so that the weak can serve them. His argument, that 'might is right', echoes the Sophist approach that embraces a kind of 'legal positivism', or in other words the view that the validity of a norm depends, not on its intrinsic merits, but on its actual sources:

[THRASYMACHUS]: Listen, then, he said; I proclaim that justice is nothing else than the interest of the stronger. [...] Have you never heard that forms of government differ; there are tyrannies, and there are democracies, and there are aristocracies? [...] And the government is the ruling power in each state? [...]

And the different forms of government make laws democratical, aristocratical, tyrannical, with a view to their several interests; and these laws, which are made by them for their own interests, are the justice which they deliver to their subjects, and him who transgresses them they punish as a breaker of the law, and unjust. And that is what I mean when I say that in all states there is the same principle of justice, which is the interest of the government; and as the government must be supposed to have power, the only reasonable conclusion is, that everywhere there is one principle of justice, which is the interest of the stronger. [...]

[SOCRATES]: Now I understand you, I said; and whether you are right or not I will try to discover. [...] It will be better that I should ask you a question: Is the physician, taken in that strict sense of which you are speaking, a healer of the sick or a maker of money? And remember that I am now speaking of the true physician.

[THRASYMACHUS]: A healer of the sick, he replied.

[SOCRATES]: And the pilot — that is to say, the true pilot — is he a captain of sailors or a mere sailor?

[THRASYMACHUS]: A captain of sailors.

[SOCRATES]: The circumstance that he sails in the ship is not to be taken into account; neither is he to be called a sailor; the name pilot by which he is distinguished has nothing to do with sailing, but is significant of his skill and of his authority over the sailors.

[THRASYMACHUS]: Very true, he said. [...]

[SOCRATES]: [...] Suppose you were to ask me whether the body is self-sufficing or has wants, I should reply: Certainly the body has wants; for the body may be ill and require to be cured, and has therefore interests to which the art of medicine ministers; and this is the origin and intention of medicine, as you will acknowledge. Am I not right?

[THRASYMACHUS]: Quite right, he replied.

[SOCRATES]: But is the art of medicine or any other art faulty or deficient in any quality in the same way that the eye may be deficient in sight or the ear fail of hearing, and therefore requires another art to provide for the interests of seeing and hearing — has art in itself, I say, any similar liability to fault or defect, and does every art require another supplementary art to provide for its interests, and that another and another without end? Or have the arts to look only after their own interests? Or have they no need either of themselves or of another? — having no faults or defects, they have no need to correct them, either by the exercise of their own art or of any other; they have only to consider the interest of their subject-matter. For every art remains pure and faultless while remaining true — that is to say, while perfect and unimpaired. Take the words in your precise sense, and tell me whether I am not right.

[THRASYMACHUS] Yes, clearly.

[SOCRATES]: Then medicine does not consider the interest of medicine, but the interest of the body?

[THRASYMACHUS]: True, he said. [...]

[SOCRATES]: [...] But surely, Thrasymachus, the arts are the superiors and rulers of their own subjects? [...] Then, I said, no science or art considers or enjoins the interest of the stronger or superior, but only the interest of the subject and weaker? [...] Then, I continued, no physician, in so far as he is a physician, considers his own good in what he prescribes, but the good of his patient; for the true physician is also a ruler having the human body as a subject, and is not a mere money-maker; that has been admitted? [...] And the pilot likewise, in the strict sense of the term, is a ruler of sailors and not a mere sailor? [...] And such a pilot and ruler will provide and prescribe for the interest of the sailor who is under him, and not for his own or the ruler's interest?

He gave a reluctant "Yes."

[SOCRATES]: Then, I said, Thrasymachus, there is no one in any rule who, in so far as he is a ruler, considers or enjoins what is for his own interest, but always what is for the interest of his subject or suitable to his art; to that he looks, and that alone he considers in everything which he says and does.

(*Republic*, 338c, 338d–339a, 341c–d, 341e–342e)

We have quoted this passage at such length, because of the influence and popularity of this sophistical, "relativist" approach to the notion of justice it seeks to combat. In fact, it is possible to align the views expressed by various interlocutors in the *Republic* and the *Gorgias* with those of subsequent political thinkers: the position taken by Thrasymachus, that justice serves the interests who those who are stronger by nature, re-emerges in the critique of Karl Marx; the contrasting position held by Callicles (in the *Gorgias*), that justice serves the interests of the mediocre masses who are, by nature, weaker, sounds like an early version of Nietzsche's *On the Genealogy of Morals* (1887); while Glaucon's argument (358e–361d) that justice in fact serves the interests of all, by protecting each individual against aggression, potential or actual, from his or her fellow citizens, anticipates the view of the state expressed by Thomas Hobbes (1588–1679), for whom *homo homini lupus est*, i.e., each individual is a wolf to his fellow individual.[19]

In his responses to Thrasymachus (see above), Socrates introduces an important idea, which as we shall see is developed elsewhere in the *Republic*: the notion of the "ship of state." What makes the captain of a ship a captain, he argues, is not "the circumstance that he sails in the ship," nor that he is called a sailor, but he is the pilot of the ship solely because of "his skill and of his authority over the sailors" (341c–d). Similarly, the position of a doctor results from his medical skill, or that of a horseman from his ability to control horses: the key idea here is that having the right kind of knowledge is essential to exercising the function of leadership.

As we have seen, a position contrary to that of Thrasymachus is held by Glaucon, who puts three basic propositions forward to Socrates. He argues that the origin of justice in social **contracts**—and here we see the important notion of the **contract** being adduced in Plato's dialogue—[20] is based on the aim of preventing injustice when an individual is unable to take revenge for himself or herself. He further argues that all those who practise justice do so, in fact, unwillingly, and they do so only out of fear of punishment. And finally he concludes that, all things considered, the life of an unjust individual is far more blissful than of the just individual. This argument, the inverse of what Thrasymachus has been advancing, is underpinned by Glaucon using the mythical tale of the ring of Gyges (358e–361d)[21]:

> Now that those who practise justice do so involuntarily and because they have not the power to be unjust will best appear if we imagine something of this kind: having given both to the just and the unjust power to do what they will, let us watch and see whither desire will lead them; then we shall discover in the very act the just and unjust man to be proceeding along the same road, following their interest, which all natures deem to be their good, and are only diverted into the path of justice by the force of law. The liberty which we are supposing may be most completely given to them in the form of such a power as is said to have been possessed by Gyges the ancestor of Croesus the Lydian. According to the tradition, Gyges was a shepherd in the service of the king of Lydia; there was a great storm, and an earthquake made an opening in the earth at the place where he was feeding his flock. Amazed at the sight, he descended into the opening, where, among other marvels, he beheld a hollow brazen horse, having doors, at which he stooping and looking in saw a dead body of stature, as appeared to him, more than human, and having nothing on but a gold ring; this he took from the finger of the dead and reascended. Now the shepherds met together, according to custom, that they might send their monthly report about the flocks to the king; into their assembly he came having the ring on his finger, and as he was sitting among them he chanced to turn the collet of the ring inside his hand, when instantly he became invisible to the rest of the company and they began to speak of him as if he were no longer present. He was astonished at this, and again touching the ring he turned the collet outwards and reappeared; he made several trials of the ring, and always with the same result — when he turned the collet inwards he became invisible, when outwards he reappeared. Whereupon he contrived to be chosen one of the messengers who were sent to the court; where as soon as he arrived he seduced the queen, and with her help conspired against the king and slew him, and took the kingdom. Suppose now that there were two such magic

rings, and the just put on one of them and the unjust the other; no man can be imagined to be of such an iron nature that he would stand fast in justice. No man would keep his hands off what was not his own when he could safely take what he liked out of the market, or go into houses and lie with any one at his pleasure, or kill or release from prison whom he would, and in all respects be like a God among men. Then the actions of the just would be as the actions of the unjust; they would both come at last to the same point. And this we may truly affirm to be a great proof that a man is just, not willingly or because he thinks that justice is any good to him individually, but of necessity, for wherever any one thinks that he can safely be unjust, there he is unjust. For all men believe in their hearts that injustice is far more profitable to the individual than justice, and he who argues as I have been supposing, will say that they are right. If you could imagine any one obtaining this power of becoming invisible, and never doing any wrong or touching what was another's, he would be thought by the lookers-on to be a most wretched idiot, although they would praise him to one another's faces, and keep up appearances with one another from a fear that they too might suffer injustice.

(*Republic*, 358e–360d)

Glaucon's argument is a threat to Socrates's position, but it is so in a different way from Thrasymachus's challenge. For what the story of the ring of Gyges, a magical ring that grants its owner the power to become invisible at will, enables him to explore is the *psychology* behind justice. Would, he asks, any intelligent person be moral, if he or she did not fear being caught and punished? What if we could do anything we wanted—and get away with it? What would we do then, and what does this tell us about what we really feel about justice?

A further counterpoint to Thrasymachus (and, by the same token, to Socrates's counter-arguments) can be found in Callicles's argument in the *Gorgias*. According to the Irish classical scholar E.R. Dodds (1893–1979), the *Gorgias* is the most "modern" of Plato's dialogues, because "the twin problems which it exposes — how to control the power of propaganda in a democracy, how to re-establish moral standards in a world whose traditional standards have disintegrated — these are also the central problems of the twentieth century."[22] Correspondingly, Callicles's argument that the laws have been framed by the majority, who are weak, in order to prevent the stronger gaining advantage over them, taps into today's culture of resentment and grievance: over and against the law, Callicles appeals to the idea of "natural justice," where the strong can exercise their advantages over the weak (*Gorgias*, 483b–484c; cf. 502d–505b, 507a–508c, 513e–514a, 517b–518c, 521d–522c):

> The reason, as I conceive, is that the makers of laws are the majority who are weak; and they make laws and distribute praises and censures with a view to themselves and to their own interests; and they terrify the stronger sort of men, and those who are able to get the better of them, in order that they may not get the better of them; and they say, that dishonesty is shameful and unjust; meaning, by the word injustice, the desire of a man to have more than his neighbours; for knowing their own inferiority, I suspect that they are too glad of equality. And therefore the endeavour to have more than the many, is conventionally said to be shameful and unjust, and is called injustice [cf. *Republic*, 538-539], whereas nature herself intimates that it is just for the better to have more than the worse, the more powerful than the weaker; and in many ways she shows, among men as well as among animals, and indeed among whole cities and races, that justice consists in the superior ruling over and having more than the inferior. For on what principle of justice did Xerxes invade Hellas, or his father the Scythians? (not to speak of numberless other examples). Nay, but these are the men who act according to nature; yes, by Heaven, and according to the law of nature: not, perhaps, according to that artificial law, which we invent and impose upon our fellows, of whom we take the best and strongest from their youth upwards, and tame them like young lions, — charming them with the sound of the voice, and saying to them, that with equality they must be content, and that the equal is the honourable and the just.
>
> But if there were a man who had sufficient force, he would shake off and break through, and escape from all this; he would trample under foot all our formulas and spells and charms, and all our laws which are against nature: the slave would rise in rebellion and be lord over us, and the light of natural justice would shine forth. And this I take to be the sentiment of Pindar, when he says in his poem, that
>
> "Law is the king of all, of mortals as well as of immortals" [23];
> this, as he says,

"Makes might to be right, doing violence
with highest hand; as I infer
from the deeds of Heracles, for without buying them—"[24]
— I do not remember the exact words, but the meaning is, that without buying them, and without their being given to him, he carried off the oxen of Geryon, according to the law of natural right, and that the oxen and other possessions of the weaker and inferior properly belong to the stronger and superior. And this is true, as you may ascertain, if you will leave philosophy and go on to higher things: for philosophy, Socrates, if pursued in moderation and at the proper age, is an elegant accomplishment, but too much philosophy is the ruin of human life.

(*Gorgias*, 483b–484c)

In these final words, and in some later ones—"For, as Euripides says, 'Every man shines in that and pursues that, and devotes the greatest portion of the day to that in which he most excels,' but anything in which he is inferior, he avoids and depreciates, and praises the opposite from partiality to himself, and because he thinks that he will thus praise himself. The true principle is to unite them. Philosophy, as a part of education, is an excellent thing, and there is no disgrace to a man while he is young in pursuing such a study; but when he is more advanced in years, the thing becomes ridiculous" (*Gorgias*, 484d–485a)—Callicles betrays his real, anti-intellectual inclinations. Nevertheless, his argument has introduced an important theme in political thought, one that will recur in Hegel and in Nietzsche: the fundamental opposition between the **master** and the **slave**.

While the exact function of the quotations from Pindar and the allusion to the myth of Hercules and his tenth labour, stealing the cattle of Geryon, remains obscure and controversial,[25] Callicles's masterful evocation of "a man who had sufficient force," who would "shake off and break through, and escape from all this; he would trample under foot all our formulas and spells and charms, and all our laws which are against nature," so that "the slave would rise in rebellion and be lord over us, and the light of natural justice would shine forth," sounds a revolutionary (and, in some cases, troubling) tone we shall hear again in later thinkers.

In response to Callicles's arguments, Socrates poses a fundamental question that goes to the heart of this dialogue's concerns: what is the relationship between rhetoric and justice (*Gorgias*, 502d–505b)?

> And what do you say of that other rhetoric which addresses the Athenian assembly and the assemblies of freemen in other states? Do the rhetoricians appear to you always to aim at what is best, and do they seek to improve the citizens by their speeches, or are they too, like the rest of mankind, bent upon giving them pleasure, forgetting the public good in the thought of their own interest, playing with the people as with children, and trying to amuse them, but never considering whether they are better or worse for this? [...] Rhetoric is of two sorts; one, which is mere flattery and disgraceful declamation; the other, which is noble and aims at the training and improvement of the souls of the citizens, and strives to say what is best, whether welcome or unwelcome, to the audience [...]. [...] And will not the true rhetorician who is honest and understands his art have his eye fixed upon these, in all the words which he addresses to the souls of men, and in all his actions, both in what he gives and in what he takes away? Will not his aim be to implant justice in the souls of his citizens and take away injustice, to implant temperance and take away intemperance, to implant every virtue and take away every vice?
> (*Gorgias*, 502d–e, 503a, 504d–e)

In this part of the dialogue, we see a number of key themes being addressed. To begin with, we can clearly see how Socrates opposes Callicles's definition of virtue—"the satisfaction of our own desires and those of others"—with his own, according to which "the satisfaction of some desires makes us better, and of others, worse, and we ought to gratify the one and not the other, and there is an art in distinguishing them." In order to underscore this definition, Socrates returns to the analogy with craftmanship—an analogy based on having acquired a knowledge of *form*: "Will not the good man, who says whatever he says with a view to the best, speak with a reference to some standard and not at random; just as all other artists, whether the painter, the builder, the shipwright, or any other look all of them to their own work, and do not select and apply at random what they apply, but strive to give a definite form to it?" (503d–e).

The usual roll-call of examples is then invoked: the captain of a ship, the medical doctor, the artist (503e, 504a–b); on this occasion, Socrates develops medicine as an analogy for virtue. For he goes on to compare what a sound diet and gymnastics do for the body with an analogous discipline for the soul (504b–505b). (In the *Republic*, this discipline is called the "dialectic."[26] In another dialogue, the *Phaedrus*, Plato offers a more formal exposition of the dialectic, while such Neoplatonists as Plotinus develop and refine this path of ascent to the Good.)[27] In turn, he goes to set up an analogy between "lawfulness and law" in the sphere of this discipline of the soul and "temperance and justice" in the sphere of morality and virtue (504d–e). What health is for the body, justice is for the soul and for society alike; justice, he is arguing, is *good for you.*

Up until now, we have largely seen Socrates in a critical mode, but at this point in the *Gorgias* he begins to expound his ethics more positively. In summary, his view is that that an undisciplined individual is an unhappy one, and can only be made happy by being restrained and subjected to justice (*Gorgias*, 507a–508c):

Therefore, Callicles, the temperate man, being [...] also just and courageous and holy, cannot be other than a perfectly good man, nor can the good man do otherwise than well and perfectly whatever he does; and he who does well must of necessity be happy and blessed, and the evil man who does evil, miserable: now this latter is he whom you were applauding — the intemperate who is the opposite of the temperate. [...] Then I further affirm that he who desires to be happy must pursue and practise temperance and run away from intemperance as fast as his legs will carry him: he had better order his life so as not to need punishment; but if either he or any of his friends, whether private individual or city, are in need of punishment, then justice must be done and he must suffer punishment, if he would be happy. This appears to me to be the aim which a man ought to have, and towards which he ought to direct all the energies both of himself and of the state, acting so that he may have temperance and justice present with him and be happy, not suffering his lusts to be unrestrained, and in the never-ending desire satisfy them leading a robber's life. Such a one is the friend neither of God nor man, for he is incapable of communion, and he who is incapable of communion is also incapable of friendship.

(*Gorgias*, 507c–e)

On this account, the "temperate" soul is "good," while the "intemperate" soul is "bad"; and from this definition, Socrates proceeds to draw the conclusion that a happy individual is one who will pursue and practise temperance; he or she will flee indiscipline; and he or she will accept punishment and discipline, if he or she (or indeed if anyone else, individual or collective), requires it. What Socrates is saying is more than just an empirical description (and he is fully aware that in some respects it is hardly an empirical description at all); rather, the point is that the individual should act in his or her private and public life *so that* justice and temperance shall dwell in the individual who seeks happiness …

Behind the discourse about "fellowship" and "friendship" lies the idea of a **cosmic order**, evoked in the lines where Socrates says that "communion and friendship and orderliness and temperance and justice bind together heaven and earth and gods and men, and that this universe is therefore called Cosmos or order, not disorder or misrule" (*Gorgias*, 508a). The belief in the existence of such a cosmic order is implicit in the allegory of the cave, with its hierarchical structure of lower (objective) and higher (ideal) existence; and it also finds expression in the importance attached to geometry. (This "faith in geometry" is something Plato may well have derived from Pythagoras, and it recurs in the "geometrical method" of Spinoza.)[28] In other words, happiness comes to the happy individual (or indeed the happy society) through the possession of temperance and justice.

Correspondingly, Socrates conceives his task as being to serve the city and its citizens (through making those citizens as good as possible):

> And must we not have the same end in view in the treatment of our city and citizens? Must we not try and make them as good as possible? For we have already discovered that there is no use in imparting to them any other good, unless the mind of those who are to have the good, whether money, or office, or any other sort of power, be gentle and good.
>
> (*Gorgias*, 513e–514a)

In other words, Socrates's task, precisely in his capacity as a philosopher, is an eminently political one. In its turn, this conception of the task of the philosopher leads in the *Gorgias* to a consideration of those who describe themselves as politicians. (As he does so, we find an oddly self-reflexive moment of meta-critique, where Plato recognizes the sometimes circular structure of the dialogue as an argumentational form) (*Gorgias*, 517b–581c):

O, my dear friend, I say nothing against them [= earlier statesmen] regarded as the serving-men of the State; and I do think that they were certainly more serviceable than those who are living now, and better able to gratify the wishes of the State; but as to transforming those desires and not allowing them to have their way, and using the powers which they had, whether of persuasion or of force, in the improvement of their fellow citizens, which is the prime object of the truly good citizen, I do not see that in these respects they were a whit superior to our present statesmen [...]. There are two kinds of operations which have to do with the body, and two which have to do with the soul: one of the two is ministerial, and if our bodies are hungry provides food for them, and if they are thirsty gives them drink, or if they are cold supplies them with garments, blankets, shoes, and all that they crave. [...] The purveyor of the articles may provide them either wholesale or retail, or he may be the maker of any of them, — the baker, or the cook, or the weaver, or the shoemaker, or the currier; and in so doing, being such as he is, he is naturally supposed by himself and every one to minister to the body. For none of them know that there is another art — an art of gymnastic and medicine which is the true minister of the body, and ought to be the mistress of all the rest, and to use their results according to the knowledge which she has and they have not, of the real good or bad effects of meats and drinks on the body. All other arts which have to do with the body are servile and menial and illiberal; and gymnastic and medicine are, as they ought to be, their mistresses. Now, when I say that all this is equally true of the soul, you seem at first to know and understand and assent to my words, and then a little while afterwards you come repeating, Has not the State had good and noble citizens? and when I ask you who they are, you reply, seemingly quite in earnest, as if I had asked, Who are or have been good trainers? — and you had replied, Thearion, the baker, Mithoecus, who wrote the Sicilian cookery-book, Sarambus, the vintner: these are ministers of the body, first-rate in their art; for the first makes admirable loaves, the second excellent dishes, and the third capital wine; — to me these appear to be the exact parallel of the statesmen whom you mention.

(*Gorgias*, 517b–c, 517d–518b)

Once again, the direction of Plato's argument moves from the physical to the spiritual, from the body to the soul, and he does so by taking the distinction between **mastery** and **slavery**, rendering it internal to the individual. For if some things *serve* the body (for instance, food or drink or clothes), while some things *lead* it (for instance, gymnastics or medicine), then the same thing applies to the soul…

Hence Socrates describes himself as being the *true statesman*, since in his discourses he aims, not at what is most pleasant, but at what is best. Correspondingly, he enjoins his listeners to take bitter draughts and compels them to hunger and thirst, while (Sophistic) politicians flatter them with sweetmeats (*Gorgias*, 521d–522c):

[SOCRATES]: I think that I am the only or almost the only Athenian living who practises the true art of politics; I am the only politician of my time. Now, seeing that when I speak my words are not uttered with any view of gaining favour, and that I look to what is best and not to what is most pleasant, having no mind to use those arts and graces which you recommend, I shall have nothing to say in the justice court. And you might argue with me, as I was arguing with Polus: — I shall be tried just as a physician would be tried in a court of little boys at the indictment of the cook. What would he reply under such circumstances, if some one were to accuse him, saying, "O my boys, many evil things has this man done to you: he is the death of you, especially of the younger ones among you, cutting and burning and starving and suffocating you, until you know not what to do; he gives you the bitterest potions, and compels you to hunger and thirst. How unlike the variety of meats and sweets on which I feasted you!" What do you suppose that the physician would be able to reply when he found himself in such a predicament? If he told the truth he could only say, "All these evil things, my boys, I did for your health," and then would there not just be a clamour among a jury like that? How they would cry out! […] And I too shall be treated in the same way, as I well know, if I am brought before the court. For I shall not be able to rehearse to the people the pleasures which I have procured for them, and which, although I am not disposed to envy either the procurers or enjoyers of them, are deemed by them to be benefits and advantages. And if any one says that I corrupt young men, and perplex their minds, or that I speak evil of old men, and use bitter words towards them, whether in private or public, it is useless for me to reply, as I truly might: — "All this I do for the sake of justice, and with a view to your interest, my judges, and to nothing else." And therefore there is no saying what may happen to me.

(*Gorgias*, 521d–522a, 522b–c)

There is a particular poignancy to these final words, inasmuch as Socrates was to be accused of corrupting the minds of the youth of Athens and of impiety (that is, of "not believing in the gods of the state"). In the course of his trial Socrates provocatively suggested that a fitting punishment for his "crimes" would be to be paid a wage by the government and to be given free dinners for the rest of his life![29] But the court, inevitably, decided otherwise: Socrates was sentenced to death by drinking a mixture containing hemlock, a poison.

The extracts from the *Gorgias* help contextualize the following passages from the *Republic*, to which we now return. In book 1, Socrates had engaged with the question: "What is justice?" (cf. 331c); in book 2, he had, in reply to Glaucon and to Adeimantus, made the methodological suggestion of looking for justice in a city, rather than in an individual human being: "If we should watch a city coming into being in speech, would we also see its justice coming into being, and its injustice?" (369a); and in book 4 he had restated this thesis: "The just man will not be any different from the just city with respect to the form itself of justice, but will be like it" (434b). In book 6, Socrates returns yet again to one of his favourite metaphors, the image of the ship of the state. It becomes clear that what the pilot or captain is to the ship, or what the doctor is to the body, the philosopher is to the political state (*Republic*, 488a–489c):

Imagine then a fleet or a ship in which there is a captain who is taller and stronger than any of the crew, but he is a little deaf and has a similar infirmity in sight, and his knowledge of navigation is not much better. The sailors are quarrelling with one another about the steering — every one is of opinion that he has a right to steer, though he has never learned the art of navigation and cannot tell who taught him or when he learned, and will further assert that it cannot be taught, and they are ready to cut in pieces any one who says the contrary. They throng about the captain, begging and praying him to commit the helm to them; and if at any time they do not prevail, but others are preferred to them, they kill the others or throw them overboard, and having first chained up the noble captain's senses with drink or some narcotic drug, they mutiny and take possession of the ship and make free with the stores; thus, eating and drinking, they proceed on their voyage in such a manner as might be expected of them. Him who is their partisan and cleverly aids them in their plot for getting the ship out of the captain's hands into their own whether by force or persuasion, they compliment with the name of sailor, pilot, able seaman, and abuse the other sort of man, whom they call a good-for-nothing; but that the true pilot must pay attention to the year and seasons and sky and stars and winds, and whatever else belongs to his art, if he intends to be really qualified for the command of a ship, and that he must and will be the steerer, whether other people like or not — the possibility of this union of authority with the steerer's art has never seriously entered into their thoughts or been made part of their calling. Now in vessels which are in a state of mutiny and by sailors who are mutineers, how will the true pilot be regarded? Will he not be called by them a prater, a star-gazer, a good-for-nothing? [...] The pilot should not humbly beg the sailors to be commanded by him — that is not the order of nature; neither are "the wise to go to the doors of the rich" — the ingenious author of this saying told a lie —[30] but the truth is, that, when a man is ill, whether he be rich or poor, to the physician he must go, and he who wants to be governed, to him who is able to govern. The ruler who is good for anything ought not to beg his subjects to be ruled by him; although the present governors of mankind are of a different stamp; they may be justly compared to the mutinous sailors, and the true helmsmen to those who are called by them good-for-nothings and star-gazers.

(*Republic*, 488a–489a, 489b–c)

Indeed, in book 5 Socrates had been led to make one of his most famous—and, in the reception of the Platonic tradition, what is sometimes regarded as one of his most notorious—statements. For this school of thought, it is none other than the philosopher—that is, the person who demonstrates "love" (*philia*) for "wisdom" (*sophia*)—who should be king (*Republic*, 473c–473d):

Until philosophers are kings, or the kings and princes of this world have the spirit and power of philosophy, and political greatness and wisdom meet in one, and those commoner natures who pursue either to the exclusion of the other are compelled to stand aside, cities will never have rest from their evils, — nor the human race, as I believe, — and then only will this our State have a possibility of life and behold the light of day.

(*Republic*, 473c–d)

Now why should this be the case? If we remember the allegory of the cave, and think of the philosopher as the person who has liberated himself from his chains, made his way into the realm of ideal forms, and *nevertheless returned back into the cave*, then is not the philosopher now in the position of the captain of a ship, or the doctor treating a patient? Is it not the philosopher who, of all individuals, understands what the Good actually is, and therefore how society is to be run (500b–500e)?

[SOCRATES]: For he, Adeimantus, whose mind is fixed upon true being, has surely no time to look down upon the affairs of earth, or to be filled with malice and envy, contending against men; his eye is ever directed towards things fixed and immutable, which he sees neither injuring nor injured by one another, but all in order moving according to reason; these he imitates, and to these he will, as far as he can, conform himself. [...] And if a necessity be laid upon him of fashioning, not only himself, but human nature generally, whether in States or individuals, into that which he beholds elsewhere, will he, think you, be an unskilful artificer of justice, temperance, and every civil virtue? [...] And if the world perceives that what we are saying about him is the truth, will they be angry with philosophy? Will they disbelieve us, when we tell them that no State can be happy which is not designed by artists who imitate the heavenly pattern? [...] They will begin by taking the State and the manners of men, from which, as from a tablet, they will rub out the picture, and leave a clean surface. This is no easy task. But whether easy or not, herein will lie the difference between them and every other legislator, — they will have nothing to do either with individual or State, and will inscribe no laws, until they have either found, or themselves made, a clean surface. [...] And when they are filling in the work, as I conceive, they will often turn their eyes upwards and downwards: I mean that they will first look at absolute justice and beauty and temperance, and again at the human copy; and will mingle

and temper the various elements of life into the image of a man; and thus they will conceive according to that other image, which, when existing among men, Homer calls "the form and likeness of God".[31]
(*Republic*, 500b–c, 500d, 500e–501a, 501b)

Thus theology in Plato serves to underline his approach to politics. For the philosopher understands what justice is: it is things being in their right place. As Socrates puts it to Glaucon in book 4, justice is related to the idea of minding one's own business, "not with respect to a man's minding his external business, but with respect to what is within, with respect to what truly concerns him and his own" (443c). (Here Plato draws an analogy between justice—"to establish the part of the soul in a relation of mastering, and being mastered by, one another that is according to nature"—and good health: "To establish the parts of the body in a relation of mastering, and being mastered by, one another that is according to nature, while to produce sickness is to establish a relation of ruling, and being ruled by, one another that is contrary to nature" [444d].)

This principle applies alike to the tripartite division of the soul (into an appetitive part, a spirited part, and a rational part) and to the tripartite division of society (into producers, guardians, and philosopher-kings). Indeed, we can now understand that the *Republic*, in which Socrates seeks to explain justice for the individual by comparing it to justice for the city, is a text *both* about politics and about spirituality. For someone "whose mind is fixed upon true being" is "ever directed towards things fixed and immutable," which he sees as "all in order" and "moving according to reason."

Thus at the conclusion to the allegory of the cave, which can serve as a conclusion to this chapter about Plato, we find the following moving declaration (517b–517c):

My opinion is that in the world of knowledge the Idea of good appears last of all, and is seen only with an effort; and, when seen, is also inferred to be the universal author of all things beautiful and right, parent of light and of the lord of light in this visible world, and the immediate source of reason and truth in the intellectual; and that this is the power upon which he who would act rationally, either in public or private life, must have his eye fixed.

(*Republic*, 517b–517c)

For all the mystical connotations in this passage, it is important to see how the liberation of the prisoners from the cave and how access to the realm of Ideas are achieved by the application of reason or *logos*. In other words, Plato insists that the dialectic is an essentially *rational* process, and the state he describes—however odd it might look from a modern perspective—is one ultimately founded on reason.

Notes

1. Martin Bernal, *Black Athena: The Afroasiatic Roots of Classical Civilization*, 3 vols (New Brunswick, NJ: Rutgers University Press, 1991–2006). In some respects, Bernal's thesis of a major influence by the ancient Egyptians and ancient Phoenicians on the ancient Greeks restates an earlier tradition, according to which Plato studied under an Egyptian priest for 13 years (see James McEvoy, "Plato and the Wisdom of Egypt," *Irish Philosophical Journal* 1 (1984), 1–24), and it is accepted that Pythagoras studied mathematics and astronomy under the priests of the Egyptian temples. Bernal's thesis, however, remains contentious; see Mary Lefkowitz and Guy MacLean Rogers (eds), *Black Athena Revisited* (Chapel Hill, NC: University of North Carolina Press, 1996); and Mary Lefkowitz, *Not Out of Africa: How Afrocentrism Became an Excuse to Teach Myth as History* (New York: Basic Books, 1996; revised 1997).
2. For an overview of the work of the thinkers from this period, see Jean-Paul Dumont (ed.), "Préface," in *Les Présocratiques* (Paris: Gallimard, 1988), ix–xxv; and Patricia Curd and Daniel W. Graham (eds), *The Oxford Handbook of Presocratic Philosophy* (New York: Oxford University Press, 2008).
3. See Friedrich Nietzsche, *The Pre-Platonic Philosophers*, ed. and trans. Greg Whitlock (Urbana and Chicago: University of Illinois Press, 1995), based on lecture series given by Nietzsche at Basel in the summer of 1872, in 1873, and in 1876. On Heidegger and the pre-Socratics, see George Joseph Seidel, *Martin Heidegger and the Pre-Socratics:*

An Introduction to His Thought (Lincoln, NE: University of Nebraska Press, 1984); and David C. Jacobs, *The Presocratics After Heidegger* (Albany, NY: State University of New York Press, 1999); as well as Martin Heidegger, *Early Greek Thinking*, trans. David Farrell Krell and Frank A. Capuzzi (New York: HarperSanFrancisco, 1984) (containing "The Anaximander Fragment" from *Holzwege* [1950], and "Logos," "Moira," and "Aletheia" from *Vorträge und Aufsätze* [1954]); and Martin Heidegger and Eugen Fink, *Heraclitus SEMINAR 1966/67*, trans. Charles H. Seibert (University, AL: University of Alabama Press, 1979).

4. See Karl Marx, *The Difference Between the Democritean and Epicurean Philosophy of Nature* [1841], in Karl Marx and Friedrich Engels, *Collected Works*, vol. 1 (Moscow: Progress Publishers, 1975), 25–105.

5. Karl Popper, "Back to the Pre-Socratics," *Proceedings of the Aristotelian Society* [NS] 59 (1958–1959), 1–24; reprinted in *Conjectures and Refutations: The Growth of Scientific Knowledge* [1963] (London and New York: Routledge, 2002), 183–223.

6. For further discussion, see "The Quest for the Historical Socrates," in John Bussanich and Nicholas D. Smith (eds), *The Bloomsbury Companion to Socrates* (London: Bloomsbury Academic, 2013), 1–19.

7. W.K.C. Guthrie, *The Sophists* (Cambridge: Cambridge University Press, 1971); and Michel Onfray, *Les sagesses antiques: De Leucippe à Diogène d'Oenanda* [*Contre-histoire de la philosophie*, vol. 1] (Paris: Grasset, 2006).

8. While the *Protagoras* and the *Gorgias* are classified among Plato's early dialogues, see also on the subject of Sophism Plato's late dialogue, the *Sophist*.

9. David Hoffman, "Justice and Self: A Reading of Plato's *Gorgias*," in *Anistoriton*, no. E024 (8 December 2002). Available online HTTP: http://www.anistor.gr/english/enback/e024.htm. For further discussion of Plato and rhetoric, see James D. Williams (ed.), *An Introduction to Classical Rhetoric: Essential Readings* (Chichester, West Sussex: Wiley-Blackwell, 2009), 108–221; and Marina McCoy, *Plato on the Rhetoric of Philosophers and Sophists* (New York: Cambridge University Press, 2008).

10. Excerpted from Gorgias, "Encomium to Helen," §8 and §10–§14, in Kathleen Freeman, *Ancilla to The Pre-Socratic Philosophers: A Complete Translation of the Fragments in Diels, "Fragmente der Vorsokratiker"* [1948] (Cambridge, MA: Harvard University Press, 1983), 132–133.

11. Benjamin Jowett, *The Republic of Plato: Translated into English with Introduction, Analysis, Marginal Analysis and Index*, 3rd edn (Oxford: Clarendon Press, 1888), i.

12. For discussion of the metaphorical and scientific reality of light and its cognitive significance, see Arthur Zajonc, *Catching the Light: The Entwined History of Light and Mind* (New York and Oxford: Oxford University Press, 1993).

13. This citation from Homer—to be precise, from the lament of Achilles in the *Odyssey*, book 11, ll. 489–491—has already been quoted in full by Socrates at the beginning of book 3 of the *Republic* (386c). Its significance has been discerned by Allan Bloom in his edition of the *Republic* (427–428 and 435–436). In his lament, Achilles bewails his fate, expressed in his preference for being alive as a serf instead of ruling over the dead. This sentiment is used by Socrates to support his argument for censorship in books 2 and 3 and in the allegory of the cave in book 7. In book 10, Socrates relates the myth of Er, an account of a visit to the other world based on the account of Odysseus's visit to the dead in book 11 of the *Odyssey*. Er relates that, in the underworld, he met the shade of Ajax, but not the shade of Achilles: why not? According to Bloom, the passages cited in book 3 serve as examples of what is unacceptable in art and hence what should be banned, since his complaint about Hades is a critique of the order of the world. So when Er mentions Ajax, whom Odysseus saw on his descent to the underworld as the twentieth shade of the dead, as the twentieth soul whom *he* saw, we are to conclude that "Achilles no longer exists, alive or dead, in the new poetry or the new Socratic world" ("Interpretive Essay," in Allan Bloom, *The Republic of Plato: Translated with Notes and an Interpretive Essay* [1968] (New York: Basic Books, 1991), 436). For a discussion of the myth of the underworld journey in Plato's *Phaedo* as a parallel case to the *Republic*, see Radcliffe G. Edmonds III, *Myths of the Underworld Journey: Plato, Aristophanes, and the "Orphic" Gold Tablets* (New York: Cambridge University Press, 2004).

14. R.G. Tanner, "ΔIANOIA and Plato's Cave," *Classical Quarterly* 20, no. 1 (1970), 81–91; and Peter Losin, "Education and Plato's Parable of the Cave," *Journal of Education* 178, no. 3 (1996), 48–65.

15. See Robert J. Fogelin, "Three Platonic Analogies," *The Philosophical Review* 80, no. 3 (July 1971), 371–382.

16. David Lay Williams, *Rousseau's Platonic Enlightenment* (University Park, PA: Pennsylvania State University Press, 2007), 135.

17. For further discussion, see John Malcolm, "The Line and the Cave," *Phronesis* 7, no. 1 (1962), 38–45; and "The Cave Revisited," *Classical Quarterly* 31, no. 1 (1981), 60–68.

18. For an account of Socrates's trial and death, see the *Apology*, the *Phaedo*, and Xenophon's *Memorabilia* and *Apology*.

19. The source of this Latin proverb is manifold: in Plautus's play *The Comedy of Asses*, we find the line, "Man is no man, but a wolf, to a stranger" (*lupus est homo homini, non homo, quom qualis sit non novit* (l. 495; in Plautus, *Amphitryon; The Comedy of Asses; The Pot of Gold; The Two Bacchuses; The Captives*, trans. Paul Nixon (London and New York: Heinemann and Putnam, 1916), 176–177). By contrast, Seneca declared in one of letters to Lucilius (Letter 95, §33) that "man [is] an object of reverence in the eyes of man" (*homo, sacra res homini*) (Seneca, *Ad Luciulium Epistulae morales*, trans. Richard M. Gummere, vol. 3 (Cambridge, MA and London: Harvard University Press and Heinemann, 1971), 78–79). Cf. Hobbes's aphorisms in the "Epistle dedicatory" of his *De Cive* (1651) (i.e., "On the Citizen"): "To speak impartially, both sayings are very true; That Man to Man is a kind of God; and that Man to Man is an errant Wolfe. The first is true, if we compare Citizens amongst themselves; and the second, if we compare Cities" (Hobbes, *On the Citizen*, ed. Richard Tuck and Michael Silverthorne (Cambridge: Cambridge University Press, 1998), 5). Hobbes's metaphor participates in a tradition that compares human faculties to those of animals, from John Gregory's *A Comparative View of the State and Faculties of Man with Those of the Animal World* (1774) to Jacques Derrida's *The Beast and the Sovereign*, trans. Geoffrey Bennington (Chicago: University of Chicago Press, 2009). For further discussion, see Brad Pasanek, "Animals," in *Metaphors of Mind: An Eighteenth-Century Dictionary* (Baltimore: Johns Hopkins University Press, 2015), 28–49.

20. For further discussion, see H.D. Lewis, "Plato and the Social Contract," *Mind* [NS] 48, no. 189 (January 1939), 78–81.

21. On the role of myth in Plato, see John Alexander Stewart (trans.), *Myths of Plato* (London: Macmillan, 1905); Luc Brisson, *Platon, les mots et les mythes: Comment et pourquoi Platon nomma le mythe?* (Paris: Maspero, 1982; 2nd edn, Paris: Éditions La Découverte, 1994), translated as *Plato the Myth Maker*, ed. and trans. Gerard Naddaf (Chicago and London: University of Chicago Press, 1998); Luc Brisson,

Introduction à la philosophie du mythe: Sauver les mythes, vol. 1 (Paris: Vrin, 1996), translated as *How Philosophers Saved Myths: Allegorical Interpretation and Classical Mythology*, trans. Catherine Tihanyi (Chicago and London: University of Chicago Press, 2004); and Plato, *Selected Myths*, ed. Catalin Partenie (New York: Oxford University Press, 2004).

22. Plato, *Gorgias: A Revised Text with Introduction and Commentary*, ed. E.R. Dodds (Cambridge: Cambridge University Press, 1959), 386.

23. Pindar, fragment 169; cf. "Law, the lord of all, mortals and immortals, carrieth everything with a high hand, justifying the extreme of violence" (Pindar, *The Odes, Including the Principal Fragments*, trans. John Sandys (London and New York: Heinemann and Putnam, 1927), 605).

24. Cf. Pindar, "This I infer from the labours of Heracles; for he drave to the Cyclopian portals of Eurystheus the kine of Geryon, which he had won neither by prayer nor by price" (*Odes, including the Principal Fragments*, 605). In this part of the dialogue, as at the beginning of the *Republic*, book 3, there is a concerted effort to advance the argument by means of literary allusion and quotation. Shortly afterwards, in the *Gorgias*, Callicles cites a fragment from a lost play of Euripides, his *Antiope* (fragment 20). For further discussion of this allusion, see Andrea Wilson Nightingale, "Plato's 'Gorgias' and Euripides' 'Antiope': A Study in Generic Transformation," *Classical Antiquity* 11, no. 1 (April 1992), 121–141.

25. See Marian Demos, "Callicles' Quotation from Pindar in the *Gorgias*," *Harvard Studies in Classical Philology* 96 (1994), 85–107; and Dale Grote, "Callicles' Use of Pindar's NOMOS BASILEUS: *Gorgias* 484B," *The Classical World* 90 (1994), 21–31.

26. For Socrates's description of the dialectic, see *Republic*, 532a–532b: "And so, Glaucon, [Socrates] said, we have at last arrived at the hymn of dialectic. This is that strain which is of the intellect only, but which the faculty of sight will nevertheless be found to imitate; for sight, as you may remember, was imagined by us after a while to behold the real animals and stars, and last of all the sun himself. And so with dialectic; when a person starts on the discovery of the absolute by the light of reason only, and without any assistance of sense, and perseveres until by pure intelligence he arrives at the perception of the absolute good, he at last finds himself at the end of the intellectual world, as in the case of sight at the end of the visible"; and 532b–532d: "But the release of the

prisoners from chains, and their translation from the shadows to the images and to the light, and the ascent from the underground den to the sun, while in his presence they are vainly trying to look on animals and plants and the light of the sun, but are able to perceive even with their weak eyes the images in the water (which are divine), and are the shadows of true existence (not shadows of images cast by a light of fire, which compared with the sun is only an image) — this power of elevating the highest principle in the soul to the contemplation of that which is best in existence, with which we may compare the raising of that faculty which is the very light of the body to the sight of that which is brightest in the material and visible world — this power is given, as I was saying, by all that study and pursuit of the arts which has been described."

27. See *Phaedrus*, 265d–266b; Plato's *Phaedrus*, trans. R. Hackforth (Cambridge: Cambridge University Press, 1952), 134–137. And see Plotinus, *Ennead* I.3, "On Dialectic," in Plotinus, *Porphyry on Plotinus; Ennead I*, trans. A.H. Armstrong, vol. 1 (Cambridge, MA and London: Harvard University Press, 1966), 149–165.

28. For the relevant Pythagorean texts and an analysis of them, see Kenneth Sylvan Guthrie (ed. and trans.), *The Pythagorean Sourcebook and Library: An Anthology of Ancient Writings Which Relate to Pythagoras and Pythagorean Philosophy*, ed. David R. Fideler (Grand Rapids, MI: Phanes Press, 1987). For further discussion of the links between Pythagoreanism and Neoplatonism, see Dominic J. O'Meara, *Pythagoras Revived: Mathematics and Philosophy in Late Antiquity* (Oxford: Clarendon Press, 1989).

29. "Reflecting that I was really too honest a man to follow in this way and live, I did not go where I could do no good to you or to myself; but where I could do the greatest good privately to everyone of you, thither I went, and sought to persuade every man among you that he must look to himself, and seek virtue and wisdom before he looks to his private interests, and look to the state before he looks to the interests of the state; and that this should be the order which he observes in all his actions. [...] There can be no more fitting reward than maintenance in the Prytaneum, O men of Athens, a reward which he deserves far more than the citizen who has won the prize at Olympia in the horse or chariot race, whether the chariots were drawn by two horses or by many. For I am in want, and he has enough; and he only gives you the

appearance of happiness, and I give you the reality" (*Apology*, 36c–37a). The Prytaneum was one of the most important buildings in Athens, containing the sacred fire of the city and housing the members of the Council.

30. Cf. Aristotle, *Rhetoric*, book 2, §16 (1391a): "Hence the saying of Simonides about wise men and rich men, in answer to Hiero's wife, who asked him whether it was better to grow rich or wise. 'Why, rich,' he said; 'for I see the wise men spending their days at the rich men's doors'" (Aristotle, *Complete Works*, ed. Jonathan Barnes, 2 vols (Princeton, NJ: Princeton University Press, 1984), vol. 2, 2216).

31. In various places, Homer uses the epithet "god-like" to describe such heroes as Achilles and Telemachus; cf. *Iliad*, book 1, l. 131; book 24, l. 630; and *Odyssey*, book 3, l. 416. See Plato, *Apology; Crito; Phaedo; Symposium; Republic*, ed. Louise Ropes Loomis, trans. Benjamin Jowett (Toronto, New York, and London: Van Nostrand, 1942), 386.

3

Aristotle and the Empirical Approach

In his famous painting *The School of Athens*, Raphael places at the centre of this work the two figures of Plato and Aristotle. Aristotle was a disciple of Plato in the Academy at Athens, but following the death of Plato (c. 348/347 BCE) he left Athens and became tutor for some years to Alexander the Great. (The school subsequently associated with Aristotle is known as the Peripatetic School; a name originally derived from the colonnades, or *peripatoi*, of the Lyceum in Athens where its members met, but also recalling the legend started by Hermippus of Smyrna that Aristotle was a "peripatetic" teacher, that is, that he walked about while he was teaching.)

Raphael's painting illustrates in an iconic way the difference in emphasis between the founder of the Academy, Plato, and its most famous pupil, Aristotle of Stagira.[1] Plato is seen pointing upward to the heavens: upward, that is, to the realm of the Ideal Forms and to the Idea of the Good. By contrast, Aristotle is presented as gesturing downward, toward the earth and to the concrete detail of the everyday. While Plato and Aristotle share a good deal in terms of outlook, this difference in approach is crucial: it is reflected in the fact that Aristotle wrote treatises on physics, biology, and medicine,[2] whereas these topics appear not to

© The Author(s) 2019
P. Bishop, *German Political Thought and the Discourse of Platonism*,
https://doi.org/10.1007/978-3-030-04510-4_3

have been of interest to Plato. And while Plato begins with the first-order questions (what is justice? what is the Good?), Aristotle begins with what is actually happening on the ground, and builds up his system from there.[3]

Hence it is useful to note that Norbert Hoerster describes Aristotle's approach to the state as being one that sees it as "a natural precondition for a happy life."[4] Two terms are important here: first, Aristotle places great emphasis on the idea of nature,[5] and sees nature as something to be positively valued[6]; and second, there is the significance he attaches to "happiness"—or, to be specific, to *eudaimonia*.[7] This kind of happiness is different from happiness in the superficial sense in which the term is sometimes used today, as well as different from the kind of happiness described as "hedonism." Whereas hedonism often describes a crude and material kind of happiness—smoking cigars, drinking champagne, enjoying the company of attractive women or attractive men (or both)—,[8]*eudaimonia* implies a richer, deeper, more interior kind of happiness. Rather than believing that happiness lies in money, status, and the possession of material goods, the *eudaimonia* that is found in the "good life" is more focused on virtue and excellence.

This difference between Plato and Aristotle is reflected in the opening paragraph of his *Politics* (*Politeia*),[9] where book 1 begins as follows:

> Every state is as we see a sort of partnership, and every partnership is formed with a view to some good (since all the actions of all mankind are done with a view to what they think to be good). It is therefore evident that, while all partnerships aim at some good the partnership that is the most supreme of all and includes all the others does so most of all, and aims at the most supreme of all goods; and this is the partnership entitled the state, the political association. (*Politics*, 1252a1–a25)[10]

To begin with, let's note that Aristotle starts with what we see: his approach is empirical, based on what is actually at hand. What is important about every state, he argues, is that it is a "partnership" or a community, and in turn each partnership or community exists for the sake of some good. Whereas Plato talks about *the* Good, Aristotle here talks about *a plurality* of goods: this could be a good or that could be a good, depending on what kind of partnership or community is being formed.

In the sections that follow, we should note the emphasis that Aristotle places on methodology:

> Those then who think that the natures of the statesman, the royal ruler, the head of an estate and the master of a family are the same, are mistaken (they imagine that the difference between these various forms of authority is one of greater and smaller numbers, not a difference in the kind [...]). And a proof that these people are mistaken will appear if we examine the question in accordance with our regular method of investigation.

Here Aristotle is implicitly attributing to Plato (see *The Statesman*, 258c–259d) the view he is criticizing. As becomes clear, the method Aristotle is using as a basis for this critique could be described as *analytic*—

> it is necessary to analyze the composite whole down to its uncompounded elements (for these are the smallest parts of the whole); so too with the state, by examining the elements of which it is composed we shall better discern in relation to these different kinds of rulers what is the difference between them, and whether it is possible to obtain any scientific precision in regard to the various statements made above.

— and as *genetic*:

> the best method of investigation is to study things in the process of development from the beginning. The first coupling together of persons then to which necessity gives rise is that between those who are unable to exist without one another: for instance the union of female and male for the continuance of the species (and this not of deliberate purpose, but with man as with the other animals and with plants there is a natural instinct to desire to leave behind one another being of the same sort as oneself); and the union of natural ruler and natural subject for the sake of security (for he that can foresee with his mind is naturally ruler and naturally master, and he that can do these things with his body is subject and naturally a slave; so that master and slave have the same interest). (*Politics*, 1252a1–1252a25)

These two aspects, the analytic and the genetic, belong together.[11] Whereas Plato's approach is very much focused on the whole—say, on justice or the Good—, Aristotle's analysis examines the *relation* between part and whole (that is, between the individual human being and the state). He makes the following important methodological statement: he seeks to combat the views of those who oppose him by examining the question of the government of the state "in accordance with our regular method of investigation," that is, by "study[ing] things in the process of development from the beginning."

Whereas Plato is primarily interested in Being (and hence in the realm of Ideal forms), Aristotle is interested in Becoming (and hence in how individual things come into being). Thus Aristotle's approach is historical or, to use a term used later by Nietzsche (and, in turn, by Foucault), it is genealogical.[12] We should note, however, the subtleties of Aristotle's account of historical or genealogical coming-into-being. For in his *Metaphysics* (book 5, 1013a), Aristotle distinguishes between four different kinds of reasons for why things come-into being. In other words, he distinguishes between four causes or types of causality (or, to put it another way, between four different kinds of "be-causes").

We might illustrate these four causes by considering an object—say, for example, a magnificent Greek temple—and asking ourselves how it came-into-being. On Aristotle's account, we can approach this question in four different ways, viz.:

- via the material cause, i.e., the temple is made out of stone, and without these stones we would not have a temple
- via the formal cause, i.e., these stones are arranged in a particular order: vertically (to create the columns), horizontally (to create the steps, the floor, and the platform for the roof), and diagonally (to support the structure of the roof itself)
- via the efficient cause, i.e., these stones did not just fall into place: they had to be quarried, transported, cut, and hoisted into place; the details of the frieze had to be chiselled, and together the architect and an army of slaves brought the temple into being
- via the final (or "purposive") cause, i.e., why was the temple built in the first place at all? The end or purpose of its construction is to

worship the gods, to give the people a place to pray, and to offer a home for the altar where the priests hold sacrifice.

All these four causes apply to any object, and not just to a temple. It is thanks to these different kinds of cause that we are able, if we choose, to construct a piece of furniture from IKEA. The material cause is found in the pieces of wood and the nails and screws to be found in the flat-pack; the formal cause is found in the assembly instructions, without which we are unable to assemble the piece of furniture; the efficient cause is to be found in ourselves, when we decide to embark on the project of purchasing, transporting, and assembling the piece of furniture; the final or purposive cause is why we decided to assemble the cupboard, the shelves, or whatever in the first place (so we have somewhere to hang our clothes, or to display our books, etc.).

All these different kinds of causes inform Aristotle's account of the origin of the state. It begins with the family or individual household (*oîkos*), of which several join together to form a village (*komé*); in turn, these join together to form a regional unity, which Aristotle called a kingdom (*basileía*); finally, these join together to form the city-state (*pólis*), which he describes as being the "perfect society" (*koinonía téleios*). Each of these four stages (cor)responds to a different kind of need: the household or family is necessary for the survival of the individual, the village offers the advantages of the division of labour, the "kingdom" allows for the formal construction of settlement around a central castle, while the city state arises not so much out of necessity as from the desire to establish a community:

On the other hand the primary partnership made up of several households for the satisfaction of not mere daily needs is the village. The village according to the most natural account seems to be a colony from a household, formed of those whom some people speak of as "fellow-sucklings", sons and sons' sons. It is owing to this that our cities were at first under royal sway and that foreign races are so still, because they were made up of parts that were under royal rule; for every household is under the royal rule of its eldest member, so that the colonies from the household were so too, because of the kinship of their members. And this is what Homer means: "And each one giveth law / To sons and eke to spouses —",[13] for his Cyclopes live in scattered families; and that is the way in which people used to live in early times. Also this explains why all races speak of the gods as ruled by a king, because they themselves too are some of them actually now so ruled and in other cases used to be of old; and as men imagine the gods in human form, so also they suppose their manner of life to be like their own. (*Politics*, 1252b15–1252b27)

As Ernest Barker emphasizes, Aristotle regards the state as something natural, *not* because the associations from which it grows are natural, but because of the way it *develops* from them. Hence, for Aristotle, the state is "natural *in itself*," as "the completion, end, or consummation" of humankind and humankind's development (and this is so because "the essentially natural condition of anything" is its "final, or complete, or perfect condition")[14]:

The partnership finally composed of several villages is the city-state; it has at last attained the limit of virtually complete self-sufficiency, and thus, while it comes into existence for the sake of life, it exists for the good life. Hence every city-state exists by nature, inasmuch as the first partnerships so exist; for the city-state is the end of the other partnerships, and nature is an end, since that which each thing is when its growth is completed we speak of as being the nature of each thing, for instance of a man, a horse, a household. Again, the object for which a thing exists, its end, is its chief good; and self-sufficiency is an end, and a chief good. From these things therefore it is clear that the city-state is a natural growth, and that man is by nature a political animal, and a man that is by nature and not merely by fortune citiless is either low in the scale of humanity or above it (like the "clanless, lawless, heartless" man reviled by Homer,[15] for one by nature unsocial is also "a lover of war") inasmuch as he is solitary, like an isolated piece at draughts. (*Politics*, 1252b28–1253a6)

In his *Nicomachean Ethics* (Book 9, Chapter 9), Aristotle underscores the social dimension of our being. It would be "strange," he writes, "to make the supremely happy man a solitary; for no one would choose the whole world on condition of being alone," and the reason for this is that "man is a political creature and one whose nature is to live with others" (1169b18–22).[16] In fact, this notion is at the core of Aristotle's *Ethics*, for he argues (in Book 1, Chapter 7): "Man is born for citizenship" (1097a12).[17]

Aristotle's political analysis reflects his metaphysical assumptions. As this passage continues, he explores the principle that the whole is prior to the part, in the sense that the part presupposes the whole; or, as Barker explains, "the idea of the whole must be there first before the part can be understood, and the whole must first be there before the part can have or exercise a function" (cf. *Politics*, 1253a19–1253a29).[18] Again, it is important to note the interconnectedness between these two aspects of Aristotle's argument. First, the polis exists "by nature" in the sense that "it is the whole to which man naturally moves in order to develop his innate capacity" (and in which "he is thus included as part"); and second, *because* it is "the whole, of which the individual is necessarily a part", the polis is "prior to the individuals who are its parts," since wholes—see above—are logically prior to their parts.

Aristotle underscores that just because the state is "natural," this does not mean it grows without human action, interaction, and volition. In the political sphere, we find a union of two key philosophical categories, art and nature: both are independent, yet both can also cooperate, and "the volition and action of human agents 'construct' the state in co-operation with a natural immanent impulse"[19]:

> Therefore the impulse to form a partnership of this kind is present in all men by nature; but the man who first united people in such a partnership was the greatest of benefactors. For as man is the best of the animals when perfected, so he is the worst of all when sundered from law and justice. For unrighteousness is most pernicious when possessed of weapons, and man is born possessing weapons for the use of wisdom and virtue, which it is possible to employ entirely for the opposite ends. Hence when devoid of virtue man is the most unholy and savage of animals, and the worst in regard to sexual indulgence and gluttony. Justice on the other hand is an element of the state; for judicial procedure, which means the decision of what is just, is the regulation of the political partnership. (*Politics*, 1252a30–1253a40)

Here the concept of justice is shown to underpin Aristotle's conception of the state, just as it does Plato's, and at the beginning and end of his *Nicomachean Ethics* and at the beginning of his *Rhetoric* he underscores this importance of justice.[20] In this passage, we also see Aristotle arguing that the function of the state is self-sufficiency or autarky. Or in other words, freedom. It is, however, a freedom of a quite specific kind, as we shall see.

Not only is the goal or the *telos* of the state described as freedom or autarky, but Aristotle tells us that it exists "by nature"; and it does so, because it is composed of human beings, and human beings are "by nature" political beings. Famously, Aristotle describes the human being as the *zoon politikon*, the "political animal," and this explains why he makes the following statements: "A man that is by nature and not merely by fortune citiless is either low in the scale of humanity or above it," and even more strongly: "While a man who is incapable of entering into partnership, or who is so self-sufficing that he has no need to do so, is no part of a state, so that he must be either a lower animal or a god."[21]

In other words, Aristotle's major insight is that the state is not a limitation on individual freedom or *autarky*, but rather it is a precondition for it. How so? Because it is *in our nature* to be sociable beings, and it is only in a society that we can realize our nature and become fully human. If we could live entirely on our own, we would not need a state; but we cannot live in complete isolation.[22] For a start, living in isolation can drive us mad[23]; then again, we cannot feed, clothe, and look after ourselves in complete isolation; but above all, because it is in our nature to be sociable, it is only in society that we can become fully human.

This explains why Aristotle says that "the city-state is prior in nature to the household and to each of us individually," for the state is the *telos* of the human being. Historically, the state proceeds from the "kingdom," which in turn proceeds from the "village", which in turn proceeds from the "household"; but ontologically it is prior to the individual, because the sociable nature of the human being presupposes there will be a social realm in which this nature will be able to realize itself. And logically it is prior to the individual, because "the whole must necessarily be prior to the part." It also explains why Aristotle says that, while "the impulse to form a partnership of this kind is present in all men by nature," "the man who first united people in such a partnership was the greatest of benefactors." The founder of the state is the greatest of all benefactors, because that person allows every one else to realize his or her true nature as a *zoon politikon*.

Now whereas, for Aristotle, the founder of the state is "the greatest of benefactors," in the thought of Rousseau we shall see that the individual who invents property is the worst of all benefactors, bequeathing us with the system of property that Rousseau regards as a curse: "The first man who, having enclosed a piece of ground, bethought himself of saying *This is mine*, and found people simple enough to believe him, was the real founder of civil society. From how many crimes, wars and murders, from how many horrors and misfortunes might not any one have saved mankind, by pulling up the stakes, or filling up the ditch, and crying to his fellows, 'Beware of listening to this impostor; you are undone if you once forget that the fruits of the earth belong to us all, and the earth itself to nobody'"....[24]

We should also note that Aristotle foregrounds the importance in human affairs of *language*. "Alone of the animals," he says, the human being "possesses speech," and this eminently human trait illustrates his point about the conjunction of the utilitarian (or the practical) and the political nature of the human being: "Speech is designed to indicate the advantageous and the harmful, and therefore also the right and the wrong; for it is the special property of man in distinction from the other animals that he alone has perception of good and bad and right and wrong and the other moral qualities, and it is partnership in these things that makes a household and a city-state" (*Politics*, 1253a8–1253a18).

It is, however, important to note that such autarky or self-sufficiency accrues only to the male citizen of the state: it does not apply to women, nor does it apply to slaves. Indeed, both Plato and Aristotle accept the existence of slaves, not least because slavery was part of the world in which they lived (*Politics*, 1254a15–1254a21). Yet how are we today to understand such passages as this one, where Aristotle appears to justify the existence of slavery?

Authority and subordination are conditions not only inevitable but also expedient; in some cases things are marked out from the moment of birth to rule or to be ruled. And there are many varieties both of rulers and of subjects (and the higher the type of the subjects, the loftier is the nature of the authority exercised over them, for example to control a human being is a higher thing than to tame a wild beast; for the higher the type of the parties to the performance of a function, the higher is the function, and when one party rules and another is ruled, there is a function performed between them) — because in every composite thing, where a plurality of parts, whether continuous or discrete, is combined to make a single common whole, there is always found a ruling and a subject factor, and this characteristic of living things is present in them as an outcome of the whole of nature, since even in things that do not partake of life there is a ruling principle, as in the case of a musical scale. (*Politics*, 1254a22–1254a33)

We should pause to consider Aristotle's musical metaphor. A musical scale or "mode" (for example, the Dorian, corresponding to the modern minor scale, or the Phrygian or Lydian, corresponding to the two forms of major scale) is characterized by having a dominant "key-note"! The argument here, as problematic as it is today, does not just relate to external or physical aspects of slavery:

Hence in studying man we must consider a man that is in the best possible condition in regard to both body and soul, and in him the principle stated will clearly appear,— since in those that are bad or in a bad condition it might be thought that the body often rules the soul because of its vicious and unnatural condition. [...] And the same must also necessarily apply in the case of mankind as a whole; therefore all men that differ as widely as the soul does from the body and the human being from the lower animal (and this is the condition of those whose function is the use of the body and from whom this is the best that is forthcoming) these are by nature slaves, for whom to be governed by this kind of authority is advantageous, inasmuch as it is advantageous to the subject things already mentioned. [...] The intention of nature therefore is to make the bodies also of freemen and of slaves different — the latter strong for necessary service, the former erect and unserviceable for such occupations, but serviceable for a life of citizenship (and that again divides into the employments of war and those of peace); but as a matter of fact often the very opposite comes about — some persons have the bodies of free men and others the souls; since this is certainly clear, that if persons were born as distinguished only in body as are the statues of the gods, everyone would say that those who were inferior deserved to be these men's slaves. And if this is true in the case of the body, there is far juster reason for this rule being laid down in the case of the soul; but beauty of soul is not so easy to see as beauty of body. (*Politics*, 1254a38–1254b2; 1254b15–1254b19; 1254b25–1255a2)

When reading passages such as these it is important to consider whether Aristotle and Plato are (only) interested in talking about slavery as such, or rather whether they are (also) interested in the structure of **mastery and slavery**, a structure that was to become, as we shall see, so fundamental to the thought of Hegel and of Nietzsche. In other words, whether they are approaching the problem of slavery "by theory" (as Plato does) or "empirically" (as Aristotle does), it is important to note how both Plato and Aristotle map the **master/slave** distinction onto the **soul/body** division.

For Plato and Aristotle alike, the soul should rule the body, but not the other way around. And why? Not so much because for the body to rule the soul is immoral (as the Judeo-Christian tradition would argue), but because it is in the nature of the soul to give guidance to the appetites and desires (in themselves, unproblematic) of the body. And both thinkers are (as indeed is Rousseau later) concerned with slavery, not just in the condition of those who are slaves, but in those who are (or believe themselves to be) masters.

For the goal of the state is at once utilitarian and something else. While anchoring his discussion in the concrete specificities of his time and place (here, the city-states of Megara and Corinth), Aristotle highlights what he regards as his political ideal. This ideal is aligned with Plato's notion of the Idea of the Good, but it is articulated in a different and more concrete way: Aristotle calls it the "good life" (1280a32).

All those [...] who are concerned about good government do take civic virtue and vice into their purview.[25] Thus it is also clear that any state that is truly so called and is not a state merely in name must pay attention to virtue; for otherwise the community becomes merely an alliance, differing only in locality from the other alliances, those of allies that live apart. And the law is a covenant or, in the phrase of the sophist Lycophron,[26] a guarantee of men's just claims on one another, but it is not designed to make the citizens virtuous and just. (*Politics*, 1280b5–1280b11)

For Aristotle, *nomos* or the law is a matter of great significance. By *nomos*, however, Aristotle does not mean legislation in the sense that we understand it today. Rather, *nomos* is "an old formulation [...] which transcends strict law and may enter the domain of social ethics"; in this respect, there is an important distinction between *nomos* and *lex*, a specifically legal or legislative act in intention and scope (*Politics*, 1280b12–1280b30).[27] It is typical of Aristotle's approach that his definition of the state or *polis* involves an abstract ideal—"attaining a perfect and self-sufficing existence"—and a biological condition, here defined as ties of contiguity (i.e., being neighbours) and consanguinity (i.e., a blood relationship by descent from a common ancestor)[28]:

It is manifest therefore that a state is not merely the sharing of a common locality for the purpose of preventing mutual injury and exchanging goods. These are necessary preconditions of a state's existence, yet nevertheless, even if all these conditions are present, that does not therefore make a state, but a state is a partnership of families and of clans in living well, and its object is a full and independent life. (*Politics*, 1280b30–1280b35)

Again, we should note the emphasis on the "good life," and the relation (in Aristotle's eyes) between the good life and the married state. In his *Nicomachean Ethics* (Book 8, Chapter 12), Aristotle argued that marital relations were more important than political ones, for "man is naturally inclined to form couples — even more than to form cities, inasmuch as the household is earlier and more necessary than the city" (1162a16–18).[29] As Barker has explained, the associations of husband and wife, as of master and slave—is there, feminists will ask, a difference?—are explained by Aristotle as arising from "the natural necessities of reproduction and self-preservation," and the *polis* meets these same needs at a higher level. (The actual, historical development of the Greek polis bears out, it has been argued, Aristotle's account.)[30]

> At the same time this will not be realized unless the partners do inhabit one and the same locality and practise intermarriage; this indeed is the reason why family relationships have arisen throughout the states, and brotherhoods and clubs for sacrificial rites and social recreations. But such organization is produced by the feeling of friendship, for friendship is the motive of social life; therefore, while the object of a state is the good life, these things are means to that end. And a state is the partnership of clans and villages in a full and independent life, which in our view constitutes a happy and noble life; the political fellowship must therefore be deemed to exist for the sake of noble actions, not merely for living in common. Hence those who contribute most to such fellowship have a larger part in the state than those who are their equals or superiors in freedom and birth but not their equals in civic virtue, or than those who surpass them in wealth but are surpassed by them in virtue. (*Politics*, 1280a31–1281a8)

As Barker has noted, what Aristotle proposes is a notion of distributive justice, one enunciated in the criterion that "contribution to the specific and essential end of the state"—which is, for Aristotle, the performance of "good actions"—is "greater than either the democratic criterion," i.e., free birth, or the "oligarchical" criterion, i.e., possessing great wealth.[31]

What sort of a state is the right one to achieve what Aristotle calls the "good life"? In book 8 of the *Republic*, Plato distinguishes between five different kinds of government. Beginning with aristocracy (i.e., government based on the hereditary principle), Socrates shows Glaucon how timocracy (i.e., government in which property or a desire for honour is a qualification for office) arises, followed by oligarchy (i.e., government by a small executive class), then democracy (i.e., government in which power is vested in the people collectively), and finally, in turn, tyranny (i.e., government by an absolute ruler). Hence in Plato's *Republic* the pattern is:

- aristocracy
- timocracy
- oligarchy

- democracy
- tyranny

The best government of all, Plato concludes, would be government under the rule of the philosopher-king.

For his part, Aristotle operates with a sixfold division of the various kinds of constitution. Again, it is important to note that his approach is an empirical one, and that he judges which constitution is best on the basis of its performance, arguing that "those constitutions that aim at the common advantage are in effect rightly framed in accordance with absolute justice, while those that aim at the rulers' own advantage only are faulty, and are all of them deviations from the right constitutions; for they have an element of despotism, whereas a city is a partnership of free men" (*Politics*, 1279a17–1279a22). In other words, the preliminary classification of consitutions is remarkably simple, for it consists of two *genera*, namely right and wrong (or: normal and perverted). How each constitution is to be classified depends on the extent to which it is observes the principle that political rule is, by virtue of its very nature, in essence for the benefit, not of the rulers, but those who are ruled (*Politics*, 1279a22–1279a33).[32] Aristotle's argument here is that (a) if we consider the goal of the state and true nature of politics, we arrive at the two genera of "right" and "wrong" constitutions; so (b) each genus breaks down into three further species, i.e., monarchy, aristocracy, and "polity" (or constitutional government), as well as tyranny, oligarchy, and democracy (in the sense that Aristotle defines this term) (*Politics*, 1279a33–1279b3)[33]:

> Deviations from the constitutions mentioned are tyranny corresponding to kingship, oligarchy to aristocracy, and democracy to constitutional government; for tyranny is monarchy ruling in the interest of the monarch, oligarchy government in the interest of the rich, democracy government in the interest of the poor, and none of these forms governs with regard to the profit of the community. (*Politics*, 1279a4–1279b10)

So Aristotle draws up a table of six different constitutions or forms of government, three of which he regards as positive, three of which he regards as negative (Fig. 3.1)[34]:

+	-
• kingship	• tyranny
• aristocracy	• oligarchy
• constitutional government	• democracy

Fig. 3.1 Aristotle's six kinds of government

These six different forms of government are judged in relation to their performance in delivering the *telos* of politics, that is, the good life:

> And inasmuch as in all the sciences and arts the End is a good, and the greatest good and good in the highest degree in the most authoritative of all, which is the political faculty, and the good in the political field, that is, the general advantage, is justice, it is therefore thought by all men that justice is some sort of equality, and up to a certain point at all events they agree with the philosophical discourses in which conclusions have been reached about questions of ethics; for justice is a quality of a thing in relation to persons, and they hold that for persons that are equal the thing must be equal. (*Politics*, 1282b14–1282b22)

Now alternative translations of this last sentence would be, "the just is (a just) something and (something just) for somebody", or "justice involves two factors — things, and the persons to whom things are assigned." We should note here how Aristotle links the question of justice to the issue of equality, whereas Plato links the notion of justice to the idea of hierarchy. This is a fundamental fault-line in political thought, and it will recur in later thinkers too (especially Nietzsche, who sees justice in terms of hierarchy and emphatically *not* in terms of equality).

> But equality in what characteristics does this mean, and inequality in what? This must be made clear, since this too raises a difficulty, and calls for political philosophy. For perhaps someone might say that the offices

of state ought to be distributed unequally according to superiority in every good quality, even if the candidates in all other respects did not differ at all but were exactly alike, because men that are different have different rights and merits. Yet if this is true, those who are superior in complexion or stature or any good quality will have an advantage in respect of political rights. (*Politics*, 1282b22–1282b27)

As Barker points out, this entire passages implies a contrast between "general opinion" (or what the Greeks called *doxa*, the lowest of the four categories of knowledge in Plato's allegory of the divided line) and "political-philosophical inquiry," which dissects and analyses that (general or public) opinion. We should not get Aristotle wrong: in the *Nicomachean Ethics* (Book 10, Chapter 2), he remarks that "that which every one thinks really is so" (1172b36)[35]; in other words, in the realm of ethical matters an opinion that is generally or universally held is (in this sense or for this reason) the truth. At the same time, Aristotle is committed to the view that philosophical inquiry can test, analyse, correct, and elevate this general opinion.[36] He turns to an analogous case for an example:

Among flute-players equally good at their art it is not proper to give an advantage in respect of the flutes to those of better birth, for they will not play any better, but it is the superior performers who ought to be given the superior instruments. [...] Suppose someone is superior in playing the flute but much inferior in birth or in good looks, then, even granting that each of these things — birth and beauty — is a greater good than ability to play the flute, and even though they surpass flute-playing proportionately more than the best flute-player surpasses the others in flute-playing, even so the best flute-player ought to be given the outstandingly good flutes; for otherwise superiority both in wealth and in birth ought to contribute to the excellence of the performance, but they do not do so at all. (*Politics*, 1282b32–1283a2)

Is it really possible, Aristotle asks, for every good thing to be commensurable with every other? Aristotle's argument on this point is clarified by Barker as follows: if one says that, say, 5/8s of a perfect stature is in some sense "better" than x/8s of perfect goodness, then one would also say that ½ of a perfect stature is equal to ½ of perfect goodness. Yet to argue in this way is to make stature and goodness commensurable, and on this basis to assume that a fraction of one is as good as a fraction of the other. Yet clearly they are not commensurable, and to regard them as such is treat them purely in terms of quantity and to neglect the crucial dimension of quality.[37] In politics, "the claim to office must necessarily be based on superiority in those things which go to the making of the state" (*Politics*, 1283a14–1283a16).

So what are these things which go into the making of the state and constitute the life of the polis? Here Aristotle declares that if "wealth and freedom are indispensable for a state's existence," then "justice and civic virtue are indispensable for its good administration" (1283a20–21), and later (in Book 4, Chapter 12) Aristotle defines political qualities as "freedom, wealth, education, good birth" (1296b19–20).[38] Central to these is the notion of education or culture—in Greek, *paideia*.[39]

Correspondingly, Aristotle decided that the best form of government is not democracy, but a mixed form consisting of oligarchical and democratic elements (*Politics*, 1287b38–1288a15). This mixed form of "constitutional government" became an important idea in ancient Roman and in medieval political thought alike.

"Governing under a law that distributes the offices among the well-to-do in accordance with merit" (1288a15) is a phrase that raises a lot of questions. If these offices are distributed on the basis of wealth, how can they also be distributed on the basis of merit? If they are distributed on the basis of merit, are they also distributed only among those with wealth? And should not offices be distributed among *all* citizens, providing they can demonstrate merit? (One solution to the difficulties posed by this passage is proposed by Barker, who suggests that the military context is important here: in other words, the wealthy refers here to those wealthy enough to provide themselves with armour for military duties.)[40] Central to Aristotle's position is the idea that the ideal holder of political office shares the same qualities as the ideal state:

Since in the first part of the discourse it was proved that the virtue of a man and that of a citizen in the best state must of necessity be the same,

> it is evident that a man becomes good in the same way and by the same means as one might establish an aristocratically or monarchically governed state, so that it will be almost the same education and habits[41] that make a man good and that make him capable as a citizen or a king. (*Politics*, 1288a38–1288b3)

By "citizen," Aristotle means here a statesman or *politikos*, someone who exercises authority over a society of equals or peers; in this case, a statesman in an ideal aristocracy where all are peers or equals in goodness.[42] Although we do not have space here to examine in detail Aristotle's theory of kingship (see *Politics*, Book 3, Chapters 14–18), it is worth noting the sense in which he talks about the "political" in the sense that power or authority is exercised in a free polis or constitutional state. In particular, it is important to note five words derived from Aristotle's concept of the political: first, *polis*, the "state"; second, *politēs*, the member of the state or the "citizen"; third, *politeia*, the "constitution"; fourth, *politeuma*, the "civic body," or the body established as sovereign by the state's constitution; and fifth, *politicos*, the "statesman"—but not the politician in the modern sense in which we use the word today.[43]

The emphasis placed by Aristotle on the role of the statesman or the kind reminds us that, significantly, two of the thinkers that stand at the beginning of the tradition of Western political thought in general and German political thought in particular, Plato and Aristotle, are not friends of democracy …

But Aristotle *is* a friend of due political process. In particular, he understands that it is important for the state to avoid corruption, especially of a financial kind (*Politics*, 1308b10–1308b19). Nevertheless, the question of the relation of political power and economic advantage is one that exercised Aristotle then as it does us now, and he was keenly alert to the danger that political power might be used to secure economic advantage. In *Politics*, Book 3, Chapter 6, he laments that "nowadays, for the sake of the advantage which is to be gained from the public revenues and from office, men want to be always in office" (1279c13–14).[44] In this respect, Aristotle is at one with the ancient world as a whole—with Plato and with Thucydides—and with the modern world as well—with Marx. In the *Republic*, Socrates remarks to Glaucon:

If you discover a life better than ruling for those who are going to rule, it is possible that your well-governed city will come into being. For here alone will the really rich rule, rich not in gold but in those riches require by the happy man, rich in a good and prudent life. But if beggars, men hungering for want of private goods, go into public affairs supposing that in them they must seize the good, it isn't possible. When ruling becomes a thing fought over, such a war — a domestic war, within the family — destroys these men themselves and the rest of the city as well. (520d–521a)[45]

And in *The Peloponnesian War* (Book 3, Chapter 82, §8), Thucydides noted in the context of the revolutionary dissensions that broke out in Corcyra in 427, the summer of the fifth year of the war: "The cause of all this was power pursued for the sake of greed and personal ambition, which led in turn to the entrenchment of a zealous partisanship."[46] It is not hard to see here a theme which, centuries later, Karl Marx will place, in an amplified and varied form, at the heart of his political critique.[47] Aristotle continues by suggesting that, "to prevent peculation [i.e., embezzlement] of the public property, let the transfer of the funds take place in the presence of all the citizens, and let copies of the lists be deposited for each brotherhood, company and tribe; and to get men to hold office without profit there must be honors assigned by law to officials of good repute" (*Politics*, 1309a10–1309a15). In ancient Athens, financing of the chorus and the actors for comedies and tragedies, and sponsoring ceremonial torch-races, were done as public services by single individuals, much as today companies sponsor sporting or cultural events; and Aristotle urged moderation in this kind of expenditure (*Politics*, 1309a15–1309a27).

In book of 3 of his *Politics*, Aristotle discussed how these "supreme offices of state" or "sovereign offices of the constitution" served as a deliberative organ (embodied in the council or the assembly), but he is probably referring to executive offices when he writes that "it is expedient both in a democracy and in an oligarchy to assign to those who have a smaller share in the government — in a democracy to the wealthy and in an oligarchy to the poor — either equality or precedence in all other things excepting the supreme offices of state; but these should be entrusted to those prescribed by the constitution exclusively, or to them for the most part" (*Politics*, 130a27–1309a32).[48]

And so Aristotle's political thought displays a combination of the practical and the pragmatic together with a sense for ideal values which he finds best expressed in the field of the aesthetic. (In fact, as well as writing on logic, physics, psychology, medicine, metaphysics, ethics, and politics, Aristotle also wrote a treatise on rhetoric and a treatise on poetics.) Significantly, he also turns (as in the passage above from *Politics*, 1282b32–1283a2) to aesthetics to communicate something important about the ideals of politics.

For Aristotle, "one thing must not be overlooked which at present is overlooked by the deviation-forms of constitution — the middle party; for many of the institutions thought to be popular destroy democracies, and many of those thought oligarchical destroy oligarchies" (*Politics*, 1309b18–1309b20). As Barker notes, it is entirely logical for Aristotle's argument to move from the doctrine that, in order to be legitimate, a constitution should be supported by a majority, to a doctrine of moderation, according to which allegiance can be commanded by a moderate constitution, neither too right nor too left.[49] Aristotle seeks to clinch the argument with an appeal to the aesthetics of human beauty:

> The adherents of the deviation-form, thinking that this form is the only right thing, drag it to excess, not knowing that just as there can be a nose that although deviating from the most handsome straightness towards being hooked or snub nevertheless is still beautiful and agreeable to look at, yet all the same, if a sculptor carries it still further in the direction of excess, he will first lose the symmetry of the feature and finally will make it not even look like a nose at all, because of its excess and deficiency in the two opposite qualities (and the same is the case also in regard to the other parts of the body), so this is what happens about constitutions likewise; for it is possible for an oligarchy and a democracy to be satisfactory although they have diverged from the best structure, but if one strains either of them further, first he will make the constitution worse, and finally he will make it not a constitution at all. (*Politics*, 1309b22–1309b35)

In his commentary, Ernest Barker perhaps speaks for all more recent readers of the *Politics* when he reacts with scepticism to Aristotle's suggestion that, if property is equalized, a democracy ceases to be a democracy. But Barker also reminds us that democracy is not meant here in the modern sense of the word, i.e., as the government of the people by the people for the people (as Abraham Lincoln memorably put it in the Gettysburg Address). Rather, Aristotle understands democracy as rule by one of the sections of society, just as oligarchy is rule by a different social section.[50] (So if all social sections disappear, these forms of government will disappear too—another anticipation of Marx?):

> Therefore the legislator and the statesman must not fail to know what sort of democratic institutions save and what destroy a democracy, and what sort of oligarchical institutions an oligarchy; for neither constitution can exist and endure without the well-to-do and the multitude, but when an even level of property comes about, the constitution resulting must of necessity be another one, so that when men destroy these classes by laws carried to excess they destroy the constitutions. (*Politics*, 1309b18–1310a1)

Earlier in the *Politics*, Aristotle had illustrated the principle that "the whole must necessarily be prior to the part" with reference to the body and to sculpture, writing that "when the whole body is destroyed, foot or hand will not exist except in an equivocal sense, like the sense in which one speaks of a hand sculptured in stone as a hand; because a hand in those circumstances will be a hand spoiled, and all things are defined by their function and capacity" (1253a22).[51] In this later section he uses the analogy from aesthetics more positively: if an object overconforms to a norm, it risks becoming unattractive, just as it risks becoming unattractive if it deviates too much from a norm. If a face is deformed, it is usually said to be ugly; but equally, a face that is exactly symmetrical is also judged to be less beautiful than one that has natural variation in it.

Aristotle's plea for the middle way stands in contrast to the extreme rigour with which Plato—in the *Republic*, and even more in his

Laws—presents his case for the subordination of society to the Idea of the Good. In relation to the analogy of the cave, Aristotle would reject the dual ontology which this allegory is often (but, in fact, incorrectly) thought to imply.[52] Yet it is true that Aristotle's emphasis on the sense is different from Plato's, as becomes clear from one of the early statements in his *Metaphysics* (book 1): "We do not regard any of the senses as Wisdom; yet surely these give us the most authoritative knowledge of particulars. But they do not tell us the 'why' of anything — e.g., why the fire is hot; they only say *that* it is hot" (981b10–12).[53] Aside from the different value attached to the senses, however, Plato and Aristotle— in this respect, fully representatives of the philosophical tradition in ancient Greece—agree on the importance of wisdom.

***

In medieval times, Plato tends to be forgotten while Aristotle becomes *the* philosopher. He exercised a key influence on Scholasticism, the primary form of philosophical discussion in the Middle Ages (c. 1100–1500 CE). As Bertrand Russell observed, "the Aristotelian logic of the Schoolmen was narrow, but afforded a training in a certain kind of accuracy."[54] Similarly, his *Politics* remained influential, in Russell's eyes, until the end of the Middle Ages.[55] Indeed, the shift from the medieval to the modern world could be said to coincide with the rise of a critique of Aristotle.

Yet although—or because—Aristotle is hailed as the father of science, there is also a tradition of critiquing Aristotle for the inaccuracy of his accounts of the Presocratics, the thinkers who preceded Plato. For example, in the twelfth century the Persian philosopher Shahab al-Din Yahya ibn Habash Suhrawardi (1154–1191), the founder of the Illuminationist (or Ishraqi) school of philosophy, attacked Aristotle for leading philosophy away from his roots in the teachings of Pythagoras and Empedocles. Thanks to Aristotle, Suhrawardi argued, "the traces of the paths of the ancient sages disappeared," and "their directions were either effaced, or corrupted and distorted."[56] Then again, in the late sixteenth century the Venetian philosopher and scientist Franciscus Patricius (1529–1597) published his *Discussionem Peripateticum* (Basel, 1581), a four-volume critique of Aristotle, especially of his treatment of the Presocratics. Despite this opposition to Aristotelianism, Patricius worked on geometry, history, and military strategy, at the same time as being interested in Hermeticism and editing the Hermetic texts.[57] In fact, in the Renaissance the very name of Aristotle came to be regarded by the innovative thinkers of the Renaissance as being (in the words of Thomas Whittaker) "the synonym of intellectual oppression"![58]

In the twentieth century, the American classicist and historian Harold F. Cherniss (1904–1987) took Aristotle to task for the accuracy of his presentation and interpretation of the Presocratics and, indeed, of Plato.[59] And more recently, Peter Kingsley has argued that, whereas it is conventionally assumed that Arab and medieval writers preserved original Greek material at the cost of trivializing or misunderstanding it, a much more complex picture emerges if one becomes aware of the extent of the damage inflicted on the Presocratics by Aristotle and by his school. Because then, "[i]nstead of Greek philosophy assuming the appearance of a dead-straight line which was bound to be refracted in the medium of Christian, Muslim, or medieval culture," a very different picture emerges which suggests that "the course of Greek philosophy is itself a kind of curve," and one that "needed a further deviation to return — via the detour of Platonic and Aristotelian misunderstanding — closer to the original Presocratic point of view."[60]

On this account, instead of falling into the stereotypical intellectual trap of "try[ing] to drive a wedge between mere ideas and the living of them," we should instead accommodate ourselves to the increasingly appreciated need "to view ancient philosophy in terms of a way of life" and "to understand philosophical documents against a wider contextual background."[61] This contextual background is, Kingsley suggests, a "magical" one, and specifically, he argues, we need to understand the teaching of Empedocles "in the context of Sicilian mythology, mystery, and magic"; or in other words, "in an initiatory context."[62] This might strike us surprising, unless we recall the legend that Plato had, at the age of 49, been initiated into the Greater Mysteries in an underground chamber below the Great Pyramid at Gaza.[63] So we might ask ourselves whether Aristotle is one of those thinkers who has helped us to move outside Plato's cave or someone who teaches us how best to live inside it.

Note 1

As we have seen, central to Aristotle's political outlook is his view that, from the beginning, the human being was a social or a gregarious being or animal. The phrase *animal sociale* can be found in numerous other thinkers, including Seneca (see his essays *On Benefits* [*De Beneficiis*], 27.17[64]; and *On Mercy* [*De Clementia*], 1.3)[65]; Macrobius, *On the Dream of Scipio* [*Somnium Scipionis*], 1. 8.6)[66]; Lactantius, *Divine Institutes* [*Institutiones Divinae*], 6.10.10[67]; and St. Bernard of Clairvaux, *Miscellaneous Sermons* [*Sermones de diversis*], 16.3, in *Opera*, I, 2350 D.[68] In his *History of Animals* (book 1, 488a), Aristotle draws a distinction between various kinds of animals—between the "gregarious" (*agelaia zoa*), the "dispersed" (*sporadikha*), and the "solitary" (*monadikha*):

> [T]he following differences are manifest in [animals'] modes of living and in their actions. Some are gregarious, some are solitary, whether they be furnished with feet or be fitted for a life in the water; and some partake of both characters. And of the gregarious, some are social, others independent. [...] Man partakes of both characters.[69]

Among those creatures he describes as "gregarious" (*agelaia*) he distinguishes further "civic" or "urban" animals (*politikha zoa*)—that is to say, those such as bees, wasps, ants, or men, who work in collaboration. The nature of this collaboration is, Aristotle is keen to emphasize, quite varied:

> Social creatures are such as have some one common object in view; and this property is not common to all creatures that are gregarious. Such social creatures are man, the bee, the wasp, the ant, and the crane. Again, of these social creatures some submit to a ruler, others are subject to no rule: as, for instance, the crane and the several sorts of bee submit to a ruler, whereas ants and numerous other creatures are subject to no rule.[70]

For some commentators, as Robert Eisler (1882–1949) pointed out, the gregarious nature of the human species—or as Rudolf Jordan called us, *homo sapiens socialis*—proves that we are not descended, not from the large apes such as the chimpanzee, the gorilla, or the orang-utan, but from a social species such as the gibbon or the siamang.[71] Whatever the facts of the evolutionary case may be, Aristotle brings the same empirical approach that he does to the study of animals to the study of human politics.

Note 2

Both Plato and Aristotle are interested in two key aspects of politics, what the ancient Greeks referred to as *nomoi* and *ethea*. These terms may be translated as "law" and "ethics," but the sense of these terms is not quite the same as our contemporary one.[72]

Plato's last (and longest) dialogue is called *Nómoi*, or *The Laws*, but the word retains here its fundamental sense, not so much of "statute" as of solemn "custom." For *Nomos* refers to usage or custom before it has been written down, as well as to the written form of statutory law.

Similarly, *ethea* may originally have derived from the "lair" or "haunt" of an animal, and in the sense that Aristotle uses the word as a term for "ethics," it acquires the meaning of a personal pattern of behaviour or even personal character. Between the original use of the words *nomos* and *ethos* in the Greek poet Hesiod (c. 750–650 BCE), who speaks in his *Theogony* of "the laws of all and the goodly ways of the immortals,"[73] and their use in Aristotle, these terms undergo a significant shift from the concrete to the abstract. The difference between them is defined by the area to which they refer: *nomoi* to public law and *ethea* to the private sphere of the individual or the family; it is not that *ethea* are any less binding than *nomoi*, but *nomos* refers to a larger field and *ethos* to the realm of the household, the family, and the feelings of the individual.[74] After all, in a sense there is nothing more binding upon the individual than the duty of being what she or he is. And this is why, for Aristotle, politics is so closely related to ethics.

Notes

1. For further discussion of this fundamental dichotomy between Plato and Aristotle, in relation to the motif of the cave, see Arthur Herman, *The Cave and the Light: Plato Versus Aristotle, and the Struggle for the Soul of Western Civilization* (New York: Random House, 2013).
2. On the likely construction of these and other treatises from Aristotle's lectures by Aristotle himself or later editors (and on the stylistic consequences), see Jonathan Barnes, *Aristotle: A Very Short Introduction* (Oxford: Oxford University Press, 2000), 5.
3. As Peter Kreeft has pointed out, Aristotle is nonetheless a Platonist, inasmuch as he does not deny that Platonic Forms are real, but he does deny the *horismos*, i.e., the "separation" of the Forms from things. The differences between Plato and Aristotle can be summarised as (a) in metaphysics, hylomorphism (i.e., the doctrine that being or *ousia* is a compound of matter and form); (b) in epistemology, empiricism and abstraction; (c) in anthropology, psychosomatic unity; and (d) in ethics, happiness in *this* world (Peter Kreeft, *The Platonic Tradition* (South Bend, IN: St Augustine's Press, 2018)). For further discussion, see A.E. Taylor, *Aristotle* (London and Edinburgh: Jack, 1919).
4. Norbert Hoerster (ed.), *Klassische Texte der Staatsphilosophie* (Munich: dtv, 1976), 48.
5. Cf. Socrates's notion of producing justice as "to establish the parts of the soul in a relation of mastering, and being mastered by, one another that is according to nature" and producing injustice as "to establish a relation of ruling, and being ruled by, one another that is contrary to nature" (*Republic*, 444d).
6. That a potential problem lies in this emphasis in nature is noted elsewhere by Hoerster, cf. *Klassiker der Staatsphilosophie*, 23. Nature returns as an important philosophical category in the thought of Nietzsche.
7. See J.L. Ackrill, "Aristotle on *eudaimonia*," *Proceedings of the British Academy* 60 (1974), 339–359; T.H. Irwin, "Conceptions of Happiness in the *Nicomachean Ethics*," in Christopher Shields (ed.), *The Oxford Handbook of Aristotle* (Oxford and New York: Oxford University Press, 2012), 495–528.
8. For a correction to this conventional but biased view of hedonism, see the work of Michel Onfray, especially *La Puissance d'exister: Manifeste hédoniste* (Paris: Grasset, 2006); *Manifeste hédoniste* (Paris: Éditions

Autrement, 2011); the five volumes of his *Journal hédoniste*, vols 1–4 (Paris: Grasset, 1996–2007), vol. 5 (Paris: Flammarion, 2013).

9. For a helpful overview of this work, see Pierre Pellegrin, "Aristotle's *Politics*," in Shields (ed.), *The Oxford Handbook of Aristotle*, 558–585.

10. The translation used here is Aristotle, *Politics*, trans. H. Rackham (Cambridge, MA and London: Harvard University Press and Heinemann, 1944).

11. Compare with Ernest Barker's remark that the "analytic method" is *in effect identical with* the "genetic method," because the genetic method begins with simple elements and "thus implies the use of analysis" (*The Politics of Aristotle*, trans. Ernest Barker (Oxford: Clarendon Press, 1952), 3, n. 1).

12. For Nietzsche's great work on genealogy, see *On the Genealogy of Morals* (1887), and its subsequent discussion by Foucault in "Nietzsche, Genealogy, History" (1971), in Paul Rabinow (ed.), *The Foucault Reader* (Harmondsworth: Penguin, 1984), 76–100. For further discussion, see Michael Mahon, *Foucault's Nietzschean Genealogy: Truth, Power, and the Subject* (Albany, NY: State University of New York Press, 1992).

13. See *The Odyssey*, book 9, l. 114. This passage is also quoted by Aristotle in his *Nicomachean Ethics*, Book 10, Chapter 9, 1180a, as well as the Athenian Stranger in Plato's *Laws*, book 3, 680b. In the *Laws*, the passage is cited in the context of a discussion contrasting "dynasty" (or *dunasteia*, i.e., "arbitrary rule"), law (or *themis*, i.e., "the law regulating a family-clan society"), and justice (or *dikē*, i.e., "the law regulating relations with those who do not belong to the clan") (*The Laws of Plato*, trans. Thomas Pangle (Chicago and London: University of Chicago Press, 1980), 521).

14. Barker, *Politics of Aristotle*, 5, n. 2.

15. See the *Iliad*, book 9, l. 63.

16. Aristotle, *Basic Works*, ed. Richard McKeon (New York: Random House, 1941), 1088.

17. Aristotle, *Basic Works*, 942.

18. Barker, *Politics of Aristotle*, 6, n. 1.

19. Barker, *Politics of Aristotle*, 7, n. 1.

20. For further discussion, see Appendix I, "Aristotle's Conception of Politics in the *Ethics* and the *Rhetoric*," and Appendix II, "Aristotle's Conception of Justice, Law, and Equity in the *Ethics* and the *Rhetoric*," in Barker, *Politics of Aristotle*, 354–361, 362–372.

21. Cf. Nietzsche's play on this passage in *Twilight of the Idols*, where he says: "To live alone one must be an animal or a god — says Aristotle. There is yet a third case: one must be both — a *philosopher*" ("Maxims and Arrows," §3; in *Twilight of the Idols and The Anti-Christ*, trans. R.J. Hollingdale (Harmondsworth: Penguin, 1968), 23).

22. Cf. "A city, I believe, comes into being because each of us isn't self-sufficient but is in need of much" (*Republic*, 369b).

23. Cf. Sara Maitland's *A Book of Silence* (London: Granta, 2008), 80–115.

24. Jean-Jacques Rousseau, *The Social Contract and Discourses*, trans. G.D.H. Cole (London: Dent, 1973), 76.

25. Or "to secure a system of good laws well obeyed" (Barker, *Politics of Aristotle*, 119), i.e., *eunomia*. Eunomia was the Greek goddess of law and legislation, the offspring of Themis (a Titaness) and Zeus (the king of the gods). Solon contrasts her to Dysnomia—"lawlessness," and according to Hesiod one of the daughters of Eris (or "strife," "chaos," "discord").

26. Lycophron's fame has been assured largely through Aristotle's references to him, including the critical remark made here. Thought to have been a pupil of the sophist Gorgias, Lycophron here proposes a contractual theory of law—although not on the Aristotelian basis that the state should exist to make its citizens just and good. See W.K.C. Guthrie, *The Sophists* (Cambridge: Cambridge University Press, 1971), 139–140, 313–314. The surviving fragments of Lycophron's writings barely cover three pages (*Les Présocratiques*, ed. Jean-Paul Dumont (Paris: Gallimard, 1988), 1051–1053).

27. Barker, *Politics of Aristotle*, 119, n. 1, cf. p. lxxi.

28. Barker, *Politics of Aristotle*, 120, n. 2.

29. Aristotle, *Basic Works*, 1073.

30. See Barker, *Politics of Aristotle*, Note B, "The Development of the *Polis* in Aristotle's View and in Greek History," 7–8.

31. Barker, *Politics of Aristotle*, 120, n. 2. As Barker goes on to note, "those who contribute more to the performance of good actions in and by the association, and who thus show a greater 'civic excellence' (i.e. a higher quality of membership of the association), deserve more from the polis — even if, on the ground of free birth, they are only equal or even inferior, and even if, on the ground of wealth, they are actually inferior" (ibid.).

32. Barker, *Politics of Aristotle*, "Note V: The Basis of the Classification of Constitutions," 113.

33. Barker, 114, n. 1.

34. For further discussion of these different kinds of constitution, see R.G. Mulgan, *Aristotle's Political Theory: An Introduction for Students of Political Theory* (Oxford: Clarendon Press, 1977), 53–77.

35. Aristotle, *Basic Works*, 1095.

36. Barker, *Politics of Aristotle*, 129–130, n. 4.

37. Barker, *Politics of Aristotle*, 131, n. 1.

38. Aristotle, *Basic Works*, 1223.

39. Barker, *Politics of Aristotle*, 131, n. 2. For an extensive discussion of the notion of *paideia*, as a kind of training in excellence, see the three-volume study by Werner Jaeger (1888–1961), *Paideia: The Ideals of Greek Culture* [1933–1947], trans. Gilbert Highet (New York: Oxford University Press, 1939–1944).

40. Barker, *Politics of Aristotle*, 151, Note GG, "The Interpretation of the 'Polity'."

41. See Richard Kraut, "Aristotle on Becoming Good: Habituation, Reflection, and Perception," in Shields (ed.), *The Oxford Handbook of Aristotle*, 529–557.

42. Barker, *Politics of Aristotle*, 152, n. 2.

43. Barker, *Politics of Aristotle*, Note S, "The Word *Polis* and Its Derivatives," 106.

44. Aristotle, *Basic Works*, 1185. (Aristotle contrasts this position with earlier times; cf. 1279a7–12; cf. book 2, 1261a37–b6.)

45. Plato, *The Republic*, trans. Allan Bloom (New York: Basic Books, 1991), 199.

46. Thucydides, *The Peloponnesian War*, ed. Walter Blanco and Jennifer Tolbert Roberts, trans. Walter Blanco (New York and London: Norton, 1998), 131.

47. Barker, *Politics of Aristotle*, Note SS, "Political Power and Economic Advantage," 230.

48. Barker, *Politics of Aristotle*, 229, n. 4.

49. Barker, *Politics of Aristotle*, 232, n. 2. Cf. *Politics*, Book 4, Chapter 12 (1296b35–1297a12).

50. Barker, *Politics of Aristotle*, 232–233, n. 3.

51. This image recurs in the Neoplatonic tradition represented by Plotinus who, in his *Enneads*, writes: "Withdraw into yourself and look. And if you do not find yourself beautiful yet, act as does the creator of a statue that is to be made beautiful; he cuts away here, he smoothes

there, he makes this line lighter, this other purer, until a lovely face has grown upon his work. So do you also: cut away all that is excessive, straighten all that is crooked, bring light to all that is overcast, labour to make all one glow of beauty and never cease chiselling your statue, until there shall shine out on you from it the godlike splendour of virtue" (Plotinus, *Enneads*, 1.6.9; in Plotinus, *The Enneads*, trans. S. MacKenna, 4th edn, rev. B.S. Page (London: Faber and Faber, 1969), 63). For further discussion, see Michel Onfray, *La Sculpture de soi: La morale esthétique* (Paris: Grasset, 1993), 77–90.

52. Although a two-world view is conventionally ascribed to Plato, it would be incorrect to describe Plato's outlook as a dualism: rather, both the ideal realm and the sensory realm stand in a relationship to each other, and the idea of the Good serves as the ultimate ground of Being. Thus there is a relationship not simply of correspondence but also of imitation: the world of ideas and the sensory world relate to teach other as the original (*paradeigma*) does to the copy (see Henning Ottmann, *Geschichte des politischen Denkens*, vol. 1, *Die Griechen*, part 2, *Von Platon bis zum Hellenismus* (Stuttgart and Weimar: Metzler, 2001), 7).

53. Aristotle, *Basic Works*, ed. Richard McKeon (New York: Random House, 1941), 690.

54. Bertrand Russell, *A History of Western Philosophy* (London: Unwin, 1985), 481.

55. Russell, *A History of Western Philosophy*, Chapter 21, 'Aristotle's Politics', 196–205 (196).

56. Suhrawardi, *Kitab hikmat al-ishraq* (*The Philosophy of Illumination*), 5.19–6.6; cited in Kingsley, *Ancient Philosophy, Mystery, and Magic: Empedocles and Pythagorean Tradition* (Oxford: Clarendon Press, 1995), 387; translated from Henry Corbin (trans.), C. Jambet (ed.), *Sohravardi: Le Livre de la sagesse orientale: Kitab Hikmat al-Ishraq* (Lagrasse: Verdier, 1986), 80–81. For further discussion, see John Walbridge, *The Leaven of the Ancients: Suhrawardi and the Heritage of the Greeks* (Albany, NY: State University of New York Press, 1999), Chapter 8, "Aristotle and the Peripatetics."

57. Kingsley, *Ancient Philosophy, Mystery, and Magic*, 386.

58. Thomas Whittaker, *The Neo-Platonists: A Study in the History of Hellenism*, 2nd edn (Cambridge: Cambridge University Press, 1918), 195.

59. Harold Cherniss, *Aristotle's Criticism of Presocratic Philosophy* (Baltimore: Johns Hopkins Press, 1935 and reprinted New York: Octagon Books, 1964); *Aristotle's Criticism of Plato and the Academy*

(Baltimore: Johns Hopkins Press, 1944). See Kingsley, *Ancient Philosophy, Mystery, and Magic*, 4, 386–387.

60. Kingsley, *Ancient Philosophy, Mystery, and Magic*, 208–209.

61. Kingsley, *Ancient Philosophy, Mystery, and Magic*, 228, 297. See Pierre Hadot, *What Is Ancient Philosophy?* trans. Michael Chase (Cambridge, MA and London: Belknap Press of Harvard University Press, 2002; rev. edn, 2004); *Philosophy as a Way of Life: Spiritual Exercises from Socrates to Foucault*, ed. Arnold Davidson, trans. Michael Chase (Malden, MA and Oxford: Blackwell, 1995).

62. Kingsley, *Ancient Philosophy, Mystery, and Magic*, 297, 359.

63. In his history of the esoteric tradition, the Candian-born history of occultism, Manly P. Hall (1901–1990), attributed this view to Thomas Taylor (1758–1835), the nineteenth-century English translator and latter-day Neoplatonist (see *The Secret Teachings of All Ages: An Encyclopedic Outline of Masonic, Hermetic, Qabbalistic and Rosicrucian Symbolical Philosophy* [1928] (New York: Tarcher/Penguin, 2003), 162).

64. "For how else do we live in security if it is not that we help each other by an exchange of good offices? It is only through the interchange of benefits that life becomes in some measure equipped and fortified against sudden disasters. Take us singly, and what are we? The prey of all creatures, their victims, whose blood is most delectable and most easily secured. For, while other creatures possess a strength that is adequate for their self-protection, and those that are born to be wanderers and to lead an isolated life have been given weapons, the covering of man is a frail skin; no might of claws or of teeth makes him a terror to others, naked and weak as he is, his safety lies in fellowship" (Seneca, *Moral Essays*, trans. John W. Basore (London: Heinemann, 1928–1935), vol. 3, 241).

65. "That no one of all the virtues is more seemly for a man, since none is more human, is a necessary conviction not only for those of us who maintain that man is a social creature, begotten for the common good, but also for those who give man over to pleasure, whose words and deeds all look to their own advantage" (Seneca, *Moral Essays*, vol. 1, 365).

66. "Man has political values because he is a social animal," (Macrobius, *Commentary on the Dream of Scipio*, trans. William Harris Stahl (New York: Columbia University Press, 1990), 121).

67. "For God, since He is kind, wished us to be a social animal" (*The Works of Lactantius*, trans. William Fletcher (Edinburgh: T & T Clark,

1871), vol. 1, 375; cf. Book 5, Chapter 19, "the nature of man is social and beneficent, in which respect alone he bears a relation to God" (334)).

68. Cf. Bernard of Clairvaux, *Monastic Sermons*, trans. Daniel Griggs (Collegeville, MN: Liturgical Press, 2016), "Introduction," xxvi. For further discussion, see Michael Casey, "*In communi vita fratrum:* St Bernard's Teachings on Cenobitic Solitude," *Analecta Sacri Ordinis Cisterciensis* 46 (1990), 243–261; David Appleby and Teresa Olsen Pierre, "Upright Posture and Human Dignity According to Bernard of Clairvaux," in David Appleby and Teresa Olsen Pierre (eds), *On the Shoulders of Giants: Essays in Honor of Glenn W. Olsen* (Toronto: Pontifical Institute of Medieval Studies, 2015), 159–178.

69. Aristotle, *Complete Works*, ed. Jonathan Barnes, 2 vols (Princeton, NJ: Princeton University Press, 1984), vol. 1, 776.

70. Aristotle, *Complete Works*, vol. 1, 776–777.

71. Rudolf Jordan, *Homo Sapiens Socialis: Principles of the Philosophy of Responsibility* (South Africa: Central News Agency, 1944). See Robert Eisler, *Man into Wolf: An Anthropological Interpretation of Sadism, Masochism, and Lycanthropy* (London: Spring Books, 1951), 29.

72. For this analysis of the correct distinction between *nomos* and *ethos*, see Eric A. Havelock, *Preface to Plato* (Cambridge, MA and London: Belknap Press of Harvard University Press, 1963), 62–63.

73. *Theogony*, l. 69; in Hesiod, *The Homeric Hymns and Homerica*, trans. Hugh G. Evelyn-White (Cambridge, MA and London: Harvard University Press and Heinemann, 1982), 83.

74. Havelock, *Preface to Plato*, 63.

4

Rousseau and the Social Contract

In this chapter we leap several centuries from Plato and Aristotle to Rousseau. In doing so, we must leap over much: over the late classical thought of Cicero (106 BCE–43 BCE)[1]; the early and medieval Christan thought of Augustine of Hippo (354–430) and Thomas Aquinas (1225–1274), both saints—and hence representative of the Catholic tradition of political thought; the Renaissance thought of Niccolò Machiavelli (1469–1527), author of *Il Principe* or *The Prince* (1513) and Thomas Hobbes of Malmesbury (1588–1679), author of *Leviathan* (1651); to say nothing of the Enlightenment tradition in England, Scotland, and France, represented by John Locke (1632–1704), David Hume (1711–1776), and Montesquieu (1689–1755).

Yet the thought of Jean-Jacques Rousseau (1712–1778) offers a good point to pick up our analysis of political thought as an attempt to find a way out of Plato's cave—that is, out of the cave described in the allegory in book 7 of the *Republic*. For an important background to Rousseau's thinking is the debate between Platonism and materialism that had taken place (and was still taking place) in early modern Europe.[2] Moreover, as David Lay Williams has argued, in order to understand Rousseau properly, we must understand "two important elements of his

© The Author(s) 2019
P. Bishop, *German Political Thought and the Discourse of Platonism*,
https://doi.org/10.1007/978-3-030-04510-4_4

education," namely, "the impression made on him by Plato" and "his complex relationship with the materialists."[3] The difference between these two schools has been summarized by Williams as follows:

Platonism	Materialism
• Embraces existence of immaterial (i.e., ideal) substance	• Denies existence of immaterial substance
• Embraces doctrine of free (human) will	• Asserts that human behaviour is pre-determined (by matter in motion)
• Open to notion of an immaterial God	• Finds notion of an immaterial God highly problematic

This materialist tradition can be found in the thought of Thomas Hobbes, especially in his *Leviathan* of 1651, revised in its Latin version of 1668. Born in Westport near Malmesbury, Hobbes witnessed at first hand the political crisis arising from the English Civil War (1642–1651). He applied his interest in the physics of motion and in the body to the political sphere, developing a contractarian theory which argued for the rule of an absolute sovereign, compared to the biblical figure of Leviathan, a huge sea monster (see Job 41: 24). Hobbes spent a number of years living in Paris,[4] and this materialist tradition can also be found in a number of prominent French thinkers as well, such as Julien de La Mettrie (1709–1751), Claude Helvétius (1715–1771), Paul-Henri Thiry (Baron) d'Holbach (1723–1789), and, most famously, in Denis Diderot (1713–1784). All these thinkers have recently been discussed by Michel Onfray and placed in the category of those thinkers whom he describes as *les ultras des Lumières*.[5]

La Mettrie presented an out-and-out materialist account of humankind in his celebrated treatise *Man A Machine* (1748). In *De l'esprit* or *On the Mind* (1758), Helvétius argued that there are only two sources of ideas, sensations and memories of those sensations: that "the physical sensibility and memory, or, to speak more exactly, that sensibility alone, produceth all our ideas," and hence that "every thing is reducible to feeling," i.e., to sense experience.[6] In his *System of Nature* (1770), Holbach drew out the deterministic consequences of materialism. "Man's life," he asserted, "is a line that nature commands him to describe upon the surface of the earth, a line that nature commands him to describe without his ever being able to swerve from it, even for an instant."[7] And Diderot, one of the chief editors with Jean le Rond d'Alembert (1717–1783) of the *Encyclopédie* (1751–1772), was equally firm in deriving determinism from materialism and in developing a strictly utilitarian ethics.

Yet while materialism became an increasingly vocal position within the tradition of the Enlightenment, it was not the only one. Following the closure of Plato's Academy in 529 CE on the orders of the Emperor Justinian I, the Platonic tradition—founded by Plato, continued by the Middle Platonists, and developed into a remarkably sophisticated system by the Neoplatonists—came to an end. Or rather, it changed so that it could persist in other forms, notably Scholasticism and mysticism, until its revival in the Renaissance in Italy in the form of the Florentine Academy led by Marsilio Ficino (1433–1499). Other members of this Academy included Pico della Mirandola (1463–1494) and Cristoforo Landino (1424–1498), and its Platonic outlook has been summarized by Paul Oskar Kristeller (1905–1999) as follows:

[The mind] is capable of turning away from the body and the external world, and of concentrating upon its own inner substance. Thus purifying itself from things external, the soul enters the contemplative life and attains a higher knowledge, discovering the incorporeal or intelligible world that is closed to it while engaging in ordinary experience and in the troubles of external life.[8]

Elsewhere the Platonic tradition began to reassert itself too. For instance, in the seventeenth century in Cambridge, a group of figures began to emerge known as the Cambridge Platonists. These included Henry More (1614–1687), Ralph Cudworth (1618–1689), and Benjamin Whichcote (1609–1683). The titles of Cudworth's works such as *A Treatise on Eternal and Immutable Morality* and *Of Freewill* reveal the direction of thought: in particular, in constructing an argument *against* the materialism and relativism of Hobbes.

There are also clearly Platonic elements in the thought of René Descartes (1596–1650), a philosopher widely identified as being the "father of modern philosophy" and whose *Meditations on First*

Philosophy (1641) has been described by Christia Mercer as "a handbook on how to escape the shadows of the cave and discover the illuminating truth beyond."[9] The Platonic strain in Descartes's thought can be identified in the following three respects: first, in the belief that certain truths are innate; second, in his distrust in the information provided by the senses; and third, in his insistence that intellect alone can discover truths.[10]

Likewise, in the German tradition, such scholars as Jakob Thomasius (1622–1684) and Johann Adam Scherzer (1628–1683) drew on Plato, as well as on Philo, Plotinus, Proclus, St. Augustine, and Johann Reuchlin (1455–1522), to establish a Platonist tradition not only in Leipzig, but in German-speaking Europe as a whole.[11] Their work, along with the work of such other Platonists as Athanasius Kircher (1602–1680), Johann Heinrich Alsted (1588–1638), and Erhard Weigel (1625–1699), was influential on another of the major philosophers of the modern period, Gottfried Wilhelm von Leibniz (1646–1716).

Leibniz fits into the tradition of a continuing tradition of Platonism in European thought that opposed materialism, determinism, and positivism in general and Hobbes in particular.[12] Without the notion of freedom, Leibniz argued in his *Theodicy* (1710), "the morality of actions [is] destroyed and all justice, divine and human, shaken" (§2).[13] For Hobbes, all normative standards are voluntaristic: that is, humans can choose which standards to embrace and which not to embrace. This approach is positivist, inasmuch as it discerns these standards in empirical circumstances, not via any kind of transcendental argumentation. For Leibniz, however, justice is not just something observed, but something innate—it is "the natural law written in our hearts."[14]

In France, the Platonic tradition advanced in the thought of the early Enlightenment. For instance, Nicolas Malebranche (1638–1715) advanced an understanding of causality dubbed "occasionalism." On this account, every event can be understood as arising from a dual causality: on the one hand, the "occasional" cause, something random or contingent, and, on the other, the real cause, that is, the will of God. In this way, Malebranche sought to reconcile (physical) causality with the existence of (divine) freedom. As well as embracing an ontological

Platonism, he advanced an epistemological Platonism, too: arguing that we know things only because we can access the realm of ideas through our intellect.[15]

As a consequence, there is an ethical Platonism to be found in Malebranche's thinking as well. In terms of the allegory from the *Republic*, if we stick with our senses, we remain in the cave: "A man who judges all things by his senses and loves only what flatters him, is in the most wretched state of mind possible. In this state he is infinitely removed from the truth and from his good." Nevertheless, it is possible to find the exit from the cave, and we can do so using our reason: "When a man judges things only according to the mind's pure ideas, when he carefully avoids the noisy confusion of creatures, and when entering into himself, he listens to his sovereign Master with his senses and passions silent, it is impossible for him to fall into error," he wrote in his preface to *The Search After Truth* (1674).[16]

The ethical implications of Platonism were equally important for François de Fénelon (1651–1716), a French theologian who was the Roman Catholic archbishop in Cambrai. Fénelon was the author of *The Adventures of Telemachus* (1699; reprinted 1717), a didactic novel centred around Homer's *Odyssey*. In this work, Fénelon recounts the educational journey undertaken by Telemachus, the son of Odysseus, under the tutelage of Mentor, who turns out to be the goddess of wisdom, Minerva, in disguise. The work is replete in Platonic echoes, from its opening in a cave to a discourse between Hazael and Mentor in book 4 that is saturated with Platonic images and vocabulary: the "First Power which produced the heavens and the earth," the "infinite and immutable Intelligence which communicates itself to all, but is not divided," the "sovereign and universal Truth which illuminates intellectual nature, as the sun enlightens the material world," the "dictates of eternal reason," the "guiding ray that is vouchsafed from above," as opposed to "fleeting illusions by a glimmering and deceitful light," "unsubstantial vapours, that are every moment changing their colour and shape, and at length fade into total obscurity," the "gaudy phantoms of imagination."[17] As Williams observes, Fénelon's commitment to "the central Platonic ontological doctrine of transcendence and its attendant virtues, in addition to its epistemic Platonism," shows itself to be beyond question.[18]

Hence it is no exaggeration to talk about the persistence of Platonic discourse in early modern European philosophy. And there is good evidence that Rousseau was familiar with modern European Platonism, although in varying degrees. For instance, it is unlikely he ever read the Cambridge Platonists or the German pre-Leibnizian Platonists; he never cites the work of Ficino, but he used Ficino's Latin translations of Plato's works; while we know he read Descartes, Leibniz, Malebranche, and Fénelon. Indeed, in the wake of the Lisbon earthquake of 1755, Rousseau responded in his "Letter to Voltaire" (1756) to Voltaire's critique of optimism in his "Poem on the Lisbon Disaster" (1756) by defending Leibniz's doctrine of the best of all possible worlds[19]; while in his novelistic treatise *Émile*, Rousseau chose Fénelon's *Telemachus* to be the book that Émile should take with him into the real world …

Equally, Rousseau's doctrine of "inner sentiment" stands in complete opposition to the teachings of the materialists. And while he was friends with Diderot, d'Holbach, and to a certain extent Helvétius, he was also acquainted with such deists and antimaterialists as Abbé Guillaume-Thomas Raynal (1713–1796) and Jean-François Marmontel (1723–1799). Marmontel's notion in his *Bélisaire* (1767) of the "inner voice" of conscience is, in important respects, remarkably close to Rousseau's notion of "inner sentiment." Having taken into account the influence of Platonism on Rousseau and his complex relationship with the materialist tradition, let us turn to a consideration of some of his texts.

In 1750, Rousseau responded to an advertisement placed by the Academy of Dijon to submit for consideration for a prize essays responding to the question, "Has the restoration of the sciences and arts contributed to the purification of morals?" The essay Rousseau wrote for this competition, known as the "Discourse on the Sciences and Arts" (known as the first *Discourse*), won first prize. Four years later a similar competition was organised by the Academy of Dijon, this time the question being, "What is the origin of inequality among people, and is it authorized by natural law?", and again Rousseau submitted an essay. This time, Rousseau did not win a prize (instead, it went to a cleric called François Xavier Talbert), but nevertheless in 1755 Rousseau published his essay he had submitted under the title "Discourse on the

Origin and Basis of Inequality Among Men" (known as the second *Discourse*). Given that, for us today, it has been reckoned that just 1% of the world's richest people own about 50% of the world's wealth, and the eight richest people in the world own as much as all of the people in the bottom 50% of income, the question remains remarkably pertinent—as does Rousseau's answer.

As Rousseau makes clear from the outset, he takes as the starting-point for his thinking the idea of the "state of nature." While this idea is closely associated with his name, Rousseau is not its inventor. For instance, we find the term in the thought of St Thomas Aquinas (see *De Veritate*, question 19, article 1, answer 13).[20] Aquinas follows Aristotle in arguing that the state of nature is not something prior to the foundation of the political community, but rather it *is* that political community. After all, for Aristotle, the human being is the *zoon politikon*, and it lies in our nature as human beings to organise ourselves into political communities.

Then again, we also find the term the "state of nature" in the work of Thomas Hobbes, in many respects the target against which Rousseau directs many of his arguments. Given the background of the English Civil War (1642–1651), which pitted "Roundheads" against "Cavaliers," i.e., Parliamentarians against Royalists, as well as Protestants against Catholics, but also given the background of his own fundamental pessimism, Hobbes concluded that the "state of nature" was, in fact, a dismal thing. In his *Leviathan*, he argued that the state came into being in order to prevent human beings fighting among themselves: for him, the state of nature is a condition of war. This war is a war of "every man, against every man"[21]; in it, "every man is Enemy to every man"; and so each individual is like a wolf to his or her fellow individuals (or, to use the Latin phrase, *homo homini lupus est*) and, as a consequence, the individual's life is "solitary, poore, nasty, brutish, and short."[22] And so the state comes into being (by means of mutual contracts).

These positions recall the arguments put forward in Plato's *Republic* about the origin and nature of justice. Just as Thrasymachus argued that justice serves the interests of those who are stronger by nature and Glaucon argued that justice serves the interests of all by protecting each individual against the aggression of his or her fellow citizens, so Aristotle (and, in turn, Aquinas) and finally Hobbes propose the view that the political state comes into being as a response to something in or about humankind when it is in the state of nature. Yet by making the appeal to the notion of the **contract**, however, such thinkers as Aristotle, Hobbes, and Rousseau in effect "de-transcendentalize" justice and the state. That is to say, the state does not—as it does in Plato—come into being as a result of meditation on the idea of the Good; rather, it arises from the ground up by means of establishing different local, and finally a universal, contracts.[23]

The idea of the state of nature is also prominent in the thought of John Locke in his *Second Treatise on Civil Government* (1680s), for Montesquieu in his *The Spirit of the Laws* (1748), and for David Hume in his *A Treatise of Human Nature* (1739). In the twentieth century, the idea makes a notable come-back in the thought of the contemporary American political philosopher John Rawls (1921–2002), who develops his argument about justice in *A Theory of Justice* (1971) in relation to the postulate of an "original position," and in the work of another American philosopher, Robert Nozick (1938–2002), who argues in *Anarchy, State, and Utopia* (1974), a libertarian response to Rawls, that a minimal state of property right and basic law enforcement would arise out of a state of nature.

That said, it is important, as we saw it was in the case of Aristotle, to distinguish between the logical and temporal priority of the state of nature. Is it prior to the human being as a being that becomes socialized in the political state, or is it an argument about history? Does the idea of the state of nature assume the empirical existence of a time in the history of humankind where there was no political organisation? Or is it trying to get at something much closer to the experience of every human being?

After all, is not each one of us born in a state of nature? That is, as a human being we enter the world as a baby, in a state that is pure biology, completely lacking in any socialization of any kind. Then, we gradually commence the path of socialization, including the education we receive in the home, at school, and in other institutitions.

In other words, the transition from the state of nature to the "civilized" state is one that each of us undergoes in the process of—**education**.

Hence the importance for Rousseau of education, a theme he develops not least in his important novelistic treatise of 1762, entitled *Émile, or On Education*.[24] It cannot be underscored how significant the issue of education is for Rousseau as it is for the Enlightenment as a whole. (Kant, for instance, defined Enlightenment as an essentially educative process, as the emergence of the individual from his or her self-imposed tutelage.)[25] Whatever we think of Rousseau's own decision, for which he has become notorious, to abandon the five children he had with Thérèse Levasseur by handing them over to a foundling hospital, it is interesting that in his *Confessions*, book 9, he argues that he made this decision for pragmatic (indeed, pedagogical) reasons: "Children came, who might have filled [the void in the heart]; but that made things even worse. I trembled at the thought of entrusting them to that badly brought-up family, to be brought up even more badly. The risks of their upbringing by the Foundling Hospital were considerably less."[26]

More important, the question of education is a definite link back to the question of how to read Plato's cave. For the allegory of the cave can be interpreted along so many different lines, including the epistemological or metaphysical, the educational, and the political. These last two are perhaps particularly closely linked. After all, Socrates introduces the allegory by saying it is "an image of our nature in its education and want of education" (514a), and the prisoners in the cave are described as being with their legs and necks in bonds "from childhood" (514a). By having one of these prisoners break free and be led by the hand *up into the world outside the cave*, Plato has presented us with an awe-inspiring allegory about the power of "upbringing."

So it is no surprise that Rousseau, in his second *Discourse*, presents the proposal of the social contract—"Let us join [...] to guard the weak from oppression, to restrain the ambitious, and secure to every man the possession of what belongs to him" (*SD*, 221)—in relation to the metaphor of chains: "All ran headlong to their chains, in hopes of securing their liberty; for they had just wit enough to perceive the advantages of political institutions, without experience enough to enable them to foresee the dangers" (*SD*, 221).[27] In this *Discourse*, he emphasizes the theme of the happy slave: "I know that [they]"—i.e., the poor who have been duped in the social contract—"are for ever holding forth in praise of the tranquillity they enjoy in their chains, and that they call a state of wretched servitude a state of peace [...]" (*SD*, 225).[28]

Nor is it a surprise that Rousseau, in *Émile*, praises Plato's *Republic* as "the most beautiful educational treatise ever written," and it should give us pause for thought that he describes it as "not at all a political work, as think those who judge books only by their titles."[29] Moreover, the image of chains plays an important role in this text. As Williams has noted, "the parallels with Plato are again striking," and the text's vocabulary—"chains," "slavery," "illusion," "deception," "opinion"—is "remarkably reminiscent of the Platonic lexicon."[30] Once again, we should recall that *Émile* is written as a response to an earlier fictional work by a Platonist, Fénelon, and that his novel, *Telemachus* (1699), is the work with which, holding it in his hand, Émile is sent as a young adult into the world.

In the opening paragraph of his *Discourse on the Origin and Basis of Inequality Among Men* (1755) we find Rousseau introducing the notion of the "state of nature" (*SD*, 175). From the outset of his second *Discourse*, Rousseau recognizes that he is working within a pre-existent tradition of thought, acknowledging the contribution of previous "philosophers [...] who have inquired into the foundations of society." At the same time, he sounds a critical tone: while they have all "felt the necessity of going back to a state of nature," he believes that "not one of them has got there." What strongly emerges from this opening paragraph is a sense of the plurality of existing views, recalling the discussion in Plato's *Republic* of the differing views about the nature of justice. At the same time, there emerges a common thread that links all of them, namely that "in speaking of the savage"—that is, the "primitive" (or more correctly the individual prior to the process of civilization, i.e., socialization)—all these thinkers are, in fact, describing the socialized individual. In other words, the "state of nature"—this term associated with Rousseau, but also found in such earlier thinkers as Aquinas, Hobbes, and Locke—is no such thing, but a description of the "civilized" human being.

As the second *Discourse* proceeds, it becomes clear that Rousseau wishes to take particular issue with the position proposed by Hobbes (*SD*, 195–197). The idea of the natural state of humankind as Rousseau conceives it represents a break with at least two previous thinkers. To begin with, it is a break with the thought of Aristotle, and the idea of the natural sociability of the human being, or that the human being is the *zoon politikon*. And it is a break with the thought of Hobbes, and his thesis that human beings are naturally evil. "Let us not conclude," Rousseau argues, taking aim at Hobbes by name, that "because man has no idea of goodness, he must be naturally wicked; that he is vicious because he does not know virtue"; for Hobbes, in Rousseau's view, has overlooked something fundamental: he "did not reflect that the same cause, which prevents a savage from making use of his reason, as our jurists hold, prevents him also from abusing his faculties, as Hobbes himself allows: so that it may be justly said that savages are not bad merely because they do not know what it is to be good" (*SD*, 195–197).[31]

In his exploration of the human being in the state of nature, Rousseau introduces a terminology that seeks to distinguish an important emotional component in the process of civilization. Thus he distinguishes between "compassion" and *amour de soi*, between the capacity for empathy and an essentially egotistical drive (*SD*, 199–200). Here Rousseau introduces a number of key distinctions we need to examine in order to understand his thought:

- *amour de soi* or "love of self," the need for food, clothes, shelter; these are what Epicurus would call "natural and necessary desires"
- *amour propre*, or social esteem depending on the opinion of others; the desire for honour, status, prestige; this is what Epicurus would call "vain and empty" desires
- *pitié*, or "compassion"; today we might call this a capacity for empathy.

In this extract Rousseau explicitly engages with the Platonic idea, which he swiftly dismisses, that reason alone is adequate for a virtuous life. No, there must, he believes, be an emotional component too, for "although it might belong to Socrates and other minds of the like craft to acquire virtue by reason, the human race would long since have ceased to be, had its preservation depended only on the reasonings of the individuals composing it" (*SD*, 199–200).

What did the state of nature actually look like? In the opening sentence of the following extract, Rousseau paints a picture of a life characterized chiefly by lack:

> Let us conclude then that man in a state of nature, wandering up and down the forests, without industry, without speech, and without home, [was] an equal stranger to war and to all ties, neither standing in need of his fellow-creatures nor having any desire to hurt them, and perhaps even not distinguishing them one from another; [...] If I have expatiated at such length on this supposed primitive state, it is because I had so many ancient errors and inveterate prejudices to eradicate, and therefore thought it incumbent on me to dig down to their very root, and show, by means of a true picture of the state of nature, how far even the natural inequalities of mankind are from having that reality and influence which modern writers suppose. (*SD*, 203–204)

The lack which characterizes the state of nature could equally well characterize the state in which a young child finds itself: wandering up and down the forests (or the living room), without industry (or any homework), without speech (but simply crying or gurgling), without home (but simply sleeping whenever or wherever it can) ... The young child, before the Lacanian mirror stage, does not recognize other babies as other individuals, and so can harbour no desire to harm them—or to help them.

In the final paragraph, Rousseau makes a significant acknowledgment. For here he concedes that the notion of a state of nature is an assumption ("a true picture"), and not a concrete historical fact; as Freud will later do in *Totem and Taboo* (1913) in relation to the "primal horde,"[32] Rousseau acknowledges he is not in a position to provide concrete empirical evidence, but believes that the notion has an argumentational value. So what Rousseau calls here an assumption, "expatiat[ing] at length on this supposed primitive state," is something empirically observable in the life of every individual human; although its projection back in time to a putative historical moment is, of course, just as speculative as the memorable scene depicting the life of primitive human beings that opens the film version of Arthur C. Clarke's *2001: A Space Odyssey* (directed by Stanley Kubrick, 1968).[33]

This propositional or argumentational (as opposed to factual or empirical) value of the notion of "the state of nature" clearly emerges at the opening of the second part of the second *Discourse*. Whereas in *Totem and Taboo* Freud will argue that the great foundational act underpinning civilization was an act of gross and brutal violence (i.e., the killing of the primal father by the resentful sons of the primal horde), Rousseau here argues that civilization is founded by an act that is in itself less violent, but has equally horrific consequences: the invention of property:

> The first man who, having enclosed a piece of ground, bethought himself of saying *This is mine*, and found people simple enough to believe him, was the real founder of civil society. From how many crimes, wars and murders, from how many horrors and misfortunes might not any one have saved mankind, by pulling up the stakes, or filling up the ditch, and crying to his fellows, "Beware of listening to this impostor; you are undone if you once forget that the fruits of the earth belong to us all, and the earth itself to nobody." (*SD*, 207)

The figure with which Rousseau here presents us stands in contrast to the individual of whon Aristotle said that, while "the impulse to form a partnership of this kind is present in all men by nature," it was "the man who first united people in such a partnership" who was "the greatest of benefactors."

Now the putative *historical* perspective taken by Rousseau in his second *Discourse* informs the political analysis of the contemporary situation undertaken in his treatise, *The Social Contract* (1762), which he subtitled "Principles of Political Right." In its arresting opening lines, we find ourselves back in the world of Plato's cave: that is to say, we find ourselves in **chains**:

Man is born free; and everywhere he is in chains. One thinks himself the master of others, and still remains a greater slave than they. How did this change come about? I do not know. What can make it legitimate? That question I think I can answer.

If I took into account only force, and the effects derived from it, I should say: "As long as a people is compelled to obey, and obeys, it does well; as soon as it can shake off the yoke, and shakes it off, it does still better; for, regaining its liberty by the same right as took it away, either it is justified in resuming it, or there was no justification for those who took it away." But the social order is a sacred right which is the basis of all other rights. Nevertheless, this right does not come from nature, and must therefore be founded on conventions. Before coming to that, I have to prove what I have just asserted. (*SC*, 6; Book 1, Chapter 1)

This striking image of chains plays an almost obsessive role in the thought of Rousseau. Moreover, it is significant that, as in Plato's allegory of the cave, the chains are not recognized as being chains, and the prisoners who wear them mistakenly regard themselves as being free. In his first *Discourse*, Rousseau speaks of "the arts, literature, and the sciences" as flinging "garlands of flowers over the chains which weigh [people] down" and of making men and women "love their own slavery" (*FD*, 130–131). "Happy slaves!"—this is how Rousseau addresses the "civilized peoples" (*FD*, 131). As Williams has noted, all of this vocabulary of "chains, slaves, garlands, appearances [...] borrows extensively from Plato"; after all, in the *Republic* Socrates specifically remarks in book 8 that, living in a democratic society, individuals end up cherishing what are really "vices" and crowning them with "garlands" (560e).

What, in the context of this opening paragraph of *The Social Contract*, does Rousseau mean by "freedom"? Does he mean physical freedom, the right to unrestricted movement? Or does he mean moral freedom, what the Greeks called *sophrosyne* or self-control, the freedom to make good moral choices? As Plato observes in the *Republic*, "the real tyrant is, even if he doesn't seem so to someone, in truth a real slave to the greatest fawning and slavery, and a flatterer of the most worthless men" (579d). Is Rousseau simply concerned to liberate us from the (illegitimate) chains of tyranny, opinion, and ill-guided emotion? Or is he trying to replace them with the (legitimate) chains of the eternal laws (of nature)?[34]

In his elaboration of this initial and striking image of the chains, Rousseau introduces a dialectic of **MASTER and SLAVE**.[35] Like the prisoners in the Platonic cave, we believe ourselves to be "masters," yet we are in fact "slaves." "How did this change come about?", Rousseau asks, to which he coyly replies, "I do not know" (*SC*, 5; Book 1, Chapter 1). Yet it is clear that this posture of Socratic ignorance, of knowing that he only knows nothing, is a pretence; Rousseau goes on to elaborate a detailed explanation of how this situation has arisen by introducing another key concept, the idea of the **CONTRACT** (*SC*, 8–9; Book 1, Chapter 3).

Not for Rousseau the simple opposition of the strong and the weak, as found in the arguments of Thrasymachus and Glaucon in Plato's *Republic*. Instead, as he goes on to argue in a chapter of *The Social Contract* entitled "Of Slavery," even those who are strong are no more free than are the dwellers in the Platonic cave:

> It will be said that the despot assures his subjects civil tranquillity. Granted; but what do they gain, if the wars his ambition brings down upon them, his insatiable avidity, and the vexatious conduct of his ministers press harder on them than their own dissensions would have done? What do they gain, if the very tranquillity they enjoy is one of their miseries? Tranquillity is found also in dungeons; but is that enough to make them desirable places to live in? The Greeks imprisoned in the cave of the Cyclops lived there very tranquilly, while they were awaiting their turn to be devoured. (*SC*, 9–10; Book 1, Chapter 4)

Or to be more accurate, Rousseau alludes here to yet another cave: not this time, it is true, the allegory of the cave in the *Republic*, but the cave of the Cyclops in book 9 of Homer's *Odyssey*. (When Odysseus and his men arrive in the land of the Cyclops, they explore the mainland and come across a cave overlooking a beach: "There we saw a cave on the verge, close to the sea / High up, overhung with laurel"[36]; trapped inside his cave by Polyphemus, Odysseus and his men wait to be eaten by him, two at a time, until Odysseus blinds the Cyclops and effects his crew's escape.)

Yet as Williams points out, there are a number of important similarities between Homer's cave from the *Odyssey* and Plato's cave in the *Republic*. First, the cave of the Cyclops is clearly a cave of despotism, pointing to the political dimension of both caves. In the allegory of the cave and in the *Odyssey*, human beings are victims of an oppressive, even sinister, regime. Second, Rousseau repeatedly emphasizes (although it is not actually in the Greek text) the "tranquillity" of the cave and the life of those imprisoned in it. Correspondingly, the prisoners in Plato's cave feel more tranquil underground, for those who are released feel "pain" and are "dazzled" by the light of the fire, their eyes "hurt" and they want to "flee," are "distressed and annoyed" at being dragged up to the sun, find their eyes "full of beams and unable to see" in the light of the sun; the release and ascent from the cave is a painful process.

Correspondingly, there are a number of important similarities between the allegory of the cave in Plato and the image of the cave as used by Rousseau:

- both Plato and Rousseau characterize their highest principles as eternal: as "eternal laws of nature" and "eternal justice" in Rousseau's *Émile* (473 and 292), as "the idea of the good" and as knowing "what is always, and not [...] what is at any time coming into being and passing away" (526d and 527b)
- both Plato and Rousseau reject social convention or agreement as a source of such highest principles
- both Plato and Rousseau deny that empirical data can serve as a source of these ideas (i.e., both reject reductionism)
- both believe (and this makes them controversial) that these principles are valid across all cultures (i.e., both reject relativism)

Central to Rousseau's thinking is the question of freedom, and this is a point on which he insists. But what, he is also interested in asking, does it mean for one to be free? "To renounce liberty is to renounce being a man, to surrender the rights of humanity and even its duties," he writes: "For him who renounces everything no indemnity is possible. Such a renunciation is incompatible with man's nature" (*SC*, 10; Book 1, Chapter 4). In order to bring out the radical nature of his emphasis on freedom, Rousseau has recourse to an extreme hypothetical example:

> Even if we assume this terrible right to kill everybody, I maintain that a slave made in war, or a conquered people, is under no obligation to a master, except to obey him as far as he is compelled to do so. By taking an equivalent for his life, the victor has not done him a favour; instead of killing him without profit, he has killed him usefully. So far then is he from acquiring over him any authority in addition to that of force, that the state of war continues to subsist between them: their mutual relation is the effect of it, and the usage of the right of war does not imply a treaty of peace. A convention has indeed been made; but this convention, so far from destroying the state of war, presupposes its continuance.
>
> (*SC*, 12–13; Book 1, Chapter 4)

And this leads Rousseau to the central question of *The Social Contract*, and he explains the construction and content of the **social contract** at considerable length (*SC*, 14–16; Book 1, Chapter 6; cf. *SC*, 16–18; Book 1, Chapter 7):

> What man loses by the social contract is his natural liberty and an unlimited right to everything he tries to get and succeeds in getting; what he gains is civil liberty and the proprietorship of all he possesses. If we are to avoid mistake in weighing one against the other, we must clearly distinguish natural liberty, which is bounded only by the strength of the individual, from civil liberty, which is limited by the general will; and possession, which is merely the effect of force or the right of the first occupier, from property, which can be founded only on a positive title.
>
> We might, over and above all this, add, to what man acquires in the civil state, moral liberty, which alone makes him truly master of himself; for the mere impulse of appetite is slavery, while obedience to a law which we prescribe to ourselves is liberty. [...].
>
> (*SC*, 18–19; Book 1, Chapter 8)

In these extracts Rousseau introduces another key set of distinctions in his thought:

- individual will, i.e., the will of the individual
- *volonté générale*, or "general will"

The problem which the social contract tries to solve is this: namely, how to find "a form of association which will defend and protect with the whole common force the person and goods of each associate, and in which each, while uniting himself with all, may still obey himself alone, and remain as free as before." And the solution which it provides is this: "Each of us puts his person and all his power in common under the supreme direction of the general will, and, in our corporate capacity, we receive each member as an indivisible part of the whole."

In other words, each of us has to subsume his or her individual will to the general will, yet in so doing we are not simply renouncing our individual will, but we are discovering the extent to which we are participants in the *volonté générale*. In the remarkable—and, for some, chilling—phrase which Rousseau uses, "whoever refuses to obey the general will shall be compelled to do so by the whole body," or in other words such an individual must "be forced to be free."

Thus in Rousseau's words the passage from the "state of nature" to a civil state produces a remarkable change in the individual. And herein lies the paradoxical nature of the social contract: on the one hand, it results in a loss of natural liberty, inasmuch as we are no longer free simply to do as we please; yet it also results in a gain of civil liberty—and in a gain of moral liberty too!

Yet how are all these individual wills to discover themselves in the collective general will? After all, as experience shows us, if we get a group of people in a room, we get as many opinions as there are people in the room (and sometimes, even more!). So how does the general will emerge? Or how is the individual to be compelled to obey the general will? Who will force the individual to be free?

At this point Rousseau introduces the figure of the legislator or lawgiver (*législateur*). The legislator is the embodiment of the general will, and it forms part of the "de-transcendentalization" of political liberty that is so important for Rousseau. Rather than sovereignty residing in the divine right of kings, sovereignty resides in the people—and the legislator is their voice. In the allegory of the cave in Plato's *Republic*, there must be someone who escapes from the cave and discovers there is the idea of the Good, and whose task is then to return to the cave with this insight. Correspondingly, Rousseau brings Book 1, Chapter 9, of *The Social Contract* to the following conclusion:

> Instead of destroying natural inequality, the fundamental compact substitutes, for such physical inequality as nature may have set up between men, an equality that is moral and legitimate, and that men, who may be unequal in strength or intelligence, become every one equal by convention and legal right. Under bad governments, this equality is only apparent and illusory: it serves only to keep the pauper in his poverty and the rich man in the position he has usurped. In fact, laws are always of use to those who possess and harmful to those who have nothing: from which it follows that the social state is advantageous to men only when all have something and none too much.
>
> (*SC*, 21–22)

from which he moves into Book 2, Chapters 1 and 2:

> I hold then that Sovereignty, being nothing less than the exercise of the general will, can never be alienated, and that the Sovereign, who is no less than a collective being, cannot be represented except by himself: the power indeed may be transmitted, but not the will. [...]
>
> This does not mean that the commands of the rulers cannot pass for general wills, so long as the Sovereign, being free to oppose them, offers no opposition. In such a case, universal silence is taken to imply the consent of the people.
>
> (*SC*, 22–23; Book 2, Chapter 1; cf. *SC*, 23–24; Book 2, Chapter 2)

As David Lay Williams emphasizes, both the Platonic philosopher-king and the Rousseauian legislator are "charged with heady duties." In the case of the former, he or she must undertake not only the difficult ascent, but also the even more difficult return to the cave: "So you must go down, each in his turn, into the common dwelling of the others and get habituated along with them to seeing the dark things," Socrates says. "And," he continues, "in getting habituated to it, you will see ten thousand times better than the men there, and you'll know what each of the phantoms is, and of what it is a phantom, because you have seen the truth about fair, just, and good things" (520c). In the case of the latter, the legislator faces the no less difficult task of articulating the general will.

On the account that Rousseau puts forward, the general will is always right because it tends to the public advantage. Nevertheless, people's individual decisions can be wrong, and if they can err as individuals, they can err as a mass. Hence Rousseau distinguishes further between the "general will" (or *volonté générale*) and the "will of all" (or *volonté de tous*):

> It follows from what has gone before that the general will is always right and tends to the public advantage; but it does not follow that the deliberations of the people are always equally correct. Our will is always for our own good, but we do not always see what that is; the people is never corrupted, but it is often deceived, and on such occasions only does it seem to will what is bad.
>
> There is often a great deal of difference between the will of all and the general will; the latter considers only the common interest, while the former takes private interest into account, and is no more than a sum of particular wills: but take away from these same wills the pluses and minuses that cancel one another, and the general will remains as the sum of the differences.
>
> (*SC*, 25–26; Book 2, Chapter 3)

In this extract Rousseau invokes a number of historical examples in support of his argument. "If the general will is to be able to express itself", he argues, "there should be no partial society within the State, and [...] each citizen should think only his own thoughts," invoking the example of Lycurgus of Sparta.

This great figure created the constitution of the ancient Greek city-state of Sparta (or Lacedaemon), dividing the territory into equal parts and thus suppressing social inequality. (Lycurgus also went further: in accordance with the command of the Oracle of Apollo at Delphi, he established the military-oriented reform of Sparta into a great military power. Thanks to his reforms, the citizens of Sparta embraced not just equality but also military fitness and an austere life-style.) Other models for the legislator as conceived by Rousseau are Solon, the Athenian lawgiver, who divided citizens into four different classes depending on their income; Numa Pompilius, the legendary second kind of Rome, who overcame the division between Romans and Sabines by creating a number of trade associations; and Servius Tullius, the legendary sixth king of Rome, who divided the population into a number of *centuriae* (or groups of a hundred men). Such measures, Rousseau argues, ensure that the general will can always be discerned—and the people never err.

There is, in other words, an important analogy between the power of the individual and the power of the state: "As nature gives each man absolute power over all his members, the social compact gives the body politic absolute power over all its members also; and it is this power which, under the direction of the general will, bears, as I have said, the name of Sovereignty" (*SC*, 26–27; Book 2, Chapter 4). Similarly, we might recall that, in Plato's *Republic*, Socrates draws a parallel in book 2 between the "justice of one man" and the "justice of a whole city" (368e), which has a crucial methodological implication for the rest of the dialogue: "If we should watch a city coming into being in speech," he says, we would also see "its justice coming into being, and its injustice" (369a). On this basis, he concludes in book 4, "the just man will not be any different from the just city with respect to the form itself of justice, but will be like it" (435a–b).

What we have to realize, Rousseau continues, is that there is a fundamental agreement between the "interest" of individuals and "justice" itself (*SC*, 28–32; Book 2, Chapters 4–5), a harmony which he explains as follows. Seen within the context of this agreement between individual "interest" and "justice," Rousseau concludes, the social contract is not so much an act of renunciation as one of advantageous exchange (*SC*, 33–34; Book 2, Chapter 6). Rousseau characterizes a state that is governed by laws of the kind he has been describing as a "republic." Rejecting in a footnote both aristocracy and democracy, Rousseau ascribes full political legitimacy to a government that works in accordance with the general will.

In Book 2, Chapter 7, which is specifically titled "The Legislator," Rousseau engages explicitly with the views expressed alike by Caligula and in the course of the Platonic dialogue called *The Statesman*, before going on to offer an picture of the abstraction of the political individual that would later be cited by Marx, in "On the Jewish Question" (1844).[37] What is important about the figure of the legislator is his or her charismatic power, which derives not so much from any personal qualities as from his or her "genius" and his or her political office (*SC*, 36; Book 2, Chapter 7).

Thus the figure of the legislator constitutes the positive counterpart to the individual who instituted the notion of property, and forms an equivalent to the "benefactor" (of whom Aristotle had spoken in *Politics*, 1253a) who was responsible for founding the state.

As Rousseau goes on to explain, it is the free vote of the people that assures that a particular will is in uniformity with the general will. The apparently paradoxical task of legislation brings Rousseau to a discussion of two further matters: the problem of language, of communication, of rhetoric; and the question of the political function of religion (*SC*, 36–38; Book 2, Chapter 7). Here Rousseau demonstrates a more positive understanding of the political role for communication and presentation skills than one finds in Plato, given his scepticism about the rhetorical arts of his Sophist opponents. Yet both thinkers attach great importance to religion, albeit in varying ways. For Plato, it is important that the religion of the state be upheld; as the Athenian Stranger puts it in *The Laws*, of all evils "the gravest are the unrestrained and insolent things done by the young," especially "when they offend against things that are public as well as hallowed" (884a).[38] In the *Republic*, Socrates is particularly concerned in books 2 and 3 about how the gods are presented in the works of Homer and Hesiod, while book 10 concludes with the myth of Er, sustaining a belief about judgement in the afterlife. For Rousseau, it is important to relocate divine authority in the figure of the charismatic legislator, and he expresses admiration in particular for Judaism and for Islam.

In fact, Rousseau explicitly engages with the position of William Warburton (1698–1779), the Bishop of Gloucester and the author of treatises on the relation between religion and politics. In what was his best known work (and is today but one among his many forgotten works), *Divine Legislation of Moses demonstrated on the Principles of a Religious Deist* (1737–1741), Warburton defends the Mosaic writings in the Hebrew bible against the deist critique that the absence of any attempt to inculcate a belief in a future life constitutes a valid objection to those arguing for their divine authority. For, Warburton argued, the omission of any such belief that would have provided a sanction for the moral code itself served to prove that it was no human legislator who stood at the origin of the Mosaic law.

Rousseau's and Plato's comments raise the question: is the understanding of the function of religion in the German political tradition the same as that of the adherents of such religions? Is a political philosopher's belief in religion the same as that of its other believers? After all, there would be seem to be a major difference between the greatest good as conceived by religious thought—namely, that there exists a greatest Good, or what Plato calls the idea of the Good—and what Rousseau regards as "the greatest good of all," namely "liberty" and "equality" (*SC*, 45–46; Book 2, Chapter 11). In terms of how his ideas would work in practice, Rousseau seems to be in no doubt about the indestructibility of the general will, and its compatibility with *bon sens* or "common sense":

> As long as several men in assembly regard themselves as a single body, they have only a single will which is concerned with their common preservation and general well-being. In this case, all the springs of the State are vigorous and simple and its rules clear and luminous; there are no embroilments or conflicts of interests; the common good is everywhere clearly apparent, and only good sense is needed to perceive it.
>
> (*SC*, 90; Book 4, Chapter 1)

And in the fourth and final book of *The Social Contract*, Rousseau recapitulates his fundamental theses about this contract. Namely, that there is only one law which, by its very nature (*par sa nature*), demands unanimous consent on the part of all citizens: this is, of course, the social contract. Then, he reminds us that civil association is the most voluntary of all acts (and, by implication, that the social contract is the most voluntary of all contracts, despite or precisely because it involves involuntary aspects). Finally, because the social contract shows how every individual can be his or her master, no individual can be born a slave. All of which leads to the central paradox of Rousseau's political theory of the social contract: how can an individual be free and at the same time forced to conform to the will of others?

> There is but one law which, from its nature, needs unanimous consent. This is the social compact; for civil association is the most voluntary of all acts. Every man being born free and his own master, no one, under any pretext whatsoever, can make any man subject without his consent. To decide that the son of a slave is born a slave is to decide that he is not born a man.
>
>   [...]
>
> The citizen gives his consent to all the laws, including those which are passed in spite of his opposition, and even those which punish him when he dares to break any of them. The constant will of all the members of the State is the general will; by virtue of it they are citizens and free. When in the popular assembly a law is proposed, what the people is asked is not exactly whether it approves or rejects the proposal, but whether it is in conformity with the general will, which is their will. Each man, in giving his vote, states his opinion on that point; and the general will is found by counting votes. When therefore the opinion that is contrary to my own prevails, this proves neither more nor less than that I was mistaken, and that what I thought to be the general will was not so. If my particular opinion had carried the day I should have achieved the opposite of what was my will; and it is in that case that I should not have been free.
>
> This presupposes, indeed, that all the qualities of the general will still reside in the majority: when they cease to do so, whatever side a man may take, liberty is no longer possible.
>
>   (*SC*, 93–94; Book 4, Chapter 2)

The conclusion of *The Social Contract* turns around the question of the following paradox: "How can a man can be both free and forced to conform to wills that are not his own? How are the opponents at once free and subject to laws they have not agreed to?" Rousseau resolves this question by arguing that to pose it in these terms is itself erroneous.

For if I oppose the general will, I am in some way opposing my own individual will, which is subsumed in that general will. So if I vote in a particular way and discover that the opposing vote has carried the day, this merely confirms, in Rousseau's view, that I must have been mistaken in my view ... And yet, Rousseau nevertheless acknowledges that there may come a time when the qualities of the general will no longer reside in the view of the majority. At this point, he notes, the political game is over—and "liberty is no longer possible."

In conclusion, one might say that Rousseau's political thought is built on the following dialectic: first, a thesis—the state of nature is good, the social state is bad; second, an antithesis—it is impossible to return to the state of nature, so we must come to terms with the social state; and third, a synthesis—we must improve the social state by bringing it closer to the state of nature.[39] The implementation of this synthesis involves the idea of a natural education, promulgated in his great novelistic treatise, *Émile*. As paradoxical as this idea sounds, anyone involved in education today will recognize the force of Rousseau's remarks in the context of the contemporary regime of tests, assessments, exams, rankings, and league tables. Rousseau's goal of freedom is political, to be sure, but it is also personal, existential, even metaphysical. Of the simple experience of walking, he writes: "There is something about walking that animates and activates my ideas; I can hardly think at all when I am still; my body must move if my mind is to do the same. The pleasant sights of the countryside, the unfolding scene, the good air, a good appetite, the sense of well-being that returns as I walk [...] all of this releases my soul, encourages more daring flights of thought, impels me, as if were, into the immensity of beings [...]."[40]

Two final points. First, Rousseau, like Plato before him, is a figure who points to the problematic relationship between certain aspects of this kind of political thought and the danger of a rise of totalitarianism. Rousseau places liberty at the forefront of his political ambitions, but surely the rhetoric of "forcing the individual to be free" runs the risk of allowing an absolute totalitarianism to come into being? Even though this is clearly not Rousseau's intention, some have argued that this is an inevitable, if unforeseen, consequence of his ideas.[41]

Second, and at a deeper level, Rousseau confronts us with the problem of freedom, even more radically (if that is possible) than is the case with Plato. On this account, we have to distinguish between (illusory) freedom, where we think we are free but are not, and (real) freedom, where in some respects we might not be free, but in a richer sense we are more free than in a state of illusory freedom. In other words, for this school of thought the following statements may all be true:

- even though we may think we are free, we are not;
- we are least free, especially when we think we are;
- and the fact that we think we are free is, in fact, proof that, in reality, we are not ….!

As Rousseau puts it in the *Social Contract*, Book 1, Chapter 8, "moral liberty […] alone makes [man] truly master of himself; for the mere impulse of appetite is slavery, while obedience to a law which we prescribe to ourselves is liberty" (*SC*, 19).

Or as Goethe expresses it in a famous poem:

> *Wer Großes will, muß sich zusammenraffen;*
> *In der Beschränkung zeigt sich erst der Meister,*
> *Und das Gesetz nur kann uns Freiheit geben.*
> Who seeks great gain leaves easy gain behind.
> None proves a master but by limitation
> And only law can give us liberty.[42]

In relation to Plato, we have noted the important areas of affinity and agreement between Rousseau and his Greek predecessor in the field of political theory, but there are also some important areas of difference and disagreement too. Williams has summarized these as epistemological, institutional, and political. First, on the epistemological level, for Plato philosophical enlightenment is only available to those who have undergone a rigorous philosophical training, whereas for Rousseau "eternal ideas" are available to anyone, because they are "engraved in the human heart" (*Emile*, p. 473). This highly biblical phrase recurs in his

Reveries of the Solitary Walker or *Rêveries du promeneur solitaire* (1776–1778; pub. 1782), in which Rousseau speaks of "the eternal truths which have been accepted at all times and by all wise men, recognized by all nations, and indelibly engraved on the human heart."[43]

Second, there are important divergences between Plato and Rousseau in respect of the institutional roles played by liberty, equality, and sovereignty in their philosophical theories. For Rousseau, liberty and equality are "the greatest good of all" or "the end of every system of legislation" (*SC*, 45; Book 2, Chapter 11). By contrast, for Plato liberty and equality are less important than justice: in the *Republic*, political freedom is frankly seen as a danger against which the state is to be guarded, as his discussion of democracy in book 8 underscores. And equality in its contemporary sense is something toward which Plato is outwardly hostile; after all, the Platonic state divides its citizens into three classes—into the producers, the guardians, and the rulers (philosopher-kings), with very little social mobility envisaged between these divisions. Whereas Rousseau holds firmly to the principle of popular sovereignty, Plato looks for the guidance of society to the self-elected minority of the philosopher-kings.

Given their differing attitudes towards sovereignty, it is not surprising that Plato and Rousseau diverge on the status of the social contract. For Rousseau, the social contract is the essential foundation of society, whereas Plato barely considers the question of contracts in the founding of his regime. Yet it would be wrong to conclude that he is entirely uninterested in the question of contracts; Glaucon argues that the origin of justice can be found in agreement among the people prevent suffering wrong and being unable to exact revenge (*Republic*, 359a–b).

Following an analysis offered by Laurence D. Cooper, Williams identifies three further institutional differences between Rousseau and Plato that correspond to the "three waves" of book 5 of the *Republic*.[44] Where Plato recommended that political offices (including that of ruler) be open to women, Rousseau followed the misogyny of his age in excluding women from any leading role. Where Plato argued that the traditional family should be abolished for all citizens serving the state as guardians, Rousseau defended—in theory, if not in practice—the institution of the family. And while Plato maintained that philosophers should become kings, the philosopher-king in Rousseau's state is replaced by the analogous, but very different, figure of the legislator.

True, Cooper argues that even in these points there are underlying affinities between Rousseau and Plato. In Rousseau's conception of the moral person, there is a "bisexual" combination of both masculine and feminine components (while Helena Rosenblatt has defended Rousseau against accusations of misogyny).[45] In Plato's proposal to abolish the family, we can see an attempt to divert affection from the family to the idea of the Good, from the immanent to the transcendent. And common to both Rousseau and Plato is a belief in the guiding role of reason in the conduct of the soul. So although Plato looks to the philosopher-king to be a ruler and Rousseau seeks to place power in the hands of the many, for both "the *institutional* question of where power should reside is contingent upon the *epistemic* question of who is wise, and wisdom itself is contingent upon the *metaphysical* question of the ideas, such as justice and good."[46]

The perennial nature of the topics addressed by Rousseau is illustrated by the way in which, as Pankaj Mishra has remarked, the kinds of attack launched by Rousseau on cosmopolitan élites now seems prophetic in the light of the outcome of the US presidential election of 2016.[47] And with President Trump as with Rousseau himself, the suspicion remains that ultimately they represent an appeal to those susceptible to authoritarianism and social dominance orientation.[48] Leaving Trump to one side, the accusation of authoritarianism, often levelled at Plato and Rousseau alike, is a recurrent motif in the critique of the discourse of Platonism.

Notes

1. For further discussion, see William H.F. Altman, *The Revival of Platonism in Cicero's Late Philosophy:* Platonis aemulus *and the Invention of Ciccero* (Lanham, ML: Lexington Books, 2016).
2. For further discussion, see Douglas Hedley and Sarah Hutton (eds), *Platonism at the Origins of Modernity: Studies on Platonism and Early*

Modern Philosophy (Dordrecht: Springer, 2008); and Guido Giglioni and Anna Corrias (eds), *Brill's Companion to Medieval and Early Modern Platonism* (Leiden and Boston: Brill, forthcoming).

3. David Lay Williams, *Rousseau's Platonic Enlightenment* (University Park, PA: Pennsylvania State University Press, 2007), 49.
4. It was during his 11 years of exile in Paris (1640–1651) that Hobbes moved, so Bernd Ludwig has argued, from the Stoic-informed political philosophy of his *Elements of Law* (1640) and *De Cive* to a rediscovery and a revival of a tradition of natural law deriving from Epicurus; see *Die Wiederentdeckung des Epikureischen Naturrechts: Zu Thomas Hobbes' philosophischer Entwicklung von „De Cive" zum „Leviathan" im Pariser Exil 1640–1651* (Frankfurt am Main: Klostermann, 1998).
5. Michel Onfray, *Les ultras des Lumières* [*Contre-histoire de la philosophie*, vol. 4] (Paris: Grasset, 2007).
6. C.A. Helvétius, *De l'esprit* [1758], in *De l'esprit, Or, Essays on the Mind and its Several Faculties* (London: Albion, 1810), 6–7.
7. Baron d'Holbach, *The System of Nature: Or, The Law of the Moral and Physical World* [1770], trans. H.D. Robinson, 2 vols (New York: Matsell, 1835), vol. 1, 88.
8. Paul Kristeller, *Eight Philosophers of the Italian Renaissance* (Stanford: Stanford University Press, 1964), 44.
9. Christia Mercer, "Platonism and Philosophical Humanism on the Continent," in Steven Nadler (ed.), *A Companion to Early Modern Philosophy* (Madden, MA and Oxford: Blackwell, 2002), 25–44 (37).
10. For further discussion, see John Cottingham, "Plato's Sun and Descartes's Stove: Contemplation and Control in Cartesian Philosophy," in Michael Ayers (ed.), *Rationalism, Platonism, and God: A Symposium on Early Modern Philosophy* (Oxford: Oxford University Press, 2007), 15–44.
11. For further discussion, see Alan Kim (ed.), *Brill's Companion to German Platonism* (Leiden and Boston: Brill, forthcoming).
12. For further discussion, see Christia Mercer, "Platonism in Early Modern Natural Philosophy: The Case of Leibniz and Conway," in Christoph Horn and James Wilberding (eds), *Neoplatonism and the Philosophy of Nature* (Oxford: Oxford University Press, 2012), 103–126.
13. Leibniz, *Theodicy: Essays on the Goodness of God, the Freedom of Man and the Origin of Evil*, trans. E.M. Huggard (La Salle, IL: Open Court, 1985), 124.

14. Leibniz, "Opinions on the Principles of Pufendof" [1706], in Patrick Riley (ed.), *Political Writings*, 2nd edn (Cambridge: Cambridge University Press, 1988), 64–75 (69).

15. Malebranche, *Trois Lettres de l'auteur de la Recherche de la Vérité* (Rotterdam: Leers, 1685), letter 1, 3–155; cf. *Trois Lettres touchant la défense de M. Arnauld*, in *Œuvres complètes*, ed. André Robinet (Paris: Vrin, 1963), 199–200.

16. Nicolas Malebranche, *The Search After Truth*, ed. Thomas M. Lennon and Paul J. Olscamp (Cambridge: Cambridge University Press, 1997), xxxvii.

17. Salignac de la Mothe-Fénelon, *The Adventures of Telemachus, the Son of Ulysses*, trans. John Hawkesworth (Manchester: Thomas Johnson, 1847), 71.

18. Williams, *Rousseau's Platonic Enlightenment*, 39–40.

19. For further discussion, see Russell R. Dynes, "The Dialogue Between Voltaire and Rousseau on the Lisbon Earthquake: The Emergence of a Social Science View," *International Journal of Mass Emergencies and Disasters* 18, no. 1 (March 2000), 97–115.

20. See Thomas Aquinas, *Quaestiones Disputatae de Veritate: Questions 10–20*, trans. James V. McGlynn (Chicago: Henry Regnery, 1953), Question 19, Answers to Difficulties, §13.

21. In *De Cive* ("On the Citizen") (1642; trans. 1651), Hobbes uses the famous phrase *bellum omnium contra omnes* ("war of all against all"): "I demonstrate, in the first place, that the state of men without civil society, which state we may properly call the state of nature, is nothing else but a mere war of all against all" (Thomas Hobbes, *Man and Citizen* (Indianapolis, IN: Hackett, 1998), 101).

22. Thomas Hobbes, *Leviathan: Revised Student Edition*, ed. Richard Tuck (Cambridge: Cambridge University Press, 1996), 88–89.

23. For further discussion, see Alex Schulman, *The Secular Contract: The Politics of Enlightenment* (New York: Continuum, 2011). The current relevance of the notion of the contract is indicated by the recent decision of the Royal Swedish Academy of Sciences to award the Nobel Prize in Economic Sciences for 2016 to Oliver Hart of Harvard University and Bengt Holmström of MIT for their contributions to contract theory.

24. Jean-Jacques Rousseau, *Emile, or On Education*, trans. Allan Bloom (New York: Basic Books, 1979).

25. *"Enlightenment is man's emergence from his self-incurred maturity"* (Kant, "An Answer to the Question: 'What Is Enlightenment?'," in Immanuel Kant, *Political Writings*, ed. Hans Reiss and trans. H.B. Nisbet, 2nd edn (Cambridge: Cambridge University Press, 1991), 54–60 [54]). This arresting opening phrase has been translated in myriad ways.

26. Rousseau, *The Confessions*, trans. J.M. Cohen (Harmondsworth: Penguin, 1953), 387. For further discussion, see Matthew D. Mendham, "Rousseau's Discarded Children: The Panoply of Excuses and the Question of Hypocrisy," *History of European Ideas* 41, no. 1 (January 2015), 131–152. Critics have tended to remain unpersuaded by Rousseau's claims in book 8 that, "in ensuring that they become labourers and peasants rather than adventurers and fortune-seekers, I believed that I was acting as a true citizen and father, and I looked upon myself as a member of Plato's republic" (Rousseau, *Confessions*, ed. Patrick Coleman and trans. Angela Scholar (Oxford: Oxford University Press, 2000), 348)!

27. The translation used here is by G.D.H. Cole in Jean-Jacques Rousseau, *The Social Contract & Discourses* (London and Toronto: Dent; New York: Dutton, 1913). The following abbreviations have been used: *FD* = first *Discourse*; *SC* = *The Social Contract*; *SD* = second *Discourse*).

28. At this point Rousseau cites Tacitus's *Histories*, 4.7: "The most wretched slavery they call peace" (*miserriman servitutem pacem appellant*).

29. Rousseau, *Emile*, 40.

30. Williams, *Rousseau's Platonic Enlightenment*, 144.

31. When Rousseau adds that "it may be justly said that savages are not bad merely because they do not know what it is to be good: for it is neither the development of the understanding nor the restraint of law that hinders them from doing ill; but the peacefulness of their passions, and their ignorance of vice" (*SD*, 197), he is alluding to Justin in *Histories*, 2.2, "So much more does the ignorance of vice profit the one sort than the knowledge of virtue the other" (*tanto plus in illis proficit vitiorum ignoratio, quam in his cognitio virtutis*).

32. See Sigmund Freud, *Totem and Taboo: Some Points of Agreement Between the Mental Lives of Savages and Neurotics*, trans. James Strachey (London: Routledge and Kegan Paul, 1960), 141–142. In a footnote Freud adds the following caveat: "The lack of precision in what I have written in the text above, its abbreviation of the time factor and its compression of the whole subject-matter, may be attributed to

the reserve necessitated by the nature of the topic. It would be foolish to aim at exactitude in such questions as it would be unfair to insist upon certainty" (142–143). In other words, can Freud's account of the murder of the father by the patriarchal horde be read, like Plato's story of the cave and Rousseau's account of the origin of property, as an allegory?

33. For further discussion of the mysterious black monoliths that appear in the opening scene, see Jean-Paul Dumont and Jean Monod, *Le fœtus astral: Essai d'analyse structurale d'un mythe cinématographique* (Paris: Bourgeois, 1970).

34. Williams, *Rousseau's Platonic Enlightenment*, 148–149. For the notion of 'eternal laws of nature', see *Émile*, book 5: "Laws! Where are there laws, and where are they respected? Everywhere you have seen only individual interest and men's passions reigning under this name. But the eternal laws of nature and order do exist. *For the wise man, they are written in the depth of his heart by conscience and reason. It is to these that he ought to enslave himself in order to be free.* The only slave is the man who does evil, for he always does it in spite of himself. Freedom is found in no form of government; it is in the heart of the free man. He takes it with him everywhere. The vile man takes his servitude everywhere" (*Emile*, 473; my emphasis).

35. For further discussion of this dialectic as it later appears in the thought of G.W.F. Hegel (1770–1831), see Paul Redding, "The Independence and Dependence of Self-Consciousness: The Dialectic of Lord and Bondsman in Hegel's *Phenomenology of Spirit*," in Frederick C. Beiser (ed.), *The Cambridge Companion to Hegel and Nineteenth-Century Philosophy* (Cambridge: Cambridge University Press, 2008), 94–110.

36. *Odyssey*, book 9, ll. 181–182; Homer, *The Odyssey*, ed. and trans. Albert Cook, 2nd edn (New York and London: Norton, 1993), 95.

37. See Eugene Kamenka (ed.), *The Portable Karl Marx* (New York: Viking Penguin, 1983), 96–114 (114). After citing this passage from Rousseau's *Social Contract*, Marx concludes: "All emancipation is the *leading back* of the human world and of human relationships and conditions, to *man himself*" (114).

38. *The Laws of Plato*, trans. Thomas Pangle (Chicago and London: Chicago University Press, 1980), 280.

39. Alexander von Gleichen-Rußwurm, *Philosophische Profile: Erinnerungen und Wertungen* (Stuttgart: Strecker und Schröder, 1922), Chapter 1, "Der Glaube an die Idee (Jean-Jacques Rousseau)," 11–19 (11).

40. Jean-Jacques Rousseau, *Rêveries of the Solitary Walker*, trans. Russell Goulbourne (Oxford and New York: Oxford University Press, 2011), "Sixth Walk," 58.

41. Robert A. Nisbet, "Rousseau and Totalitarianism," *The Journal of Politics* 5, no. 2 (May 1943), 93–114.

42. Johann Wolfgang von Goethe, *Selected Poems* [Goethe Edition, vol. 1], ed. Christopher Middleton and trans. Michael Hamburger (Boston: Suhrkamp/Insel Publishers, 1983), 164–165.

43. Rousseau, *Rêveries of the Solitary Walker*, trans. Goulbourne, 30–31.

44. See Laurence D. Cooper, "Human Nature and the Love of Wisdom: Rousseau's Hidden (and Modified) Platonism," *The Journal of Politics* 64, no. 1 (February 2002), 108–125. For further discussion, see Laurence D. Cooper, *Eros in Plato, Rousseau, and Nietzsche: The Politics of Infinity* (University Park, PA: Penn State University Press, 2008).

45. For further discussion, see Helena Rosenblatt, "On the 'Misogyny' of Jean-Jacques Rousseau: The Letter to d'Alembert in Historical Context," *French Historical Studies* 25, no. 1 (Winter 2002), 91–114.

46. Williams, *Rousseau's Platonic Enlightenment*, 182

47. Pankaj Mishra, "How Rousseau Predicted Trump," *The New Yorker*, 1 August 2016. Available online HTTP http:www.newyorker.com/magazine/2016/08/01/how-rousseau-predicted-trump.

48. Beckly L. Choma and Yaniv Hanoch, "Cognitive Ability and Authoritarianism: Understanding Support for Trump and Clinton," *Personality and Individual Differences* 106 (February 2017), 287–291.

5

Kant and the Categorical Imperative

In this chapter we move from Geneva in Switzerland to Königsberg in Prussia, the city where Immanuel Kant was born—and where he spent the entirety of his life from 1724 to 1804.[1] In his sparsely decorated study Kant had only one picture: a portrait of Rousseau, hung over the writing desk. This simple fact of interior decoration points to a deeper connection between the two men—and between the traditions of political thought both represent.[2]

Rousseau is a figure of the Enlightenment, the intellectual movement known in France as the *siècle des lumières* and in Germany as the *Aufklärung*.[3] For the Enlightenment was an international movement: based in Scotland, in England, and in Ireland (Hume in Edinburgh, Hobbes in Malmesbury, Locke in Bristol, Berkeley in Kilkenny, not to mention to the entire coffee-house culture in London), as well as in the Netherlands (Spinoza in Amsterdam), in France (Voltaire in Paris, Descartes in Tours, Pascal in Clermont-Ferrand, and Montesquieu in Bordeaux), and in the states that made up Germany (Leibniz in Leipzig, Wolff in Breslau), especially such important centres as Berlin, Frankfurt, and (in Austria) Vienna. From the north of Europe in Königsberg to

© The Author(s) 2019
P. Bishop, *German Political Thought and the Discourse of Platonism*,
https://doi.org/10.1007/978-3-030-04510-4_5

the south of Europe in Naples (where Vico was born and worked), the Enlightenment was international in its reach and ambition.

For his part, Kant belongs fairly and squarely to this tradition of the Enlightenment. One of his most famous essays, published in the *Berlinische Monatsschrift* in 1784, was entitled "Answering the Question: What Is Enlightenment?". Here Kant famously answered this question with the following definition: it is "the emergence of the individual from his or her self-imposed immaturity."[4] Yet at the same time Kant can be seen in terms of another tradition, not necessarily co-terminous with the Enlightenment, and to some extent representing a reaction and a response to the Enlightenment—in other words, with Romanticism. (In fact, German Romanticism, a movement associated with literature, music, and the visual arts, has a significant political dimension, reflected in the writings of Novalis, the *nom de plume* of Friedrich von Hardenberg (1772–1801), and Friedrich Schlegel (1772–1829) in particular.[5] At the same time, Schegel is arguably one of the first figures of another intellectual tradition known as *Lebensphilosophie*,[6] and frequently, if inaccurately, associated with irrationalism—and the political Right.) Or to put it another way, Kant should also be seen in the context of the tradition of German Idealism, a tradition distinct from yet not unrelated to Platonic idealism.[7] As a movement, German Idealism could be found across the states making up Germany in the late eighteenth and early nineteenth centuries, and was associated with such cities as Berlin, Halle, Weimar, Jena, with Frankfurt, Würzburg, Heidelberg, and Nuremberg, not to mention Stuttgart, Tübingen, and Munich.[8] One thinks, for example, of Johann Gottlieb Fichte (1762–1814), himself an important political thinker[9]; Friedrich Ernst Schleiermacher (1768–1834), Friedrich Wilhelm Schelling (1775–1854), and Georg Wilhelm Friedrich Hegel (1770–1831), a figure to whom we shall return in the following chapter. In all these cases, their thought in some respects represents a reaction and a response to the thought of Kant. As we shall see, both the Enlightenment and German Idealist inform Kant's thought in general and hence his political thought in particular.

Kant's thinking is notable for its complexity, reflected in three major systematic works he wrote, the *Critique of Pure Reason* (1781; second edition, 1787), the *Critique of Practical Reason* (1788), and the *Critique of Judgement* (1790). Taken together, these works represent a remarkably detailed explanation of how we can know things (i.e., the epistemology of the first *Critique*), of what things we should do (i.e., the morality of the second *Critique*), and of how we can appreciate art and do science (i.e., the aesthetics and teleology of the third *Critique*). In turn, these works feed into Kant's political thought, reflected in the two works examined in this chapter, the *Metaphysics of Morals* (1797) and "On the Common Saying: This May be True in Theory but It Does Not Apply in Practice" (1793) (Fig. 5.1).

The entire systematic philosophy of Kant is designed to answer a simple, but extremely difficult, problem. The problem can be stated thus. On the one hand, we live in a world of causality. We know that if we drop an object, it will fall; that if we push someone, he or she will fall over; that if he or she gets up and pushes us back, we will fall over—that is, if we are pushed hard enough. In other words, the law of cause and effect seems to be an iron one. On the other hand, however, we think of ourselves and of other people as being free, as having free will, and as

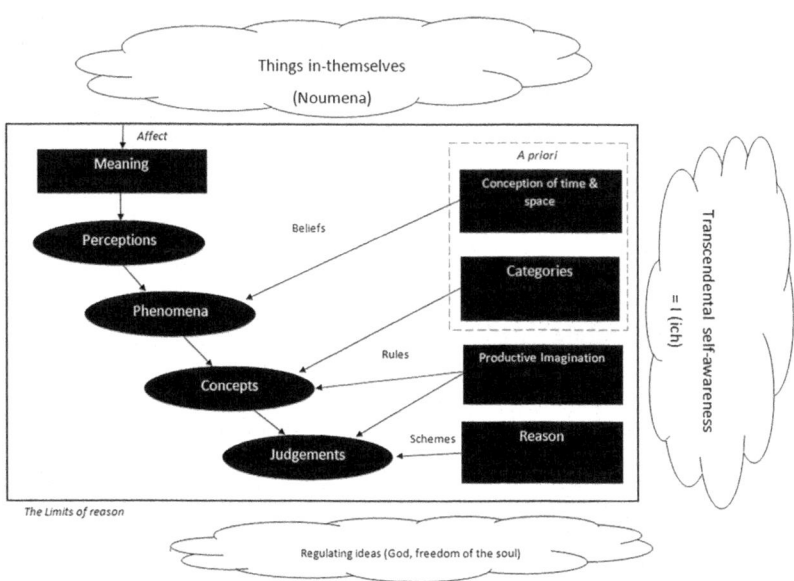

Fig. 5.1 Outline of Kant's system

being able to exercise that free will. Without free will, moral judgments and distinctions become pointless. For how can we judge someone as morally "good" or "bad," if he or she is simply obeying the iron law of causality?

Throughout his philosophy, Kant proposes to preserve the law of causality, while at the same time preserving the notion of free will. This seemingly impossible task involves the introduction of a kind of dualism of perspective, and so we find ourselves going back to Plato's allegory of the cave.[10] In that allegory, we see how Socrates makes a distinction between the realm of the cave and the realm outside the cave, between the realm of images and objects known through opinion (*eikasia*) and belief (*pistis*) and the realm of mathematical objects and Platonic Ideas known through reflection (*dianoia*) and insight (*noësis*).

Corresponding to this distinction in the allegory of the cave and the allegory of the divided line is Kant's distinction between the realm of the phenomenon and the realm of the noumenon, between the realm of things-for-us and the realm of the thing-in-itself. Everything we see in the world we perceive in space and in time, but for Kant, space and time are "forms of sensory intuition," rather than objects of sensory intuition. We know an object is here rather than there, or there rather than here; we know that it has been there for a long time, or a short time, or intermittently; but we do not know time or space *in themselves*. In fact, we do not know what anything is *in itself*, and so what Kant calls the *Ding-an-sich* (the "thing-in-itself") could also be *Dinge-an-sich* ("things-in-themselves"), because singularity and plurality depend on being in time and in space.

Now clearly we exist in the phenomenal realm; we exist as physical objects, in a temporal-spatial context, obedient to the laws of physical causality. But do we not also exist as *noumenon* or *noumena*? Are we not also participants in our own right in the noumenal realm, and so outside the forms of time and space, and outside the laws of causality? And would that not also mean: *we are free?* In other words, inasmuch as we exist in the temporal-spatial context, we are objects of causality. But inasmuch as we also exist as things-in-themselves, we can choose how we act: which means, we are free. Thus freedom is intimately bound up with the question of action—*moral action*.

This form of argumentation has two important implications for Kant's political thought. First, it means that Kant is working with a kind of dualism, which is nevertheless (as with Plato) not really a dualism. For instance, Kant argues that time and space have "empirical reality," that is, they are objectively valid for how external objects appear to us, but time and space also have "transcendental ideality," that is, they are pure *forms of intuition*, in themselves they have no content. Yet it is not as if there are two times and two spaces—a real time and space, and an ideal time and space. Time and space are both "empirically real" *and* "transcendentally ideal," and the same is true for us: seen in one way, we are *phenomena*, subject to the laws of causality; seen in another way, we are *noumena*, and we are free to act as we choose.

Second, we can see how the notion of freedom comes to play an important role in Kant's thought. But this freedom is not simply about behaving in a random or spontaneous manner; rather, freedom is said to lie in the ability to make *moral choices*. And Kant takes his entire metaphysical, moral framework and applies it to the realm of politics. This move has, as we shall see, some surprising consequences for his conception of political freedom.

The link between Kant's moral philosophy and his political thought lies precisely in the identity of the formula that Kant deploys to serve as a guide to conduct in both. In his second *Critique*, dedicated to the question of "practical reason," Kant tries to relate the natural realm of causal necessity and the autonomous realm of freedom to a complex web of concepts: to legality and morality; to motivation, will, and duty; and ultimately to inclination and reason. What relates all these different realms, faculties, and aspects together is what Kant calls the "categorical imperative." The "categorical imperative" is something we must do (hence *imperative*), and it is valid at all times (hence *categorical*). So what does the categorical imperative tell us we must do at all times?

There are three different formulations, all found in Kant's work entitled *Grounding for the Metaphysics of Morals* (1785):

1. Act only according to that maxim whereby you can at the same time will that it should become a universal law without contradiction;

2. Act in such a way that you treat humanity, whether in your own person or in the person of any other, never merely as a means to an end, but always at the same time as an end;
3. Therefore, every rational being must so act as if he or she were through his or her maxim always a legalising member in the universal kingdom of ends.[11]

These formulae, particularly the first, are very close to a formulation in a work with a confusingly similar name, *The Metaphysics of Morals* (1797), as we shall see. But they are also very close to what is called the "Golden Rule," or the principle of "do-as-you-would-be-done-by": in this form, "do unto others as you would have them do unto you," is Kant linking into a tradition that includes Confucianism, Hinduism, Buddhism, Taoism, and Zoroastrianism, not to mention—Christianity?

Yet what is important about the categorical imperative is not that it has been declaimed by a prophet or a representative of the deity; or, rather, what it is important is that it has *not* been declaimed by a prophet or a representative of the deity, but rather that it constitutes—for Kant, at least—a postulate of *reason*. The categorical imperative is, in Kant's view, entirely *rational*; in this respect, Kant is linking back into the Socratic tradition that sees immoral behaviour essentially as a consequence of ignorance.[12]

For we must, Kant believes, behave as rational beings in accordance with the dictate of the categorical imperative. For instance, we should not steal. Why? Not because, on Mount Horeb, Yahweh included among the Ten Commandments given to Moses the injunction, "Thou shalt not steal." But rather because—rationally—I cannot find it acceptable to steal. For if I were to steal something from you, someone else could then come and steal it from me: the maxim of stealing things from other people cannot be turned into a universal maxim, and so stealing cannot be part of moral behaviour. Let us see how these arguments—and how this kind of argumentation—inform Kant's political thinking.

In his *Metaphysics of Morals*, Kant undertakes to answer the question: What is right?[13] In other words, what is the essence of the law? In answering this question, Kant proposes to leave the Aristotelian path, i.e., to put empirical principles to one side, and to embark on a more Platonic path, i.e., to look for the idea of right by searching in the realm of pure reason. This transcendental manoeuvre is central to Kant's thinking, and he underlines its importance with a reference to a tale by the Roman fabulist, Phaedrus (c. 15 BCE–50 CE). In "The Fox and the Tragic Mask," Phaedrus relates a tale in which a fox, happening by chance to catch sight of a tragic mask, declares: "Ah! as great as its beauty, still it has no brains!"—the point being that "a merely empirical system that is void of rational principles is, like the wooden head in the fable of Phaedrus, fine enough in appearance, but unfortunately it wants brain."[14] In his *Metaphysics of Morals* Kant identifies right with "the whole of the conditions under which the voluntary actions of any one person can be harmonized in reality with the voluntary actions of every other person, according to a universal law of freedom"[15]; that is to say, the universal principle of right is identical with what, elsewhere, Kant calls the categorical imperative. And he restates the maxim that defines the categorical imperative: "Every action is right which in itself, or in the maxim on which it proceeds, is such that it can coexist along with the freedom of the will of each and all in action, according to a universal law."[16]

From this position, two conclusions follow. First, a practical law that helps us decide what to do: "Act externally in such a manner that the free exercise of thy will may be able to coexist with the freedom of all others, according to a universal law."[17] And second, as a consequence and as a back-up to this law, all right is accompanied by a warrant to bring compulsion to bear on anyone who violates it: "according to the logical principle of contradiction, all right is accompanied with an implied title or warrant to bring compulsion to bear on any one who may violate it in fact."[18] Whereas, for Rousseau, an individual may be forced to be free; so, for Kant, an individual may be forced to comply with law (and, in so being compelled, be forced to be moral).

In expounding his position in the *Metaphysics of Morals*, Kant distinguishes between "natural right", i.e., pure (or a priori) rational principles, and "positive" (or "statutory") right, or a form of right which proceeds from the will of a legislator. (To exemplify this distinction, one might compare the inherent right to life as a "natural" right with a particular legal declaration to this effect, for instance, the first clause of the German *Grundgesetz*, which declares that "the dignity of the individual is inviolable".) For Kant, there is essentially one innate, inalienable right accorded to any human being: the right to freedom.

> Freedom is independence of the compulsory will of another; and in so far as it can coexist with the freedom of all according to a universal law, it is the one sole original, inborn right belonging to every man in virtue of his humanity. There is, indeed, an innate equality belonging to every man which consists in his right to be independent of being bound by others to anything more than that to which he may also reciprocally bind them. [...] But all these rights or titles are already included in the principle of innate freedom, and are not really distinguished from it, even as dividing members under a higher species of right.[19]

If there is one innate right, freedom, where does that leave another right frequently proclaimed by the Enlightenment and by the French Revolution, i.e., equality? For Kant, equality is essentially another aspect of freedom, that is, equality is the right to independence from others (aside from any reciprocal ties one might have). The conception of freedom developed by Kant is anything other than abstract: it includes the principle of the presumption of innocence, the right to common action, and the right to communication.

How these rights are to be secured, and the political implications flowing from them, inform an essay written in 1793 entitled "On the Common Saying: This May be True in Theory but It Does Not Apply in Practice". This is indeed a common saying, but Kant takes it to task for its cynical implication that theory and practice, that moral law and actual conduct, do not always have to be exactly aligned. The second part of this essay is entitled "On the Relationship of Theory to Practice," and in parenthesis Kant adds the subtitle, "Against Hobbes." So the ambition of Kant's thinking in this extract is clear: what Kant is seeking to refute is the political theory of Hobbes, as expressed in his *Leviathan* (1651), while the specific target is the argument presented by Hobbes in his *De Cive* ("On the Citizen"), published in Latin in Paris (1642; 1647), and appearing in English translation as *Philosophicall Rudiments*

Concerning Government and Society (1651).[20] From the outset of this section of his essay, Kant recognizes the peculiar—indeed, in effect, the unique—nature of the social contract. What makes the social contract so special, he argues, is that it is constructed to the achievement of an *ideal* end. It is this *ideal* end—that is, its political objective of founding a civil society—that turns the social contract into a duty, and hence endows it with an ethical dimension.

According to Kant, the concept of external right is derived from the concept of freedom (and not, he emphasizes, from the concept of happiness). We might, in the words of the American Declaration of Independence, proclaim the "pursuit of happiness" to be an inalienable right; but even more fundamental than happiness, for Kant, is freedom. Yet there is a paradox here: for right involves a restriction of individual freedom, so that his or her freedom may harmonize with the freedom of others. Public right is, then, equivalent to these external laws. And so the civil constitution embodies this paradox, inasmuch as it is a relationship of free individuals who are nevertheless subject to coercive laws.

To resolve this paradox, however, means to understand it as a requirement of pure reason: after all, there are as many different conceptions of happiness as there are individuals, and for these individuals to co-exist, their freedom must be guaranteed at a collective, rather than an individual, level. Freedom is thus a product of reason, rather than a product of (individual) will. Consequently, Kant goes on to discuss three principles of the civil state (*der bürgerliche Zustand*) as a lawful state (*rechtlicher Zustand*): namely, (1) freedom (2) equality (c) and independence. At the outset, Kant reminds us that these principles are nothing less than a priori principles of pure reason: "These principles are not so much laws given by an already established state [*Staat*], as laws by which a state can alone be established in accordance with pure rational principles of external human right."[21] So far as the relation between freedom and the pursuit of happiness is concerned, Kant declares the following:

Man's *freedom* as a human being, as a principle for the constitution of a commonwealth, can be expressed in the following formula. No-one can compel me to be happy in accordance with his conception of the welfare of others, for each may seek his happiness in whatever way he sees fit, so long as he does not infringe upon the freedom of others to pursue a similar end which can be reconciled with the freedom of everyone else within a workable general law — i.e., he must accord to others the same right as he enjoys himself.[22]

For all his emphasis on freedom rather than the pursuit of happiness, Kant is at pains to explain that the former does not preclude the latter, but indeed that the former is the precondition for the latter. For happiness can, he argues, only ever be something that each individual defines or discovers for himself or herself: a paternalist government, concerned to bring about the happiness of its subjects, would actually be the greatest despotism imaginable! Hence the best form of benevolent government is not paternalistic, but patriotic, in the sense that every member of such a state is proud to affirm his or her membership of it.

The second principle of civil government is something away from which, in the later *Metaphysics of Morals*, Kant was going to shift—equality. As becomes clear, however, Kant's quarrel with equality is a limited one: in relation to the head of state, he argues, equality cannot pertain, but it should pertain in relation to all other members of the state:

Each member of the commonwealth has rights of coercion in relation to all the others, except in relation to the head of state. For he alone is not a member of the commonwealth, but its creator or preserver, and he alone is authorised to coerce others without being subject to any coercive law himself. [...] From this idea of the equality of men as subjects in a commonwealth, there emerges this further formula: every member of the commonwealth must be entitled to reach any degree of rank which a subject can earn through his talent, his industry and his good fortune. And his fellow-subjects may not stand in his way by *hereditary* prerogatives or privileges of rank and thereby hold him and his descendants back indefinitely.[23]
      [...]
      All right consists solely in the restriction of the freedom of others, with the qualification that their freedom can co-exist with my freedom within the terms of a general law; and public right in a commonwealth is

simply a state of affairs regulated by a real legislation which conforms to this principle and is backed up by power, and under which a whole people live as subjects in a lawful state [*rechtlichen Zustand*] *(status iuridicus)*. This is what we call a civil state [...].24

For Kant, the head of state is not a member of it, but rather its creator or preserver, a figure perhaps to be regarded with as much awe and gratitude as did Aristotle when he said of the founder of the state that "the man who first united people in such a partnership was the greatest of benefactors" (*Politics*, 1253a). Yet does this mean that the head of state is above the law?

Even more worrying, perhaps, is Kant's argument that equality among individuals inasmuch as they are members of the state is consistent with their inequality in material terms. On this view, then, all are equal in an abstract sense, while some are rich and others are poor. For now, let us leave on one side—as conditioned by the preconceptions and prejudices of the times in which he was writing—Kant's argument than the poor must depend on the rich as the child obeys its parents or a wife her husband; what is radically clear about Kant's conception is that all are equal as subjects before the law. Thus while allowing for inheritance, Kant argues against hereditary privileges; whether these two positions are entirely compatible in reality is again debatable. What lies behind Kant's position in this respect?

Time and again, Kant recurs to the apparent paradox that right consists in the restriction of freedom—a restriction in the freedom, that is, of others so that their freedom can co-exist with mine. In the civil state, the birth right of each individual is equal, and this is the basis for the denial of hereditary privileges. So while the right to pass on property, etc., as inheritance may—and, one is tempted to add, surely will inevitably—result in an inequality of wealth, the material advantages enjoyed by some should not prevent others from reaching their own level of attainment in society.

Whatever we may think of Kant's naiveté in this regard, he is trying to articulate something important when he declares that neither any kind of contract (presumably including the social) nor any kind of military force can make an individual cease to be his or her own master (in the phrase used by Kant, *Eigner seiner selbst*).[25] This inalienable right (or, as Kant would seem to think of it, actual fact) serves as a guarantee of some kind of happiness, to the extent that we may be considered happy, whatever condition we are in, as long as we aware that, if we do reach the same level as others, this is entirely our own fault and no-one else's. In other words, true happiness is, in a society based on hereditary privilege, impossible.

Finally, Kant turns his attention to the third principle of the civil state, that is, independence. What does, he asks, it means for the individual as a citizen, that is, as the "co-legislator" of the state, to be independent? Answering this question leads to Kant to discuss in detail his understanding of the social contract. In pursuing this argument, Kant explores the implications that "all right depends on laws," and that "a public law is an act of public will." This means that the individual will on its own cannot legislate for the state, for legislation requires the "freedom, equality and *unity* of the will of *all* the members." It is this basic law, arising from the general will of the people, that forms the basis of the social contract: "The basic law, which can come only from the general, united will of the people [*Volkswillen*], is called the *original contract* [*den ursprünglichen Vertrag*]".[26]

Accordingly, every citizen has a right to vote on legislation (while not everyone is a citizen: again, reflecting the prejudices of his age, Kant excludes—as would have Plato and Aristotle before him—children and women from the rights of full citizenship). But to the extent that he upholds this principle, Kant upholds it to the full: he argues, for instance (and against the practice of his own day?), that large landowners are only entitled to one vote. The unanimity of assent required in theory is, in practice, reflected in the acceptance of a majority of votes in favour of a decision, and it is on the basis of this contract that any valid civil constitution is founded:

> Now this is an *original contract*, on which alone a civil and hence thoroughly rightful [*rechtliche*] constitution among human beings can be based and a commonwealth established. But it is by no means necessary that this contract (called *contractus originarius* or *pactum sociale*), as a

coalition of every particular and private will within a people [*Volk*] into a common and public will (for the sake of a merely rightful legislation), be presupposed as *a fact* (as a fact it is indeed not possible) [...]. It is instead *only an idea* of reason, which, however, has its undoubted practical reality [...].[27]

Thus far, Kant's position is consistent with Rousseau's: the foundation of the state is the social contract. In Rousseau, however, this contract is seen as being in some way historical: whether it corresponds (diachronically) to a chronological moment in the history of humanity or (synchronically) to a developmental moment in the life of each individual, the establishment of the social contract is seen as an actual fact. For Kant, however, the contract is something that becomes *transcendentalized*: like the categorical imperative, it does not have to be actually enacted to be nonetheless very real.

In Kant's own words, the social contract—"based on a coalition of the wills of all private individuals in a nation to form a common, public will for the purposes of rightful legislation"—does not actually exist "as a *fact*, for it cannot possibly be so," but rather it is, in his own philosophical jargon, "merely an *idea* of reason, which nonetheless has undoubted practical reality." *An idea of reason*, which nevertheless has *practical reality*: this is how Kant's political theory bridges the gap between the noumenal and the phenomenal, or (in Platonic terms) between the realm of Ideas and the realm of the cave.

The question inevitably arises: How does this "idea of reason" attain to reality? Through the way in which a legislator is obliged to frame laws *in such a way* that they could have been produced by the united will of the populace, and to the extent that laws do this, they pass "the test of the rightfulness of every public law." This test is, of course, the same test that every moral decision has to pass: could it become a universalized maxim? Could a law have been agreed to by everybody? If yes, then it is legal; but if a law is one that everyone could never possibly agree to, then it is unjust. We should note that the test is whether it is *possible* that everyone could agree to it; not whether, in fact, everyone has, which means that if it is at least *possible* that everyone could agree to it, then it is our duty to consider the law as "just."[28] It is not the *actuality*, but the *possibility*, that everyone could agree to a piece of legislation, that constitutes "the test of rightfulness."

Thus whether or not the consent of the people is theoretically possible is what matters for Kant, and if a law passes the test, then all we have to do is obey it. And this applies, irrespective of whether it increases the happiness of all, or some, or indeed anyone: for "we are not concerned here with any happiness" and "no generally valid principle of legislation can be based on happiness," but "the highest principle" is those "rights which would [...] be secured for everyone," and it is from here that "all maxims relating to the commonwealth must begin." Citing the principle that *Salus publica suprema civitatis lex est*, i.e., "public welfare is the supreme law of the state,"[29] Kant argues that public welfare consists first and foremost in a legal constitution guaranteeing to all freedom within the law. (In this respect, Kant concedes the right to pursue happiness, so long as this pursuit and this happiness do not impinge on the rights of fellow citizens.) In this respect, however, Kant issues a warning. For he explicitly argues that laws directed towards happiness are *not* an end for which a civil constitution is established. Rather, laws are a means to establishing "a rightful state," including its defence against external aggressors, potential or actual.[30] He even goes so far as to say that the aim of government is not to "make the people happy against its will," but to ensure its continued existence as a political unity.[31] (On the account proposed by Rousseau and by Kant, then, we can be forced to be free; but we cannot be forced to be happy. And perhaps this is right.)

If, in Kant's words, a law is *irreprehensible* (i.e., it is beyond reproach), then it is *irresistible* (i.e., the state has the right, indeed, the duty, to impose it), and this leads to the thorny issue of whether, in any circumstances, the individual is entitled to resist or challenge the laws of the state. Kant's uncompromising (and controversial) view is that such resistance is *never* justified. In his critique of Hobbes, we see how Kant nevertheless proposes an uncompromising line against any kind of civil disobedience. Any resistance against the supreme legislative power is, he argues, the "greatest and most punishable crime in a commonwealth."

For resistance, he believes, undermines the very foundations of the political community. For this reason, he concludes, its prohibition is "absolute." [32]

Indeed, a subject has no right to resist even a tyrannical head of state! As shocking as this stance might seem to us, it is entirely compatible with Kant's argumentational logic. *If* it is the duty of the subject to obey the state, *then* it must be obeyed, whatever the nature of the state. For disobedience in a tyrannical state undermines the legitimacy of the state, instead of simply undermining the tyrant. Kant embeds his argument in the political discursive context of his day, engaging with the view of Gottfried Achenwall (1719–1772), a philosopher, historian, and economist based at the University of Göttingen. (Throughout his academic career, Achenwall shifted between the fields of law and philosophy, lecturing and working in both fields, as well as promoting in Germany the study of statistics.) In his two-volume study of natural law, *Jus Naturae* (1755–1756), Achenwall offers a cautious justification of the right to resist tyranny.

Kant disagrees, and he does so for two reasons. First, because of the political mechanics of organising such resistance to the state. Elsewhere in this essay, Kant argues that "even if an actual contract of the people with the head of state has been violated, the people cannot reply immediately as a *commonwealth*, but only by forming factions," for "the hitherto existing constitution has been destroyed by the people, but a new commonwealth has still to be organised"—and "at this point, the state of anarchy supervenes, with all the terrors it may bring with it." He concludes that "the wrong which is thereby done is done by each faction of the people to the others, as is clear from the case where the rebellious subjects ended up by trying to thrust upon each other a constitution which would have been far more oppressive than the one they abandoned," for "they would have been devoured by ecclesiastics and aristocrats, instead of enjoying greater equality in the distribution of political burdens under a single head of state who ruled them all."[33] (Clearly, Kant is thinking of the French Revolution here.)

Second, he disagrees because of his conception of the social contract. The idea of the social contract, he insists, is just that: an *idea*, or a basic postulate of reason. But simply because it is not a (historical) reality does not make it any less of a reality; in fact, its "ideal" nature is what makes the social contract truly real. As Kant goes on to explain, it is the existence of the social contract, not as a fact, but as a rational principle, that guarantees its effectiveness. And he embeds his argument in an analysis of constitutional affairs of his own day. As well as referring to the French revolutionary leader, Georges Jacques Danton (1759–1794), Kant examines the political-constitutional situation in Great Britain. (According to a family legend, Kant's paternal grandfather had been a Scottish immigrant, and perhaps this is one of the personal reasons for Kant's particular interest in the constitutional affairs of the United Kingdom?) After the Glorious Revolution of 1688, which saw James II overthrown and the accession of William III of Orange and Mary to the British throne, Parliament legislated for William's and Mary's accession, restricting the monarchy to the Protestant successors of James I. Kant's point is this: it is possible for the state itself to change the terms of the social contract, but not for the people themselves to initiate such change.

In so arguing, Kant underscores the inviolability of the monarch, as well as the inviolable rights of the people in relation to the head of state—excepting, that is, any rights of coercion. As Kant is aware (and as the subtitle of this chapter of his essay makes clear), this argument is intended as a challenge to Hobbes. Kant's critique of Hobbes's position in *De Cive* is set out as follows:

> In every commonwealth there must be *obedience* under the mechanism of the state constitution to coercive laws (applying to the whole), but there must also be a *spirit of freedom,* since each, in what has to do with universal human duties, requires to be convinced by reason that this coercion is in conformity with right [*rechmäßig*], lest he fall into contradiction with himself. [...] For it is a natural calling [*Naturberuf*] of humanity to communicate with one another, especially in what concerns people generally; hence those societies would disappear if such freedom were favored. And how else, again, could the government get the knowledge it requires for its own essential purpose than by letting the spirit of freedom, so worthy of respect in its origin and in its effects, express itself?[34]

(This idea that human beings are naturally communicative is one that will recur, as we shall see, in the thought of Jürgen Habermas.) Taking issue with what Hobbes says in *De Cive* (Chapter 7, §14), Kant argues that the subject must assume that the ruler has no wish to commit injustice. To this extent, it seems as if Kant envisages the ruler in Platonic terms as a kind of philosopher-king, or at any rate as being a good Kantian; at the back of Kant's mind must surely have been the enlightened despotism of the Prussian king, Frederick the Great.

Kant accepts that a ruler may commit an injustice through an error or through ignorance, and accordingly, he argues, the subject has the right to express an opinion. On this account, the freedom of the pen is the primary safeguard of the right of the people. Yet even here, Kant is cautious: such criticism should not be disrespectful. As always, Kant's primary concern is to establish an unassailable position from which to judge political decisions. (His motivation to do this is, for historical reasons, clear: along with a collapse of the belief in God goes the collapse of the belief in the divine right of kings. Just as, in his first *Critique*, Kant argued that he wanted to limit knowledge in order to find room for belief,[35] so in his political theory Kant wants to limit civil disobedience in order to provide for a stable society.)

Thus the people may judge to be negative whatever it believes has not been decreed in good will by the supreme legislation of the state; or, as Kant puts it (in line with his maxim above), "whatever a people cannot impose upon itself, cannot be imposed upon it by the legislator, either." Accordingly, it is important to be balanced and to see the nuances in Kant's political theory. If, on the one hand, he is arguing for obedience to the laws of the state which may legitimately be regarded as coercive, he is also, on the other hand, arguing for the presence of a "spirit of freedom" in society, so that each individual embraces the coercion implied in such laws for, without so doing, he or she would be in a state of self-contradiction. In the paradox of freedom, as Kant understands it, it is no loss of freedom to give up one's freedom. Indeed, true freedom involves precisely this giving up of freedom, as we sacrifice doing what we want in favour of doing what is our duty.

So morality, for Kant, is at once paradoxical and liberating. In obeying the law, we are doing our duty; and in doing our duty, we are discovering a new, exciting freedom: we are discovering the freedom to be moral beings. Doing one's duty is not just a restriction of one's freedom to do whatever one wants, it leads us into a realm where we are free to be moral. (And lest this all sound very abstract, Kant anchors this idea in a contemporary problem for European states at the time of the Enlightenment: he condemns the existence of secret societies.)[36]

When reading Kant today, his position can sometimes seem perverse. To be moral, we have to do our duty; and one sometimes has the sense that the less we enjoy doing our duty, the more moral we are being. As a reaction and a response to this (perceived) deficiency on the part of Kant, the poet, playwright and historian Friedrich Schiller (1759–1805) proposed the idea that it was possible to imagine duty (what one ought morally to do) and inclination (what one actually wants to do) coinciding. If duty and inclination coincide, he argued, one would be something extremely rare—one would become a beautiful soul.[37]

Yet inevitably our sense of unease with Kant comes from our position of reading him in the twenty-first century, with our knowledge of all the events that happened in the twentieth century. When Kant argues that one must *always* obey the law, we cannot help asking: is this also true if one is a member of a totalitarian society? Should one have followed this precept of absolute obedience, even if one had been a German citizen in the 1930s and 1940s, living under the National Socialist rule of the Third Reich?

Piquancy is added to this debate by the work of Hannah Arendt (1906–1975), the German-born political theorist and an important commentator on Kant's political thought.[38] During the autumn semester of 1970, Arendt gave a series of lectures at the New School for Social Research, based on material she had presented earlier at the University of Chicago in 1964, 1965 and 1966. These lectures have subsequently been published as *Lectures on Kant's Philosophy*. But her most famous intervention in the question of how to interpret Kant's political philosophy against the backdrop of the Third Reich came in her study of the trial of Adolf Eichmann (1906–1962) in Jerusalem. In *Eichmann in Jerusalem* (1963), Arendt reports how, during his police examination, Eichmann "suddenly declared with great emphasis that he had lived his whole life according to Kant's moral precepts, and especially according to a Kantian definition of duty."[39] At the trial, Eichmann was pressed on this point by the judge, perhaps curious about Eichmann's statement or indignant at his invocation of Kant.

> And, to the surprise of everybody, Eichmann came up with an approximately correct definition of the categorical imperative: "I meant by my remark about Kant that the principle of my will must always be such that it can become the principle of general laws" (which is not the case with theft or murder, for instance, because the thief or the murderer cannot conceivably wish to live under a legal system that would give others the right to rob or murder him.) Upon further questioning, he added that he had read Kant's *Critique of Practical Reason*.[40]

Armed with this knowledge of Kant, it seems, Eichmann had been able to reconcile himself to organising the Holocaust with perfect equanimity. He had succeeded, as Arendt points out, in harmonizing Kant's ethics with the dictates of the Nazi terror, as another Nazi, Hans Frank (1900–1962), had also been able to do:

> [Eichmann] proceeded to explain that from the moment he was charged with carrying out the Final Solution he had ceased to live according to Kantian principles, that he had known it, and that he had consoled himself with the thought that he no longer "was master of his own deeds," that he was unable "to change anything." What he failed to point out in court was that in this "period of crimes legalized by the state," as he himself now called it,[[41]] he had not simply dismissed the Kantian formula as no longer applicable, he had distorted it to read: Act as if the principle of your actions were the same as that of the legislator or of the law of the land — or, in Hans Frank's formulation of "the categorical imperative in the Third Reich", which Eichmann might have known: "Act in such a way that the Führer, if he knew your action, would approve of it". (*Die Technik des Staates*, 1942, pp. 15–16)[42]

On the basis of this account in Arendt's *Eichmann in Jerusalem*, the French philosopher Michel Onfray has written a play, *Le Songe d'Eichmann* (2008), in which Kant, Eichmann, and Nietzsche are shown in intense debate about what is and what is not morally good.[43]

Yet Arendt is more nuanced. On the one hand, she defends Kant against this outrageous misinterpretation at the hands of Frank and of Eichmann: "Kant, to be sure, had never intended to say anything of the sort; on the contrary, to him every man was a legislator the moment he started to act: by using his 'practical reason' man found the principles that could and should be the principles of law".[44] On the other hand, Arendt is well aware how open this philosophical position is to abuse:

> But it is true that Eichmann's unconscious distortion agrees with what he himself called the version of Kant "for the household use of the little man". In this household use, all that is left of Kant's spirit is the demand that a man do more than obey the law, that he go beyond the mere call of obedience and identify his own will with the principle behind the law — the source from which the law sprang. In Kant's philosophy, that source was practical reason; in Eichmann's household use of him, it was the will of the Führer.[45]

Yet is the real problem here nothing to do with Kant at all, but with a culturally specific aspect of the German character? Certainly this is what Arendt herself concludes is the case:

> Much of the horribly painstaking thoroughness in the execution of the Final Solution — a thoroughness that usually strikes the observer as typically German, or else as characteristic of the perfect bureaucrat — can be traced to the odd notion, indeed very common in Germany, that to be law-abiding means not merely to obey the laws but to act as though one were the legislator of the laws that one obeys. Hence the conviction that nothing less than going beyond the call of duty will do.[46]

That said, there is another way in which to approach this problem and to appreciate the radicalness of Kant's thinking in this respect. In an essay entitled "The Republic of Silence" (1944), the French Existentialist philosopher Jean-Paul Sartre (1905–1980) declared: "We were never more free than during the German Occupation," and he explained this astonishing phrase as follows:

We had lost all right, beginning with the right to talk. Every day we were insulted to our faces and had to take it in silence. Under one pretext or another, as workers, Jews, or political prisoners, we were deported *en masse*. Everywhere, on billboards, in the newspapers, on the screen, we encountered the revolting and insipid picture of ourselves that our oppressors wanted us to accept. And, because of all this, we were free. Because the Nazi venom seeped even into our thoughts, every accurate thought was a conquest. Because an all-powerful police tried to force us to hold our tongues, every word took on the value of a declaration of principles. Because we were hunted down, every one of our gestures had the weight of a solemn commitment. The circumstances, as atrocious as they often were, finally made it possible for us to live, without pretence or false shame, the hectic and impossible existence that is known as the lot of man.[47]

Sartre's description here—aside from the existential anguish implied in the reference to "the hectic and impossible existence that is known as the lot of man"—is entirely in line with what Kant is trying to say. It is not so much that, in the Third Reich, the oppressed citizens of France were more free than they had been previously. Rather, the extreme circumstances of invasion and occupation throw into the light the nobility (or potential nobility) of human existence.

For Kant, we exist in the limited realm of time and space, and hence as phenomena. But to the extent that we can use our reason, we have access to the noumenal realm, and through obedience to the categorical imperative, we can (in the paradoxical dialectic of freedom) have freedom in the here-and-now. It is as if Kant were harking back to the Stoical tradition which declares: I know, to the extent that I align myself with the universal *logos*, that in some way I am eternal. Or as Baruch Spinoza (1632–1677) tells us in his *Ethics*, we know—indeed, he says that we *experience*—that we are "eternal": in his words, "We feel and know by experience that we are eternal."[48]

And it is this sense of being both temporal and eternal, phenomenal and noumenal, that links Kant with the discourse of Platonism in the German tradition of political thought. For despite the relative paucity of Kant's direct references to Plato, and despite the normative (i.e., rule-based) emphasis of Kant's ethics as compared with the prudential (i.e., virtue-based) emphasis of Plato's, there are—as noted in the introduction to this chapter—important parallels between Kant and Plato.

In the "Introduction" to the first *Critique*, Kant initially criticizes Plato for "abandon[ing] the world of the senses because it posed so many hindrances for the understanding, and dar[ing] to go beyond it on the wings of the Ideas, in the empty space of pure understanding" (A5/B9).[49] In the "Transcendental Dialectic," book 1 (A313–320/ B370–377), Kant expounds his understanding of the Platonic doctrine of the Idea, alluding to the *Republic* where Socrates speaks of how the eye of the soul "must be turned around from that which is *coming into being* [...] until it is able to endure looking at that which *is* and the brighest part of that which *is*," i.e., looking at the Good (517d).[50] Yet in the "Transcendental Dialectic," book 2, Kant aligns his critical philosophy with Plato's metaphysics, writing that "what is an Ideal to us, was to Plato an Idea in the divine understanding, an individual object in that understanding's pure intuition, the most perfect thing of each species of possible beings and the original ground of all its origins in appearance" (A568/B596).[51]

In this way Kant activates, using the discourse of Platonism, the important notion of the *ideal*, in the specific sense that this term is used in German Idealism. (Unlike today, where we dismissively speak of something being "just an ideal," Kant wants to assert the reality of the ideal, and hence the realism of idealism.)[52] On this account, abstract notions like goodness or justice lose none of their force as the object of ethical imperatives because they are abstract.[53] Plato's epistemological tendency towards abstraction is matched by Kant's insistence on a purely formal definition of the good in the form of the categorical imperative—so that we act only according to maxims that could become universal laws, never treat other people as a means rather than as an end, and regard ourselves, even and especially in the political realm, as members of a *universal kingdom of ends*. And Kant is thoroughly Platonic when, in the *Grounding for the Metaphysics of Morals*, he envisages the contemplation of virtue:

To behold virtue in her proper form is nothing other than to present morality stripped of all admixture of what is sensuous and of every spurious adornment of reward or self-love. How much then she eclipses all else that appears attractive to the inclinations can be easily seen by everyone with the least effort of his reason, if it be not entirely ruined for all abstraction.[54]

In the thought of one of Kant's successors in the tradition of German thought, G.W.F. Hegel, the idea of the Idea of the state undergoes a process of conceptual articulation and elaboration, as we shall see in the following chapter.

Notes

1. For an evocation of the Prussian world in which Kant lived, the reader could do worse than read the novels by Michael Gregorio (the pseudonym of Michael G. Jacob and Daniela De Gregorio), *Critique of Criminal Reason* (London: Faber and Faber, 2006); *Days of Atonement* (London: Faber and Faber, 2007); *A Visible Darkness* (London: Faber and Faber, 2009).

2. As Hans Reiss notes, the first extant notes of Kant's thinking on political theory date from the 1760s, when he was studying Rousseau and natural law. It was not, however, until 1767 that Kant gave his first lecture-course on the Theory of Right; a course he was to repeat twelve times (Hans Reiss, "Introduction," in *Kant's Political Writings*, ed. Hans Reiss, trans. H.B. Nisbet (Cambridge: Cambridge University Press, 1970), 1–38 [15]). For further discussion of Rousseau's influence on the development of Kant's critical philosophy, see David James, *Rousseau and German Idealism: Freedom, Dependence and Necessity* (Cambridge: Cambridge University Press, 2013).

3. Although one blithely talks about *the* Enlightenment, in reality the matter is more complex. As well as the mainstream Enlightenment tradition, other kinds have been identified by historians and critics as well: a "Rosicrucian" Enlightenment (Frances Yates), a "covert" Enlightenment (Alfred J. Gabay), a "religious" Enlightenment (David Sorkin), and even a "Catholic" Enlightenment (Ulrich L. Lehner), while others have identified *les anti-Lumières* as a tradition linking the eighteenth

century and the Cold War (Zeev Sternhell) or described such thinkers as Jean Meslier, La Mettrie, Maupertuis, Helvétius, d'Holbach, and the Marquis de Sade as *les ultras des Lumières* (Michel Onfray). See, most recently, the book that has been published by Ulrich L. Lehner entitled *The Catholic Enlightenment* (New York: Oxford University Press, 2016).

4. Kant, "An Answer to the Question: 'What Is Enlightenment?'", in *Political Writings*, ed. Hans Reiss, trans. H.B. Nisbet, 2nd edn (Cambridge: Cambridge University Press, 1991), 54–60 (54): "*Enlightenment is man's emergence from his self-incurred maturity.*"

5. See Frederick Beiser (ed. and trans.), *The Early Political Writings of the German Romantics* (Cambridge: Cambridge University Press, 1996).

6. See Robert Josef Kozljanič, *Lebensphilosophie: Eine Einführung* (Stuttgart: Kohlhammer, 2004), Chapter 1, "Friedrich Schlegel: Begründung und Methodik einer 'Philosophie des Lebens'" (29–40).

7. For further discussion of Plato's relationship to German Idealism, see Burkhard Mojvisch and Orrin F. Summerell (eds), *Platonismus im Idealismus: Die platonische Tradition in der klassischen deutschen Philosophie* (Munich and Leipzig: Saur, 2003).

8. For an introduction to the thinking of German Idealism, see Ernst Behler (ed.), *Philosophy of German Idealism* (New York: Continuum, 1987); Rüdiger Bubner, *German Idealist Philosophy* (Harmondsworth: Penguin, 1997), translated from Rüdiger Bubner, *Deutscher Idealismus* [*Geschichte der Philosophie in Text und Darstellung*, vol. 6] (Stuttgart: Reclam, 1978); Brian O'Connor and Georg Mohr, *German Idealism: An Anthology and Guide* (Chicago: University of Chicago Press, 2006). And for further discussion, see Robert C. Solomon and Kathleen M. Higgins (eds), *The Age of German Idealism* [*Routledge History of Philosophy*, vol. 6] (London and New York: Routledge, 1993); Karl Ameriks (ed.), *The Cambridge Companion to German Idealism* (Cambridge and New York: Cambridge University Press, 2000); Matthew C. Altman, *The Palgrave Handbook of German Idealism* (Houndmills, Basingstoke, and New York: Palgrave Macmillan, 2014).

9. See, for instance, Fichte, *Addresses to the German Nation*, trans. Gregory Moore (Cambridge and New York: Cambridge University Press, 2008).

10. For further discussion of the relation between Kant and Plato, see the following: Heinz Heimsoeth, "Kant and Plato," *Kant-Studien* 56 (1965), 349–372; and "Platon und Kants Werdegang," in Martial Guéroult et al., *Studien zu Kants philosophischer Entwicklung* (Hildesheim: Olms, 1967), 127–143.

11. Kant, *Grounding for the Metaphysics of Morals* [1785], trans. James W. Ellington, 3rd edn (Indianapolis: Hackett, 1993), 30, 36, 40.

12. See, for instance, *Meno*, 77b 78b; *Gorgias*, 467c–468c; *Protagoras*, 354e–357c; and *Laws*, 860c-e and 731c. For further discussion, see Harold Cherniss, "The Sources of Evil According to Plato," *Proceedings of the American Philosophical Society* 98, no. 1 (February 1954), 23–30; Jeffrey H. Silver, "Wrongdoing and Ignorance: Socrates Defended," *Philosophy Today* 40, no. 4 (Winter 1996), 496–503.

13. The translation used is from Immanuel Kant, *The Philosophy of Law: An Exposition of the Fundamental Principles of Jurisprudence and the Science of Right*, trans. William Hastie (Edinburgh: T. & T. Clark, 1887).

14. Kant, *The Philosophy of Law*, 44.

15. Kant, *The Philosophy of Law*, 45.

16. Kant, *The Philosophy of Law*, 45.

17. Kant, *The Philosophy of Law*, 46.

18. Kant, *The Philosophy of Law*, 47.

19. Kant, *The Philosophy of Law*, 56–57.

20. Kant, *Political Writings*, 73.

21. Kant, *Political Writings*, 74.

22. Kant, *Political Writings*, 74.

23. Kant, *Political Writings*, 74–75.

24. Kant, *Political Writings*, 75–76.

25. Is this phrase one of the sources for the provocative later work, *Der Einzige und sein Eigentum* (*The Ego and His Own*) (1845) by the renegade anarchist thinker, Max Stirner (1806–1856), in which the individual who creates himself or herself beyond conventional ethical norms is called *der Eigner*?

26. Kant, *Political Writings*, 77.

27. Kant, "On the Common Saying: That May be Correct in Theory, but It Is of No Use in Practice," in *Practical Philosophy*, ed. and trans. Mary J. Gregor (Cambridge: Cambridge University Press, 1996), 273–309 (296).

28. As an example of how such a test would function, Kant cites the example of a war tax. If a war tax is imposed on the citizens of the state, they cannot claim that it is unjust, simply because it is oppressive and because the war is unnecessary. Why? Because, in Kant's view, the citizens are simply not in a position to judge the issue. Maybe the war *is* inevitable and maybe the tax *is* unavoidable. In this sense, the tax is rightful; what *would* be wrong would be to impose the tax only on

some while exempting others, since "an unequal distribution of burdens can never be considered just" (Kant, *Political Writings*, 79; Kant, *Practical Philosophy*, 297).

29. Cf. the principle *Salus populi suprema lex esto*, "Let the health of the people be the supreme law", derived from Cicero, *De Legibus* (*On the Laws*), book 3, part 3, §8; cited by Hobbes in his *Leviathan* (1651), Chapter 30; by Spinoza in his *Theological-Political Treatise* (1670); and by John Locke in the second of his *Two Treatises on Government* (1689).

30. Kant, *Practical Philosophy*, 298.

31. As an instance of how happiness might, with good reason, be restricted, Kant gives the example of placing restrictions on imports, to support the livelihood of certain citizens rather than give advantage to foreign industries, "since a state, without the prosperity of the people, would not possess enough strength to resist foreign enemies or to maintain itself as a commonwealth" (Kant, *Practical Philosophy*, 298).

32. Kant, *Practical Philosophy*, 298–299.

33. Kant, *Political Writings*, 83.

34. Kant, *Practical Philosophy*, 303.

35. "I had to deny *knowledge* in order to make room for faith" (*Ich mußte also das Wissen aufheben, um zum Glauben Platz zu bekommen*), in Immanuel Kant, *Critique of Pure Reason*, ed. and trans. Paul Guyer and Allen W. Wood (Cambridge: Cambridge University Press, 1997), "Preface to the Second Edition," B xxx (117).

36. For further discussion of the role played by secret societies in the imaginary (and in the reality) of Kant's time, see Stefan Andriopoulos, "Occult Conspiracies: Spirits and Secret Societies in Schiller's 'Ghost Seer,'" *New German Critique* 103 (2008), 65–81; Ritchie Robertson, "Freemasons vs Jesuits: Conspiracy Theories in Enlightenment Germany," *Times Literary Supplement*, 12 October 2012, 13–15.

37. See Schiller's definition of the beautiful soul in "On Grace and Dignity" (1793): "One refers to a beautiful soul when the ethical sense has at last so taken control of all a person's feelings that it can leave affect to guide the will without hesitation and is never in danger of standing in contradiction of its decisions. For this reason the actions of a beautiful soul are not themselves ethical, but the character as a whole is so. [...] The beautiful soul has no other merit besides being" (Jane V. Curran and Christophe Fricker (eds), *Schiller's "On Grace and Dignity" in Its Cultural Context* (Rochester, NY: Camden House, 2005),

152). For further discussion, see Robert E. Norton, *The Beautiful Soul: Aesthetic Morality in the Eighteenth Century* (Ithaca, NY, and London: Cornell University Press, 1995); and Frederick Beiser, *Schiller as Philosopher: A Re-examination* (Oxford: Clarendon Press, 2005), 80–85.

38. See Hannah Arendt, *Lectures in Kant's Political Philosophy*, ed. Ronald Beiner (Chicago and London: University of Chicago Press, 1992). For further discussion, see Allen Wood, "Kant's Political Philosophy," in Altman (ed.), *The Palgrave Handbook of German Idealism*, 165–185.

39. Hannah Arendt, *Eichmann in Jerusalem: A Report on the Banality of Evil* (New York: Penguin, 2006), 135–136.

40. Arendt, *Eichmann in Jerusalem*, 136.

41. Compare with the arguments proposed by Carl Schmitt (1888–1985) to justify the actions of the Third Reich as legitimate in legal terms. For further discussion, see Seyla Benhabib, "Carl Schmitt's Critique of Kant: Sovereignty and International Law," *Political Theory* 40, no. 6 (December 2012), 688–713.

42. Arendt, *Eichmann in Jerusalem*, 136. Hans Frank worked as a German lawyer for the National Socialist Party, then directly for Adolf Hitler. Found guilty at Nuremberg of war crimes and crimes against humanity, Frank was executed.

43. Michel Onfray, *Le Songe d'Eichmann* (Paris: Galilée, 2008).

44. Arendt, *Eichmann in Jerusalem*, 136.

45. Arendt, *Eichmann in Jerusalem*, 136–137.

46. Arendt, *Eichmann in Jerusalem*, 137.

47. Jean-Paul Sartre, "Paris Under the Occupation", *Sartre Studies International* 4, no. 2 (1998), 1–15 (2–3).

48. Spinoza, *Ethics*, part 5, proposition 22, scholium, in *Selections*, ed. J. Wild (London: Scribner, 1928), 385. Spinoza explains this remarkable claim as follows: "Although, therefore, we do not recollect that we existed before the body, we feel that our mind, insofar as it involves the essence of the body under the form of eternity, is eternal, and that this existence of the mind cannot be limited by time nor manifested through duration" (385).

49. Kant, *Critique of Pure Reason*, 129, 140.

50. Kant, *Critique of Pure Reason*, 395–399. Cf. too *Meno* (81), *Phaedo* (73–77), *Phaedrus* (243–257).

51. Kant, *Critique of Pure Reason*, 551.

52. See Jeremy Dunham, Iain Hamilton Grant, and Sean Watson, *Idealism: The History of a Philosophy* (Durham: Acumen, 2011; reprinted Abingdon and New York: Routledge, 2014).
53. For further discussion, see Allen D. Rosen, *Kant's Theory of Justice* (Ithaca and London: Cornell University Press, 1993).
54. Kant, *Grounding for the Metaphysics of Morals*, 34, fn. 19.

6

Hegel and the Dialectic

In moving from Kant to Georg Wilhelm Friedrich Hegel (1770–1831) we retain many of the great themes of Kantian thought, yet we find them enriched, enhanced, and developed in the work of this great philosopher.[1] His reception has proved remarkably important in the genesis of existentialism, psychoanalysis, and post-structuralism in the twentieth century. And yet, above all in his political philosophy, the discourse of Platonism continues to make its subterranean presence felt.

A glance at the famous portrait of Hegel made in 1831 by Johann Jakob Schlesinger (1792–1855), currently on display in the Nationalgalerie in Berlin, will show us what sort of man we are dealing with. Finished shortly before Hegel's death due to a cholera outbreak in Berlin, it shows us Hegel looking greying, haggard, yet resolute and undeterred. It shows us someone unforgiving, even ruthless: and it is true that, for such readers as Karl Popper (1902–1994), Hegel belongs to a tradition of totalitarian thought which, on Popper's account, begins with Plato.[2]

Hegel's complete works are voluminous, and notoriously difficult to understand. To guide us through the labyrinth of his thought in general and through that part of the labyrinth devoted to political thought

© The Author(s) 2019
P. Bishop, *German Political Thought and the Discourse of Platonism*,
https://doi.org/10.1007/978-3-030-04510-4_6

extracted for us here, let us consider three guiding ideas in Hegel's thought. First, there is the basic Hegelian principle, clearly articulated in his *Elements of the Philosophy of Right* (1821). This principle states that "what is rational, is real; and what is real, is rational" (*Was vernünftig ist, das ist wirklich; und was wirklich ist, das ist vernünftig*).[3] How are we to understand this remarkable statement? We shall return to this statement in its context, but for now, let us note how it is glossed by Norbert Hoerster, who reads it as saying that what should be and what is, what is rational and what is real, the ethical ideal of the state and the historical reality of the state coincide.[4] Does this mean: what is, is right?

No. What Hegel is trying to get at is this: however problematic reality may be, there is something rational about or behind it. (Indeed, we have to recognize there is something rational about or behind it, or we would not be able to recognize reality as problematic in the first place.) Hegel is not trying to argue that the ideal—in this case, the ethical ideal of the state—is, at any particular moment in history, ever fully realized. His point rather is that this ideal is realized *in the course of* history as it dialectically unfolds.[5] What is really real at any particular historical moment is not the entirety of reason, but it is moving towards the most rational form that it is possible to attain at that moment in history.[6]

A second key idea is something to which we have just referred—the dialectic. Now we already encountered the notion of the dialectic in Plato's *Republic* (e.g. 532a–d, 533b–d), and in fact there are many different sorts of dialectic.[7] Some of these different sorts of dialectic are summarized below:

- Platonic dialectic: the function of the dialectic for Plato is to allow us to discover the truth about the human condition, to cultivate our understanding, to distinguish between different levels of reality, and to lead to the spiritual knowledge of the divine[8];
- Kantian dialectic: for Kant, the dialectic is an activity that tries to work through what appear to be the inherent illusions of the understanding;
- Hegelian dialectic: for Hegel, the dialectic is a movement of thought that generates its own oppositions and resolves them, turning his

philosophy into the culmination of all that has preceded it and into the system of all systems;

• Marxist dialectic: for Marx, dialectical materialism is the study of what appear to be inherent contradictions in the processes of social and economic development;

• Buddhist-Nagarjuna dialectic: in this Eastern philosophical school, the dialectic is used to deny all views in such a way as to empty the mind of its beliefs; in so doing, it functions as a kind of religious catharsis.

And there are other kinds of dialectic too: in addition to the famous dialectic of capital as analysed by Marx, there is the dialectic of psychology found in Freudian psychoanalysis and in Jungian psychotherapy, the dialectic of social science as found in the work of Charles Sanders Peirce (1839–1914)[9] and of Erving Goffman (1922–1982), the dialectic of phenomenology, the dialectic of contemporary social thought (Slavoj Žižek and Giorgio Agamben), and so on. Even the Hegelian dialectic undergoes its own dialectical reversal at the hands of the thinkers of the Frankfurt School, when Theodor W. Adorno (1903–1969) introduces the notion of "negative dialectics."[10]

For all the significant differences between Plato and Hegel in relation to the dialectic, there is an equally significant common element. Glenn Alexander Magee has pointed to the underlying affinity between Hegelian and Platonic dialectic as being, in both cases, "a recollection and explication of [...] wisdom": in the Platonic dialectic, "attempts are made to define some universal, all of which prove inadequate, but each of which builds on the previous attempt" (cf. the discussion of justice in the *Republic*, book 1) and the "key to the dialectic" is that "the participants already know, in some sense, the meaning of the terms they aim at defining"; while, in Hegel's *Logic*, each category constitutes "a provisional definition of the Absolute," but proves "partial and inadequate, forcing us to inquire further, and so the dialectic pushes on."[11]

According to the British Idealist philosopher, J.M.E. McTaggart (1866–1925), in the dialectic Hegel's primary object is "to establish the existence of a logical connection between the various categories which are involved in the constitution of experience," while teaching that "this connection is of such a kind that any category, if scrutinised with sufficient care and attention, is found to lead on to another [...]."[12] McTaggart insists that the dialectic must be regarded "as a process, not of construction, but of reconstruction," revealing that "the lower categories have no independent existence, but are only abstractions from the highest" and that "no category except the highest can be completely rational, since every lower one involves its contrary." This argument informs Hegel's view of the relation between the Absolute and reality: "The Absolute Idea is present to us in all reality, in all the phenomena of experience, and in our own selves," for "everywhere it is the soul of all reality" yet, "although it is always present to us, it is not always explicitly present."[13]

For Plato (and indeed for Plotinus) and for Hegel alike, dialectic is "the means whereby the world makes itself intelligible," as Jeremy Dunham, Iain Hamilton Grant, and Sean Watson have observed.[14] In his (*Greater*) *Logic*, Hegel defined logic as "the science of things grasped in thoughts," and dialectic as the means whereby these "thought-determinations" are thinkable.[15] Thus dialectic is "the very nature of thinking," and the insight that the dialectic, "as understanding, [...] must fall into the negative of itself, into contradictions, is an aspect of capital importance in the Logic."[16] For Hegel, the dialectic enables us to understand that "reason is the soul of the world, inhabits it, and is immanent in it, as its own, innermost nature, its universal."[17]

Thus for Hegel there exists an intrinsic logic in the world, manifest in nature, self-consciousness, and history alike. Dialectic reveals how the Idea unfolds in all these areas, moving through consecutive phases of [1] unity, [2] multiplicity, and [3] unity in multiplicity. Or, in Hegel's words, dialectic is:

[...] the genuine nature that properly belongs to the determinations of the understanding, to things, and to the finite in general. [...] The dialectic [...] is the *immanent* transcending, in which the one-sidedness and restrictedness of the determinations of the understanding displays itself as what it is, i.e., as their negation. [...] Hence the Dialectical constitutes the moving soul of scientific progression, and it is the principle through which alone *immanent coherence and necessity* enter into the content of science.[18]

The third guiding idea in Hegel's thought is in his relation to Kant. Although Hegel is greatly indebted to Kant, he belongs to a series of thinkers who try to shape and adapt the methods and the conclusions of the critical philosophy. These thinkers include the lyric poet Friedrich Hölderlin (1770–1843) and the philosopher F.W.J. Schelling (1775–1854), both of whom were friends of Hegel at the Stift in Tübingen, as well as J.G. Fichte (1762–1814). So one can read Hegel as a thinker who, while remaining true to the insights of Kant's understanding of morality, operates a shift away from the moral (as individual) to the ethical (as collective). The German word for ethics, *Sittlichkeit*, echoes the German term for customs, *Sitten*; while, on a Kantian/individual/moral level it is good, for instance, to be friendly and hospitable towards strangers, on the Hegelian/collective/ethical there are particular customs, traditions and practices that embody this friendship and hospitality. In particular, Hegel pays greater attention than Kant did to the institutions and organisations that embody the ethical life. For Hegel, the institutions and organisations that embody the state are ultimately ethical agencies.

One of the works where Hegel sets out his political views most clearly is his *Elements of the Philosophy of Right* (sometimes translated as *Outlines of the Philosophy of Right*).[19] In this first extract, taken from the Preface to this work, Hegel draws a connection between the ethical world, the state, and the realization of reason in self-consciousness:

> But a further difficulty lies in the fact that man thinks, and seeks freedom and a basis for conduct in thought. Divine as his right to act in this way is, it becomes a wrong, when it takes the place of thinking. Thought then regards itself as free only when it is conscious of being at variance with what is generally recognised, and of setting itself up as something original.
>
> The idea that freedom of thought and mind is indicated only by deviation from, or even hostility to what is everywhere recognised, is most persistent with regard to the state. The essential task of a philosophy of the state would thus seem to be the discovery and publication of a new and original theory.

When we examine this idea and the way it is applied, we are almost led to think that no state or constitution has ever existed, or now exists. We are tempted to suppose that we must now begin and keep on beginning afresh for ever. We are to fancy that the founding of the social order has depended upon present devices and discoveries. As to nature, philosophy, it is admitted, has to understand it as it is. The philosophers' stone must be concealed somewhere, we say, in nature itself, as nature is in itself rational. Knowledge must, therefore, examine, apprehend and conceive the reason actually present in nature. Not with the superficial shapes and accidents of nature, but with its eternal harmony, that is to say, its inherent law and essence, knowledge has to cope. But the ethical world or the state, which is in fact reason potently and permanently actualised in self-consciousness, is not permitted to enjoy the happiness of being reason at all. On the contrary, the spiritual universe is looked upon as abandoned by God, and given over as a prey to accident and chance. As in this way the divine is eliminated from the ethical world, truth must be sought outside of it. And since at the same time reason should and does belong to the ethical world, truth, being divorced from reason, is reduced to a mere speculation. Thus seems to arise the necessity and duty of every thinker to pursue a career of his own. Not that he needs to seek for the philosophers' stone, since the philosophizing of our day has saved him the trouble, and every would-be thinker is convinced that he possesses the stone already without search. But these erratic pretensions are, as it indeed happens, ridiculed by all who, whether they are aware of it or not, are conditioned in their lives by the state, and find their minds and wills satisfied in it. These, who include the majority if not all, regard the occupation of philosophers as a game, sometimes playful, sometimes earnest, sometimes entertaining, sometimes dangerous, but always as a mere game.

(Preface, *Elements of the Philosophy of Right*)[20]

Indeed, Hegel goes so far as to identify these three things—the ethical world, the state, and the realization of reason in self-consciousness—, claiming that "the ethical world or the state" is in fact "reason potently and permanently actualised in self-consciousness." At the same time, however, he laments that philosophy has hitherto not fully understood this fact. Hegel wants to defend philosophy against the charge that is merely a game, and he intends to do this by demonstrating that philosophy alone can comprehend reality, including political reality.

In fact, on Hegel's account philosophy is nothing less than "the inquisition into the rational, and therefore the apprehension of the real and present," as he explains:

> The real world is in earnest with the principles of right and duty, and in the full light of a consciousness of these principles it lives. With this world of reality philosophic cob-web spinning has come into open rupture. Now, as to genuine philosophy it is precisely its attitude to reality which has been misapprehended. Philosophy is, as I have already observed, an inquisition into the rational, and therefore the apprehension of the real and present. Hence it cannot be the exposition of a world beyond, which is merely a castle in the air, having no existence except in the error of a one-sided and empty formalism of thought.
>
> (Preface, *Elements of the Philosophy of Right*)[21]

At this point Hegel goes on to wrap himself in the mantle of Plato, while at the same time suggesting that he, Hegel, is in a position to understand philosophy in a way that Plato, because of the limitations of his time, could not: "Even Plato's *Republic*, now regarded as the byword for an empty ideal, has grasped the essential nature of the ethical observances of the Greeks," for "he knew that there was breaking in upon Greek life a deeper principle, which could directly manifest itself only as an unsatisfied longing and therefore as ruin." Hegel continues: "Moved by the same longing Plato had to seek help against it, but had to conceive of the help as coming down from above, and hoped at last to have found it in an external special form of Greek ethical observance," and he "exhausted himself in contriving how by means of this new society to stem the tide of ruin, but succeeded only in injuring more fatally its deeper motive, the free infinite personality." Yet the means by which, according to Hegel, Plato has "proved himself to be a great mind" is "because the very principle and central distinguishing feature of his idea is the pivot upon which the world-wide revolution then in process turned."[22] And what is this principle? As we have seen, Hegel enunciates it as follows:

> What is rational, is real;
> And what is real, is rational.

Following on from this brief, but significant, discussion of Plato's *Republic*, which establishes Hegel's thought in relation to the discourse of Platonism, and after the introduction of this central distinguishing feature of his conception of philosophy, Hegel proceeds to analyse and gloss this principle as follows:

> Against the doctrine that the idea is a mere idea, figment or opinion, philosophy preserves the more profound view that nothing is real except the idea. Hence arises the effort to recognise in the temporal and transient the substance, which is immanent, and the eternal, which is present. The rational is synonymous with the idea, because in realising itself it passes into external existence. It thus appears in an endless wealth of forms, figures and phenomena. It wraps its kernel round with a robe of many colours, in which consciousness finds itself at home. Through this varied husk the conception first of all penetrates, in order to touch the pulse, and then feel it throbbing in its external manifestations.
>
> (Preface, *Elements of the Philosophy of Right*)[23]

In these lines we find Hegel presenting the core of his philosophy and his philosophical approach to politics. First, he argues that nothing is real except the idea. Hearing this today, this claim might strike us as odd, but it is as central to Hegel's conception of philosophy as it is to Plato's.[24] What he is trying to get at is that the ideal is more real than the real: in other words, while there are individuals who are friendly with each other, the idea of friendship is larger than all these individual relationships; while there are individual acts of kindness, the idea of charity or care for the other is larger than these individual cases; or while are individual instances where justice is done (and seen to be done), the principle of justice itself is something so major, so fundamental, even so cosmic (cf. the ancient Greek concept of *dike*),[25] that it outstrips those individual instances.

Yet how do we attain to knowledge of the idea or the ideal? We must, says Hegel, learn to recognize in "the temporal and the transient" what is the substance and the eternal; we must understand, in the here-and-now (in the "immanent" and in the "present"), what is beyond-the-here-and-now. If we do this, Hegel argues, we shall recognise that the idea, which is the rational, is steadily realizing itself in the here-and-now and, as it realizes itself, it passes into eternal existence. Applied to the realm of politics, then, it is the task of political science (or *Staatswissenschaft*) both to conceive and to present the state as in itself something rational:

> This treatise, in so far as it contains a political science, is nothing more than an attempt to conceive of and present the state as in itself rational. As a philosophic writing, it must be on its guard against constructing a state as it ought to be. Philosophy cannot teach the state what it should be, but only how it, the ethical universe, is to be known.
>
> *Idou Podos, idou kai to pidima*
> *Hic Rhodus, hic saltus.*
>
> To apprehend what is is the task of philosophy, because what is is reason. As for the individual, every one is a son of his time; so philosophy also is its time apprehended in thoughts. It is just as foolish to fancy that any philosophy can transcend its present world, as that an individual could leap out of his time or jump over Rhodes. If a theory transgresses its time, and builds up a world as it ought to be, it has an existence merely in the unstable element of opinion, which gives room to every wandering fancy.
> (Preface, *Elements of the Philosophy of Right*)[26]

In so writing, Hegel alludes to one of Aesop's fables, in which an athlete makes the boastful claim that, during a competition held on the island of Rhodes, he had achieved an incredibly large long jump across the whole of the island. To which a sceptical onlooker issues the challenge: "Here is Rhodes, now jump!" How does this saying apply to Hegel's argument?

Hegel places himself at a distance from Plato's attempt in the *Republic* to construct the ideal state (assuming that, of course, this is what Plato was trying to do...). While holding on to the ideal, Hegel wants philosophy to show how that ideal has already been realized—that is, made real or *is being made* real—in the state as it already exists, that is, in the state as it existed in nineteenth-century Prussia. It is in the *here*, and in the *now*, that philosophy has to demonstrate its intellectual prowess; hence the allusion to Aesop. At the same time, this allusion contains a warning.

In apprehending the real or what "is," philosophy undertakes its most important task: namely, the task of revealing that what "is," is rational, *is* reason, *is* reason realizing itself in history and in time. Consequently, the activity of philosophy is bound by history and by time as well: and it is as impossible for philosophy not to reflect and be bound by the age in which it is being thought as it would be for an individual to jump across the entire island of Rhodes ... Yet this is not an insuperable problem for philosophy, since—for Hegel—its task is to understand reason or the idea as it unfolds or realizes itself in historical time.[27]

Now this interest in the historical, or the empirical, or the concrete is reflected in the very structure of Hegel's argumentation in his *Elements of the Philosophy of Right*. In this work he distinguishes between three different moments in its outline of politics: first, the individual or the "concrete" person; second, civil society; and third, the state itself. Even in this simple outline, we can see the organisation or "systematicity" of approach for which Hegel would become famous—or notorious. (As Nietzsche once remarked, "I mistrust all systematizers and avoid them," for "the will to a system is lack of integrity.")[28]

Turning to the first of these three elements or moments, the concrete person is on the one hand the incarnation of the principle of individuality, while on the other it provides evidence of the need to think above the level of the individual, i.e., to think on the level of the universal:

> The concrete person, who is himself the object of his particular aims, is, as a totality of wants and a mixture of caprice and physical necessity, one principle of civil society. But the particular person is essentially so related to other particular persons that each establishes himself and finds satisfaction by means of the others, and at the same time purely and simply by means of the form of universality, the second principle here.
> [....]
> In the course of the actual attainment of selfish ends — an attainment conditioned in this way by universality — there is formed a system of complete interdependence, wherein the livelihood, happiness, and legal status of one man is interwoven with the livelihood, happiness, and rights of all. On this system, individual happiness, etc., depend, and only in this connected system are they actualized and secured.
> (*Elements of the Philosophy of Right*, §182 and §183)[29]

Hegel's point is that we claim rights for ourselves not just for ourselves as individuals, but for all. It is not simply Mr or Ms X's right to walk down the street, or to participate in a political protest, or to cast a vote; it is the right of all citizens to do this. (Of course, we have to be careful about the question about who, for Hegel, is and who is not a citizen: while, for Hegel, women are citizens, he insists on gender distinction in their duties and commitments.) Examining the individual will, dialectically, lead us to consider the universal. The next step toward this is the collectivity of individuals known as civil society (*bürgerliche Gesellschaft*):

> Civil society contains three moments:
> (A) The mediation of need and one man's satisfaction through his labour and the satisfaction of the needs of all others — the *system of needs*.
> (B) The actuality of the universal principle of freedom therein contained – the protection of property through the *administration of justice*.
> (C) Provision against contingencies still lurking in systems (A) and (B), and care for particular interests as a common interest, by means of the *police* and the *corporation*.
> (*Elements of the Philosophy of Right*, §188)[30]

In its turn, civil society contains three different elements (or, as Hegel calls them, moments): first, there is the system of needs. The system of needs means the world of work; it corresponds, within Plato's three classes in the *Republic*, to the producers (the craftsmen, artisans, farmers etc.). Second, there is "moment" of justice: over and above the satisfaction of human beings' material needs, there is the longing for the guarantee of freedom, the protection of property, in short: a system of law. And third, there is the "moment" that Hegel identifies with such institutions as the police and the corporations (or, as we might call them, guilds or trade unions). This level of institutional organisation leads us to the next level: to the state.

Hegel's praise for the state seemingly knows no bounds, and his language here is one of the reasons that some critics—notably, Karl Popper—have identified Hegelian thought with totalitarian politics. Hegel's description and evaluation of the state, however, must be judged within their argumentational context:

The state is the actuality of the ethical Idea. It is ethical mind *qua* the substantial will manifest and revealed to itself, knowing and thinking itself, accomplishing what it knows and in so far as it knows it. The state exists immediately in *custom* [*Sitte*], mediately in individual self-consciousness, knowledge, and activity, while self-consciousness in virtue of its sentiment towards the state, finds in the state, as its essence and the end-product of its activity, its substantive freedom. [...]

The state is absolutely rational inasmuch as it is the actuality of the substantial will which it possesses in the particular self-consciousness once that consciousness has been raised to consciousness of its universality. This substantial unity is an absolute unmoved end in itself, in which freedom comes into its supreme right. On the other hand this final end has supreme right against the individual, whose supreme duty is to be a member of the state.

(*Elements of the Philosophy of Right*, §257 and §258)[31]

Just as Hegel situates his argument in relation to Plato, so he engages with such predecessors as Rousseau and Fichte, taking issue with their respective notions of the "social contract" and the "will"—and seeing in their philosophical insufficiencies the intellectual source of the violent consequences of the French Revolution (i.e., the Terror):

Remark: The philosophical treatment of these topics is concerned only with their inward side, with the *thought of their concept*. The merit of Rousseau's[32] contribution to the search for this concept is that, by adducing the *will* as the principle of the state, he is adducing a principle which has *thought* both for its form and its content, a principle indeed which is thinking itself, not a principle, like gregarious instinct, for instance, or divine authority, which has thought as its form only. Unfortunately, however, as Fichte did later,[33] he takes the will only in a determinate form as the *individual* will, and he regards the universal will not as the absolutely rational element in the will, but only as a "general" will which proceeds out of this individual will as out of a conscious will. The result is that he reduces the union of individuals in the state to a *contract* and therefore to something based on their arbitrary wills, their opinion, and their capriciously given express consent; and abstract reasoning proceeds to draw the logical inferences which destroy the absolutely divine principle of the state, together with its majesty and absolute authority. For this reason, when these abstract conclusions came into power, they afforded for the first time in human history the prodigious spectacle of the overthrow of the constitution of a great actual state and its complete reconstruction *ab initio* on the basis of pure thought alone, after the destruction of all existing and given material. The will of its re-founders was to give it what they alleged was a purely rational basis, but it was only abstractions that were being used; the Idea was lacking; and the experiment was ended in the maximum of frightfulness and terror.

Above all, Hegel's description and evaluation of the state must be seen in the context of his argument that rationality or reason (*die Vernünftigkeit*) lies in the unity of the universal and the particular: "Rationality, taken generally and in the abstract, consists in the thorough-going unity of the universal and the single." Such a unity can only be achieved in the political realm if the individual sees himself or herself as being—more precisely, his or her "highest form of duty" as being—"a member of the state."

Thus the state exists at a level beyond the level of civil society. Of course, some political traditions dispute this fact; some are not even keen on the idea of society. The former British Prime Minister Margaret Thatcher famously once remarked: "There is no such thing as society," and she added: "There are individual men and women, and there are families."[34] Clearly, Mrs. Thatcher had not been reading Hegel; just as the individual must transcend his or her personal interests, sacrificing some of them but only being able to attain some of them through being a member of society, so society itself must see beyond its particular interests to understand that its highest task is to embody the principles of reason and the ethical idea through contributing to the construction and maintenance of the state.

Confusingly, Hegel says that "this idea"—he means the unity of objective freedom and subjective freedom, of general will and individual will—is "the absolutely eternal and necessary being of mind" (or, to translate it another way, "the eternal and necessary being of spirit"). Now "spirit" or *Geist* is one of the central categories of Hegelian thought, and at the same time one of the most notoriously difficult to translate. Some translate *Geist* as "mind," some as "spirit," but what does Hegel actually mean by *Geist*? Again, this is not an easy question to answer, but his conception of *Geist* seems to be akin to the ancient idea of the *spiritus mundi* or the "spirit of the world," a dimension of the universe that penetrates the material world and yet is not limited to it, that represents the teleological unfolding of the idea through history yet is more than simply "fate" or "destiny." Or as the South African philosopher J.N. Findlay (1903–1987) glossed the term, *Geist* as Spirit or Mind refers to "a common rational life, whose typical activity is the ordering of diverse items or materials under the dominance of simplifying universals, and whose Ego, whose self, if the word be appropriate at all, lies in rational categories and rational goals and common rational norms of procedure"; or in other words, "a life in which all conscious individual persons may share, to the extent that they employ the common categories, norms and standards in which that rational life consists."[35]

By arguing for the "spiritual" (in a non-religious sense of the term)[36] dimension of the state, Hegel sought, as we saw, to set himself decisively apart from Fichte—and from Rousseau.[37] On the one hand, Hegel agrees with Rousseau's notion that the principle of the state is to be found in the will; in other words, that the state is something that is *willed into being* by the people. On the other hand, however, Hegel disagrees with Rousseau that the "general will" is the same as the universal will, because this, in his view, "reduces the union of individuals in the state to a contract." Thus Hegel does not take issue with the notion of the social contract as such, but he regards Rousseau's account as deficient, because it does not take into account the universal, or rational, aspect of the state. For Rousseau, the state is the product of the social contract; for Hegel, the state is also so much more, as he explains:

> The state in and by itself is the ethical whole, the actualization of freedom; and it is an absolute end of reason that freedom should be actual. The state is mind on earth and consciously realizing itself there. In nature, on the other hand, mind actualizes itself only as its own other, as mind asleep. Only when it is present in consciousness, when it knows itself as a really existent object, is it the state. [...] The march of God in the world,

that is what the state is. [...] The state is no ideal work of art; it stands on earth and so in the sphere of caprice, chance, and error, and bad behaviour may disfigure it in many respects. But the ugliest of men, or a criminal, or an invalid, or a cripple, is still always a living man. The affirmative, life, subsists despite his defects, and it is this affirmative factor which is our theme here.

(*Elements of the Philosophy of Right*, §258, Addition)[38]

This remarkable view of the state is elaborated further in a series of lectures on the philosophy of history, delivered in 1822, 1828, and 1830, and only published posthumously; sometimes these lectures are referred to under the title "Reason in History," which captures well their content.[39] (The extracts in this chapter are largely taken from an English translation of the edition prepared from Hegel's manuscripts by his son, Karl Hegel, and published in 1840.)[40]

In these lectures, Hegel poses the existential necessity of the state in the most radical possible of terms: it is only in the state, he argues, that we, as human beings, can have a "rational existence." Indeed, as human beings, we only exist at all within the state, and to the state we owe our entire existence. This has implications for the priority of the state over the individual: Hegel claims that the state does not exist for the sake of the individual, but rather the individual exists for the sake of the state. In other words, to paraphrase the famous words of the inaugural address given by John F. Kennedy, we ought not to ask what the state can do for us, but what we can do for the state ... And Hegel does not shy away from declaring that there is something godlike about the state, inasmuch as what is divine about the state is that it is the idea as it is made manifest on earth:

The moral Whole, the State, [is] that form of reality in which the individual has and enjoys his freedom; but on the condition of his recognizing, believing in, and willing that which is common to the Whole. And this must not be understood as if the subjective will of the social unit attained its gratification and enjoyment through that common Will; as if this were a means provided for its benefit; as if the individual, in his relations to other individuals, thus limited his freedom, in order that this universal limitation — the mutual constraint of all — might secure a small space of liberty for each. Rather, we affirm, are Law, Morality, Government, and they alone, the positive reality and completion of Freedom. Freedom of a low and limited order is mere caprice; which finds its exercise in the sphere of particular and limited desires. [...] In the history of the World, only those peoples can come under our notice which form a state. For it must be understood that this latter is the realization of Freedom, i.e., of the absolute final aim, and that it exists for its own sake. It must further be understood that all the worth which the human being possesses — all spiritual reality, he possesses only through the State. For his spiritual reality consists in this, that his own essence — Reason — is objectively present to him, that it possesses objective immediate existence for him. Thus only is he fully conscious; thus only is he a partaker of morality — of a just and moral social and political life. For Truth is the Unity of the universal and subjective Will; and the Universal is to be found in the State, in its laws, its universal and rational arrangements. The State is the Divine Idea as it exists on Earth.[41]

How can Hegel make such apparently extravagant claims? The answer lies in the argumentation also contained in the paragraph above: and this is essentially an argument about ethics. What activates or realizes itself in history is, says Hegel, the "subjective will" (or what he also calls "passion"). But this passionate, subjective will can realize itself in a concrete and ethical way, bearing within it "the idea" as an "inner essence," while the state constitutes "the reality of the ethical life in the present." What Hegel is trying to get at is that our ethical conduct depends on a concrete, structured social environment where such conduct is possible. Out in the desert, or in the heart of the jungle, it is impossible to be ethical; there: only the law of survival pertains. By contrast, in the state we have the chance to lead ethical lives.

Hegel underscores this argument with a historical reference to the figure of Antigone in Sophocles' great tragic drama of the same name, citing this line: "The divine commands are not of yesterday, nor of today; no, they have an infinite existence, and no one could say whence they came." Hegel's interpretation of Antigone is complicated and it has received a good deal of commentary, especially from French thinkers and psychoanalysts.[42] In essence, however, Hegel's case is the following. Sophocles' *Antigone* opens after two brothers, Eteocles and Polyneices, on opposing sides in a civil war, have fought each other to death for the throne. Thebes' new ruler, Creon, decrees that one brother, Eteocles, will receive honours, while the other, Polyneices, will be publicly disgraced by being left, unburied, on the battlefield. At the beginning of the play, Polyneices' sister, Antigone, meets her other sister, Ismene, late at night outside the palace gates, to ask for her help in burying Polyneices' body. Ismene refuses, so Antigone goes to bury her brother alone—thereby defying the edict of Creon. Sophocles' drama stages a compelling conflict between the personal and the political, between legal and moral duty, between love for one's brother and love for the state. Yet the lines cited by Hegel suggest that individual morality cannot supersede the law, because there is something divine about the commands of the state.

As he continues, Hegel places his argument about the state in the context of the question of freedom: to be precise, the question of what makes freedom real. His argument here follows the classic dialectical pattern, when he states that (a) freedom is identified with the subjective will; (b) the nature of the state is the unity of the objective and general will; (c) in this unity the subjective will is *aufgehoben* or "sublated," that is, it renounces its particularity:

We have in it, therefore, the object of History in a more definite shape than before; that in which Freedom obtains objectivity, and lives in the enjoyment of this objectivity. For Law is the objectivity of Spirit; volition in its true form. Only that will which obeys law, is free: for it obeys itself — it is independent and so free. When the State or our country constitutes a community of existence; when the subjective will of man submits to laws — the contradiction between Liberty and Necessity vanishes. The Rational has necessary existence, as being the reality and substance of things, and we are free in recognizing it as law, and following it as the substance of our own being. The objective and the subjective will are then reconciled, and present one identical homogeneous whole.[43]

How is this unity of objective and subjective will to be achieved? Hegel tackles the opposition, still frequently found today—and arguably never more so than today—, between the people and the government. In his view, the existence of a constitution serves to secure the universal function of the government and the subjective will of the people against one another, but he thinks there is something divisive about this arrangement. In this state, he suggests, this opposition between the people and the government is overcome, for in the state the unity of the universal and the particular will is, as he says, really present. For the unity of the state has the unity of universal and particular will as its basis, and hence as its being and its substance.

But the state is not something that has always existed, it is something that has come into being: and so Hegel must turn explicitly to the question of history. In so doing, he is aware he is participating in activity that reaches back to Herodotus, the "father" of history and author of the *Histories*, and Thucydides, author of *The Peloponnesian War*, Xenophon's *Anabasis*, Caesar's *Commentaries*, Livy, and Diodorus of Sicily; and includes such more recent writers as Francesco Guicciardini (1483–1540) and his *Istoria d'Italia* (1561–1564), Frederick the Great (1712–1786) and his *Histoire de mon Temps* (1747), Johannes von Müller (1752–1809), the author of a 5-volume *History of Switzerland* (1786–1808) and a 24-volume *Universal History* (1811), and Montesquieu's *De l'esprit des lois* or *Spirit of the Laws* (1748). At one point in the drafts for his lectures, Hegel announces the thinking behind his philosophical conception of history in the following terms:

> The sole aim of philosophical enquiry is **to eliminate the contingent. Contingency is the same as external necessity, that is, a necessity which originates in causes which are themselves no more than external circumstances.** In history, we must look for a more general design, the ultimate end of the world, and not a particular end of the subjective spirit or mind; and we must comprehend it by means of reason, which cannot concern itself with particular and finite end, but only with the absolute. [...] That world history is governed by an ultimate design, that it is a rational process — whose rationality is not that of a particular subject, but a divine and absolute reason — [...] is a proposition whose truth we must assume; its proof lies in the study of world history itself, which is the image and enactment of reason.[44]

Right from the outset, Hegel wants to maintain that, in order to understand history, we have to do philosophy; and that, if we do philosophy in the right way, we shall understand history afresh. For he makes nothing less than the bold claim that "reason governs the world." And if "reason governs the world," this means that "world history is a rational process."

As we look around the world today, this might strike us as a remarkable claim. As indeed it is, except perhaps in a different way from how one might expect, for it is remarkable, Hegel believes, that we have a world—in the Greek sense of a *kosmos*—around which to look in the first place. The fact that we notice so much that is wrong in the world does not invalidate Hegel's argument; rather, it serves to validate it, for the fact that we expect, ideally, the world to look or to be in a particular way indicates that we think of the world as fundamentally a rational place. (This aspect of world history as developed by Hegel is one that Marx and Engels will pick up and run with particularly fast, as we shall see.)

True, the kind of reason in which Hegel is interested in one in which, as he puts it, the relation of "reason" to God remains unexplained. Here we can see how Hegel's view of world history is rooted in a theological conception. According to Christianity, the world was created by God through his *logos* (or "reason"), the same *logos* which became incarnated in the figure of Christ. Just as Christianity (and indeed Greek thought before it, on which Christianity explicitly drew) sees the world—and history, too—as saturated with *logos*, so Hegel sees world history as the unfolding manifestation of *Vernunft*. However, there is an important difference between the Christian outlook and the Hegelian outlook: in the tradition of St. Augustine, at least, world history is moving in one direction, in which it is the City of God (the New Jerusalem) that matters, not any city established on earth. By contrast, for Hegel the state *is* the goal of the history, and so the theological notion of the City of God is turned into something historical, concrete, and immanent.

How can philosophy demonstrate this insight? For Hegel, the task of philosophy is, as he says, to "eliminate the contingent"; in other words, it is to eliminate what he calls "external necessity," and instead it is to reveal the underlying rational necessity about history. Or, as he puts it, history has an "absolute end," and this end is something essentially rational. For this reason, he concludes, world history is nothing less than the "image" and indeed the "enactment" of reason.

In other words, we have to learn a new way of *seeing*. Just as, in Plato's *Republic*, we have to learn to see with the "eye of reason" (book 10; cf. 518c–519a, 527e, 533d), so we have to learn to see, says Hegel, with "the eye of the concept":

> Anyone who views the world purely subjectively will see it in terms of his own nature; he will know everything better than everyone else, and see how things ought to have been done and what course events ought to have taken. But the overall content of world history is rational, and indeed has to be rational; a divine will rules supreme and is strong enough to determine the overall content. Our aim must be to discern this substance, and to do so, we must bring with us a rational consciousness. Physical perception and a finite understanding are not enough; we must see with the eye of the concept, the eye of reason, which penetrates the surface and finds its way through the complex and confusing turmoil of events.[45]

So we must learn to see the world through the eye of reason and, if we do so, a new vision of the world is revealed. We shall see the world, not just from any old perspective, but from "the sum total of all philosophical perspectives":

> The last species of Reflective History [...] adopts an abstract position; yet, since it takes general points of view (e.g., as the History of Art, of Law, of Religion), it forms a transition to the Philosophical History of the World. [...] Such branches of national life stand in close relation to the entire complex of a people's annals; and the question of chief importance in relation to our subject is, whether the connection of the whole is exhibited in its truth and reality, or referred to merely external relations. In the latter case, these important phenomena (Art, Law, Religion, etc.) appear as purely accidental national peculiarities. [...] [W]hen Reflective History has advanced to the adoption of general points of view, if the position taken is a true one, these are found to constitute — not a merely external thread, a superficial series — but are the inward guiding soul of the occurrences and actions that occupy a nation's annals. For, like the soul-conductor Mercury, the Idea is in truth, the leader of peoples and of the World; and Spirit, the rational and necessitated will of that conductor,

is and has been the director of the events of the World's History. To become acquainted with Spirit in this its office of guidance, is the object of our present undertaking.[46]

On this account, the true leader of history—of whom Hegel speaks both in mythological or alchemical terms as Mercury (the god of commerce, communication, and the conduct of souls to the underworld) and in political terms as *der Führer*—as the mysterious Spirit or *Geist*.

So while there are individual "spirits" involved in the historical development of individual nations or peoples, there is an overarching, universal Spirit, and it is in this Spirit that Hegel is interested. For this Spirit is, he says, living and active, its life and its activity being reflected in history—and in everything, i.e., in religion, science, the arts, as well as in the destinies and events of history. Hence Hegel's profound and wide-ranging interest in all manner of subjects:

> The perspective adopted by the philosophical history of the world is accordingly not just one among many general perspectives, an isolated abstraction singled out at the expense of the rest. Its spiritual principle is the sum total of all possible perspectives. It concentrates its attention on the concrete spiritual principle in the life of nations, and deals not with individual situations but with a universal thought which runs throughout the whole. [...] Thus the destinies, passions, and energies of nations are not its prime considerations, with the events following on in second place. On the contrary, its chief concern is the spirit of the events themselves, the moving spirit within them, for this is the true Mercury, the leader of nations. [...] [T]he universal object is infinitely concrete, all-comprehending and omnipresent, for the spirit is eternally present to itself; it has no past, and remains for ever the same in all its vigour and strength.[47]

Thus philosophy must concern itself with the dynamic of historical progression; again, another theme that was later to be developed by Marx and by Engels.

On this account, if we examine the history of the world, we shall see in it the expression of the development of Spirit or *Geist*, and the stages of history corresponds to the national spirits, which at different points come to the fore and then recede again. (Later, Oswald Spengler (1880–1936) was to offer an account that world that was both Hegelian and Goethean—or, as he called it, "morphological"—in inspiration.)[48] In the following extract, Hegel provides a defence of the ideal and its relation to reality. For history, he explains, shows "how the world spirit gradually attains consciousness and the will to truth," and it does so from "early glimmerings," via "major discoveries," to "a state or condition of complete consciousness," which is, of course, the state:

> World history is the expression of the divine and absolute process of the spirit in its highest forms, of the progression whereby it discovers its true nature and becomes conscious of itself. The specific forms it assumes at each of these stages are the national spirits of world history, with all the determinate characteristics of their ethical life, their constitutions, their arts, their religion, and their knowledge. The world spirit has an infinite urge and an irresistible impulse to realize these stages of its development; for this sequence and its realization are its true concept. World history merely shows how the spirit gradually attains consciousness and the will to truth; it progresses from its early glimmerings to major discoveries and finally to a state of complete consciousness.[49]

In world history, we can—according to Hegel—see, if we look hard enough, or through the eye of the concept (or through the lens of Hegelian philosophy), how the "ideals of reason", that is, the "ideas of the good, the true, and all that is best in the world", are slowly realizing themselves. These ideas resonate with the ideals proposed in Plato's *Republic*, where we are told to leave the cave, to strive for excellence, and to ascend to the vision of the Idea of the Good. Only here, this vision becomes something immanent to the cave: Hegel takes the entire realm of Platonic ideas, and suggests they are unfolding within the cave itself.

Indeed, according to Eric Steinhart, Plato's allegory of the cave and the related allegory of the divided line can help us understand Hegel's argument in his early major work, *Phenomenology of Spirit* (1807).[50] Steinhart proposes a congruence between, on the one hand, the Platonic ascent of the soul, from the lowest level of knowledge and being to the intelligible world, i.e., from [1] the knowledge of images (*eikasia*) and [2] the knowledge of things (*pistis*) to [3] the knowledge of mathematical objects (*dianoia*) and [4] the knowledge of forms (*noesis*), and ultimately to [5] the knowledge of the idea of the good, and, on the other, the Hegelian evolution of consciousness. This evolution involves a development from [1] sense-certainty and [2] perception to [3] force and understanding, and then from [4] self-consciousness, reason, and spirit to [5] religion, and ultimately to [6] absolute knowledge.

In short, on this account Hegel is *historicizing* the ascent of the soul out of the cave... And in both cases, Steinhart suggests, the ascent out of the cave and the progress of spirit through history is *dialectical*. In the case of Hegel, his thought is often schematically presented as moving from [a] thesis to [b] antithesis and finally [c] synthesis, which in turn becomes the thesis for a new dialectical development.[51] This schema involves a negation, and then a negation of this negation, and Hegel's argument is that what applies on the levels of logic and of consciousness or self-consciousness also applies on the level of history.[52] If we replace the model of thesis-antithesis-synthesis with the more accurate model of a "dialectical form" consisting of determination, negation, and sublation, then we can see that negation is central to Hegel's dialectic, as the three "sides" of this triangle are not just "*parts* of the Logic," but "*moments of everything logically real.*"[53]

Where, in the allegory of the cave, the final step is to look at the sun, i.e., to contemplate the idea of the Good, in Hegel's phenomenology the final step is knowledge of the absolute.[54] The notion of the absolute is not unique to Hegel: deriving from Neoplatonism, Scholasticism, as well as Fichte and Schelling, it represents complete self-consciousness, perfect self-knowledge, or, in Hegel's terms, the ultimate identity of subject and substance in an objective and concrete way. Or as Hegel says, the movement of the Spirit is "the circle that returns into itself, the circle that presupposes its beginning and reaches it only at the end."[55]

Where, then, does this leave all in the world that is manifestly unjust? Where does this leave the centuries of pain and suffering, of toil and tears? Hegel's answer can sound callous, but from his philosophical perspective, it is the only answer he can give: that is all mere empirical detail. If, as the saying goes, one needs to crack an egg to make an omelette, there must a grand cracking of eggs on a giant scale to bring into the being the cosmic-size omelette that is the history of the world! When Hegel tells us that spiritual or rational being demands "the seriousness, the anguish, the patience, and the labour of the negative,"[56] this is not just a translation into Hegelese of the phrase "they are only sent to try us" which Hegel, according to J.N. Findlay, "doubtless heard again and again from his pious parents,"—it is "his central philosophical assertion."[57]

We could put this question another way. Where, in this grand scheme of things, does this leave the individual? Again, Hegel's answer will probably strike us as unsentimental to the point of brutality: the individual only matters in relation to the whole, that is to say, in relation to the state. Consequently, the morality of the individual consists in fulfilling the duties imposed upon him or her by society. As in Kant, the key notion here is doing one's duty:

> The worth of individuals is measured by the extent to which they reflect and represent the national spirit, and have adopted a particular station within the affairs of the state as a whole. And one of the conditions of freedom in a state is that this decision should be left to the individual, and that the occupation he takes up should not be laid down in advance by any kind of caste system. The individual's morality will then consist in fulfilling the duties imposed upon him by his social station; these can be recognized without difficulty, and their particular form will depend on the particular class to which the individual belongs. The substantial nature of such relationships, i.e., the rational element they embody, is universally known, and its expression is what we call duty.[58]

Hegel insists that "duty is rooted in the soil of civil life: individuals follow their appointed profession, and hence also their appointed duty; and their morality consists in acting in accordance with this duty"; in this respect, one might compare and contrast his notion of duty with Plato's definition of justice in the *Republic* as "not with respect to a man's minding his external business, but with respect to what is within, with respect to what truly concerns him and his own," so that "he doesn't let each part in him mind other people's business or the three classes in the soul meddle with each other, but really sets his own house in good order and rules himself".[59] The exact kinds of duties imposed on the individual will depend on his or her position in society (or, as Hegel calls it, his or her "station"). We have not yet developed the idea of class that will be so important for Marx, but already we can find the seed in Hegel's thought.

In fact, Hegel works out the elaborate relations between all the different parts of society, in a way that has been captured by Kenneth Westphal in the form of a diagram (presented in a slightly modified form below).[60] These different parts include, at the top, the Monarch and the Supreme Council, which conduct the state's foreign relations through diplomacy and, where necessary, military means. Below are the Executive and Legislative organs of the state, the former concerned with the administration of justice and various public authorities responsible for health, safety, education and law enforcement, the latter consisting of various parliamentary bodies, including an upper house and a lower house. These represent the lowest tier of Hegel's state, described by him as the "system of needs." Under this category fall the business class (i.e., crafts, manufacture, and trade) and the agricultural class, while on the lowest level there are, in a sort of Thatcherite way, individuals and their families.

This complex division of different organs and institutions falls, perhaps somewhat undialectically, into two distinct societal divisions: on the one hand, the "system of needs" (the business class and the agricultural class), the administration of justice, and the public authorities, which Hegel calls *civil society* (or the "state external"); on the other, the legislature (the advisory body, the estates assembly, and the upper and lower houses), the higher advisory officials of the executive, and the crown (the monarch and the supreme council), which Hegel calls the *political state* (or the government). Taken together, both civil society and the political state constitute the state proper, understood in its full systematic sense. And yet here, too, the dialectic is present: for the administration of justice and the public authorities fall into both categories, civil society *and* the political state. In this way, and typically for Hegel's political outlook, the organs and institutions of public administration and services turn out to be the most important ones in his analysis. What counts above all in Hegel's system is what, for Thatcherites and others, has to be "rolled back"—what conservative politics in the Anglo-American world colloquially calls *the state* (Fig. 6.1).

As well as noting the complex interrelationship between all these different organisations, institutions, or (if one will) classes, we should

	THE CROWN	
Foreign relations (Military/Diplomacy)		
EXECUTIVE	EXECUTIVE	LEGISLATURE
Higher Advisory Officials	Higher Advisory Officials	
		Advisory Body
Administration of Justice	Public Authority	Estates Assembly Upper House Lower House
• courts • promulgation of law • assessment and revision of statutes	• public health • public safety • public works • public education • economic regulation • poverty relief • chartering of corporations • certification of corporate officials • law enforcement	
SYSTEM OF NEEDS		SYSTEM OF NEEDS
Business Class (Crafts, Manufacture, Trade)		Agricultural class
Corporations		
Individuals and their families		

Fig. 6.1 Organisational diagram of Hegel's state

notice that Hegel sees the relationship between them as essentially an harmonious one; by contrast, for Marx, the relationship will be an entirely antagonistic one. (By the same token, one might also note that, for Hegel, the agricultural class is represented by the upper house, while the business or industrial class is represented by the lower house; by the time of Marx, however, industrialization will have begun effectively to reverse this order of priority…)

Returning to Hegel's strictures on individuals and morality: as the passage above indicates, moral relationships thus turn out, in a highly Kantian way, to be ones that are characterized by duty. For instance, duty to one's children and one's parents; the duty to pay one's debts (a typically German priority, as the Greeks recently discovered during their government-debt crisis of 2015); and the duty to be a good citizen. For Hegel, profession and duty constitute the basis of civil life in general. (On this point, as on many others, one might well ask whether Hegel underestimates the extent to which he is turning culturally specific expectations into universal laws …)

But profession and duty do not, he adds, apply to all; for some, their duty is a more serious and at the same time a more spectacular one. This duty applies to those whom Hegel describes as "world-historical indi-viduals"; those such as Napoleon, for instance, whom Hegel saw at the Battle of Jena, and whom he once famously described as *the world spirit sitting on a horse*.[61] To these individuals falls a task equivalent in signif-icance and urgency to the role of the philosopher-king in the *Republic*; in terms of the allegory of book 7, to descend back into the cave and to engage with the world one finds there. For such world-historical individuals as Hegel conceives them, a grave task is at hand: they must understand what is going in the world (its "universal principle"), they must understand what changes are about to befall the world in the unfolding self-realization in history of reason, and they must be pre-pared to become drivers for that change, to the extent even of sacrificing their own self-interests:

> World-historical men — the Heroes of an epoch — must, therefore, be recognized as its clear-sighted ones; *their* deeds, *their* words are the best of that time. Great men have formed purposes to satisfy themselves, not

others. Whatever prudent designs and counsels they might have learned from others, would be the more limited and inconsistent features in their career; for it was they who best understood affairs; from whom *others* learned, and approved, or at least acquiesced in — their policy. For that Spirit which had taken this fresh step in history is the inmost soul of all individuals; but in a state of unconsciousness which the great men in question aroused. Their fellows, therefore, follow these soul-leaders; for they feel the irresistible power of their own inner Spirit thus embodied. If we go on to cast a look at the fate of these World-Historical persons, whose vocation it was to be the agents of the World-Spirit — we shall find it to have been no happy one. They attained no calm enjoyment; their whole life was labor and trouble; their whole nature was nought else but their master-passion. When their object is attained they fall off like empty hulls from the kernel. (32/30–31)

A World-historical individual is not so unwise as to indulge a variety of wishes to divide his regards. He is devoted to the One Aim, regardless of all else. It is even possible that such men may treat other great, even sacred interests, inconsiderately; conduct which is indeed obnoxious to moral reprehension. But so mighty a form must trample down many an innocent flower — crush to pieces many an object in its path. (34/32)[62]

It is worth noting that, while the examples of world-historical individuals cited by Hegel include eminently political or military ones, such as Caesar conquering Gaul, Alexander the Great, or Napoleon (cf. *The Philosophy of History*, 31–32), he also includes such intellectual-cultural figures as Sophocles and Aristophanes, or Thucydides—and Plato. (In this respect, Hegel will be imitated half a century later by one of his most formidable critics, Nietzsche, who describes the *Übermensch* in terms that are sometimes political—e.g., Julius Caesar, Frederick the Great—but more often than not aesthetic, e.g., Homer, Aristophanes, Leonardo da Vinci, Raphael, or Goethe.)[63]

Given the presence of military individuals in the roll-call of those whom Hegel dubs "world-historical," it will undoubtedly be the case that, in the course of history, many a fair flower will be trampled, and that those who do the trampling will be the world-historical individuals. What they do, may *appear* to be wrong, but in advancing the cause of the history (and the unfolding of the next stage of the Spirit), they have, so Hegel says, "absolute right in their side."

In this account of world history (and the onward match of the Spirit), it is important to grasp Hegel's emphasis on the dynamic and changing nature of this process. As he puts it, "the state or condition of the world is not yet known," and so "the aim is to give it reality." To do this is the goal of the world-historical individuals, for it is they who have always been "the first to formulate for their fellow human beings what they really want." To resist such world-historical individuals is, then, futile, for their course is ultimately, he concludes, the right one.

Within Hegel there is a curious tension between his argument in favour of the Prussian state as the instantiation of world reason, and his emphasis on the dynamics of historical change. This tension will result in two different Hegelian schools, referred to as the "Right" and the "Left" Hegelians. On the one hand, the "Right" Hegelians read Hegel as an essentially conservative thinker. (These include such philosophers, theologians or historians as Carl Friedrich Göschel (1781–1861), Georg Andreas Gabler (1786–1853), Johann Philipp Gabler (1753–1826), Hermann Friedrich Wilhelm Hinrichs (1794–1861), Carl Daub (1765–1836), Heinrich Leo (1799–1878), Leopold von Henning (1791–1866), and Heinrich Gustav Hotho (1802–1873), as well as Karl Rosenkranz (1805–1879), Eduard Gans (1797–1839), Karl Ludwig Michelet (1801–1893), Philipp Konrad Marheineke (1780–1846), Wilhelm Vatke (1806–1882), Johann Eduard Erdmann (1805–1892), Eduard Zeller (1814–1908), Max Schasler (1819–1903), and Albert Schwegler (1819–1857); and hence, by and large, thinkers who have made little historical impact.)

On the other hand, there are the "Left" or so-called Young Hegelians, whose impact has been somewhat greater.[64] Among these one might include David Friedrich Strauss (1808–1874), Bruno Bauer (1809–1882), Ludwig Feuerbach (1804–1872) (an important and unjustly neglected thinker), Carl Nauwerck (1810–1891), Arnold Ruge (1881–1945), not to mention Max Stirner (1806–1856) (a complex thinker, sometimes associated with the tradition of anarchism), as well as August von Cieszkowski (1814–1894) and Karl Schmidt (1819–1864) (usually regarded as the last of the Young Heglians, and author of *The Realm of the Understanding and the Individual* of 1846). (Are the Young Hegelians the intellectual forebears of those modern commentators who propose the standard "non-metaphysical" or "anti-theological" reading of Hegel, such as Kenley Royce Dove, William Maker, Terry Pinkard, and Richard Dien Winfield?[65] If so, to what extent is there a relation between a more politically conservative reading of Hegel and the "onto-theological" reading propounded by Heidegger as well as such scholars as Walter Jaeschke, Emil Fackenheim, Cyril O'Regan, Malcolm Clark, Albert Chapelle, Claude Bruaire, and Iwan Iljin?)[66] Among the Young Hegelians are also included two big names—Karl Marx (1818–1883) and Friedrich Engels (1820–1895), and it is to their place in the discourse of Platonism in German Political Thought that we shall next turn.

While Hegel can, with good reason, be regarded as the main forerunner of Marx, it should be noted that Hegel continued to exercise a major influence alongside Marx in the twentieth century, especially in France. Rejecting the "Hegel of the Absolute" of Jean Wahl (1888–1974) and the "religious Hegel" of Gabriel Marcel (1889–1973), two thinkers defined Hegel studies in France: Alexandre Kojève (1902–1968) and Jean Hippolyte (1907–1968). These two thinkers have given rise in turn to two further schools of Hegel interpretation, an "erotic" Hegel arising from Kojève and promoted by Georges Bataille (1897–1962) and other members of the so-called College of Sociology, and a "rationalist" Hegel arising from Hyppolite who engaged, as Jacques Lacan (1901–1981) did, with Platonism, negation, and the philosophy of nature.[67] In the form of an investigation of the erotic, the religious, and Platonism itself, the discourse of Platonism underwent new transformations and received new inflections in German Political Thought. After all, in Hegelianism, as Findlay argued, "the Idea, the final, all-explanatory goal of everything, is simply rationality which sees itself to be the goal of everything," and to this extent, so Findlay concluded, "these Hegelian ideas do not so much [...] point to a way *beyond* the cave in which we are immured, and whose arrangements we find so absurd, as that they seek to transform our life *in* the cave."[68]

Notes

1. For further discussion, see Paul Guyer, "Thought and Being: Hegel's Critique of Kant's Theoretical Philosophy," in Frederick C. Beiser (ed.), *The Cambridge Companion to Hegel* (Cambridge: Cambridge University Press, 1993), 171–209; George Armstrong Kelly, *Idealism, Politics and History: Sources of Hegelian Thought* (Cambridge: Cambridge University Press, 1969), Part 3, "Immanuel Kant: The Rationalization of the Chimera," 75–178.
2. See Karl Popper, *The Open Society and Its Enemies*, vol. 1, *The Spell of Plato*, vol. 2, *The High Tide of Prophecy: Hegel, Marx, and the Aftermath* (London: Routledge, 1945). A one-volume edition of this work was published, together with an introduction by Alan Ryan and an accompanying essay by E.H. Gombrich as *The Open Society and Its Enemies* (Princeton, NJ and Oxford: Princeton University Press, 2013). For a discussion of the controversial reception of Popper's central thesis concerning the link between totalitarianism and Plato, see Renford Bambrough (ed.), *Plato, Popper and Politics: Some Contributions to a Modern Controversy* (Cambridge and New York: Heffer and Barnes & Noble, 1967).
3. Cf. G.W.F. Hegel, *Elements of the Philosophy of Right*, ed. Allen W. Wood, trans. H.B. Nisbet (Cambridge: Cambridge University Press, 1991), 18:
   "What is rational, is actual;
   and what is actual, is rational."
   Cf. G.W.F. Hegel, *The Encyclopedia Logic: Part I of the Encyclopedia of Philosophical Sciences with the Zusätze*, trans. Théodore F. Geraets, W.A. Suchting, and H.S. Harris (Indianapolis, IN: Hackett, 1991), Introduction, §6 (29).
4. Norbert Hoerster (ed.), *Klassische Texte der Staatsphilosophie* (Munich: dtv, 2011), 230.
5. For further discussion of Hegel's idealism, see Thomas B. Wartenberg, "Hegel's Idealism: The Logic of Conceptuality," in Beiser (ed.), *Cambridge Companion to Hegel*, 102–128; Robert Stern, "Hegel's Idealism," in Frederick C. Beiser (ed.), *The Cambridge Companion to Hegel and Nineteenth-Century Philosophy* (Cambridge: Cambridge University Press, 2008), 135–173.

6. Hoerster (ed.), *Klassische Texte der Staatsphilosophie*, 230–231. Cf. the discussion of Hegel's notion of "actuality" in the notes in Hegel, *Elements of the Philosophy of Right*, ed. Wood, trans. Nisbet, 389–390.
7. For further discussion, see Pierre Grimes and Regina L. Uliana, *Philosophical Midwifery: A New Paradigm for Understanding Human Problems, with Its Validation* (Costa Mesa, CA: Hyparxis Press, 1998), Chapter 13, "Comparative Study of the Dialectic," 145–165; Geoffrey L. Skoll, *Dialectics in Social Thought: The Present Crisis* (New York: Palgrave Macmillan, 2014).
8. Cf. *Republic*, book 7, where Socrates defines the dialectic as taking place when someone tries "by discussion — by means of argument without the use of any of the senses — to attain to each thing itself that *is* and doesn't give up before he grasps by intellection itself that which is good itself" and hence comes to "the very end of the intelligible realm" (532a–b; *The Republic of Plato*, ed. and trans. Allan Bloom (New York: Basic Books, 1991), 211). On this account, the dialectic is the highest form of "the arts" (comprising arithmetic, geometry, sold geometry, astronomy, harmony, and the dialectic), whose entire activity has "the power to release and lead what is best in the soul up to the contemplation of what is best in the things that *are*" (532c; 211).
9. See Gary Shapiro, "Peirce's Critique of Hegel's Phenomenology and Dialectic," *Transactions of the Charles S. Peirce Society* 17, no. 3 (Summer, 1981), 269–275.
10. See Theodor W. Adorno, *Negative Dialectics* [1966], trans. E.B. Ashton (New York and London: Continuum, 1973). For further discussion, see Brian O'Connor, "Adorno's Reconception of the Dialectic," in Stephen Houlgate and Michael Baur (eds), *A Companion to Hegel* (Malden, MA and Oxford: Wiley Blackwell, 2011), 537–555.
11. Glenn Alexander Magee, *Hegel and the Hermetic Tradition* (Ithaca and London: Cornell University Press, 2001), 89–90. For further discussion, see Michael Foster, "Hegel's Dialectical Method," in Beiser (ed.), *Cambridge Companion to Hegel*, 130–169.
12. John McTaggart Ellis McTaggart, *Studies in the Hegelian Dialectic*, 2nd edn (Cambridge: Cambridge University Press, 1922), 1.
13. McTaggart, *Studies in the Hegelian Dialectic*, 3.
14. Jeremy Dunham, Iain Hamilton Grant, and Sean Watson, *Idealism: The History of a Philosophy* (Durham: Acumen, 2011; reprinted Abingdon and New York: Routledge, 2014), 31.

15. Introduction, §24, in Hegel, *The Encyclopedia Logic: Part I*, trans. Geraets, Suchting, and Harris, 56. In §24, Addition 1, Hegel goes on to explain that "the Logical is to be sought in a system of thought-determinations in which the antithesis between subjective and objective (in its usual meaning) disappears," linking "this meaning of thinking and of its determinations" back to "the Ancients when they say that *nous* governs the world, or by our own saying thay there is reason in the world [...]" (56).

16. Hegel, Introduction, §11, in *The Encyclopedia Logic: Part I*, trans. Geraets, Suchting, and Harris, 56.

17. Hegel, Introduction, §11, in *The Encyclopedia Logic: Part I*, trans. Geraets, Suchting, and Harris, 56.

18. Hegel, Part 1, *The Science of Logic*, §81, in *The Encyclopedia Logic*, trans. Geraets, Suchting, and Harris, 128; cf. Dunham, Grant, and Watson, *Idealism*, 154–155.

19. The translation used here is *Hegel's Philosophy of Right*, trans. Samuel Walters Dyde (London: Bell, 1896). For further discussion of this work, see Kenneth Westphal, "The Basic Structure and Context of Hegel's *Philosophy of Right*," in Beiser (ed.), *Cambridge Companion to Hegel*, 234–268; Dudley Knowles, *Hegel and the "Philosophy of Right"* (London: Routledge, 2002); Allen W. Wood, "Hegel's Political Philosophy," in Houlgate and Baur (eds), *A Companion to Hegel*, 297–311. A powerful account of Hegel's thinking can be found in the works of one of the first generation of Frankfurt School thinkers, Herbert Marcuse (1898–1979), who had studied under Edmund Husserl (1859–1938) and later under Martin Heidegger (1889–1976). See his *Habilitation*, entitled *Hegel's Ontology and the Theory of Historicity* [1932], trans. Seyla Benhabib (Cambridge, MA and London: MIT Press, 1987); and his eminently readable study, *Reason and Revolution: Hegel and the Rise of Social Theory* [1941; 2nd edn, 1955] (London: Routledge & Kegan Paul, 1986).

20. Hegel, *Philosophy of Right*, trans. Dyde, xviii–xxi.

21. Hegel, *Philosophy of Right*, trans. Dyde, xxvi.

22. Hegel, *Philosophy of Right*, trans. Dyde, xxvi–xxvii.

23. Hegel, *Philosophy of Right*, trans. Dyde, xxvii–xxviii.

24. For further discussion of Hegel and Plato, see M.B. Foster, *The Political Philosophies of Plato and Hegel* (Oxford: Clarendon Press, 1935); Huntington Cairns, *Legal Philosophy from Plato to Hegel* (Baltimore:

Johns Hopkins Press, 1949); Robert Bruce Ware, "Freedom as Justice: Hegel's Interpretation of Plato's *Republic*," *Metaphilosophy* 31, no. 3 (April 2000), 287–310; Gary K. Browning, *Plato and Hegel: Two Modes of Philosophizing About Politics* [1991] (London and New York: Routledge, 2013).

It has been proposed that Plato's divided line and the myth of the cave are essential for understanding the evolution of consciousness presented in Hegel's *Phenomenology of Spirit* (1807), see the website created by Eric Steinhart (1998); available http://www.ericsteinhart.com/progress/HEGEL/DEFAULT.HTM, consulted 29.07.2016. At the same time, other commentators have insisted on the importance of Aristotle, not Plato, for Hegel's conception of the idea: "Hegel identifies the idea not with Plato's archetype but with Aristotle's formal-final cause. Hegel saw Aristotle, not Plato, as the proper founder of absolute idealism" (Frederick Beiser, *Hegel* (New York and Abingdon: Routledge, 2005), 66), citing Hegel's *Lectures on the History of Philosophy* (1825–1826): "Aristotle surpassed Plato in speculative depth, in that he was familiar with the most fundamental speculation and that, with all his most far-reaching empirical breadth, he stands essentially, and deeply rooted, in the idealist tradition" (G.W.F. Hegel, *Lectures on the History of Philosophy, 1825–6*, vol. 2, *Greek Philosophy*, ed. Robert F. Brown, trans. R.F. Brown and J.M. Stewart (Oxford: Clarendon Press, 2006), 226).

25. For the ancient Greeks, *Dike* was the goddess of justice. In *Philosophy in the Tragic Age of the Greeks* (c. 1873), Nietzsche presents Heraclitus as asking, "But where law and Zeus's daughter *Dike* rule alone, as they do in this world, how could there be the sphere of guilt, of penance, of judgment?" (§5, in *Philosophy in the Tragic Age of the Greeks*, trans. Marianne Cowan (Washington, DC: Regnery, 1962), 51), cf. Heraclitus, fragments 23, 94, 28, and 80.

26. Hegel, *Philosophy of Right*, trans. Dyde, xxviii–xxix.

27. For classic discussions of Hegel's relation to history, see Rudolf Haym, *Hegel und seine Zeit* [1857] (Hildesheim: Olms, 1962); Georg Lukács, *Der junge Hegel: Über die Beziehungen von Dialektik und Ökonomie*, 2 vols (Frankfurt am Main: Suhrkamp, 1973), vol. 1; Jean Hippolyte, *Genesis and Structure of the "Phenomenology of Spirit,"* trans. Samuel Cherniak and John Heckman (Evanston: Northwestern University Press, 1974). For more recent discussion, see Frederick C. Beiser,

"Hegel's Historicism," in Beiser (ed.), *Cambridge Companion to Hegel*, 270–300; Robert Bernasconi, "'The Ruling Categories of the World': The Trinity in Hegel's Philosophy of History and The Rise and Fall of Peoples," in Houlgate and Baur (eds), *A Companion to Hegel*, 315–331. See, too, R.G. Collingwood, *The Idea of History: Revised Edition* (Oxford and New York: Oxford University Press, 1993), 87–113, for brief, but illuminating, remarks on Romanticism, Herder, Kant, Schiller, Fichte, Schelling, Hegel, and Hegel and Marx.

28. *Twilight of the Idols*, "Maxims and Arrows," §26, in Friedrich Nietzsche, *Twilight of the Idols and The Anti-Christ*, trans. R.J. Hollingdale (Harmondsworth: Penguin, 1968), 25.

29. G.W.F. Hegel, *Hegel's Philosophy of Right*, trans. T.M. Knox [1952] (London, Oxford, and New York: Oxford University Press, 1976), 122–123.

30. Hegel, *Hegel's Philosophy of Right*, trans. Knox, 126.

31. Hegel, *Hegel's Philosophy of Right*, trans. Knox, 155–157.

32. For the passages from Rousseau's *The Social Contract* which Hegel has in mind (Book 1, Chapters 3, 4, and 6) and for a critique of this work, see Hegel, *Lectures on the History of Philosophy*, trans. E.S. Haldane, 3 vols (London: Kegan Paul, Trench, Tübner, 1892), vol. 3, 400–402. For further discussion, see George Armstrong Kelly, *Idealism, Politics and History: Sources of Hegelian Thought* (Cambridge: Cambridge University Press, 1969), part 2, "J.-J. Rousseau: The Land of Chimeras and the Land of Prejudices," 25–72.

33. See Johann Gottlieb Fichte, *Foundations of Natural Right* (1796–1797), §17, in *Foundations of Natural Right*, ed. Frederick Neuhouser, trans. Michael Baur (Cambridge: Cambridge University Press, 2000), 165–182. Cf. Hegel, *Lectures on the History of Philosophy*, trans. Haldane, vol. 3, 503–504ff. For further discussion, see Kelly, *Idealism, Politics and History*, 1969, Part 4, "J.G. Fichte: The Chimera Dogmatized," 181–285.

34. At least, this is how her interview with *Woman's Own* magazine published in 31 October 1987 was quoted in *The Sunday Times*. Yet the transcript of the original interview, conducted by Douglas Keay, shows that the original context of this remark was more nuanced: "I think we have gone through a period when too many children and people […] are casting their problems on society and who is society? There is no such thing! There are individual men and women and there are families and

no government can do anything except through people and people look to themselves first. [...] There is no such thing as society. There is [a] living tapestry of men and women and people and the beauty of that tapestry and the quality of our lives will depend upon how much each of us is prepared to take responsibility for ourselves and each of us [is] prepared to turn around and help by our own efforts those who are unfortunate" (23 September 1987, Interview for *Woman's Own*; available http://www. margaretthatcher.org/document/106689. Accessed 27.7.2016).

35. J.N. Findlay, *The Discipline of the Cave* (London and New York: Allen and Unwin and Humanities Press, 1966), 218–219.
36. Some readings of Hegel emphasize precisely a religious, heterodox, or hermetic reading of Hegel, highlighting the roots of his thought in the Western esoteric tradition; see Cyril O'Regan, *The Heterodox Hegel* (Albany: State University of New York Press, 1994); Magee, *Hegel and the Hermetic Tradition*.
37. At Tübingen, Hegel refused an invitation to join a "Kant Club" formed at the *Stift*, claiming that he was too busy reading Rousseau (see Franz Wiedmann, *Hegel: An Illustrated Biography*, trans. Joachim Neugroschel (New York: Pegasus, 1968), 19).
38. Hegel, *Hegel's Philosophy of Right*, trans. Knox, 279.
39. For these texts, see G.W.F. Hegel, *Reason in History: A General Introduction to the Philosophy of History*, trans. Robert S. Hartman (Indianapolis and New York: Bobbs-Merrill, 1953); Georg Wilhelm Friedrich Hegel, *Lectures on the Philosophy of World History: Introduction: Reason in History*, trans. H.B. Nisbet (Cambridge: Cambridge University Press, 1980).
40. G.W.F. Hegel, *Lectures on the Philosophy of World History*, trans. from the third German edition by John Sibree (London: Bohn, 1861); republished as *The Philosophy of History* (Mineola, NY: Dover, 1956).
41. Hegel, *Lectures on the Philosophy of World History*, trans. Sibree, 40–41; *The Philosophy of History*, 38–39.
42. For further discussion, see the overview of the reception of *Antigone* in Douglas Cairns, *Sophocles: "Antigone"* (London and New York: Bloomsbury, 2016), 115–153 (esp. "Antigone Among the Philosophers," 122ff.). For an example of psychoanalytic approaches building on Hegel and Lacan, see Paul Allen Miller, "Lacan's *Antigone*: The Sublime Object and the Ethics of Interpretation," *Phoenix* 61, no. 1–2 (Spring–Summer 2007), 1–14. For his part, Martin Heidegger

(1889–1976) approached the *Antigone* through the prism of the translation made by Hölderlin (published in 1804), focusing in a lecture course on metaphysics (given in Freiburg in 1935) and in a course on Hölderlin's poem, "The Ister" (given in 1942–1943), on the "Ode to Man" in Sophocles' drama; see Heidegger, "The Ode on Man in Sophocles' *Antigone*," published in *An Introduction to Metaphysics*, trans. Ralph Manheim (New Haven and London: Yale University Press, 1959) and reprinted in Thomas Woodward (ed.), *Sophocles: A Collection of Critical Essays* (Eaglewood Cliffs: Prentice, 1996), 86–100.

43. Hegel, *Lectures on the Philosophy of World History*, 41; *The Philosophy of History*, 39.

44. Hegel, *Lectures on the Philosophy of World History*, Second Draft (1830), "The Philosophical History of the World," A [Its General Concept], trans. Nisbet, 28.

45. Hegel, *Lectures on the Philosophy of World History*, Second Draft (1830), "The Philosophical History of the World", A [Its General Concept], trans. Nisbet, 26.

46. Hegel, *Lectures on the Philosophy of History*, trans. Sibree, 8; *The Philosophy of History*, 8.

47. Hegel, *Lectures on the Philosophy of World History*, Second Draft (1830), "The Philosophical History of the World," A [Its General Concept], trans. Nisbet, 30–31.

48. See Oswald Spengler, *The Decline of the West* [vol. 1, *Form and Actuality*, 1918, revised 1922; vol. 2, *Perspectives of World History*, 1923], trans. Charles Francis Atkinson (New York: Knopf, 1926 and 1928).

49. Hegel, *Lectures on the Philosophy of World History*, Second Draft (1830), "The Philosophical History of the World," B [The Realisation of Spirit in History], trans. Nisbet, 65.

50. See Eric Steinhart, "Hegel's Phenomenology of Spirit Website" (1998). Available http://www.ericsteinhart.com/progress/HEGEL/DEFAULT.HTM, consulted 29.7.2016.

51. Jean Gebser (1905–1973) describes this structure of thinking as "pyramidal thinking," noting that it is "characteristic of Plato" and has "its most trenchant expression in the Hegelian axiom of thesis, antithesis, and synthesis" (*The Ever-Present Origin* [1949; 1953], trans. Noel Barstad with Algis Mickunas (Athens: Ohio University Press, 1985), 86; cf. 257).

52. As Walter Kaufmann points out, "whoever looks for the stereotype of the allegedly Hegelian dialectic in Hegel's *Phenomenology* will not find it," and he rightly points to Fichte and to Schelling (in his *On the Ego as Principle of Philosophy* (1795)) as proponents of this pattern; see Walter Kaufmann, *Hegel: A Reinterpretation* (Notre Dame, IN: University of Notre Dame Press, 1978), §37, "Dialectic," 153–162; Gustav E. Mueller, "The Hegel Legend of 'Thesis-Antithesis-Synthesis,'" *Journal of the History of Ideas* 19, no. 3 (June 1958), 411–414; reprinted in Jon Stewart (ed.), *The Hegel Myths and Legends* (Evanston, IL: Northwestern University Press, 1996), 301–305. See Fichte's "Review of *Aenesidemus*" (1794), in *Early Philosophical Writings*, ed. and trans. Daniel Breazeale (Ithaca and London: Cornell University Press, 1988), 53–78: "How Is Synthesis Possible Without Presupposing Thesis and Antithesis?" (63); and "Outline of the Distinctive Character of the *Wissenschaftslehre* with Respect to the Theoretical Faculty" (1795), in *Early Philosophical Writings*, 233–306, where he says of the self-positing of the ego: "The action here described is simultaneously *thetic*, *antithetic*, and *synthetic*. It is *thetic* insofar as it posits an absolutely unperceivable, opposing acitivity outside of the I. [...] The same action is *antithetic* insofar as, by positing or not positing a certain condition, it opposes one and the same activity of the I to itself. It is *synthetic* insofar as, by positing the opposing activity as a contingent condition, it posits this activity as one and the same" (249).

53. See Hegel, *The Encyclopedia Logic: Part I*, trans. Geraets, Suchting, and Harris, §79, 125.

54. For Hegel's use of the term "the absolute," deriving from Nicholas of Cusa's term *absolutum* to refer to God, and used by such post-Kantian philosophers as Fichte and Schelling to refer to ultimate, unconditioned reality, see Michael Inwood, *A Hegel Dictionary* (Oxford: Blackwell, 1992), 27–29; Glenn Alexander Magee, *The Hegel Dictionary* (London and New York: Continuum, 2010), 19–22.

55. G.W.F. Hegel, *Phenomenology of Spirit*, trans. A.V. Miller (Oxford: Oxford University Press, 1979), para. 802 (488). For further discussion, see Tom Rockmore, *Cognition: An Introduction to Hegel's "Phenomenology of Spirit"* (Berkeley, Los Angeles, and London: University of California Press, 1997); Robert Stern, *Hegel and the "Phenomenology of Spirit"* (London and New York: Routledge,

2002); Peter Kalkavage, *The Logic of Desire: An Introduction to Hegel's "Phenomenology of Spirit"* (Philadelphia: Paul Dry Books, 2007); Donald Phillip Verene, *Hegel's Absolute: An Introduction to Reading the "Phenomenology of Spirit"* (Albany: State University of New York Press, 2007); Kenneth R. Westphal (ed.), *The Blackwell Guide to Hegel's "Phenomenology of Spirit"* (Malden, MA and Oxford: Wiley-Blackwell, 2009); Stephen Houlgate, *Hegel's "Phenomenology of Spirit": A Reader's Guide* (London and New York: Bloomsbury, 2012).

56. Hegel, *Phenomenology of Spirit*, "Preface," para. 19 (10).
57. J.N. Findlay, *The Discipline of the Cave* (London and New York: Allen & Unwin and Humanities Press, 1966), 220.
58. Hegel, *Lectures on the Philosophy of World History*, Second Draft (1830), "The Philosophical History of the World," B: The Realisation of Spirit in History, trans. Nisbet, 80 and 81.
59. *Republic*, 443c–d; trans. Bloom, 123.
60. Kenneth Westphal, "The Basic Context and Structure of Hegel's *Philosophy of Right*," in Beiser (ed.), *Cambridge Companion to Hegel*, 234–269, esp. "Organizational Diagram of Hegel's State," 269. See also Westphal, "Hegel on Political Representation: Laborers, Corporations, and the Monarch," *The Owl of Minerva* 25, no. 1 (1993), 111–116.
61. See Hegel's letter to Friedrich Immanuel Niethammer (1766–1848) of 13 October 1806: "Last evening toward sunset I saw the shots fired by the French patrols from both Gempenbachtal and Winzerla. The Prussians were driven from Winzerla in the night, and the fire lasted until after twelve o'clock. Today between eight and nine o'clock the French advance units forced their way [into the city], with the regular troops following an hour later. It was an hour of anguish, especially because of general unfamiliarity with the right which everyone enjoys by the will of the French Emperor himself not to comply with the demands of these light troops but just quietly to give them what is required. [...] I saw the Emperor — this world soul — riding out of the city on reconnaissance. It is indeed a wonderful sensation to see such an individual, who, concentrated here at a single point, astride a horse, reaches out over the world and masters it" (Hegel, *The Letters*, trans. Clark Butler and Christine Seiler (Bloomington: University of Indiana Press, 1984), 114).
62. Hegel, *Lectures on the Philosophy of World History*, trans. Sibree, 30–34; *The Philosophy of History*, 29–32.

63. See, for example, *The Will to Power*, §380: "[...] Slackness, skepticism, 'immorality', the right to throw off a faith, belong to greatness (Caesar, also Homer, Aristophanes, Leonardo, Goethe" (*The Will to Power*, ed. Walter Kaufmann, trans. Walter Kaufmann and R.J. Hollingdale (New York: Vintage, 1968), 205).

64. See the useful collection by Lawrence S. Stepelevich (ed.), *The Young Hegelians: An Anthology* (Cambridge: Cambridge University Press, 1983), which includes texts by Strauss, Cieszkowski, Feuerbach, Bruno Bauer, Ruge, Edgar Bauer (1820–1886), Engels, Marx, Moses Hess (1812–1875), Stirner and Schmidt.

65. See Magee, *Hegel and the Hermetic Tradition*, 15.

66. See "The Onto-Theo-Logical Constitution of Metaphysics" (1957), the concluding lecture in a seminar on Hegel's *Science of Logic* in the winter semester of 1956–1957, in Martin Heidegger, *Identity and Difference*, trans. Joan Stambaugh (New York: Harper & Row, 1969), 42–74.

67. Dunham, Grant, and Watson, *Idealism*, 293.

68. Findlay, *The Discipline of the Cave*, 221.

7

Marx and Engels: The Revolution

"Peoples of the world, together / Join to serve the common cause! / So it feeds us all for ever / See to it that it's now yours. / Forward, without forgetting / Where our strength can be seen now to be! / When starving or when eating / Forward, not forgetting / Our solidarity!" This rousing song by Bertolt Brecht (1898–1956), memorably set to music by Hanns Eisler (1898–1962), captures well the revolutionary fervour associated with the writings of Karl Marx (1818–1883) and Friedrich Engels (1820–1895). Its final stanza brings it to the following stirring conclusion: "Workers of the world, uniting / That's the way to lose your chains. / Mighty regiments now are fighting / That no tyranny remains! / Forward, without forgetting / 'Til the concrete question is hurled / When starving or when eating: / Whose tomorrow is tomorrow? / And whose world is the world?"[1] Yet it is sometimes hard to find this fizzing excitement in the 120 or so volumes of the *MEGA*, the *Marx-Engels-Gesamtausgabe*, the edition of their complete writings.

In some respects, the popular image of Marx precedes and to this extent hinders our perception of his contribution to German Political Thought, yet the following may help provide a clearer context for appreciating his thought:

© The Author(s) 2019
P. Bishop, *German Political Thought and the Discourse of Platonism*,
https://doi.org/10.1007/978-3-030-04510-4_7

- the most important philosophical context for Marx was the thought of Hegel. Marx took Hegel's system, and modified it in a crucial respect: he removed its idealist perspective. Marx himself talked about standing Hegel on his head; or, more accurately, he wrote that Hegel was standing on his head and he, Marx, had turned him the right way round again.[2]
- Marx can also, however, be placed in a much longer philosophical tradition, which takes us back to the ancient Greeks again. His doctoral thesis, completed in 1841, was entitled *On the Difference Between the Democritean and Epicurean Philosophy of Nature*. In it he engaged with pre-Platonic and post-Platonic thought: with Democritus, a materialist philosopher who formulated the idea that the universe is composed of atoms, and Epicurus, a later materialist philosopher who expounded an ethical philosophy of *ataraxia* (detachment, tranquillity, or *Gelassenheit*).

In *The German Ideology* (1845) Marx explains what is meant by standing Hegel the right way up:

> In direct contrast to German philosophy which descends from heaven to earth, here it is a matter of ascending from earth to heaven. That is to say, not setting out from what men say, imagine, conceive, nor from men as narrated, thought of, imagined, conceived, in order to arrive at men in the flesh; but setting out from real, active men, and on the basis of their real life-process demonstrating the development of the ideological reflexes and echoes of this life-process. [...] It is not consciousness that determines life, but life that determines consciousness.[3]

Consequently, in his *Contribution to the Critique of Political Economy* (1859), Marx begins by proposing that the legal relations and political forms—or what Hegel called "civil society"—originate in the material conditions of life. From the outset, Marx takes issue with Aristotle and with Rousseau. He rejects the idea that legal relations and political forms can be comprehended in themselves, as Aristotle proposed to do when he said that "the best method of investigation is to study things in the process of development from the beginning" and undertook a comparative analysis of different kinds of political constitution. And Marx rejects the idea that legal relations and political forms can be understood "on the basis of a so-called general development of the human mind," of the kind that Rousseau can be understood to be proposing, according to one reading of *The Social Contract*.

Instead, Marx takes Hegel's idea (in turn derived from English and French thinkers) of civil society—and he turns it on its head (or, if one prefers, the right way round). Marx turns it on its head (or sets it on its feet) because, instead of deriving the totality from the unfolding in history of the Idea, he argues that this totality is rooted in "the material conditions of life" and, in particular, in "political economy."

What does Marx mean by "political economy"? As he explains in the Preface to his *Critique of Political Economy*, "in the social production of their existence, men inevitably enter into definite relations, which are independent of their will, namely relations of production appropriate to a given stage in the development of their material forces of production." Here he introduces the idea of a *base* and a *superstructure*: the base is "the economic structure of society, the real foundation," and the superstructure is something "legal and political," corresponding to "forms of social consciousness." The base determines the superstructure: in other words, the economic reality determines how we think and the idea we have. On this point, Marx could not be clearer: "The mode of production of material life conditions the general process of social, political and intellectual life," he says, or to put it in more abstract terms, "it is not the consciousness of men that determines their existence, but their social existence that determines their consciousness." And what is also clear is that this model of base and superstructure is not static, but dynamic:

> At a certain stage of development, the material productive forces of society come into conflict with the existing relations of production or — this merely expresses the same thing in legal terms — with the property relations within the framework of which they have operated hitherto. From forms of development of the productive forces these relations turn into their fetters.
>
> (*Contribution to a Critique of Political Economy*, Preface)[4]

The changes in the economic foundation "lead sooner or later to the transformation of the whole immense superstructure," he says, and so begins "an era of social revolution."

One should note that while Marx argued his case by using evidence from economics, his political theory also serves as a starting-point for Marxist aesthetics. For while one can trace "the material transformation of the economic conditions of production, which can be determined with the precision of natural science," this transformation will also be reflected in "the legal, political, religious, artistic or philosophic — in short, ideological forms," forms in which we become conscious of this conflict and in which we can pursue the cause of struggle.

Just as Hegel in his *Lectures on the Philosophy of World History* offered a complete account of historical progress, so Marx suggests that—"in broad outline," as he puts it—the Asiatic, ancient, feudal and modern bourgeois modes of production could be described as "epochs marking progress in the economic development of society." This final stage, i.e., "the bourgeois mode of production," is, however, the crucial one, for it is, according to Marx, "the last antagonistic form of the social process of production," in the sense that the antagonism it involves does not simply pit individuals against individuals, or classes against classes, but "the productive forces developing within bourgeois society create also the material conditions for a solution of this antagonism." In other words, we stand on the threshold of a historical turning-point.

The passage we have been discussing has introduced us to the important Marxist distinction between "base" and "superstructure," as well as to the notion of *ideology*. For Marx, ideology is the forms taken by the superstructure, forms which at the same time obscure that this is what they are and hence obscure the economic base. Marx also uses the word in a more specific context, when in 1846 he and Engels wrote the set of manuscripts later published as *The German Ideology*. This work is a critical, indeed polemical one, directed against such Young Hegelians as Bruno Bauer (1809–1882), Ludwig Feuerbach (1804–1872), and the anarchist thinker, Max Stirner (1806–1856). More positively, in this work Marx and Engels outline what is sometimes called a materialist conception of history (see *The German Ideology*, part 1: Feuerbach).[5]

Central to this account of historical development is the notion of the *alienating* effect of the division of labour. For Marx, separating out different aspects of work and distributing them to people so that each performs only a limited repertoire of activities, has profoundly distressing consequences.[6] Together with the division of labour, the existence of private property leads to an increasingly problematic contradiction between, on the one hand, general interests and, on the other, individual interests. (As a contemporary example, one might think about the problem inherent in the UK housing market: the increase in house prices makes it ever more difficult for young people to get a foot on the housing-ladder, but no one who already owns a house wants house prices to go down!)

Why is the division of labour, in Marx's eyes, such a problem? First, because it disguises, through the notion of the "general interest," the far more genuine "mutual interdependence of the individuals among whom the labour is divided." Second, because through the division of labour, something essentially *natural* escapes our control and, in turn, it controls us. In other words, we become *alienated*. Against the alienation of bourgeois capitalist society, Marx paints a contrasting picture of human activities in a famous passage that constitutes a Communist idyll: no longer forced, under the division of labour, to decide whether he or she is a hunter, a fisherman, a herdsman, or a cultural critic, the human being can choose to go hunting in the morning, to go fishing in the afternoon, to rear cattle in the evening, and—after dinner, of course—to be a critic. (Lest one sneer, the era of late capitalism is steering us in this direction as the idea of a job for life disappears to be replaced by a need to reskill and change career …)

Although this passage contains a sly dig at the career choice of the critic, in it Marx is harking back to an important tradition in Political Thought. For in the *Republic*, Socrates describes the life of the individual attached to the law of equality in the following terms: he "lives along day by day, gratifying the desire that occurs to him, at one time drinking and listening to the flute, at another downing water and reducing; now practising gymnastics, and again idling and neglecting everything; and sometimes spending his time as though he were occupied with philosophy" (561c–d).[7]

What, for Plato, is a negative image is, for Marx, a positive one. To this extent, then, Marxism is not just Hegel, but Plato, stood on his feet.

And the entire thrust of Marx's argumentation is, of course, thoroughly anti-Platonic. It cannot be sufficiently emphasized how Marx saw his work as a contribution to the science of economics. Even if, nowadays, his economic analysis is usually dismissed out-of-hand, it is, in the environment after the 2007–2012 financial crash, making something of a comeback through, for instance, the work of Thomas Piketty or Yanis Varoufakis. How seriously Marx took this aspect of his work can be gauged from the following extract from *Value, Price and Profit*, a speech given to the First International Working Men's Association in 1865 (and published in 1898).

This speech takes as its starting-point a remark made by Thomas Hobbes in his *Leviathan* where he states that "the value, or worth, of a man is, as of all other things, his price: that is to say, so much as would be given for the use of his power."[8] Aligning himself with this statement, Marx says that it can be used as the basis for "determining the value of labour as that of all other commodities" (see Marx, *Value, Price and Profit*, Chapters 7 and 8).[9] It is worthwhile considering this analysis at some length, because it is a good example of how Marx believed— regardless of what economists today say about him—that he could draw on empirical data to support his political-theoretical conclusions.

The question Marx is trying to answer is a beguilingly simple one: "What is the value of labour?" (Given the increasingly grotesque discrepancies in income between those at the top and those at the bottom of our society, this question is still a good one to ask today.) Essentially Marx argues that the value of labour (or labouring power) is determined by the value of the necessities required to produce, to maintain, and to develop that power. And he works through a concrete example. Suppose the things necessary to support the life of a worker require six hours of labour in order to be produced. And suppose that six hours of average labour were the equivalent of 3 shillings. In this case, 3 shillings would be the "price" or monetary value of that worker's labour.

But of course, this worker is just that, a worker, and he or she must sell his or her labour. If he or she sells it at a cost of 3 shillings a day (or 18 shillings for an entire week, i.e., a six-day week), then he or she is selling his or her labour at its exact value. Suppose, Marx continues, this labourer (for the sake of argument, a man) is a spinner. If he works for six hours a day, he can add to the cotton which he spins a value of 3 shillings per day. This value turns out to be an exact equivalent for his wages, the price of his labouring power. Spending 3 shillings a day for 3 shillings' worth of value "added" to the cotton: how could the person who employs the spinner make a profit from this business? Or, to use the terms Marx does, how would the capitalist get any "surplus value," in other words, profit? Here lies, so Marx believes, the nub of the matter.

For, in buying the labouring power of the worker and paying its value, the capitalist has acquired the right to use or consume it, as if it were a commodity. But while the *value* of that labour (or labouring power) is determined (as we have just seen) by the quantity of labour required to maintain or reproduce it, its *use* is limited by such restrictions as the energy or physical strength of the worker. Now recall that to reproduce his labouring power, the worker must reproduce a daily value of 3 shillings by working six hours a day. So what does the capitalist do to make a profit?

The capitalist must make the worker work not six, but *twelve* hours a day for those same 3 shillings, meaning that the worker performs six hours' worth of extra or surplus labour. This *surplus labour* realizes or manifests itself in a *surplus produce* or a *surplus value*. In the case of the spinner, for example, this would mean the following: if he, by six hours of labour, adds 3 shillings value to the cotton, then by twelve hours of labour he adds 6 shillings value. If the capitalist pays the spinner 3 shillings, the capitalist will make a profit of 6 shillings because, although paying the value of *six* hours' labour, he will receive the value of *twelve* hours of labour.

So the capitalist pays out 3 shillings for the spinner's wages, and receives the equivalent of 6 shillings back. While 3 of these shillings must go on payment for the *next* set of wages, the capitalist is left with another 3 shillings of profit or *surplus value*. This form of exchange between capital and labour tends to reproduce the system of dependency and exploitation. Of course, the capitalist has to have the 3 shillings to pay the spinner, buy in the cotton, provide the spinning-factory in the first place; but if the capitalist has these financial resources, then the surplus value will simply continue to accrue. As a result, Marx defines the rate of surplus value as being dependent on the proportion between (a) the time required to reproduce the value of the labouring power, and (b) the surplus time that labour is performed for the capitalist. Despite the crudity of the economic model, Marx is trying to *demystify* the economics of price, labour, and that most mysterious thing in capitalism, *profit*.

Thus one part of Marx's political theory is concerned with trying to understand the present. Another part—at once much more attractive, as well as dangerous—is concerned with trying to predict, and indeed trying to mould and to bring about, the future. A rallying-cry for the future emerges clearly and memorably from the pages of one of the most famous documents associated with Marx and Engels, their *Manifesto of the Communist Party* written in 1848.[10]

In its opening lines, Marx and Engels declare that "the history of all hitherto existing history" is not, as it is in Hegel, the gradual unfolding of the Idea and the realization in history of Reason, but rather "the history of class struggles" (see *Manifesto*, §1, "Bourgeoisie and Proletariat"). Marx and Engels begin by looking back to the past and identifying different epochs, which they relate to the conflict between different "classes" (a concept crucial for their discussion). In ancient Rome, society was divided into freeman and slaves, into patricians and plebeians; in the Middle Ages, it was divided into lords and serfs, into guild-masters and journeymen; and in the modern industrial age, it is divided into the bourgeoisie and the proletariat.

According to Hegel, the function of the state is to legislate and act in the best of interests of all (which, it turned out, is the same thing as the interests of the state). For Marx and Engels, however, the state is more of a racket, protected the vested interests of just one class—the bourgeoisie:

The bourgeoisie, historically, has played a most revolutionary part.

The bourgeoisie, wherever it has got the upper hand, has put an end to all feudal, patriarchal, idyllic relations. It has pitilessly torn asunder the motley feudal ties that bound man to his "natural superiors," and has left remaining no other nexus between man and man than naked self-interest, than callous "cash payment." It has drowned the most heavenly ecstasies of religious fervour, of chivalrous enthusiasm, of philistine sentimentalism, in the icy water of egotistical calculation. It has resolved personal worth into exchange value, and in place of the numberless indefeasible chartered freedoms, has set up that single, unconscionable freedom — free trade. In one word, for exploitation, veiled by religious and political illusions, it has substituted naked, shameless, direct, brutal exploitation.

[…]

The bourgeoisie has disclosed how it came to pass that the brutal display of vigour in the Middle Ages, which reactionaries so much admire, found its fitting complement in the most slothful indolence. It has been the first to show what man's activity can bring about. It has accomplished wonders far surpassing Egyptian pyramids, Roman aqueducts, and Gothic cathedrals; it has conducted expeditions that put in the shade all former Exoduses of nations and crusades.

(*Manifesto*, §1, "Bourgeoisie and Proletarians")[11]

It may come as a surprise to see Marx and Engels describe the bourgeoisie as a "revolutionary" player in history. However, it is important to remember that while the revolution in Russia of October 1917 was a proletarian revolution, the French Revolution of 1789 had been a bourgeois revolution, overthrowing the aristocracy and the monarchy. Moreover, Marx and Engels underscore that, in the capitalist system, the bourgeois have played another revolutionary role: driving the industrial revolution which has, as they explain, "put an end to all feudal, patriarchal, idyllic relations." Before the industrial revolution, the economy was primarily agricultural. The land was tilled by peasants, tenant farmers working on the land owned by the feudal lords. But between 1760 and 1840, there was a shift away from agriculture towards industry. This changed the nature of labour away from hand production to the use of machines, and it intensified the division of labour:

The bourgeoisie cannot exist without constantly revolutionising the instruments of production, and thereby the relations of production, and with them the whole relations of society. Conservation of the old modes of production in unaltered form, was, on the contrary, the first condition of existence for all earlier industrial classes. Constant revolutionising of production, uninterrupted disturbance of all social conditions, everlasting uncertainty and agitation distinguish the bourgeois epoch from all earlier ones. All fixed, fast-frozen relations, with their train of ancient and venerable prejudices and opinions, are swept away, all new-formed ones become antiquated before they can ossify. All that is solid melts into air, all that is holy is profaned, and man is at last compelled to face with sober senses his real conditions of life, and his relations with his kind.

(*Manifesto*, §1, "Bourgeoisie and Proletarians")[12]

In effect, the bourgeois lets the industrial genie out of the bottle: and Marx and Engels compare modern bourgeois society to the figure (derived from a short story by Lucian of Samosata (c. 125—after 180), and made famous by a ballad by Goethe) of the sorcerer's apprentice.[13] The entire system, they argue, is now out of control:

[…] Modern bourgeois society, with its relations of production, of exchange and of property, a society that has conjured up such gigantic means of production and of exchange, is like the sorcerer who is no longer able to control the powers of the nether world whom he has called up by his spells. […] And how does the bourgeoisie get over these crises? On the one hand by enforced destruction of a mass of productive forces; on the other, by the conquest of new markets, and by the more thorough exploitation of the old ones. That is to say, by paving the way for more extensive and more destructive crises, and by diminishing the means whereby crises are prevented.

(*Manifesto*, §1, "Bourgeoisie and Proletarians")[14]

What drives modern bourgeois capitalism out of control is what Marx and Engels call "the epidemic of over-production." This epidemic means there is "too much civilisation, too much means of subsistence, too much industry, too much commerce"; in turn, this means that "society suddenly finds itself put back into a state of momentary barbarism."

Capitalism is barbaric, because of its destructive effects—so destructive, in fact, that it threatens itself with its own destruction. Or in the terms that Marx and Engels use, "the weapons with which the bourgeoisie felled feudalism to the ground are now turned against the bourgeoisie itself," and "not only has the bourgeoisie forged the weapons that bring death to itself; it has also called into existence the men who are to wield those weapons." Those wielders of the anti-capitalist weapons are, of course, the class that capitalism has brought into being, "the modern working class," or "the proletarians."

We saw above how, in his *Contribution to a Critique of Political Economy*, Marx had used the image of fetters, and when the image of chains is first used in the *Communist Manifesto*, it occurs in the context of how "the productive forces at the disposal of society" have become "too powerful for these conditions, by which they are fettered [*gehemmt*], and so soon as they overcome these fetters [*dies Hemmnis*], they bring disorder into the whole of bourgeois society, endanger the existence of bourgeois property." In addition, Marx and Engels focus on the relation of the proletariat to the machinery it uses in its labour. In their eyes, the machine subordinates the labourer to its mechanical demands; curiously enough, a point also made by Nietzsche in his early writings from the time of *The Birth of Tragedy*![15]

As capitalism expands, so a gradual but increasing proletarisation of the entire population takes place. In this way, the proletariat begins to become the vessel for the universal wishes of all humankind (*Manifesto*, §1, "Bourgeoisie and Proletarians").[16]

As time goes on, so one part of the bourgeoisie begins to understand what is happening. It grasps the historical moment in which it finds itself, and so it decides to join the side of the poletariat. Which part is this of the bourgeoisie? It is the part that is usually described as the intellectual vanguard. Not a part of the proletariat, but—understanding its historical destiny—the members of this intellectual vanguard leave their own class, the bourgeoisie, and align themselves with the class of the future, the proletariat (*Manifesto*, §1, "Bourgeoisie and Proletarians").[17] The function of the intellectual vanguard—the self-appointed intellectual vanguard, one is tempted to note—is to apprise the proletariat of its historical mission and to rid it of its "false consciousness."[18] This term is used by Marxists to describe how the forces of capitalist society—its structures, institutions (including its education systems …), the media—mislead the proletariat and obscure its awareness of its historical destiny. (In terms of Plato's allegory of the cave, the prisoners mistake the shadows they see projected on the wall for the real objects being carried around behind them.) To the extent that the members of the proletariat willingly accept this obscuring of its role, we are dealing with a mechanism akin to what, in psychoanalysis, would be called "repression."[19] (In terms of Plato's allegory of the cave, the prisoners willingly accept their imprisonment, to the extent of wanting to deny the actual circumstances of being held prisoner….) Furthermore, there are some members of the proletariat, right at the bottom, who have no interest in its historical role at all, and can even serve the reactionary forces of capitalism: Marx and Engels dismissively and contemptuously describe these as the *Lumpenproletariat*, or as we might say: "yobs," "neds," "feral youths."[20]

What is special about the working-class, or the proletariat, is that, unlike other historical movements: (a) it has a historical destiny, and (b) it attains to consciousness—thanks, of course, to the intellectual vanguard—of its historical destiny. It has a destiny, it knows it has a destiny, and it knows it knows. Put in terms of Plato's allegory of the cave, the members of the intellectual vanguard are like the man who finds the way out of the cave, and discovers the *real* world (which is the *ideal* world). As Socrates tells Glaucon, when this man recalls "his first home and the wisdom there, and his fellow prisoners in that time," then he will both "consider himself happy for the change"—and "pity the others" (516c). *Such a man must go back down into the cave again.* "Our job as founders" (i.e., of the city), Socrates tells Glaucon, "is to compel the best natures to go to the study which we were saying before is the greatest, to see the good and to go up that ascent; and, when they have gone up and seen sufficiently, not to permit them what is now permitted," that is, "to remain there" and "not be willing to go down again among those prisoners or share their labours and honours" (519c–d). In other words, the working-class must learn to read Plato; or, better, Marx. Hence one of the important consequences of Marxism, the tradition of working-class education in the form of public lectures and seminars;

in the early part of the twentieth century, there was an amazing explosion in pedagogical offerings made available to the working-class (reflected in the construction of public libraries, the holding of public lectures, etc.).

Evidently, there is an important difference between Plato and Marx: whereas, for Plato, the truth about the world involves the notion of transcendence, for Marx the truth about the world is something immanent, something material, something historical. In place of Plato's dialectic as an *exercice spirituel*, Marx and Engels offers the dialectic of historical materialism.[21] And there is another difference, too. In Plato's *Republic*, Socrates has to make the case to Glaucon for the man who escapes the cave to return to the prisoners. In the *Communist Manifesto* (and elsewhere), Marx and Engels emphasize the *historical inevitability* of the process of history. Sooner or later, the revolution is coming: "What the bourgeoisie therefore produces, above all, are its own grave-diggers. Its fall and the victory of the proletariat are equally inevitable" (*Manifesto*, §1, "Bourgeoisie and Proletarians").[22] This sense of historical inevitability lends Marxism its soteriological, apocalyptic, or eschatalogical dimension. Just as, in Christianity, the world is on course for the end of time, the Day of Judgment, and the establishment of the New Jerusalem; so, in Marxism, the world is on course for the revolution, the settling of political scores with the aristocracy and bourgeoisie, and the establishment of the Communist utopia.[23]

What, then, is the role of Communism? What is its function, if what is going to happen—i.e., the revolution—is going to happen anyway? The function of Communism is both to speed up the arrival of the revolution, but also to bring about an understanding of these historical processes. While Marx and Engels place great emphasis on the importance of historical and material conditions in determining consciousness, they also propose an argument that an understanding of historical inevitability can help bring about those inevitable events themselves.

But Communism also propounds some clear political principles, obviously. Chief among these is a theme dear to the heart of, for example, Jean-Jacques Rousseau—the abolition of private property. Recall that, in his *Discourse on the Origin and Basis of Inequality Among Men*, Rousseau had written that "the first man who, having enclosed a piece of ground, bethought himself of saying *This is mine*, and found people

simple enough to believe him, was the real founder of civil society."
For Marx, one could rewrite this along the following lines: "The first
man who, having enclosed a piece of ground, bethought himself of saying *This is mine*, and found people simple enough to believe him, was
the real founder of *capitalist society*." Marx and Engels remind us that,
just as the French Revolution of 1789 had "abolished feudal property
in favour of bourgeois property," so, in the forthcoming revolution, the
proletariat will achieve in turn the abolition of all private property. Why
must private property be abolished? To understand this point takes us to
the heart of Marx's and Engel's thinking about the economy.

Because property, in "its current form," or so they argue, is based on
"the antagonism of capital and wage labour." In other words, thinking
about property reveals the essentially antagonistic nature of capitalist
society. This antagonism is the antagonism between capital and wage
labour, i.e., between those who own the businesses, the factories, the
offices, and those who work in them. "To be a capitalist," Marx and
Engels explain, "is to have not only a purely personal, but a social status in production." In other words, in capitalist society, even (and especially) the personal is the political, but in a bad way. (By contrast, in the
Communist society, the personal is the political, but in a good way.)
Accordingly, capital is "a collective product," it is "not only personal; it
is a social power." On the other hand, there is wage-labour, and those
who sell their labour for a wage. Wage-labour, as we have seen, is essentially exploitative: it keeps the workers in an impoverished state, while
allowing the property-owning capitalists to enrich themselves.

Understanding the essentially antagonistic nature of capitalist society allows Marx and Engels to highlight the difference between bourgeois and Communist societies. One of these differences, they claim, is
that in bourgeois society, "the past dominates the present," whereas in
Communist society, "the present dominates the past." And they go on
to explain how, in their view, the abolition of private property will permit other changes, too: the abolition of freedom and individuality, or
to be precise, the abolition of *bourgeois* freedom and *bourgeois* individuality (which are neither true freedom nor true individuality). For by
"freedom," what the bourgeois means is the freedom of selling and buying; if this form of economic exchange is abolished, then this "freedom"

obviously falls away, but a much greater freedom is attained. The abolition of private property, they argue, is already underway: so much of the property in which nine-tenths of the population live is already owned by one tenth of the population (one might think of the current debate surrounding property ownership in the centre of London …). And bourgeois "individuality" is not real individuality, it is merely a question of owning certain kinds of objects or properties; in this respect, one can see how Marx and Engels lay the groundwork for the development of Marxism as a form of cultural critique.

Indeed, this aspect of their work is of fundamental importance: culture and education (*Bildung*), they argue, has become reduced to "a mere training to act as a machine." What appears to bourgeois eyes (and to unenlightened proletariat ones) to be a law of nature (and one recalls Rousseau's hypothesis of a state of nature), is, in fact, something socially, economically, and historically constructed (*Manifesto*, §2, "Proletarians and Communists").[24] *Things don't have to be the way they are*, so Marx and Engels want to tell us, and they let us in on a world-historical secret: *and they are not going to be like this for much longer.…*

Central to the argument propounded by Marx and Engels is the insight they discern into the relationship between consciousness and material production. According to them, the entire history of ideas serves to proves this fundamental point: that "intellectual production changes its character in proportion as material production is changed," or to put it another way, that "the ruling ideas of each age have ever been the idea of its ruling class" (*Manifesto*, §2, "Proletarians and Communists").[25] Although Marx and Engels emphasize the inevitability of the historical change they are talking about, they also highlight the agency of the class responsible for driving this change, i.e., the proletariat. According to their own definition of political power, this power is "the organised power of one class for oppressing another." So their goal is a revolution to remove the ruling class, with a paradoxical end in view—the triumph of the proletariat which, with its triumph, simultaneously abolishes itself *qua* being the proletariat, paving the way to true political freedom (that old dream of the German Political Tradition …), in which "the free development of each is the condition for the free development of all" (*Manifesto*, §2, "Proletarians and Communists").[26]

So the goal of Marxism is freedom; just as it was for Rousseau, for Kant, and for Hegel. But at the beginning of the tradition of German Political Thought stands Plato: his concern, one will recall, is not so much with freedom as with justice.

And in other respects, too, the contrast between, on the one hand, Marx and Engels, and, on the other, Plato, could not be more evident. At its most fundamental level, this difference is an essentially ontological one: Plato gives the ontological priority to *ideas*, whereas Marx and Engels give the ontological priority to the *material world* in its *historical* development. Plato is a thinker of *transcendence*, Marx and Engels are thinkers of *immanence*. Yet, as we have seen, there are some surprising parallels between them—the task of the Platonic philosopher being to return to the cave and to liberate the remaining prisoners, the task of the Marxist or radical philosopher being to go among the working-class, trapped in their factories and work-places, and to prepare them for the coming liberation of the revolution. So it is telling that, in the resounding and well-known conclusion to the *Communist Manifesto*, Marx and Engels return to an image that is well-known to us by now: the images of the proletariat as being enslaved by bourgeois, capitalist society, and as being—precisely as the prisoners in Plato's cave—bound up in chains; in the chains of economic independence, social repression, and false consciousness:

> The Communists disdain to conceal their views and aims. They openly declare that their ends can be attained only by the forcible overthrow of all existing social conditions. Let the ruling classes tremble at a Communistic revolution. The proletarians have nothing to lose but their chains. They have a world to win.
>
> Working men of all countries, unite!
>
> (*Manifesto*, §4, "Position of the Communists in Relation to the Various Existing Opposition Parties")[27]

Clearly, then, the *Communist Manifesto* is a call to arms; it is an appeal to the proletariat to assume its historical responsibility and—with the guidance of the intellectual vanguard, not least Marx and Engels themselves—to lead humankind out of the cave of capitalist exploitation and into the Communist world of authentic human existence. What might such a Communist world look like?

To describe what the world might look like after the revolution has always been a problem for the Left. Something which is not just quantitatively, but qualitatively, different—can we, in our current state of alienation (whether economic or existential), even conceive what such a world might look like? On the other hand, any political system that describes itself as "scientific," as Marxist thought did,[28] must surely be able to say something about what a Communist society would be like? After all, even Plato could tell us what life outside the cave would be like: the philosopher would first make out "the shadows," then reflections ("the phantoms of the human beings and the other things in water"), then "the things themselves," until finally—"And from there he could turn to beholding the things in heaven and heaven itself" (516a). This chapter concludes with extracts from two texts, one by Marx, the other by Engels, which address themselves to this question of the nature of a Communist society.

In 1875, Marx wrote a text now known as "Marginal Notes to the Programme of the German Workers' Party" in order to address what he saw as the deficiencies or shortcomings in the political programme of a political party, the Social Democratic Workers' Party of Germany (SDAP). (This party should not be confused with the German Workers' Party, the predecessor of the National Socialist German Workers' Party—abbreviated to the Nazi Party—which belongs to a completely different wing of the political spectrum.) Sometimes this text, which Marx himself described in a letter to Bracke of 5 May 1875 as "a long scrap of paper," is known as the *Critique of the Gotha Programme*, because in it Marx voiced his criticisms of a document written as the basis for a proposed union between the SDAP and the General German Workers' Association (ADAV) to create a party that became the future Social Democratic Party of Germany (SPD), still a major political force in German politics today. So this text by Marx is an early critique from the Communist standpoint of the "watering-down" of its principles to form democratically acceptable (and electable) political parties. As Paresh Chattopadhyay has suggested, it is a text that contains "a condensed discussion of the most essential elements of the capitalist mode of production, its revolutionary transformation into its opposite, and a rough portrayal, in a few bold strokes, of what Marx had called in *Capital* the 'union of free individuals'[29] destined to succeed the existing social order."[30] To this extent, the text can be considered as a second "Communist Manifesto," albeit one written this time by Marx on his own.

In these "Marginal Notes," Marx explores the idea of a "co-operative society," that is, a society based on common ownership of the means of production, not based (as now) on "exchange." As part of a discussion of "equal rights," he distinguishes between the "first phase" of Communist society, something that emerges (after, as he puts it, "prolonged birth pangs") from existing capitalist society, and a later (or "higher") phase of Communist society, where the "division of labour" has been overcome and where "bourgeois rights" have been replaced by a more just principle that Marx famously articulates as follows: "From each according to his ability, to each according to his needs!" (*Marginal Notes to the Programme of the German Workers Party*, §1).[31]

As part of his critique of the Gotha Programme, Marx returns to his attack on those less radical reformers who demand, not revolution, but reform. As we saw above, Marx regarded "the cry for an *equality of wages*" as "rest[ing] upon a mistake" and being "an inane wish never to be fulfilled"; it is "an offspring of that false and superficial radicalism that accepts premises and tries to evade conclusions." Here Marx, using the same logic that Plato does in his allegory of the cave, tries to understand why those slaves who have begun to realize they are slaves, nevertheless fail to grasp the full implications of this insight. In Plato, the benighted prisoners are so invested in their system of "honours, praises, and prizes" (516c) that they mock and scorn the returning philosopher, and—"if they were somehow able to get their hands on and kill the man who attempts to release and lead up, wouldn't they kill him?" (517a). In Marx, those who argue for the abolition of the wage system in general (and the "iron law of wages," propounded by the economist Ferdinand Lassalle (1825–1864), in particular),[32] have accepted the socialist premise—but rejected the revolutionary conclusion. "It is as if," Marx wrote, "among the slaves who have at last got behind the secret of slavery and broken out in rebellion, a slave still in thrall to obsolete notions were to inscribe on the programme of the rebellion"—and here Marx's sarcasm becomes palpable: "Slavery must be abolished because the feeding of slaves in the system of slavery cannot exceed a certain low maximum!"[33]

In his discussion of the transition from the present form of society, a capitalist one, to the future Communist society, Marx coins another famous phrase: "the dictatorship of the proletariat." Marx notes that, in present-day society—by which, of course, he means the society of 1875, but his remark largely applies to our Western society today—there are different states or different countries, but despite their "diversity of form" they are all based on modern bourgeois society, i.e., they are all, to a greater or lesser exent, capitalistically developed. So how does one get from where we are to where we want (or at least Marx wants us) to go, that is, from capitalism to Communism?

To answer this question, Marx remembers his Hegelian roots. In his account of history, Hegel argued that, in order to cook a world-historical omelette, one must crack a few world-historical eggs. Or as he memorably put it, "a world-historical individual is devoted to the one aim, regardless of all else," and he added: "It is even possible that such men may treat other great, even sacred interests inconsiderately; conduct which is indeed obnoxious to moral reprehension. But so mighty a form must trample down many an innocent flower or crush to pieces many an object in its path."[34] Similarly, Marx was sufficiently realistic to understand that the transition from capitalist to Communist society would not be an easy one, and so he proposed that the transition would take place in three stages: (1) the starting-point, capitalist society; (2) the revolutionary dictatorship of the proletariat; and (3) the ultimate goal, Communist society (*Marginal Notes*, §4).[35]

Although the actual term "dictatorship of the proletariat" was coined, not by Marx or Engels, but by an early socialist supporter, Joseph Weydemeyer (1818–1866),[36] it becomes a distinctive feature of Marxist thought in explaining how the transition from capitalism to Communism, that is, from private ownership of the means of production to its collective ownership, would be achieved. In other words, the dictatorship of the proletariat is not an end in itself, but a means to an end—the placing of political power in the hands of the working class has the objective of achieving the transition to Communism. In an essay written in 1880 called "The Development of Utopian Socialism," Engels tells us a bit more about what the Communist society will look like.

As we have noted, Engels already described the kind of socialism proposed by himself and Marx as "scientific," but there is also a utopian dimension to their thought as well. Now, the term "utopian socialism" is used to describe an early current of socialist thinking, one associated with the work of such political thinkers as Henri de Saint-Simon (1760–1825), Charles Fourier (1772–1837), and Robert Owen (1771–1858), the founder of a utopian socialist experiment at New Lanark in Scotland.[37] The specifically "utopian" dimension of their thought lies not so much in its goal, a socialist society, as in their belief that it can be achieved without violent struggle or revolution.

By contrast, Engels argues that there must be a moment of negation on the path to achievening the great positive of Communism. (In this respect, of course, Engels is also being a good Hegelian.) But in this essay he is not so much thinking of violent revolution but of the abolition of what, for Hegel, was the outcome and the crowning glory of the historical process—the state. For Engels, the abolition of class distinctions and class antagonisms means the abolition of the structure that maintains these distinctions and anatagonisms, the state.

He argues that the state, as a representative of society as a whole, has always been the state of that class which itself represented society as a whole. So in antiquity (i.e., in the ancient Greece of Plato and Aristotle), the state was a state of citizens owning slaves; in the Middle Ages, the state was a state of feudal lords; and in the modern age, the state is represented by the ruling class, the bourgeoisie. But when the state becomes the real representative of the *whole of society*, then the state has achieved something hithero unimaginable: it has rendered itself unnecessary. And to this extent, Engels shares the thinking of the utopian socialists. For such a state is not actually going to be abolished, bur rather it will abolish itself or, as he puts it, *it fades away* or *dies out*:

> The first act by virtue of which the state really constitutes itself the representative of the whole of society — the taking possession of the means

of production in the name of society — this is, at the same time, its last independent act as a state. State interference in social relations becomes, in one domain after another, superfluous, and then dies out of itself; the government of persons is replaced by the administration of things, and by the conduct of processes of production. The state is not "abolished." *It dies out.* This gives the measure of the value of the phrase: "a free state," both as to its justifiable use at times by agitators, and as to its ultimate scientific inefficiency; and also of the demands of the so-called anarchists for the abolition of the state out of hand.[38]

In this work we should note Engels's polemic against another radical political tradition, that of the anarchists. Although the anarchist tradition is one not represented in this survey of German Political Thought, its mention here reminds us that, although Marxism became the dominant form of political radicalism, in the nineteenth and twentieth centuries it was by no means the only one.[39]

In conclusion, what can we say about the participation of Marx and Engels in the discourse of Platonism and about their contribution to German Political Thought? As far as the former is concerned, Marxism as a form of materialist philosophy is clearly a rejection of Platonism. Indeed, Marx himself demonstrated his anti-Platonist credentials as early as 1841 in his doctoral thesis, *The Difference Between the Democritean and Epicurean Philosophy of Nature*, examining the thought of two ancient Greek atomist thinkers.[40] As far as the latter is concerned, their influence in the twentieth century has obviously been massive. Basing themselves on the thought of Marx and Engels, political parties took charge of large parts of the globe, notably in Russia, Eastern Europe, South America, and China. Despite the "collapse of Communism" and the introduction of market economics into China, Marxism has maintained a presence in political thought, particularly in the wake of the financial crash of 2007–2008 and the resulting global financial crisis.

Nevertheless, some of the deficits of Marxist thought have become clearer over time. First, it is relatively uninterested in questions of gender. While some feminists are Marxist, not all Marxists are feminists; and there are doubtless patriarchal assumptions underlying the writings of Marx and Engels, even if Engels—in his *Origins of the Family, Private Property and the State* (1884)—was interested in theories of matriarchy. Second, its analysis of capitalism in economic terms has proved to be wrong; or, at least, not right in the way that Marx thought it was. After all, capitalism has not collapsed; although, as it currently lurches from crisis to crisis, this does not exclude its collapse in the future... Third, Marxism has strong roots in Hegelianism, and this arguably limits its applicability: if Hegel gets things wrong, so will Marx as well. Common to Hegelianism and Marxism is a remarkable confidence in their methodological approach, one that tends to overlook cultural or other sorts of difference. To a certain extent, this reflects a peculiarly Germanic trait, characteristic of many systems of thought originating in Germany: a strong drive to systematization, albeit systematization in its own terms, and no-one else's. (Perhaps the most extreme form of this trait is Freud's famous argument about the truth of his own school of psychoanalysis. The more the patient says "no," Freud argues, the more the patient *means* "yes"; a logical vicious circle from which it can be difficult to exit, until or unless one rejects the entire logic of the system of thought completely.) Perhaps it was for this reason that Nietzsche once observed, "the will to a system is a lack of integrity" ...[41]

Yet Marxism has also proved to be a remarkably fertile tradition of thought, and aside from its economic analysis, its political forms (such as the Communist Party), and its responsibility for some of the greatest massacres of the twentieth century, it forms the basis in the West for a critical tradition that has become known as Western Marxism. In this form, it has developed into a major kind of cultural critique, and in this way it was taken up, along with Nietzsche, into the work of the thinkers of the Frankfurt School, notably Theodor W. Adorno (1903–1969) and Max Horkheimer (1895–1973), to whose work we shall turn in Chapter 9. If, in the thought of Marx, the route out of the cave of capitalism lies only through the revolution of the proletariat, who will release themselves from their shackles and take charge of the cave, then Adorno and Horkheimer ponder a Western world (Europe and America) where this revolutionary moment seems unlikely to be ever attained, and where the ghastly truth is, in the chilling phrase of Walter Benjamin (1892–1940), "that things 'just go on' *is* the catastrophe."[42]

On this account of history, we are more than ever before held as prisoners in the cave, and more than ever before we believe ourselves, in an entirely deluded way, to be free. To show how popular culture teaches human beings to love their confinement lies at the heart of the project of *Critical Theory* pursued by the members of the Frankfurt School. Yet the influence of the discourse of Platonism on German Political Thought makes itself felt not only on the political Left, but on the political Right, too. Enter two of the nineteenth and twentieth centuries' most controversial thinkers, Friedrich Nietzsche (1844–1900) and Martin Heidegger (1889–1976).

Notes

1. Extracted from Bertolt Brecht, "Solidarity Song," in John Willett and Ralph Manheim (eds), *Poems 1913–1956* (London: Methuen, 1987), 185–186.
2. "The dialectic of the Idea became itself merely the conscious reflex of the dialectic evolution of the real world, and therefore, the dialectic of Hegel was turned upside down or rather it was placed upon its feet instead of on its head, where it was standing before" (Engels, *Feuerbach: The Roots of the Socialist Philosophy*, trans. Austin Lewis (Chicago: Kerr, 1906), 96). For further discussion, see Allen Wood, "Hegel and Marxism," in Frederick C. Beiser (ed.), *The Cambridge Companion to Hegel* (Cambridge: Cambridge University Press, 1993), 414–443; Andrew Chitty, "Hegel and Marx," in Stephen Houlgate and Michael Baur (eds), *A Companion to Hegel* (Malden, MA and Oxford: Wiley Blackwell, 2011), 477–500.
3. Marx and Engels, "The German Ideology," in *Collected Works*, vol. 5 (Moscow: Progress Publishers, 1976), 19–539 (36–37); cf. Eugene Kamenka (ed.), *The Portable Marx* (New York: Viking Penguin, 1983), 169–170.
4. Karl Marx, "A Contribution to the Critique of Political Economy," in Marx/Engels, *Collected Works*, vol. 29 (Moscow: Progress Publishers, 1987), 257–417 (263); cited in Kamenka (ed.), *Portable Marx*, 160.
5. Marx, "The German Ideology," in Marx/Engels, *Collected Works*, vol. 5, 46–47; cited in Kamenka (ed.), *Portable Marx*, 176–177.

6. To this extent, it is instructive to compare Friedrich Schiller (1759–1805) and Marx on the notion of alienation, as Vickey Rippere has done; see *Schiller and "Alienation"* (Berne: Lang, 1981). For instance, in his *On the Aesthetic Education of Humankind* (1795), Schiller argued that the fragmentation of human beings has turned them into clockwork models, engaged in a purely mechanistic life (Letter 6, §7) and that the forces which split us into two derive from both outside and within the individual (Letter 6, §10). Yet he also argues that this antagonism of faculties was both historically necessary and has proved to be the great instrument of culture (Letter 6 §11–12); see Friedrich Schiller, *On the Aesthetic Education of Man in a Series of Letters*, ed. and trans. Elizabeth M. Wilkinson and L.A. Willoughby, 2nd edn (Oxford: Clarendon Press, 1982).

7. Plato, *The Republic*, ed. and trans. Allan Bloom (New York: Basic Books, 1991), 239–240.

8. Thomas Hobbes, *Leviathan: Revised Student Edition*, ed. Richard Tuck (Cambridge: Cambridge University Press, 1996), 63.

9. Karl Marx, "Value, Price and Profit," in Marx/Engels, *Collected Works*, vol. 20 (Moscow: Progress Publishers, 1985), 101–149 (127–131); cited in Kamenka (ed.), *Portable Marx*, 405–409.

10. Marx/Engels, *Collected Works*, vol. 6 (Moscow: Progress Publishers, 1976), 477–519; cited in Kamenka (ed.), *Portable Marx*, 203–241.

11. Marx/Engels, *Collected Works*, vol. 6, 487; cited in Kamenka (ed.), *Portable Marx*, 206.

12. Marx/Engels, *Collected Works*, vol. 6, 487; cited in Kamenka (ed.), *Portable Marx*, 207.

13. See Lucian, *"Philopseudes"* (i.e., "The Lover of Lies"); and Goethe's poem, "The Sorcerer's Apprentice" (*Der Zauberlehrling*), written in 1797.

14. Marx/Engels, *Collected Works*, vol. 6, 489–490; cited in Kamenka (ed.), *Portable Marx*, 209–210.

15. See KSA 7, 3[44], 73. In his polemic against the liberal Protestant theologian David Friedrich Strauss (1808–1874), Nietzsche takes exception to a passage from Strauss's *Der alte und der neue Glaube* (*The Old Faith and the New*) (1872) and responds: "Of what consolation could it be to the worker within this machine to know that this oil is being poured on to him while the machine continues to hold him in its grip?" (*Untimely Meditations*, "David Strauss, the Confessor and the Writer" (1873), §6;

in Friedrich Nietzsche, *Untimely Meditations*, trans. R.J. Hollingdale (Cambridge: Cambridge University Press, 1983), 25). And in his next *Untimely Meditation*, "On the Uses and Disadvantages of History for Life" (1874), Nietzsche regrets "the need to make use of the jargon of the slave-owner and the employer of labour to describe things which in themselves ought to be thought of as free of utility and raised above the necessities of life; but the words 'factory,' 'labour market,' 'supply,' 'making profitable,' and whatever auxiliary verbs egoism now employs, come unbidden to the lips when one wishes to describe the most recent generation of men of learning" (UM II §7; in *Untimely Meditations*, 99).

16. Marx/Engels, *Collected Works*, vol. 6, 491–492; cited in Kamenka (ed.), *Portable Marx*, 212–213.

17. Marx/Engels, *Collected Works*, vol. 6, 494; cited in Kamenka (ed.), *Portable Marx*, 215.

18. The notion of "false consciousness" is closely related to the notion of "ideology"; see Engels's letter to Franz Mehring of 14 July 1893: "Ideology is a process accomplished by the so-called thinker consciously indeed, but with a false consciousness. The real motives impelling him remain unknown to him, otherwise it would not be an ideological process at all. Hence he imagines false or apparent motives" (Marx and Engels, *Correspondence*, trans. Donna Torr (New York: International Publishers, 1968), 434–435). The term was subsequently taken up and developed by Georg Lukács (1885–1971) in *History and Class Consciousness: Studies in Marxist Dialectics* [1920], trans. Rodney Livingstone (Cambridge, MA: MIT Press, 1971), 50: "The dialectical method does not permit us simply to proclaim the 'falseness' of this consciousness and to persist in an inflexible confrontation of true and false. On the contrary, it requires us to investigate this 'false consciousness' concretely as an aspect of the historical totality and as a stage in the historical process"); and by Herbert Marcuse (1898–1979) in *One-Dimensional Man: Studies in the Ideology of Advanced Industrial Society* [1964] (London: Ark, 1986): "To the degree to which they correspond to the given reality, thought and behavior express a false consciousness, responding to and contributing to the preservation of a false order of facts. And this false consciousness has become embodied in the prevailing technical apparatus which in turn reproduces it" (145). The problem with the notion is this: How does one know that the *other person's* consciousness is false and not one's *own* consciousness.…?

19. For the notion of repression, defined by Jean Laplanche and Jean-Bertrand Pontalis as "an operation whereby the subject attempts to repel, or to confine to the unconscious, representations (thoughts, images, memories) which are bound to an instinct" and, more loosely, as a kind of "defence" (*The Language of Psychoanalysis*, trans. Donald Nicholson-Smith (London: Karnac, 1998), 390–394), see Freud's classic paper of 1915, "Repression" (in *Standard Edition of the Collected Works of Sigmund Freud*, ed. James Strachey and Anna Freud, 24 vols (London: Hogarth Press, 1957–1974), vol. 14, 141–157); and, for a more nuanced discussion, his paper "Constructions in Analysis" (1937), in Freud, *Standard Edition*, vol. 23, 256–269. For further discussion, see Michael Billig, *Freudian Repression: Conversation Creating the Unconscious* (Cambridge: Cambridge University Press, 1999); Sergio Lewkowicz and Thierry Bolkanowski with Georges Pragier (eds), *On Freud's "Constructions in Analysis"* (London: Karnac, 2011). Again, a similar question arises as in the case of "false consciousness": Can one unquestioningly assent to the principle, conroversially utilized by Freud in his case-study of the analysis of "Little Dora," that "no" means "yes" (see *Fragment of a Case of Hysteria*, in *Standard Edition*, vol. 3, 44–45)?

20. For a popular sociological investigation of the term, see Francis Gilbert, *Yob Nation: The Truth About Britain's Yob Culture* (London: Portrait, 2007). For a critical discussion, see Rosalind Coward, "Whipping Boys," *Guardian Weekend*, 3 September 1994, 32–35.

21. For Marx's definition of "historical materialism," see *The German Ideology*, Chapter 2, "Civil Society and the Conception of History": "This conception of history depends on our ability to expound the real process of production, starting out from the material production of life itself, and to comprehend the form of intercourse connected with this and created by this mode of production (i.e., civil society in its various stages), as the basis of all history; describing it in its action as the state, and to explain all the different theoretical products and forms of consciousness, religion, philosophy, ethics, etc., and trace their origins and growth from that basis" (Marx/Engels, *Collected Works*, vol. 5; cited in *Kamenka* (ed.), *Portable Marx*, 181).

22. Marx/Engels, *Collected Works*, vol. 6, 495–496; cited in Kamenka (ed.), *Portable Marx*, 216–217.

23. Compare with the work of the Marxist philosopher, Ernst Bloch (1885–1977), where this apocalyptic or chiliastic dimension is especially evident; see his *Geist der Utopie* (1918; revised 1923), translated

as *The Spirit of Utopia*, trans. Anthony A. Nassar (Stanford, CA: Stanford University Press, 2000); and *Das Prinzip Hoffnung*, 3 vols (written 1938–1947, pub. 1954–1959), translated as *The Principle of Hope*, trans. Neville Plaice, Stephen Plaice, and Paul Knight, 3 vols (Cambridge, MA: MIT Press, 1986).

24. Marx/Engels, *Collected Works*, vol. 6, 498–501; cited in Kamenka (ed.), *Portable Marx*, 219–223.

25. Marx/Engels, *Collected Works*, vol. 6, 503; cited in Kamenka (ed.), *Portable Marx*, 225–226.

26. Marx/Engels, *Collected Works*, vol. 6, 505–506; cited in Kamenka (ed.), *Portable Marx*, 228.

27. Marx/Engels, *Collected Works*, vol. 6, 519; cited in Kamenka (ed.), *Portable Marx*, 240.

28. See Friedrich Engels, "Socialism: Utopian and Scientific" (1880), in Marx/Engels, *Selected Works*, vol. 3 (Moscow: Progress Publishers, 1970), 95–151.

29. Cf. "Let us now picture to ourselves, by way of change, a community of free individuals, carrying on their work with the means of production in common, in which the labour power of all the different individuals is consciously applied as the combined labour power of the community" (Karl Marx, *Capital: A Critique of Political Economy*, vol. 1, *The Process of Production of Capital*, Chapter 1, "Commodities," in Marx/Engels, *Collected Works*, vol. 34 (London: Lawrence & Wishart, 2010), 89).

30. Paresh Chattopadhyay, *Marx's Associated Means of Production: A Critique of Marxism* (New York: Palgrave Macmillan, 2016), 197.

31. Marx/Engels, *Collected Works*, vol. 24, 81–99 (85–87); cited in Kamenka (ed.), *Portable Marx*, 538–541.

32. According to this "iron law" (a phrase borrowing an expression from a poem by Goethe, "The Divine" (*Das Göttliche*) (from the early 1870s): "Following great, bronzen, / Ageless laws / All of us must / Fulfill the circles / Of our existence"), real wages tend in the long run to adjust themselves to the minimum wage necessary for workers to meet their basic needs.

33. Marx/Engels, *Collected Works*, vol. 24, 92; cited in Kamenka (ed.), *Portable Marx*, 547.

34. G.W.F. Hegel, *Lectures on the Philosophy of World History*, trans. from the third German edition by John Sibree (London: Bohn, 1861), 34; *The Philosophy of History* (Mineola, NY: Dover, 1956), 32.

35. Marx/Engels, *Collected Works*, vol. 24, pp. 94–95; in Kamenka (ed.), *Portable Marx*, 549–550.
36. For further discussion, see Hal Draper, *The "Dictatorship of the Proletariat" from Marx to Lenin* (New York: Monthly Review Press, 1987).
37. For a useful overview of these thinkers, see Michel Onfray, *L'Eudémonisme social* [*Contre-histoire de la philosophie*, vol. 5] (Paris: Grasset, 2008).
38. Friedrich Engels, *Socialism: Utopian and Scientific*, trans. Edward Aveling (New York: International Publishers, 1935), 69–70.
39. The anarchist tradition is associated with the thought of Pierre-Joseph Proudhon (1809–1865), author of a treatise *What Is Property? Or, An Inquiry into the Principle of Right and Government* (1840), which enunciates the principle, "Property is theft." For an acoustic introduction to anarchist thought, see Michel Onfray, *Le Post-Anarchisme expliqué à ma Grand-Mère* (Vincennes: Frémeaux & Associés, 2 CDs, 2011).
40. Marx/Engels, *Collected Works*, vol. 1 (Moscow: Progress Publishers, 1975), 25–105.
41. *Twilight of the Idols*, "Maxims and Arrows," §26, in Friedrich Nietzsche, *Twilight of the Idols and The Anti-Christ*, trans. R.J. Hollingdale (Harmondsworth: Penguin, 1968), 25.
42. "Daß es 'so weiter geht', *ist* die Katastrophe"; in Walter Benjamin, "Central Park," trans. Lloyd Spencer and Mark Harrington, *New German Critique* 34 (Winter 1985), 32–58 (50).

8

Nietzsche and Heidegger: A Glance to the Right

Even now, it is difficult to discuss Friedrich Nietzsche (1844–1900) in relation to politics, because of the many misunderstandings that—still—attend his work. This is despite—or maybe because of—his massive reception in the twentieth century. Indeed, Nietzsche has in some ways become so much part of our mental furniture that it would be easy to underestimate the impact of his thought. But according to the Expressionist writer Gottfried Benn (1885–1856), everything that his generation "had discussed, had thought out inside itself, one might say: suffered, one might also say: done to death — all that had already been expressed and exhausted in Nietzsche, had found definitive formulation; all the rest was mere exegesis."[1]

To the members of Benn's Nietzsche-influenced generation one might reckon many figures: in the fields of music and the visual arts, to say nothing of his vast philosophical reception. One might also note Nietzsche's remarkable importance, both acknowledged and unacknowledged, for psychoanalysis, as well as for a whole host of marginal (or marginalized) figures who have, with good reason, been described as "Zarathustra's children."[2] Yet the unease surrounding him tends regrettably to remain. (Teaching in a UK university in the 1990s, I was once

© The Author(s) 2019
P. Bishop, *German Political Thought and the Discourse of Platonism*,
https://doi.org/10.1007/978-3-030-04510-4_8

spotted on the way to class by a colleague from the French department. "What's that you're going to teach?" he asked, looking at the books in my hand. I barely had time to reply before he saw the books were by Nietzsche, whereupon he immediately stood bolt upright and gave a Hitler salute.) In the final chapter of the autobiographical work, *Ecce Homo*, Nietzsche asked three times: "Have I been understood?"[3] It would be fair to say that, in terms of his political influence, the answer has often been: no.[4]

If Marx is the totemic thinker for the political Left, Nietzsche has often become a reluctant taboo for the political Right. At any rate, he largely remains a taboo for the Left.[5] Nevertheless, some thinkers have proposed a libertarian reading of Nietzsche in a sense of a *nietzschéisme de gauche*, not without being contested for doing so[6]; and one critic has ingeniously argued that Nietzsche, as an essentially right-wing thinker, was nevertheless aiming to infiltrate and thereby undermine the Left.[7] The widespread association of Nietzsche with the political Right is largely due to the fact that Nietzsche was taken up and assimilated by National Socialism[8]; but can we hold Nietzsche responsible for this, given the fact that the Nazi Party was founded in 1920 and that Nietzsche had died in 1900? And how does Nietzsche fit into the picture in relation to the discourse of Platonism, given that his writings contain numerous critiques of Plato? As we shall explore in this chapter, the picture is more complicated than it might appear at a first glance.

Nietzsche

Here are some phrases taken from Nietzsche's writings:

- let the feeble perish!
- slavery belongs to the essence of a culture
- war is the archetype of the state

Taken at face value, it would seem to be an open-and-shut case: and Nietzsche could be confidently rejected as a thinker who is (to use the phrase employed by Lady Caroline Lamb to describe Lord Byron) mad, bad, and dangerous to know. Closer inspection, however, reveals that this is not necessarily the case.

One should remember that Nietzsche's biography displays an unusual trajectory. He was born in 1844 as the son of a the village pastor in Röcken, in the eastern part of Germany. As he put it in an early autobiographical sketch he wrote, "as a plant I was born close to the churchyard, and as a human being in a vicarage."[9] After going to school in the Gymnasium in Naumburg and in Schulpforta, famed for its academic rigour (and its strict discipline), he went to university in Bonn to study theology but soon switched to classical philology—and to Leipzig University, where he studied under the celebrated scholar Friedrich Ritschl (1806–1876). It is no exaggeration to describe the young Nietzsche as an academic superstar: at the age of merely twenty-four, he was appointed (thanks to the support of his mentor, Ritschl) Extraordinary Professor of classical philology at the University of Basel. Yet only ten years later, Nietzsche decided to resign from his professorship at Basel, applying to be released from the post on grounds of ill-health. For the remainder of his life, until his mental collapse in Turin in 1889 and (after a decade in what is euphemistically called "mental darkness," or *geistige Umnachtung*) his death in 1900, Nietzsche was an itinerant, independent philosopher. He moved around between Italy, France, and Switzerland—especially his beloved Sils Maria,[10] where he wrote much of his masterpiece, *Thus Spoke Zarathustra*, between 1882 and 1884. In one of his final works, provocatively entitled *The Anti-Christ*, Nietzsche wrote, "some people are born posthumously,"[11] and in a sense there is, given his tumultuous reception in the twentieth century, no one of whom this is more true than Nietzsche.

Let us go back to those phrases we have just cited and examine them a little bit more carefully. First of all, that cry: "let the feeble perish!", whose context does not seem to make things any better (or easier): "The weak and the failures shall perish: first principle of *our* love of man. And one should even give them every possible assistance."[12] As Alexandre Lacroix has pointed out, this text informs a scene in François Mauriac's novel, *The Kiss to the Leper* (*Le Baiser au lépreux*, 1922). Here its hypochondriac young hero, Jean Péloueyre, comes across Nietzsche's phrase—and feels got at. After all, Nietzsche's phrase is a provocative inversion of Matthew, 5: 3, "Blessed are the poor in spirit: for theirs is the kingdom of heaven."[13] Yet there is cunning in Nietzsche's rhetoric: rather than to respond as Jean Péloueyre does, Nietzsche is inviting us to identify ourselves with the strong, and in turn to identify ourselves with a creative philosophy of affirmation, rather than with a destructive psychology of *ressentiment*.

What about the second phrase? In an early lecture (with an implicitly political theme) entitled "The Greek State" (1871/1872), Nietzsche had argued that "*slavery belongs to the essence of a culture*," since "in order for there to be a broad, deep, fertile soil for the development of art, the overwhelming majority has to be slavishly subjected to life's necessity in the service of the minority, *beyond* the measure that is necessary for the individual."[14] Read in the light of Nietzsche's thought as a whole, however, the true sense of this apparently shocking statement is that the individual must dedicate himself or herself to a higher (i.e., cultural) cause, and in this way transcend the limitations of his or her individual self: a notion which, through the mouth of Zarathustra, Nietzsche calls *Selbst-Überwindung* and places under the sign of the *Übermensch*, the human-who-is-more-than-(just)-human. This becomes clear in *The Gay Science*, which talks about how "every strengthening and enhancement of the human type also involves a new kind of enslavement."[15]

Finally, there is the difficult question of Nietzsche's relation to war. Elsewhere in "The Greek State" Nietzsche asserted that "through war, and in the military profession, we are presented with a type, even perhaps with the *archetype of the state*," and he went on to argue: "Here we see, as the most general effect of the war tendency, the immediate separation and division of the chaotic masses into *military castes*, from which there arises the construction of a 'war-like society' in the shape of a pyramid on the broadest possible base: a slave-like bottom stratum."[16] There is a specific Greek discourse to Nietzsche's discourse on war. Although Ridley Scott's movie *Black Hawk Down* (2001) opens with a quotation attributed (or misattributed) to Plato, "Only the dead have seen the end of war,"[17] it is perhaps Heraclitus who is more famous for the fragment of his philosophy which states that "war is the father of all things."[18] In turn, this statement needs to be seen in the context of another fragment, which tells us: "They do not comprehend how, in differing, it [= the universe] agrees with itself — [it is] a backward-turning connection, like that of a bow and the lyre."[19] As in war, so in art, Heraclitus tells us, a (productive) tension is everything: the essence of the bow, the essence of the lyre, is tension—in the instrument of warfare, so in the instrument of (artistic) creation. Tension is all.

Likewise, it is against this Heraclitean background that Nietzsche's pronouncements, otherwise so grievously open to misinterpretation, are surely to be understood. For Zarathustra, "it is the good war that hallows every cause"[20]; a saying that is considered worthy of being quoted back to Zarathustra in Part 4.[21] "You should love peace as a means to new wars. And the short peace more than the long"—says Zarathustra, another maxim considered worthy of re-quotation.[22] And why is this the case? Because, in Zarathustra's words, "war and courage have done more great things than charity."[23]

But what kind of a war is Zarathustra advocating? We need to be clear about this. "You should seek your enemy," Zarathustra tells us, "you should wage your war — a war for your own thoughts"—*eure Gedanken*, your opinions, your beliefs.[24] So this is a very particular kind of war; and it is the kind of war of which, in *Twilight of the Idols* (1889), Nietzsche can say that "one has renounced *grand* life when one renounces war."[25] And this is the case, and only the case, because, as Nietzsche tells us, "one is *fruitful* only at the cost of being rich in contradictions."[26] Such a notion of war, then, is intimately bound up with Nietzsche's conception of freedom, expressed in his view that "war is a training in freedom." For "what is freedom?" Nietzsche asks, and he supplies the answer: "That one has the will to self-responsibility"; so "the free man is a *warrior*."[27]

So against this background, one can better understand why, in *Ecce Homo*, Nietzsche says of himself: "I am by nature warlike"—[28] a statement reformulated in his vivid declaration, "I am not a man, I am dynamite."[29] Here, in an apparently prophetic mode, Nietzsche tells us that "there will be wars such as there have never yet been on earth."[30] However, we should note the condition for this prediction—such wars will only take place, "when truth steps into battle with the lie of millennia."[31] This lie is the dual ontology that divides the world into the "real" and the "apparent," upon which the "morality of unselfing" is constructed.[32]

Now this dual ontology is one that, rightly or wrongly, is associated above all with Plato. And nowhere is this more clearly the case than in Nietzsche's writings. It is reflected, for instance, in his presentation of Socrates in his early and in his late writings. In *The Birth of Tragedy* (1872), Nietzsche presents Socrates as a figure who, through the work of Euripides, brings about the end of the tragic culture which Nietzsche so much admires: "This is the new opposition: the Dionysian and the Socratic — and the art of Greek tragedy was wrecked on this."[33] Recalling the account of Socrates's death in the *Apology*, and comparing it with the end of the *Symposium*, Nietzsche claims that "*the dying Socrates* became the new ideal, never seen before, of noble Greek youths: above all, the typical Hellenic youth, Plato, prostrated himself before this image with all the ardent devotion of his enthusiastic soul."[34] In short, Socrates becomes a symbol for "a type of existence unheard of before: the type of the *theoretical man*," and hence an inaugurator of the discipline of science—"once we clearly see how after Socrates, the mystagogue of science, one philosophical school succeeds another, wave upon wave; […] once we see all this clearly, along with the amazingly high pyramid of knowledge in our own time — we cannot fail to see in Socrates the one turning point and vortex of so-called world history."[35] (At the same time, even here Nietzsche wondered whether, if "the hunger for insatiable and optimistic knowledge that in Socrates has appeared exemplary" has turned into "tragic resignation and destitute need for art," then "this 'turning' [will] lead to ever-new configurations of genius"—and introduced the figure of "the *Socrates who practises music*.")[36]

Seventeen years later, in *Twilight of the Idols*, Nietzsche returned to the "problem," as he called it, of Socrates. Referring back to his analysis in *The Birth of Tragedy* of Socrates and Plato as "symptoms of decay, as agents of the dissolution of Greece, as pseudo-Greek, as anti-Greek" (§2), Nietzsche radicalized his critique even further. He rejected Socrates for his ugliness (§3), for his *décadence* (§4), for his dialectics (§5–§6), for his irony (§7), and above all for wanting to die (§12). He recounted the anecdote related in Cicero's *Tusculan Disputations* (Book 4, 37, 80) (and recounted in Lichtenberg's essay "On Physiognomics") of how a foreigner passing through Athens told Socrates that he was a *monstrum* (§3)[37]; cited the words of the dying Socrates in the *Phaedo*, "Crito, we ought to offer a cock to Asclepius" (118a),[38] which Nietzsche interpreted as meaning that "to live — that means to be a long time sick" (§1); and poured scorn on Socrates's confession in his *Apology* about the existence of his "daimonion," "a sort of voice which comes to me, and when it comes to me always dissuades me from what I am proposing to do, and never urges me on" (*Apology*, 81d),[39] describing these "auditory hallucinations" and indeed "everything about him" as "exaggerated, *buffo*, caricature" as well as "hidden, reserved, subterranean" (§4). On Nietzsche's account, Socrates was "the buffoon who *got himself taken seriously*: what was really happening when that happened?" (§5); on this account, Socrates was "a misunderstanding," and "*the entire morality of improvement, the Christian included, has been a misunderstanding*" (§11).

Yet it is not as if Nietzsche never had anything positive to say about Socrates or Plato. In particular, other remarks in Nietzsche's correspondence reveal a fundamental ambivalence in his attitude towards Plato.[40] In a letter to Lou von Salomé in 1882, for instance, Nietzsche told her that "our idea of reducing philosophical systems to the personal deeds of their originators is truly an idea from a 'kindred mind': I myself in Basel related the history of ancient philosophy in *this* way," and he chose Plato as an example of this practice: "I used to like to tell my audience: 'This system is refuted and dead — but the *person* behind it is irrefutable, the person always remains immortal'—for instance, Plato."[41] Thus while, in some sense, Plato's system might be wrong, at the same time, in another sense, Plato *himself* never could be. Then again, in a letter to Franz Overbeck of October 1883, Nietzsche remarks that, while reading a work by a philosopher at Basel, Gustav Teichmüller (1832–1888)—most likely his *The Real and the Apparent World: A New Foundation of Metaphysics* (*Die wirkliche und die scheinbare Welt: Neue Grundlegung der Metaphysik*, 1882) which he had borrowed from Overbeck—he had been struck, or "increasingly dumbfounded with astonishment," by "*how little* I know Plato and **how much** Zarathustra platonizes."[42]

Given all of which, it is not unreasonable to expect even Nietzsche to participate in and contribute to the Platonic discourse in German Political Thought.[43] After all, the opening of Nietzsche's most important work (or the work which Nietzsche regarded as his most important) opens with an astonishing reversal of the motif of Plato's cave. For it begins in a cave, but one which is in every sense the opposite of Plato's. First of all, Zarathustra leaves his home by the lake and goes *into* the cave, before exiting from it ten years later. Then, the cave is not located in subterranean regions, but is up in the mountains. Third, throughout the course of the narrative Zarathustra goes into and out of his cave, as he does at the beginning of Part 2, at the beginning of Part 4, and at the end of Part 4.

Zarathustra not only sees the sun, the symbol of the idea of the Good, but he directly addresses it: "Great star! What would your happiness be, if you had not those for whom you shine! [...] So bless me then, tranquil eye, that can behold without envy even an excessive happiness!"[44] Like the *Republic*, Nietzsche's *Zarathustra* involves an important symbolic imagery of ascent and descent[45]: just as book 1 of the *Republic* opens with Socrates relating how he on the previous day had "gone down" to the Piraeus with Glaucon to pay his devotions to the goddess (i.e., the Thracian deity, Bendis) (327a), and in the allegory of the cave the man who is led out of the cave has to go back down again to liberate the other prisoners (516e–517a; 520c), so Zarathustra has to go down to the market-place.

The market-place is also the setting for Nietzsche's most famous (anti-Christian, anti-Platonic) parable, the parable of "the madman" in §125 of *The Gay Science*. In this parable, where the madman announces that "God is dead," the earth has become "unchained" from its sun, the Platonic symbol of the idea of the Good, and is moving, "perpetually falling," "straying as through an infinite nothing" (§125). So when Zarathustra turns up in the market-place, he does not need to announce that God is dead: although we are reminded of this fact, which is regarded as something to be taken for granted, in his brief conversation with the old saint in the forest (in §2 of the Prologue). Instead, Zarathustra teaches—or tries to teach—the people in the market-place about the Superman. In the *Republic*, the return of the man from the realm outside and above the cave to the prisoners who remain within it "provoke[s] laughter," and the trapped prisoners say that "he had returned from his journey aloft with his eyes ruined and that it was not worth while even to attempt the ascent" (517a).[46]

Likewise, in *Zarathustra* the response of the people in the market-place is to laugh, and to show more interest in the entertainment provided by the tight-rope walker: "Zarathustra [...] fell silent. There they stand (he said to his heart), there they laugh: they do not understand me, I am not the mouth for these ears."[47] In the *Republic*, it is said that the prisoners, if they could lay their hand on the man who tried to release them and lead them up, would "kill him" (517a).[48] Nietzsche's *Zarathustra* perceives a similar menace on the part of the people in the market-place: "And now they look at me and laugh: and laughing, they still hate me. There is ice in their laughter."[49]

Where is the political dimension in all of this? It is true that, in *Thus Spoke Zarathustra*, there is a greater emphasis on a dimension one could call the existential. "Uncanny is human existence and still without meaning: a buffoon can be fatal to it," says Zarathustra in §7 of the Prologue; he adds, "Many things are uncanny: but none more uncanny than man," thus echoing the words of the chorus in the *Antigone*, "There is much that is strange, but nothing that is stranger than human being."[50] Yet there is an explicit engagement with political themes as well. In "Of the New Idol," Zarathustra condemns the state: "The state is the coldest of all cold monsters. Coldly it lies, too; and this lie creeps from its mouth: 'I, the state, am the people.' / It is a lie!"[51] Condemning the state's custodians of culture, newspaper journalists, and the wealthy as "superfluous people" (and describing them as "nimble apes," "clamber[ing] over one another" and "scuffl[ing] into the mud and the abyss"), Zarathustra declares: "Only there, where the state ceases, does the man who is not superfluous begin: does the song of the necessary man, the unique and irreplaceable melody, begin."[52]

In the next chapter, we find an explicit engagement with the world governed by the *ressentiment* fuelled by a competitive, capitalist economy, in "Of the Flies of the Market-Place": "The market-place is full of solemn buffoons — and the people boast of their great men!", Zarathustra declares, and adds: "These are their heroes of the hour."

"Flee, my friend, into your solitude," he urges his audience, "I see you strung by poisonous flies. Flee to where the raw, tough breeze blows! / Flee into your solitude! You have lived too near the small and the pitiable men. Flee from their hidden vengeance! Towards you they are nothing but vengeance."[53]

At the conclusion to *Zarathustra* (at least, as Nietzsche completed the work—further installments were planned), Zarathustra welcomes to his cave a lion, a sign that his time has come and that his "children" are "near," and he leaves his cave, presumably for the last time, "glowing and strong, like a morning sun emerging from behind dark mountains."[54] In this stunning conclusion, the Platonic image of the idea of the Good, i.e., the sun, is, so to speak, eclipsed by the figure of Zarathustra himself; and, to a significant extent, Nietzsche regarded his later writings as commentaries on *Zarathustra*.

For instance, he described *Beyond Good and Evil* (1886) as "saying the same thing" as *Zarathustra*—"but differently, very differently."[55] And perhaps the clearest statement of political critique in Nietzsche's writings is in *On the Genealogy of Morals* (1887), the third section of which is presented as an exegesis of one of Zarathustra's aphorisms. In this passage from *On the Genealogy of Morals*, which has become famous—or even notorious—because it is usually read as being racist, Nietzsche talks about the "blond beast." Now the "blond beast" is first mentioned in the first of Nietzsche's three essays in this work, dedicated to a discussion of the difference between two kinds of moral evaluation, "good and bad" and "good and evil." Here Nietzsche applies the label to the Roman, Arabian, Germanic, Japanese nobility, the Homeric heroes, and the Scandinavian vikings:

[O]nce they go outside where the strange, the *stranger*, is found, they are not much better than uncaged beasts of prey. There they savour a freedom from all social constraints, they compensate themselves in the wilderness for the tensions engendered by protracted confinement and enclosure within the peace of society, they go *back* to the innocent conscience of the beast of prey [...]. One cannot fail to see at the bottom of all these noble races the beast of prey, the splendid *blond beast* prowling avidly in search of spoil and victory; this hidden core needs to erupt from time to time, the animal has to get out again and go back to the wilderness [...].

(GM I §11)[56]

Here, the noble conception of the good is seen as something outside society, outside the state, outside the realm of the political. In his second essay, dedicated to discussion of "'Guilt,' 'Bad Conscience,' and the Like," Nietzsche uses the same image of the blond beast in exactly the *opposite* sense. Here he applies the term to those who have created the state:

> I employed the word "state": it is obvious what is meant — some pack of blond beasts of prey, a conqueror and master race which, organized for war and with the ability to organize, unhesitatingly lays its terrible claws upon a populace perhaps tremendously superior in numbers but still formless and nomad. That is after all how the "state" began on earth: I think that sentimentalism which would have it begin with a "contract" has been disposed of. He who can command, he who is by nature "master," he who is violent in act and bearing — what has he to do with contracts!
>
> (*GM* II §17)[57]

In so writing, Nietzsche rejects Rousseau's account of the social contract, and suggests that the social organisation embodied in the political state is responsible for placing human beings in the chains—or rather the "cage," the "torture chamber" (GM II. 16)[58]—of "bad conscience."

At the same time, we should note that, for Nietzsche, the image of chains does not necessarily have negative connotations. For instance, in aphorism §140 of *Human, All Too Human*, vol. 2, part 2, *The Wanderer and His Shadow*, entitled "Dancing in chains," Nietzsche writes that "with every Greek artist, poet and writer one has to ask: what is the *new constraint* he has imposed upon himself and through which he charms his contemporaries (so that he finds imitators)?", adding: "For that which we call 'invention' (in metrics, for example) is always such a self-imposed fetter." In short, "'dancing in chains,' making things difficult for oneself and then spreading over it the illusion of ease and facility — that is the artifice they want to demonstrate to us."[59] In so writing, Nietzsche is echoing Voltaire's letter to Deodati de Tovazzi of 24 January 1761, where he writes, "you are dancing in liberty and we are dancing in our chains" (*vous dansez en liberté et nous dansons avec nos chaînes*).[60] In terms of the Platonic allegory of the cave, the chains around the prisoners' necks are, so far as Nietzsche is concerned, not so much epistemological chains as moral ones; but the chains in which Nietzsche is really interested are the chains of *aesthetics*, in line with Goethe's motto, "None proves a master but by limitation / And only law can give us liberty" (*In der Beschränkung zeigt sich erst der Meister, / Und das Gesetz nur kann uns Freiheit geben*).[61] These chains, paradoxically, aid in the (aesthetic) construction of the self.

Thus across his writings as a whole, Nietzsche offers an account of modern politics, and this critique should be seen as part and parcel of his critique of Plato's ontology. That critique is at its most explicit in *Twilight of the Idols*, a work whose title likely alludes to Francis Bacon's critique of the "four idols" in book 1 of his *New Organon* (aphorisms 39–68).[62] These four idols are the "idols of the tribe," the "idols of the cave," the "idols of the market place," and the "idols of the theatre"; we might compare these with Nietzsche's own critique of the "four great errors," i.e., the error of mistaking cause for consequence, the error of false causality, the error of imaginary causes, and the error of free will. (Indeed, it is because he is rejecting the idols that Nietzsche subtitles his work, "How to Philosophize with a Hammer," not because he is attacking them with a sledge hammer but rather because, as he puts it in the Preface, the idols are not "idols of the age but *eternal* idols which are here touched with the hammer as with a tuning fork.")[63] On Bacon's account, the idols of the cave are "the idols of the individual man":

The idols of the cave are the illusions of the individual man. For (apart from the aberrations of human nature in general) each man has a kind of individual cave or cavern which fragments and distorts the light of nature. This may happen either because of the unique and particular nature of each man; or because of his reading of books and the authority of those whom he respects and admires; or because of the different impressions things make on different minds, preoccupied and prejudiced perhaps, or calm and detached, and so on. The evident consequence is that the human spirit (in its different dispositions in different men) is a variable thing, quite irregular, almost haphazard. Heraclitus well said that men seek knowledge in lesser, private worlds, not in the great or common world. (Book 1, §42)[64]

On Nietzsche's account, one of the greatest idols not just of the age but of all time is the idol of Plato's cave itself, and the belief in a dual ontology it is used to support. This passage makes elaborate use of an imagery of light which recalls the image of "the most brilliant light of being" in the *Republic*[65] and the image of illumination in the *Seventh Letter*,[66] and in it Nietzsche turns his back on the opposition between a "real" and an "apparent" world:

HOW THE "TRUE WORLD" FINALLY BECAME A FABLE:
History of an Error

1. The true world attainable by the wise, the pious, and the virtuous man, — he lives in it, *he embodies it.*
   (Oldest form of the idea, relatively rational, simple, and convincing. Transcription of the proposition, "I, Plato, *am* the truth.")
2. The true world unattainable at present, but promised to the wise, the pious, and the virtuous man ("to the sinner who repents").
   (Progress of the idea: it becomes more refined, more insidious, more incomprehensible, — it *becomes feminine*, it becomes Christian.)
3. The true world unattainable, undemonstrable, and unable to be promised; but even as conceived, a comfort, an obligation, and an imperative.
   (The old sun still, but shining only through mist and scepticism; the idea become sublime, pale, northerly, Königsbergian.)
4. The true world — unattainable? At any rate unattained. And being unattained also *unknown*. Consequently also neither comforting, saving, nor obligatory: what obligation could anything unknown lay upon us?
   (Grey morning. First yawning of reason. Cockcrowing of Positivism.)

5. The "true" world — an idea neither good for anything, nor even obligatory any longer, — an idea become useless and superfluous; *consequently* a refuted idea: let us do away with it!
(Full day; breakfast; return of *bon sens* and cheerfulness; Plato blushing for shame; infernal noise of all free intellects.)

6. We have done away with the true world: what world is left? perhaps the seeming? … But no! *in doing away with the true, we have also done away with the seeming world!*
(Noon; the moment of the shortest shadow; end of the longest error; climax of mankind; *INCIPIT ZARATHUSTRA*).[67]

Here, we must leave aside the question of the extent to which Plato really is a proponent of dualism,[68] and thus the extent to which Nietzsche's critique of Plato is justified.

For it is clear that Nietzsche plays a crucial role in the German reception of the discourse of Platonism, and in the history of German Political Thought. At the centre of his thought is a passionate cry for the rights—no, for the entitlement—of the individual, or at least the great individual, symbolized and embodied previously in ancient Greek myth in the figure of the hero,[69] and previously in German thought in the figure of the genius,[70] and "reincarnated" by Nietzsche in the figure of the *Übermensch*. Although, in *Zarathustra*, the silent, voiceless voice of "The Stillest Hour" tells Zarathustra, "it is the stillest words which bring the storm" and "thoughts that come on doves' feet guide the world,"[71] and although Zarathustra embraces a view of language as "rainbows and bridges of semblance":

How lovely it is, that there are words and sounds: are not words and sounds rainbows and bridges of semblance between things eternally apart?

To every soul belongs another world; for each soul, every other soul is an afterworld.

Between what is most similar, precisely there semblance tells lies most beautifully; for the smallest gap is the hardest to bridge.

For me — how could there be an outside-me? There is no outside! But we forget this because of sounds; how lovely it is that we forget!

Are not names and sounds given to things, so that humankind might refresh itself with things? Speech is a beautiful folly: with it humankind dances over all things.

How lovely is all speech, and all the lies of sounds! With sounds our love dances on many-hued rainbows,[72]

it was the thunderous pronouncement of the "death of God," a misperception of what it meant to philosophize with a hammer, and the writing in letters so large that even the blind can see,[73] that came to govern the reception of his own work. As one of Nietzsche's greatest readers, Martin Heidegger, put it:

[A] man who teaches must at times grow noisy. In fact, he may have to scream and scream, although his aim is to make his students learn so quiet a thing as thinking. Nietzsche, most quiet and shiest of men, knew of this necessity. He endured the agony of having to scream. In a decade when the world at large still knew nothing of world wars, when faith in "progress" was virtually *the* religion of the civilized peoples and nations, Nietzsche screamed out into the world: "The wasteland grows …".[74]

Heidegger

In Book 2, Chapters 47–53, Thucydides describes how, in the course of the Peloponnesian War, a great plague broke out in Athens. Thucydides, with the kind of tranquil prose that Nietzsche so much admired,[75] describes the course and consequences of this plague in the context of his account of this ancient Greek war which pitted Athens and its empire against the Sparta-led coalition of city-states known as the Peloponnesian League. "People in good health were all of a sudden attacked by violent heats in the head, and redness and inflammation in the eyes, the inward parts, such as the throat or tongue, becoming bloody and emitting an unnatural and fetid breath," recorded Thucydides, going into remarkable and shocking clinical detail about this outbreak that occurred in the summer of 430 BCE, the second year of the war. "The disorder first settled in the head, ran its course from thence through the whole of the body, and even where it did not prove mortal, it still left its mark on the extremities; for it settled in the privy parts, the fingers and the toes, and many escaped with the loss of these, some too with that of their eyes," he wrote, adding: "Others again were seized with an entire loss of memory on their first recovery, and did not know either themselves or their friends."[76]

What Thucydides' account reminds us is that history is full of disturbing events and deeds, and this is no less true of our own time and its recent past: the Holocaust, for instance, but also a plethora of other conflicts and wars, which mean that the twentieth century witnessed about a hundred million deaths: the First World War (1914–1918), the Armenian genocide (1915), the Russian Bolshevik revolution (1917), which gave rise to Leninism and Stalinism with their concentration camps, deportations, organised famines, summary executions, show trials, totalitarian society, thought police, and militarization of everyday life); the response to Marxist-Leninist dictatorship in the form of various European forms of Fascism: the rise to power of Mussolini (1922), Hitler (1933), António de Oliveira Salazar (1933), Franco (1936), and Marshal Pétain (1940); the rise of National Socialism as a racist variation on a fundamentally Fascist theme, leading to the outbreak of the Second World War (1939), the industrialization of death in the extermination camps (1942); the two atomic bombs dropped by the US on Hiroshima, then Nagasaki (1945); the liberation of the Nazi death camps and the discovery of the Holocaust or Shoah (1945).

Then, after the War there was the rise of Soviet imperialism in Eastern Europe and the installation of puppet dictatorships in East Germany, Poland, Czechoslovakia, Hungary, Rumania, and Bulgaria; the First Indochina War (1946–1954); the imitation of Leninism in Chairman Mao's China (1949); the Korean War (1950); the Algerian War (1954); the installation of a Communist regime in Cuba (1959); the system of racial segregation in South Africa (1959–1979); the Second Indochina or Vietnam War (1964–1975); the so-called "cultural" revolution in China (1965); the Generals' coup d'état and the Greek military junta of 1967–1974; the Six-Day Arab-Israeli war (1967); such European terrorism as the Red Brigade in Italy (1970), the Red Army Faction (RAF), initially known as the Baader-Meinhoff Gang in the 1970s in Germany; the US support for military coups d'état in

South America, and in Chile (1973); the Lebanese Civil War (1975); the Khmer Rouge in Cambodia (1975); the Islamic revolution in Iran (1979); the first Iraq war (1991); in the very heart of Europe, the ethnic conflict between the Bosnians and the Serbs (1992); the Rwanda genocide (1994)...[77] In his disturbing study, *Twentieth Century Book of the Dead* (1972), Gil Elliot added up the millions of men, women, and children killed in the conduct of war or by the agents of their own state, and chillingly concluded that one was less likely to be killed in time of war than in peace time.[78]

Placing the Holocaust in this context is, of course, not to relativize the extermination of six million Jews in the concentration camps run by Nazi Germany, nor to lend credence to the growing trend to deny the genocide of the Jews that is known as Holocaust denial.[79] Yet it is possible that this passage from Thucydides could have been used in precisely such a way by Martin Heidegger (1889–1976), one of the most controversial thinkers of the twentieth century. Although best known for his work as an existentialist philosopher (and for having been a member of the National Socialist Party), Heidegger is also a major figure in the tradition of German Political Thought.

At the same time (and by the same token) Heidegger is also a thinker who is closely bound up with the figure of Nietzsche.[80] Brigitte Neske used to relate, so we learn from David Farrell Krell, how the philosophically-inclined book-reading public, on finding a work with two words printed in its spine, *heidegger nietzsche*, did not know exactly what was meant by this: was it *Nietzsche* commenting on *Heidegger*, or *Heidegger* on *Nietzsche*?[81] And according to Hans-Georg Gadamer (1900–2002), in his later years Heidegger used to lament, "Nietzsche has broken me" (*Nietzsche hat mich kaputtgemacht*)—[82] a gnomic remark which suggests, even if in a negative way, the signal importance that Nietzsche held for Heidegger.

That importance is reflected in a series of seminars on Nietzsche given by Heidegger in the 1930s and early 1940s, published in two volumes in 1961.[83] In his lectures on Nietzsche in 1937, Heidegger described Nietzsche's fundamental metaphysical position as constituting nothing less than "the end of metaphysics":

Nietzsche's philosophy is the end of metaphysics, inasmuch as it reverts to the very commencement of Greek thought, taking up such thought in a way that is peculiar to Nietzsche's philosophy alone. In this way Nietzsche's philosophy closes the ring that is formed by the very course of inquiry into being as such and as a whole.[84]

Yet Heidegger is worried by his own definition, asking a series of questions: "Yet can we designate Nietzsche's way of grappling with the commencement of Western philosophy as an *end*? Is it not rather a reawakening of the commencement? Is it not therefore itself a commencement and hence the very opposite of an end?"[85] And so Heidegger prefers to think of Nietzsche's philosophy in relation to the tradition of Western metaphysics as an "accomplishment":

Because Nietzsche's fundamental metaphysical position is at the end of metaphysics in the designated sense, it performs the grandest and most profound gathering — that is, accomplishment — of all essential fundamental positions in Western philosophy since Plato and in the light of Platonism. It does so from within a fundamental position that is determined by Platonism and yet which is itself creative.[86]

So even after Nietzsche there was room for philosophy, and Heidegger regarded himself as occupying this space. In his *Introduction to Metaphysics* (published in 1953 but based on a lecture series given in 1935), Heidegger described his own work of understanding Being as "bringing [Nietzsche's] accomplishment to a full unfolding," and answering the following questions: "Does Nietzsche speak the truth? Or was he himself only the last victim of a long process of error and neglect, but as such the unrecognized witness to a new necessity?"[87]

As the choice of the seminar format to disseminate his ideas about Nietzsche suggests, Heidegger's career was essentially an academic one, and to this extent he forms part of a shift we have observed in German Political Thought from the eighteenth century onward: namely, that it becomes "professionalized," "academicized," and "universitarized." Born in Meßkirch, a small rural town in the south of Baden-Württemberg, in 1889, Heidegger was the son of the sexton (or parish officer) to the local village Roman Catholic church. Although he began his university studies in Freiburg im Breisgau as a student of theology, Heidegger soon switched to philosophy. In 1914 he completed his doctoral thesis, a study informed by Neo-Thomism (i.e., a modern revival of the philosophy of St Thomas Aquinas) and Neo-Kantianism (i.e., a revival of the philosophy of Kant) into the problem of psychologism, or the role of psychology in understanding philosophical issues. And in 1916 he completed his postdoctoral study or *Habilitation* on the thought of the Scholastic philosopher, Duns Scotus.

Heidegger embarked on a career as a university academic. In 1923, he was elected to an extraordinary professorship in philosophy at Marburg, one of Germany's great university towns. In 1927, he published his major philosophical work, *Being and Time* (*Sein und Zeit*), or at least the first part of it; the remainder of it was never published. In 1928, Heidegger was offered the professorship of philosophy at Freiburg, replacing the eminent (Jewish) phenomenologist Edmund Husserl (1859–1938) who had retired from this post. Heidegger was to stay in Freiburg for the rest of his life and his career.

On 21 April 1933, Heidegger was elected Rector of the University—an act often seen as compliance with the new National Socialist regime, given his acquisition of Party membership on 1 May 1938 and his inaugural address of 27 May 1933 (discussed further below). Yet Heidegger held the position of Rector for no more than a year, resigning the post in April 1933; he never resigned his membership of the Party, however.[88]

The nature of Heidegger's response to the rise of the National Socialist Party and to Hitler's appointment as Chancellor on 30 January 1933 can be gauged through two famous remarks apparently made by Heidegger to the philosopher and psychologist Karl Jaspers (1883–1969). Shortly after the Nazi election victory, Heidegger took leave from Jaspers in Heidelberg to return to Freiburg, remarking: "One has to join in."[89] And when, dining with Jaspers later in 1933, Jaspers asked Heidegger, "How shall a person as uneducated as Hitler rule Germany?", Heidegger is said to have replied, "Education does not matter. You should just see his wonderful hands!"[90] Curiously, after meeting the Führer in 1936, the British historian Arnold Toynbee (1889–1975) is also said to have remarked: "He has beautiful hands."[91] But could Heidegger have been thinking of a passage in Nietzsche's *Daybreak*, where Nietzsche has the following—for him, in some respects surprisingly positive—remarks to make about, of all people, Catholic priests?

> From [the spirit of countless people who joy in submission], and in concert with the power and very often the deepest conviction and honesty of devotion, [Christianity] has *chiselled out* perhaps the most refined figures in human society that have ever yet existed: the figures of the higher and highest Catholic priesthood, especially when they have descended from a noble race and brought with them an inborn grace of gesture, the eye of command, and beautiful hands and feet.[92]

(Whether one can think of Hitler's hands as being in any way particularly attractive is not something that can be decided here.)

In the postwar period, Heidegger was forbidden to teach by the French occupation authorities in charge of south-eastern Germany. He was the subject of denazification procedures until March 1949, when he was declared a sympathiser or *Mitläufer* of the regime, although no disciplinary or other measures were imposed. The winter semester of 1950–1951 saw Heidegger resume his teaching at the University of Freiburg, where he was granted emeritus status. Although he ceased regular teaching in 1958, he continued to give private seminars: such as the Zollikon Seminars, held at the private residence of the psychotherapist Medard Boss from 1959 to 1969; or the seminars held together with the French poet René Char at Le Thor (in 1966, 1968, and 1969) and in Zähringen (in 1973); or his seminar on Heraclitus, held with Eugen Fink in 1966–1967.

In the course of the twentieth century, Heidegger exercised a decisive influence on a number of thinkers, particularly in France.[93] That influence was exercised both through his writing and on a personal (sometimes, very personal) level.

In 1917, Heidegger had married Elfride Petri (1893–1992), but he is known to have conducted extramarital relationships with some of his students, including Hannah Arendt (1906–1975) and with Elisabeth Blochmann (1892–1972). (In one of her *Essays in Understanding*,

Hannah Arendt describes Heidegger as a fox: a fox, she says, who was "so lacking in shyness that he not only kept getting caught in traps but couldn't even tell the difference between a trap and a non-trap" and who, "in his shocking ignorance of the difference between traps and non-traps," decided to build "a trap as his burrow.")[94] The fact that Arendt was Jewish, and Blochmann was a Protestant of Jewish descent,[95] shows how complex and complicated it is to accuse Heidegger of anti-Semitism: an issue which has recently been raised again in the light of the publication of his *Black Notebooks*, a series of personal and reflective journals written by Heidegger between 1931 and 1941. But then, almost everything about Heidegger, not least his philosophy, is complicated: including his relation to Platonism and his role in the tradition of German Political Thought.

According to Hans-Georg Gadamer, after Heidegger had resigned from his position as rector of the University of Freiburg, one of his friends saw him in a tram and greeted him with the following question, "Back from Syracuse?"[96] The allusion here is to the attempt—and failure—to convert a tyrant to philosophy: in Plato's case, the tyrant Dionysius the Younger (or Dionysius II) of Syracuse, and in Heidegger's case the National Socialist regime. In the *Seventh Letter*, a text attributed to Plato, we find an account of how Plato "put it to the proof whether Dionysius was really all on fire with philosophy or whether the frequent reports that had come to Athens to that effect amounted to nothing" (340b):

> Now there is an experimental method for determining the truth in such cases that [...] is truly appropriate to despots, especially those stuffed with secondhand opinions, which [...] was very much the case with Dionysius. One must point out to such men that the whole plan is possible and explain what preliminary steps and how much hard work it will require, for the hearer, if he is genuinely devoted to philosophy and is a man of God with a natural affinity and fitness for the work, sees in the course marked out a path of enchantment [...]. As for those, however, who are not genuine converts to philosophy, but have only a superficial tinge of doctrine [...] as soon as they see how many subjects there are to study, how much hard work they involve, and how indispensable it is for

the project to adopt a well-ordered scheme of living, they decide that the plan is difficult if not impossible for them [...]. (340b–341a)

"This test," Plato observed, "proves to be the surest and safest in dealing with those who are self-indulgent and incapable of continued hard work," and so, alas! it turned out to be in the case of Dionysius II. Failing to turn to Dionysius into the philosopher-king envisioned in the *Republic*, Plato failed in his attempt to convert the tyrant to Platonic philosophy, and to bring about the moment he describes in the *Seventh Letter* in the following terms: "Aquaintance with [the subject of philosophy] must come rather after a long period of attendance on instruction in the subject itself and of close companionship, when, suddenly, like a blaze kindled by a leaping spark, it is generated in the soul and at once becomes self-sustaining" (341d).[97]

Can we read Heidegger's interventions in the form of his rectoral address and in his lecture series of 1933–1934 entitled *On the Essence of Truth* as just such an experimental preliminary testing of his German listeners and the German nation for the philosophical task that, in Heidegger's view, lay before it?

The Germans and the Greeks

Heidegger's relation to the Greeks in general and to Plato in particular helps clarify the relation between the discourse of Platonism and the tradition of German Political Thought. As Mark Ralkowski has pointed out, the nineteenth century had seen a revival of interest in Platonism,[98] thanks to Friedrich Schleiermacher (1768–1834), a translator and commentator of Plato.[99]

At the beginning of the nineteenth century, the German Romantic writer and critic Friedrich Schlegel (1772–1829) decided to embark on the major project of making a new translation of the entire works of Plato. To help in this task, he chose the young theologian and biblical scholar Schleiermacher, who was at that time, like Schlegel, living in Berlin. In the end, Schleiermacher ended up bearing almost sole responsibility for the project, which led to the publication of *Platons*

Werke in 6 volumes (vols. 1–5, 1804–1810; vol. 6, the *Republic*, 1828). Writing to the publisher Georg Andreas Reimer (1776–1842) in June 1803, Schleiermacher gloomily commented, "In fifty years someone else will probably do it better,"[100] but in fact his translation was to become an authoritative one, not just for his generation but into the present day. According to Wilhelm Dilthey (1833–1911), "through [Schleiermacher's translation] the knowledge of Greek philosophy first became possible,"[101] an amazing statement about the impact of Schleiermacher's work, undertaken on the basis of an impetus provided by Schlegel.

Why was Schleiermacher's translation so important? In part, because he moved the discourse around Platonism in Germany away from two schools, the sceptical and the esoteric, and towards a philological understanding. Let us briefly consider these two approaches rejected by Schleiermacher and examine what he proposed to put in its place. First, Schleiermacher rejected the view that Plato was "more of a dialectician than a logical philosopher, more desirous of contradicting others, than capable of, or caring to produce, a well-founded structure of his own"— in other words, that Plato was a sceptic. As far as Schleiermacher was concerned, this approach is "founded on nothing, and explains nothing, but leaves the whole problem as it was before."[102] But second, he also rejected those esoteric readings of Plato that regard the dialogues merely as the remnants of the "lost riches of Platonic wisdom," as a system to which we no longer have any access.[103] Instead, Schleiermacher proposed a reading of Plato based on the twin principles of inseparability and systematicity: in other words, in the dialogues artistic form and philosophical content belong inseparably together,[104] and the entirety of Plato's thinking can be completely disengaged from those dialogues.[105] Moreover, Schleiermacher's approach was an eminently philological one, based on a close analysis of Plato's language, and an attempt to "feel where and how Plato is cramped by [his language], and where he himself laboriously extends its grasp",[106] and reflecting the assumption of the renaissance in German philology at the end of the eighteenth century that, in Julia Lamm's words, "only a German, and only the German language, could uncover the soul of the classics."[107]

In particular, this final interpretative principle was to be influential on Heidegger, who is reported as asserting that only two languages are suitable for philosophizing, ancient Greek and German; and who went so far as to say that, when the French begin to think seriously, they have to switch to German.[108] This aspect of Heidegger's view of the relation between modern Germany and ancient Greece has been caricatured by Glenn W. Most when he writes that "Heidegger's Greeks are Greeks in *Lederhosen*"; or indeed, because of the ultimately Roman inspiration of Heidegger's idealized projection of specifically German virtues, "Heidegger's Greeks may be described as being Germans in togas."[109] In the summer semester of 1924, in his lecture course on Aristotle, Heidegger urged that "we need to win back the sense of rootedness and autochthony [*Bodenständigkeit*] that was alive in Greek philosophy."[110] In his *Basic Problems of Phenomenology* (1927), Heidegger offered an elegant variation on a passage from Kant's *Critique of Pure Reason*[111]: "We not only want to, but also must understand the Greeks better than they understood themselves."[112] And in the summer semester of 1930, Heidegger asserted that "only our German language has a deep and creative philosophical character to compare to the Greek":

> *Ousía tou ontos* means in translation: the beingness of being [*Seiendheit des Seienden*]. We say, on the other hand: the being of beings [*Sein des Seienden*]. "Beingness" is a very unusual and *artificial* linguistic form that occurs only in the sphere of philosophical reflection. We cannot say this, however, of the corresponding Greek word. *Ousía* is not an artificial expression which first occurs in philosophy, but belongs to the everyday language and speech of the Greeks. Philosophy took up the word from its pre-philosophical usage. If this could happen so easily, and with no artificiality, then we must conclude that the *pre-philosophical* language of the Greeks was already *philosophical*. This is actually the case. The history of the basic word of Greek philosophy is an exemplary demonstration of the fact that the *Greek language is philosophical*, i.e., not that Greek is loaded with philosophical terminology, but that it philosophizes in its basic structure and formation. The same applies to every genuine language, in different degrees to be sure. The extent to which this is so depends on the depth and power of the people who speak the language and exist within it.[113]

And Heidegger went on in a footnote to point to two figures who, in his view, bore out the validity of this assertion—the medieval German theologian and mystic, Meister Eckhart (c. 1260–1328),[114] and Hegel. What we find, then, in Heidegger's use of the discourse of Platonism is a reflection of a longstanding belief in Germany about its relation to ancient Greece, including and preeminently Plato.

Over the period of his intellectual development between 1923 and 1943, Heidegger's thinking is (on Theodore Kisiel's account) informed by three main concepts that can be labelled the phenomenological, the metontological, and the archaic-poetic. What these terms mean, and the texts from which Heidegger derives his thinking associated with them, has been discussed by Kisiel[115] and is summarized by him in the form of the table in Fig. 8.1[116]:

To be precise, Heidegger brings these three conceptual schemes to bear on the notion of the *polis* and of the political, and in the period of 1933–1935 on which we shall focus here his argumentation revolves around an interpretation of Plato's *Republic*.

If one of the main characteristics of Heidegger's thought is the consistency of his engagement with the discourse of Platonism, this is also reflected in comments to be found in his correspondence from this time. Writing to Jaspers on 8 December 1932, Heidegger remarked: "The little that is my own becomes more and more hazy to

	Period	Basic Text	Basic Concepts
Phenomenological	1923-1925	Aristotle, *Rhetoric*	pathos, ethos, logos of doxic speech situation
Metontological	1933-1935	Plato, *The Republic*	leader of people, guardians of state, 3-levelled service
Archaic-Poetic	1935-1943	Sophocles, *Antigone*	polemos of thinker, poet, and statesman as prepolitical

Fig. 8.1 Main concepts in Heidegger's thinking

me in this keen air."[117] And writing to Elisabeth Blochmann on 19 December 1932, Heidegger confessed: "The more strongly I get into my work, the more securely I am invariably forced back into the great beginnings among the Greeks. And frequently I hesitate over whether it would not be more essential to abandon all my own attempts and merely make sure that this world does not become only a pale tradition, but that it once more stands before our eyes in its exciting greatness and exemplariness."[118] Looking back on this period overy twenty years later, Heidegger told Hannah Arendt in a letter of 10 October 1954: "I would like to begin my Plato studies with [the lectures on] the *Sophist* (of 1924–1925), to go through it again, and to read Plato anew."[119]

In that lecture course on the dialogue *The Sophist*, placed among Plato's late dialogues, we can see (as Drew A. Hyland has noted) how Heidegger, still under the influence of Husserl's phenomenology, interprets such Greek thinkers as Plato and Aristotle as preparing the way for philosophy understood as "scientific research in the phenomenological mode."[120] Hyland evaluates this lecture course as "a remarkable and remarkably important text," and as being one of Heidegger's "most thorough" studies of Greek philosophy as well as an "important precursor" to his main *opus, Being and Time.*[121]

In his seminar on Plato's *Sophist*, Heidegger begins by remarking that, in this dialogue, Plato "considers human Dasein in one of its most extreme possibilities, namely philosophical existence."[122] By displaying what the sophist is, i.e., as being a non-philosopher, Plato "shows indirectly what the philosopher is." And Plato does so, Heidegger argues, not simply saying what one would have to do in order to be a philosopher, but he shows it "by actually philosophizing."[123]

This actual philosophizing involves vision, or *theoria*; but on Heidegger's account, this vision involves not just the way one sees things, but how one is in the world—it involves Dasein or our way of Being-in-the-world. As Heidegger puts it, "*theoria* is a mode of Being in which man attains his highest mode of Being, his proper spiritual health."[124] In his study based on his first lecture course of 1931–1932 called *On the Essence of Truth* (published 1988), Heidegger expresses this idea in the following terms: "The questioning which penetrates through to the *highest* idea is [...] simultaneously a questioning down into the deepest perceiving possible for man as an existing being," since it involves "a questioning of the history of man's essence that aims at understanding what empowers being and unhiddenness," i.e., *alētheia*.[125] In support of this reading, Heidegger cites the *Seventh Letter* in which Plato says: "*Only then is the perceiving of essence unfolded, the perceiving that stretches as far as possible, namely as far as the innermost capacity of man reaches*" (344b), or as another translation of this passage from this disputed text renders it, "After practicing detailed comparisons of names and definitions and visual and other sense perceptions, after scrutinizing them in benevolent disputation by the use of question and answer without jealousy, at last in a flash understanding of each blazes up, and the mind, as it exerts all its powers to the limit of human capacity, is flooded with light."[126] As Mark Ralkowksi points out, what Heidegger does in his seminar is to "phenomenologize" the doctrine of "perfectionism" found in Aristotle. That is to say, one does not contemplate the means to becoming happy in *theōria*, or as Aristotle puts it in his *Nicomeachean Ethics*, "wisdom will contemplate none of the things that will make a man happy (for it is not concerned with any coming into being)"[127]; rather, *theōria* itself literally *is* happiness, because it is *theōria* that is the activity that fulfils the human function and condition.[128] This thinking ties in with Heidegger's understanding of freedom in a political and a philosophical sense (and, for him, these senses are inseparable). For in his lecture series *On the Essence of Truth* he argues—to use entirely non-Heideggerian, even un-Heideggerian, language—that happiness is bound up with duty, or in other words: with being true to one's own self. Whether that self is conceived in an individual or on a national level is something that must be now be considered.

In this chapter, Heidegger's role in the tradition of German Political Thought is examined chiefly with reference to the following texts: his rectoral address of 1933, and his lecture course at the University of Freiburg in the winter semester 1933–1934, *On the Essence of Truth*. The title of this lecture course, in which Heidegger examined Plato's allegory of the cave in the *Republic* and his *Theaetetus* dialogue, recalls an earlier, stand-alone lecture first given in 1930 under the title

"The Essence of Truth" (first published in 1943 and subsequently in 1967 in a collection of essays under the title *Pathmarks* [in German, *Wegmarken*]).[129] In that essay, Heidegger offers a definition of truth, not as correspondence (or what Aquinas called *adaequatio intellectūs et rei*, Kant "the agreement of knowledge with its subject," and logical positivists "empirical verifiability"), but as *alētheia* (variously translated as "unconcealedness," "unclosedness," or "disclosure").[130] But he also, as Theodore Kisiel has pointed out, revealed "[a] 'German-conservative' emphasis on freedom as binding obligation, an emphasis which is muted in the first published version of 1943."[131]

In so writing, Kisiel is highlighting the intellectual connections between Heidegger and the so-called Conservative Revolutionary movement, a movement that had its roots in the work of, for example, Paul de Lagarde (1827–1891) and Julius Langbehn (1851–1907), and that was associated especially with Arthur Moeller van den Bruck (1876–1925).[132] In 1921 the novelist Thomas Mann (1875–1955), who himself swung from conservative to more progressive thought, had applied the notion of "conservative revolution" to describe the outlook of Nietzsche, describing it in the following terms: "Its synthesis is one of Enlightenment and faith, of freedom and obligation, of flesh and God, 'God' and 'world.' It is, expressed aesthetically, one of sensuousness and criticism; politically expressed, one of conservatism and revolution. For conservatism only needs to have spirit [*Geist*] to be more revolutionary that any positivistic, liberalist Enlightenment, and Nietzsche himself was from the very beginning, already in his *Untimely Meditations*, nothing other than conservative revolution."[133] But for Heidegger, it seems, the more important link was less with Nietzsche and more with Plato: in 1942, on the basis of his lecture course entitled *On the Essence of Truth* given at Freiburg in the winter semester of 1930–1931, he published an essay in a journal called *Geistige Überlieferung* with the title "Plato's Doctrine of the Essay of Truth"; he reissued this, together with another short text called "Letter on Humanism," in 1947.[134] And the notes of this lecture course confirm how Heidegger now placed Plato at the centre of his philosophical—and, by the same token, his political—thinking.

The *Rektoratsrede*

Following his election to the Rectorship of the University of Freiburg on 21 April 1933, on 27 May 1933 Heidegger gave his rectoral address, entitled "The Self-Assertion of the German University."[135] Subsequently, Heidegger himself was to write a short essay, entitled "The Rectorate 1933/34: Facts and Thoughts," when his rectoral address was republished in 1983.[136] His response at the time to the rise of National Socialism is reflected in his *Black Notebooks* but also in his correspondence. In a letter to Elisabeth Blochmann of 30 March 1933, for instance, Heidegger wrote:

> The current events have for me — precisely because so much remains obscure and uncontrolled — an extraordinarily concentrative power. It intensifies the will and the confidence to work in the service of a grand mission and to cooperate in the building of a world grounded in the people. For some time now, I have given up on the empty, superficial, unreal, thus nihilistic talk of mere "culture" and so-called "values" and have sought this new ground in *Da-sein*. We will find this ground and at the same time the calling of the German people in the history of the West only if we expose ourselves to be-ing itself in a new way and new appropriation. I thereby experience the current events wholly out of the future. Only in this way can we develop a genuine involvement and that *in-stantiation* [*Inständigkeit*] in our history which is in fact the precondition for any effective action.[137]

In this same letter to Blochmann, Heidegger claimed that the Germans had to prepare themselves for "a second, a more profound revolution."[138] How should we understand this remark? On Charles Bambach's account, "caught in the mood of euphoric self-renewal [...] Heidegger [...] interpreted the events of early 1933 not as a political transfer of power, but as an epochal shift within being itself, a radical awakening from the slumbers of Weimar politics as usual."[139] Or as Rüdiger Safranski dramatically phrases it, Heidegger "interpreted the 1933 revolution as a collective outbreak from the cave."[140]

At the end of his rectoral address, Heidegger signalled his indebtedness precisely to the discourse of Platonism by citing the following line from the *Republic*. In discussion with Adeimantus about the dangers of Sophism and the smallness of the group of real philosophers, Socrates remarks: "For all great things are precarious and, as the proverb truly says, 'fine things are hard'" (497d).[141] Or as Heidegger translates it (*ta ... megala panta episphale*), "all that is great stands in the storm" (480). The significance of this line for Heidegger is given by its immediate context, where Socrates declares that one of his themes in this dialogue is "the manner in which a state that occupies itself with philosophy can escape destruction."

As this allusion to the *Republic* suggests, the theme of Heidegger's rectoral address is the role of the philosophy in the state, not the university. In effect, Heidegger was telling his colleagues and students: ask not what the state can do for the university, ask what the university can do for the state. After his introductory remarks to the effect that he was seeking to give "*spiritual* leadership" to the university in his capacity as its rector, Heidegger quoted a line from Aeschylus's drama, *Prometheus Unbound* (l. 514), which Heidegger translated as "knowing, however, is far weaker than necessity," and glossed as follows: "All knowing about things has always already been delivered up to overpowering fate and fails before it" (472). In fact, his entire rectoral address is a meditation on the relation between knowledge—between knowing, science (or scholarship [*Wissenschaft*]), or theory (*theoria*)—and necessity. Or as Heidegger resoundingly asserted: "Science is the questioning holding of one's ground in the midst of the ever self-concealing totality of what is. This active perseverance knows, as it perseveres, about its impotence before fate" (473). What, in more concrete terms, did this mean?

What it did *not* mean was a defence of "academic freedom" as conventionally understood, i.e., as freedom to teach and to research independent of political interference. Such freedom is, Heidegger said, "not genuine," because it was "only negative" (476). Instead, science (or scholarship [*Wissenschaft*]) had, in Heidegger's view, to become "the fundamental happening of our spiritual being as part of a people" (474). And it had to face up to "the forsakenness of modern man in the midst of what is," a situation captured by Nietzsche when, in his parable of the madman in *The Gay Science* (§125), he had declared, "God is dead" (474).

So what it *did* mean was aligning (cf. the German term, *Gleichschaltung*) science (or scholarship [*Wissenschaft*]) with three bonds, embodied in the *Neues Studentenrecht* that was to be proclaimed on 1 May 1933 and would seek to organize students according to the *Führerprinzip* and to integrate German universities into the National Socialist state. Those three bonds were the bond to "the community of the people"; the bond to "the honour and destiny of the nation"; and the bond to "the mission of the German people" (476). In turn, the three bonds to the people, to the destiny of the state, and to its spiritual mission, equated to three services (*Dienste*): to the labour service (*Arbeitsdienst*), the armed service (*Wehrdienst*), and the knowledge service (*Wissensdienst*). Was Heidegger referring to the National Socialist programme of organised labour, militarization, and pedagogical *Gleichschaltung*? Or was he referring to the three stands or classes of Plato's *Republic*, the workers, the soldiers, and the philosopher-kings?[142]

Going beyond Plato, Heidegger went on to argue that these groups or services needed to "primordially coalesce and become *one* formative force" (*ursprünglich zu* einer *prägenden Kraft sich zusammenfinden*) (478), and this could only happen through battle or struggle (*Kampf*), i.e., "all faculties of will and thought, all strengths of the heart and all skills of the body, must be unfolded *through* battle, heightened *in* battle, and preserved *as* battle" (479). Well, the Third Reich would undoubtedly provide the members of Heidegger's audience with plenty of opportunities for struggle or battle: and the storm that Heidegger evoked in his final quotation from Plato's *Republic* became a horrifying reality when the consequences of Goebbel's famous cry, "Do you want total war?" (*Wollt ihr den totalen Krieg?*), led to the death and destruction of the Second World War.

On the Essence of Truth

Heidegger first gave a lecture course entitled "On the Essence of Truth" in the winter semester of 1931–1932 at Freiburg[143]; from 7 November 1933 to 27 February 1934, he repeated the course in a revised form.[144] Now this repetition and revision followed on the lecture course given in the summer semester of 1933, "The Fundamental Question of Philosophy." Given that Heidegger had been intensively lecturing on the topic of truth for about a decade,[145] this choice comes as no surprise, but it is the fact that he held this version of the course in a particular historical and political context that determines the decision to examine it here.

In his introductory remarks at the outset of the course, Heidegger addressed "the question of essence" (*ousía*) as "insidious and unavoidable." What is "essential," he argued, is what is "bound into the law and structure of beings" (70). As abstract as this sounds, Heidegger foregrounded the existential aspect of this question. "In the ordinary hustle and bustle," he continued, "a human being — indeed, often an entire people — chases and hastens after arbitrary objects and opportunities," but such human beings (or such a people) need(s) to grasp that the reverse is the case: "To create and to awaken *fundamental moods* through *originary courage* — [...] then all things become visible, decidable, and endurable," he declared. Heidegger described this as "the courage for what is originary as one's own" (70).

Analysing the famous fragment (DK 22 B 53) of Heraclitus which states that "war [or struggle] is the father of all things," and restating it as meaning that "essence essences: as struggle" (76), Heidegger turns to a consideration of two different models of truth: truth as correctness, and truth as unconcealment (in Greek, *alētheia*; in German, *Unverborgenheit*).[146] To illustrate the kind of truth in which he is interested, Heidegger gives the following examples of the kind of truths in which he is *not* interested: for instance, "2 and 1 is 3," "the earth orbits the sun," "winter follows autumn," "on 12 November the German people will cast the vote that determines its ownmost future" (i.e., the plebiscite on Germany's withdrawal from the League of Nations), "Kant is the greatest German philosopher," "there is noise in the street" (demonstrations and marches...?), "this lecture hall is heated." These are all, Heidegger says, *individual truths* (78).

The model for this kind of truth is *correctness*. But Heidegger is interested in a different kind of truth, in the "true" truth, in the truth of *alētheia* or *Unverborgenheit*. He approaches this kind of truth through a long digression on language (80–92). The most important thing about language, he argues, is not words, but silence. "Keeping silent is the origin and ground of language," he claims (84 and 86; cf. 87, 88), and one wonders about the political resonances of the importance he attaches to remaining silent …

At this point, Heidegger finally turns his attention to Plato and to the allegory of the cave in book 7 of the *Republic*, which he describes as "the single centre of Platonic philosophizing" (97). For Heidegger, the allegory of the cave is a myth, a *mūthos*, that reveals a truth, a *lógos*, and he reads this as "a sign that we stand in a decisive transition here, *decisive for two thousand years*" (97). And he underscores that his reading of the allegory of the cave is, in his eyes, not a mere exercise in philological interpretation, "a matter of introducing the techniques and mastering the methods for interpreting Platonic dialogues," but something far more significant—"it is a matter of *awakening and carrying out the question of the essence of truth*" (98). He drove home this point to his audience in the following way, by telling them that "authentic understanding of the *mūthos*" did not depend on how well (or how badly) they understood Greek, or how much (or how little) they knew about Plato; rather, it depended on whether they were ready to take seriously "the fact that you are sitting here in the lecture hall of a German university — that is, whether something unavoidable, something that has an enduring effect, speaks to you in the story of the underground cave that is to be interpreted" (98). So Heidegger was doing much more than simply giving a lecture: he was educating the German *Volk* about its historical destiny. And he was doing so through the discourse of Platonism.

How does Heidegger read the allegory of the cave? He divides it into four stages, viz. (1) the realm of shadows; (2) the realm of fire; (3) the realm of light; (4) the return to the shadows. The various elements of Heidegger's appropriation of Plato's cave allegory can be summarized, as Mark Ralkowski has done, in the form of a table in Fig. 8.2[147]:

In the first stage (514a–515c), the stage of the human being in the subterranean cave, Heidegger sees "the everyday situation of man" (105). It is, he says, "the situation of man in everydayness, insofar as he is given over to idle talk, to the customary, what lies closest at hand, the everyday, business as usual" (105–106). In *Being and Time*, Heidegger had offered extensive phenomenological analysis of all these

Elements of the allegory	Plato's interpretation	Heidegger's interpretation
Realm of the shadows	Sensibles	Entities
The fire	*Doxa*	Dasein/World
Realm of light	Forms	Being of beings
The light itself	The Good	Being as such

Fig. 8.2 Heidegger's appropriation of Plato's cave allegory

things: of *das Gerede* (idle talk), for instance, or *die Neugier* (curiosity), *die Zweideutigkeit* (ambiguity), *das Verfallen* and *die Geworfenheit* (falling and thrownness), *Angst* (anxiety), or *Sorge* (care).[148] What happens to us in "everydayness," in "the press of things"? We "lose" ourselves, we "forget" ourselves, Heidegger says (106). Or to put it in the language of Heideggerian philosophy: we do not understand what is *unconcealed* in the cave.

In the second stage (515c–515e), we begin to learn something about this unconcealment, as the human being is "liberated" within the cave. By removing the chains which bind the prisoners by leg and neck, one of them is able to turn round and look at the fire. This is, Heidegger says, "not some arbitrary event, but a happening that touches the *essence of human beings*" (108). Yet the removal of chains is not the whole truth: after all, the human being is still in the cave. But "something is happening now with unconcealment," it is "start[ing] to *move*, so to speak" (108).

Heidegger describes this first liberation as an "external liberation," but taking away those chains is "*not an actual liberation*" (110). There must be another, a further liberation, which "take[s] hold of the man in his *own Being*," "change[s] his inner condition," changes his "will" (110). For Heidegger, this question must be posed: "How must we think the essential connection between *the Being-free of humans* and their *relationship to light, concealment, and unconcealment* if we want to grasp the *inner essential structure of truth* as such?" (110).

So the third stage (515e–516e) involves this "authentic liberation," a liberation not to the light of the fire but to the "originary light." As Heidegger observes, this liberation is a transition to the unconcealed, and it involves *violence*. Liberation, Heidegger underscores, "demands effort," and it is here that "what is distinctive about *Greek* Dasein comes to light" (113). For Heidegger, violence—reflected in the way the man from the cave is dragged out (and up)—is necessary, because the Dasein of the Greeks is "a great, immense *struggle* with the most immense and darkest powers"; as he puts it, "liberation is no walk in the park" (113). Leaving aside the political implications of this emphasis on struggle and on violence, is there another political dimension to this reading of the allegory of the cave? Indeed there is—the connection between "light" and "idea," a connection regarded by Heidegger as "a fundamental element — indeed, [...] the *fundamental constitution*"—of the West. First, because Plato's doctrine of the ideas prepared the way for the Christian concept of God. Second, because it helped form the modern concept of reason and hence natural science. And third, because these two aspects—that is, rationalism and the idea of God—fused in the thinking of Hegel, who "completed Western philosophy" by "reconstructing the Greek world in a Christian way" (115).

In turn, these three developments are said to lead to three more recent ones. First, to Marxism and its doctrine of ideologies, which can (according to Heidegger) only be understood "on the basis of Hegel"; second, to Kierkegaard and his "new interpretation" of Christianity; and third, as a fusion and "innocuous blend[ing]" of these two ideas, to the "cultural philistinism" that drove Nietzsche to despair (115–116). At this point Heidegger pauses to point out the threefold significance of Nietzsche: as someone who struggles with humanism, as someone who struggles with a "baseless Christianity," and as someone who struggles with the Enlightenment (116). And it is this struggle, "the urgency of the[se] circumstances," "this tremendous moment" into which, according to Heidegger, National Socialism "is being driven today," into "the coming to be of a *new spirit of the entire earth*" (116).

So for Heidegger there is an important link between what is happening politically in Germany and with what Plato calls the journey to "the place above the heavens." Schematically, Heidegger presents his understanding of the allegory of the cave as "a sensory image of human Dasein" in the table in Fig. 8.3:

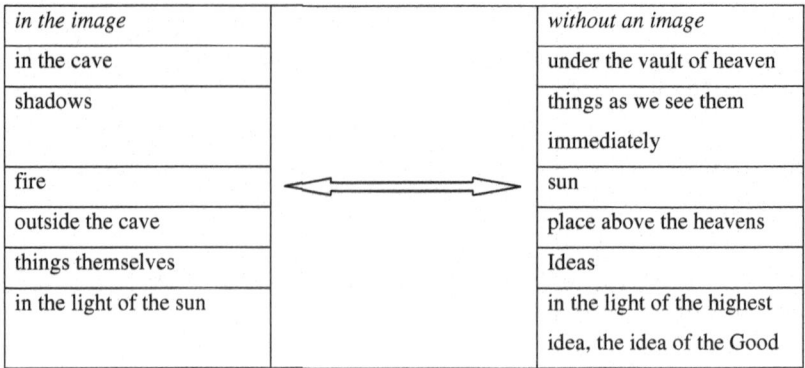

in the image		without an image
in the cave		under the vault of heaven
shadows		things as we see them immediately
fire	⟵——————⟶	sun
outside the cave		place above the heavens
things themselves		Ideas
in the light of the sun		in the light of the highest idea, the idea of the Good

Fig. 8.3 Plato's allegory of the cave as "sensory image of human Dasein"

It is in the doctrine of ideas that the influence of the Platonic system lies, or so Heidegger argues. Without the idea, no God; without the idea, no natural science; without Christian and rationalist thought, no Hegel; without Hegel, no Marxism (cf. 118). As far as Heidegger is concerned, to do philosophy is also to do politics, for Marxism "cannot be defeated once and for all unless we first confront the doctrine of ideas and its two-millennia-long history" (118).

To understand what the "idea" means for Plato, Heidegger embarks on a detailed consideration of "light" as the "sensory image" of the idea (120), and examines how our concept of cognition is oriented around "seeing" and "light"; after all, *theoría* (i.e., theoretical cognition) means nothing other than "looking," and in Christian thought (for instance, in St Augustine) God is conceived as *lumen* and human beings are endowed with the *lumen naturale* (i.e., the natural light of reason) (120).

Via the etymological link in German between *Helle* (i.e., brightness, clarity) and *Hallen* (i.e., resounding), Heidegger points out the connection between the visible and the audible, between looking and listening. And it is with Aristotle, Heidegger argues, that *hearing* comes to rule over Greek Dasein just as ideas and seeing do. In this part of Greek tradition, discourse is a "defining moment for the essence of human beings" (123). To hear, Heidegger suggests, is not just to listen, but it involves listening to someone else—"hearing a summons, lending an ear to a wish, listening to an order, assignment, and so on" (123). So it is in this context that Heidegger interprets Aristotle's famous definition of the human being as the "political animal" (*Politics*, 1.2), not as meaning that the human being is a "social being," but rather that the human being is "the sort of living being that belongs from the start to a *with-one-another in the state*"—which is a very different interpretation from the usual one (123).

In fact Heidegger's interpretation of the allegory of the cave turns out to be an unusual one. For it turns on the question of how one understands freedom. The second and third stages of the allegory with their respective forms of liberation show, Heidegger argues, that "*to be free is not to be released from something but to be led forth to something*" (124). Freedom involves not being free *from*, but free *for something*—to become free for the light. We must become free for the light, we must become "habituated" to it, we must bind ourselves to it: freedom is about binding oneself to the light. "Binding oneself to the light is what liberates," Heidegger concludes, "binding oneself in this way is the highest relation to freedom, is being-free itself" (125). As we have seen elsewhere in the tradition of German Political Thought, freedom is about not being free at all …

In a sense, Plato anticipates this conclusion when, in the allegory of the stage, he introduces the fourth stage (516e–517a): the return and descent of the liberated man back down into the cave. Not least because at this point Plato introduces the notion that the liberator, who is responsible for liberating the human beings from the cave through acts of violence, faces the prospect of being killed—of being paid back with "an overpowering counter-violence" (139). So *who* is this liberator?

In Heidegger's view, the liberator is not the politician; it is the philosopher. To understand the task of the philosopher, Heidegger turns to the *Sophist* dialogue, where Plato defines the philosopher as someone "whose thoughts constantly dwell upon the nature of reality" and who is "difficult to see because his region is so bright, for the eye of the vulgar soul cannot endure to keep its gaze fixed on the divine" (254a).[149] For Heidegger, it is the philosopher who climbs out of the cave, who gets used to the light, and who returns to the cave as the liberator of the prisoners—exposing himself to the fate of death, much as Socrates suffered death through drinking the cup of hemlock. To think that philosophers have a good life, sitting in their room and thinking their thoughts, is to misunderstand what philosophers do—and to betray a "superficial way of thinking" (140).

When he goes back down into the cave, the liberator or philosopher recognizes that although there is a certain unconcealment in the cave, what is unconcealed at the same time *covers up* genuine unconcealment: the prisoners cling to the shadows, mistaking them for the figures carried in front of the fire. Similarly, the *alētheia* outside the cave "conceals" the reality outside. In a startling reversal of most interpretations of the allegory, Heidegger argues that what the liberator or philosopher now realizes is that "in unison with unconcealment, *concealment, semblance*, and *deception* happen and must happen" (142). In so doing, the liberator gains insight into "the necessity of liberation" and realizes that "this liberation cannot lead to some tranquil enjoyment and possession outside the cave, but that unconcealment happens in history, in the constant confrontation with the false and with semblance" (142). In other words, the insight into the necessity of liberation is the liberating effect of the insight into necessity; and the realm of the necessary concealment, semblance, and deception is History.

From this analysis Heidegger derives three key conclusions. First, there is "no *truth in itself*," but rather "truth *happens*"—and it happens "in the innermost confrontation with *concealment* in the sense of *disguise* and *covering up*" (142). Second, the individual human being (insofar as he exists) is "thrust into relations on the basis of which beings and the world are revealed to him," and in this sense man *is* the truth. Third, humankind also exists as "a historical people in community," and so the human being "exists in the truth and in the untruth, in concealment and unconcealment *together*" (142). Hence to uncover the truth involves confrontation and struggle; and the process and outcome of this confrontation and this struggle is History:

> [...] The human being engaged in struggle must first of all decide for reality in *such a way* that the truly determinative forces of Dasein will *illuminate* the history and reality of a people and bring Dasein into them. Reality cannot provide the people with a place to stand; instead, spirit

and the spiritual world of a people develop within history. History is not fulfilled in a time frame that ends in 1934 or 1935 — maybe not until 1960. (142)

Such then is Heidegger's grim reading of the allegory of the cave, introduced by Socrates as "[a] compar[ison] [of] our nature in respect of education and its lack" (514a). The word used here, *paideía*, is sometimes translated in German as "education" (*Erziehung*) or "cultivation" (*Bildung*) or "formation of Greek humanity" (*Formung des griechischen Menschen*) (as Werner Jaeger [1888–1961] called it).[150] Heidegger offers a new translation, and it is not a particularly snappy one: *paideía* means "the *inner binding-fast of human Dasein on the basis of the steadfastness that holds fast* to what fate demands" (158). Its opposite, the lack of education, means "failure, powerlessness, not standing fast" (158)— the reverse of the Plato quotation in the rectoral speech! As a result, Heidegger comes up with a clear definition of philosophy: it is *not* a cultural phenomenon, *not* an opportunity for personal development, *not* an area of scholarship, *not* a worldview, and *not* a standpoint created for an individual human being. So what *is* philosophy? According to Heidegger, it is "a *fundamental happening in the history of humanity itself* [...] which has the character of a quite *distinctive questioning* [...] *in which and through which the essence of humanity transforms itself*" (159). Or to put it another way, philosophy is politics.

An example of the kind of politics in which Heidegger wishes to intervene and of the kind in which he does not is provided by Erwin Guido Kolbenheyer (1878–1962), an Austrian writer who had written a trilogy about Paracelsus (*Die Kindheit des Paracelsus*, 1917; *Das Gestirn des Paracelsus*, 1922; *Das dritte Reich des Paracelsus*, 1926), published a theoretical work (*Die Bauhütte*, 1925) which urged its readers to turn away from Judeo-Christianity, and had increasingly become seen as an artistic spokesman for the National Socialist regime. On 29 January 1934, Kolbenheyer had been in Freiburg, giving a speech on "The Value for Life and Effect on Life of Poetic Art in a People" (*Lebenswert und Lebenswirkung der Dichtkunst in einem Volke*).[151] The following day, 30 January 1934, Heidegger took the opportunity in his lecture course to make some trenchant comments about Kolbenheyer.

For Heidegger, Kolbenheyer was "the prime example of a contemporary cave dweller," someone who was "bound to the shadows" and took them as "the only definitive reality and world" (159–160). Heidegger rejected Kolbenheyer's—and, by extension, National Socialism's—outlook, based as it was on *biology*; instead, Heidegger insisted on the importance of *history*. Yet he saw the significance of history in terms of his own philosophical ontology, arguing that the "fundamental modes of conduct of historical man"—i.e., "engagement of action, responsibility in endurance and persistence, courage, confidence, faith, the strength for sacrifice"—are possibly "only on the basis of *freedom*," but freedom in the specific sense as which we have seen it defined above. Rejecting in this way Kolbenheyer, as well as rejecting Freud and Marx (161), Heidgger's remarks make it clear that while he supported the cause of National Socialism, he was no by means an average Nazi supporter. For Heidegger, National Socialism was all about "truly seeing and grasping today's *historical-political German reality*"—and about "shap[ing] the *historical-political reality* so radically in all domains of Dasein that the *new necessities of Being come to have effect and take shape without falsification*" (161). So, for Heidegger, National Socialism was nothing to do with biology, with economics, or even with nationalism, but was about finding a way out of Plato's cave.

In other words, for Heidegger National Socialism was a philosophical project, and what "this essential history of man" in the allegory of the cave teaches is that "the transformation in the individual stages" is not "the mere turning of a potsherd in the hand" but "an exit from night-like day into the real day"—and thus it is "philosophizing" (165). For Heidegger, Western civilization had arrived at a moment when it could reverse the identification of truth with "the assimilation of thinking and seeing" and go back to the notion of truth as "openness" (*alētheia*). On this account, truth is "a *happening*," and this happening involves "pulling one out of the cave, assailing the concealed, tearing beings out of concealment" (170).

On the one hand, Heidegger's account of Western history suggests it has been a giant mistake: the confusion of truth as correspondence with truth as unconcealment (*alētheia*). On the other hand, he proposes a counter-history, beginning with Homer, in which a "driving force within it" moves humankind towards the *"liberation of [humankind] to the essence of his Being"*: a counter-history that involves the foundation of the Greek city-state (the *polis*), Greek culture (religious ritual, tragedy, architecture), and "the awakening of *philosophy*" (171). Yet it also involves the movement of National Socialism under the direction of the Führer, not in the sense of "promulgating this or that slogan," but in the sense of bringing about "a *total transformation*, a *projection of a world,*" on the basis of which the Führer "educates the entire people" (171–172). On this account, the task of National Socialism was to turn the whole of Germany—and even the whole of Europe—into a university lecture-hall; more precisely, into a gigantic Heideggerian seminar on Plato.

Before moving on to the second part of his lecture course *On the Essence of Truth* and to an analysis of Plato's *Theaetetus*, Heidegger offered a clarification of three fundamental concepts: "untruth" (*pseũdos*), "forgetting" (*léthe*), and "unconcealment" (*à-létheia*) and its opposite, "concealment" (*létheia*). For Heidegger, an untruth does not simply mean getting something wrong, it means "twisting," "distorting," "turn[ing] the thing around in such a way that it is not seen as it really is" (173). And "concealment" is etymologically (and conceptually) related to "forgetting," as the ancient Greek for "I remain concealed," *léthe, látho, lantháno*, suggests. And for an example of "forgetting" as a kind of "remaining concealed," Heidegger turned to Thucydides and his account of the great plague in Athens. That final line from book 2, §49, "Others again were seized with an entire loss of memory on their first recovery, and did not know either themselves or their friends," was translated by Heidegger as "others were overcome, right after an initial recovery, by the remaining-hidden [*Verborgenheit*] of all beings," or "the remaining-hidden of all things befell them" (cf. 174).

For Heidegger, the physiological symptoms of the plague—the horrible sickness, the retching, the spasms, diarrhoea, and death—were less important than the "forgetting" experienced on recovery. No wonder, then, Heidegger had nothing to say about the horrors of totalitarianism, the murder of the Jews in the concentration camps, and the destructiveness of the Second World War. In his Bremen lectures of 1949, Heidegger was even able to use the Holocaust to offer a critique of factory farming, arguing that "agriculture is now a motorized food industry — in essence, the same as the manufacturing of corpses in gas chambers and the extermination camps, the same as the blockading and starving of nations, the same as the manufacture of atom bombs."[152] It seems that, for Heidegger, the worst thing about National Socialism was that it had "forgotten" its mission to lead the Germans out of the cave and into the liberating light of its historical destiny.

What's in a Name? Psychoanalytic Connotations

The enormity of the Holocaust and the Second World War threatens to overwhelm our comprehension, so one way to approach Heidegger's relation to twentieth-century German politics could be through psychoanalysis. For example, in a study of Freud in relation to politics entitled *De l'élection*, the Quebec-born psychoanalyst René Major provides an example of just such an approach. In the opening paragraph of this study he sets out his ambition to understand how a group (be it the Jews, be it the Germans) comes to think of itself as a chosen people, selected for a great mission, and how an individual (be it Hitler, be it Heidegger) might come to regard himself as destined to be the leader of this people, and how this decision might be unconsciously reflected in his name:

> In crucial moments of history, an unexpected coincidence of a society's loss of symbols and the overweening temptation of a man embodying those symbols in his name will always assume the form of an apocalypse. Wearing a party mask, the face of death soon reveals its grinning features. The archaic dreams of a people, even the most advanced, intertwines with a mad mission undertaken by a man to produce in reality the erased trace of his own history. Such a conjunction can shape the contours of a social insanity to which one can only submit unless one can prevent it.[153]

Consequently, Major's study revolves around the idea of the *nom propre* as "uncovering in reality the imaginary characteristics of the hidden name" (57).

He points out, for instance, that the surname of Adolf Hitler was particularly conflicted in this way, thanks to his problematic patrilineage. His father was the illegitimate child of a peasant woman called Maria Schickelgruber. She had been employed as a housekeeper in a Jewish family called Frankenberger, or so Hitler's personal lawyer, Hans Frank, was to declare during the Nuremberg Trials. (There is no evidence for this hypothesis.) Until he was in his forties, Hitler's father was known as Alois Schickelgruber, i.e., his mother's name, at which point he changed his name to Hitler, sometimes spelled *Hiedler, Hüttler,* or *Huettler.* Now if his father had not changed his name, Adolf would have been called Adolf Schickelgruber—the erasure of this repressed name would return with force in the real, Major argues, with its echoes of the gravedigger (*Gruber*): I "send" (*schicke*) "into the grave" (*in die Grube*), while to *grübeln* or *Grübeln haben* means to have "obsessive thoughts." Similarly, *Hitler* or *Hüttler* contains the word *Hütte,* meaning the Tabernacle of the ancient Jews, the shrine housing the Ark of the Covenant and other sacred objects, before the construction of the Temple. Would history have been the same, Major wonders, if the crowds had cried out, not *Heil Hitler,* but *Heil Schickelgruber* (56–57)?

Back to Heidegger. How are the "significances which are not necessary for identification by the *nom propre*" associated "in a cryptic way" with "thought or ideology" where they are preserved "as signifiers, i.e., as proper to the imaginary but not demarcated as such" (77)? If "the imaginary characteristics of the name weave the thread of a discourse without the symbolic power of the name bringing in discrimination of what is similar and what is dissimilar and without the referent itself becoming disconnected as something foreign" (77), what can this tell us about Heidegger? In his study *Crowds and Power* (*Masse und Macht,* 1960), Elias Canetti (1905–1994) pointed out how the forest (*Heide*) and the army (*Heer*) can become combined in a political imaginary (here attributed to the Germans), so that the forest became a symbol of the army (72–73).[154] In the rectoral address, there is nothing pagan or unbelieving associated with the word for the gentile (*der Heide*). Nevertheless, the fact that the word *die Heide* can mean forest or land acquires another sense, allied with the word *Heer* or "army," when it comes to symbolize, in a reduplicated way, the German nation and what (after the

First World War) the Treaty of Versailles sought to disempower for good (77). Is there a relation, Major wonders, between *Heidegger's* own name (together with its "imaginary characteristics") and his outlook on the National Socialist revolution in his rectoral address?

In his analysis of this address, Major points out how the original Greek, *episphalè*, meaning "unstable," "tottering," or "risky," is translated in German as *Sturm*, meaning not just "tempest" but also a tumult of passions or emotions, i.e., agitation, discontent, revolution (64). He also focuses on the passage where Heidegger declares that "*this* science"—i.e., Heidegger's specific politico-philosophical conception of *Wissenschaft*—"is meant when the essence of the German university is delimited as the 'high' school that, grounded in science, by means of science educates and disciplines the leaders and guardians [*die Führer und Hüter*] of the fate of the German people" ("Self-Assertion," 477; cf. *De l'élection*, 78). Evidently, the term *Führer* recalls the designation applied to Adolf Hitler, while *Hüter* recalls the *Hütte* or "hut," "booth," "tabernacle," associated with the Jewish people (79).

Towards the end the rectoral address, the allusion to Plato and the saying, "all that is great stands in the storm" (*alles Grosse steht im Sturm*), together with Heideggert's enunciation of the principle that "all leading must grant the body of followers its own strength" (*alle Führung muß der Gefolgschaft die Eigenkraft zugestehen*) and the quotation from Carl von Clausewitz (1780–1831), the author of *On War* (*Vom Krieg*), "I take leave of the frivolous hope of salvation by the hand of accident" (*ich sage mich los von der leichtsinnigen Hoffnung einer Errettung durch die Hand des Zufalls*) ("Rectoral Address," 479), brings together three strands. First, there is the motif of *die Führer und Hüter* (with its echoes of *Hütte*, "tabernacle"). Second, there is the element of "chance" or "accident" (*Zufall*) implicit in the Greek word *episphalè*, with its connotations of risk and hazard. And third, there is the motif of a kind of tempest, tumult, or agitation, associated with the word *Sturm*, which recalls the title of the weekly Nazi tabloid with its vehemently anti-Semitic and genocidal propaganda, *Der Stürmer* (79–80). Against this semantic and psychoanalytic background, the discourse of Platonism in Heidegger's rectoral address and its concluding paragraphs acquires a strange, new, and unsettling resonance.

The "Spiegel" Interview

Notoriously Heidegger never apologized for his role in the Third Reich, as limited as it was. In 1967 the poet Paul Celan (1920–1970) visited Heidegger at his "hut," his small country lodging, in Todtnauberg in the Black Forest.[155] He visited him, so he recorded in a poem, in the spirit of "a hope, today, / of a thinking man's / coming / word / in the heart" (*einer Hoffnung, heute, / auf eines Denkenden / kommendes / Wort / im Herzen*)[156]; but this hope, it seems, was in vain.

Heidegger never apologized—but he did try to explain. In 1966, Heidegger granted an interview to the German news magazine *Der Spiegel*, on the condition that it only be published after his death. (Similarly, Heidegger placed an embargo on his *Black Notebooks*, stipulating that they were to be the last volumes published in the collected works of the *Gesamtausgabe*.) On 31 May 1976, five days after Heidegger had died on 26 May 1976, the interview was published and soon became a sensation. Its notoriety derives in part from the headline under which it appeared, which quoted Heidegger directly: "Only a god can save us."[157]

In this interview conducted by Rudolf Augstein and Georg Wolff (a former SS troop-leader and secret agent), Heidegger was challenged on his record as a Nazi sympathiser through his tenure as Rector at Freiburg. Heidegger defended himself against all the charges. When asked about the line in his address, "The much celebrated 'academic freedom' is being banished from the German university; for this freedom was not genuine, since it was only negative" (475–476), Heidegger explained this remark as follows. First, he stood by his remark: "This academic 'freedom' was only too often a negative one: freedom *from* the effort to surrender oneself to what a scientific study demands in terms of reflection and meditation" (48). Second, he argued that it had to be seen in context. That context, as Augstein and Wolff pointed out, was his praise for "the splendour and the greatness of this setting out [*dieses Aufbruchs*]" (480), which could easily be read as a reference to Hitler's designation four months earlier as Chancellor. Heidegger agreed, explaining that at the time he saw "no alternative," and comparing his own reaction to the rise of National Socialism to the position held earlier by the German liberal politician and Protestant minister, Friedrich Naumann (1860–1919), a proponent in his book *Mittleuropa* (1915) of German nationalism, and to the contemporary response of the German philosopher and psychologist, Eduard Spranger (1882–1963).[158] By "self-assertion," Heidegger argued, he meant "the task of winning back a new meaning for the university, in opposition to its merely technical organization, through a reflection upon the tradition of Western European thought" (49).

As the interview unfolded, so Heidegger seized the opportunity to propose his critique of modern Western civilization: "Everything is functioning. That is precisely what is awesome, that everything functions, that the functioning propels everything more and more toward further functioning, and that technicity increasingly dislodges man and uproots him from the earth" (56). He pointed to the first pictures of earth that had recently been taken from the moon[159] as evidence of how "uprooted" humankind had become. On Heidegger's account, we are all now so lost in the forms and structures of technology and instrumental thinking that we do not even realize we are lost.[160] Consequently Heidegger conceded that even philosophy could no longer propose a solution. Philosophy, he argued, "will be unable to effect any immediate change in the current state of the world," and "this is true not only of philosophy but of all purely human reflection and endeavour"—for this reason, "only a god can save us" (57).

For some this is a shocking abnegation of the task of the philosophy, which is to think the impossible, including the impossibility of thinking the Holocaust. Yet for Heidegger, it is an inevitable conclusion, given his view that we have failed to escape the cave. In terms of the discourse of Platonism, National Socialism had failed to deliver on its promise to liberate us from the cave. For Heidegger, there now seemed to be no further prospect of ever finding the exit. We might be able to send satellites into space (and, in 1969, even send men to the moon), but we are trapped more than ever in the cave. Other thinkers, however, are not so sure. And for another thinker in the German tradition who takes a more positive view of the future of humankind, we can look to the contemporary philosopher, Jürgen Habermas, who belongs to the third generation of a set of thinkers known as the Frankfurt School.

Notes

1. Gottfried Benn, "Nietzsche — nach fünfzig Jahren" [1950], in Dieter Wellershoff (ed.), *Gesammelte Werke* (Wiesbaden: Limes, 1968), vol. 4, 1046–1057 (1046).
2. Raymond Furness, *Zarathustra's Children: A Study of a Lost Generation of German Writers* (Rochester, NY and Woodbridge: Camden House, 2000).
3. "Why I am a Destiny," §7, §8, §9; in Nietzsche, *Ecce Homo*, trans. R.J. Hollingdale (Penguin: Harmondsworth, 1992), 101–104.
4. For further discussion of Nietzsche in relation to politics, see Simone Goyard-Fabre, *Nietzsche et la question politique* (Paris: Éditions Sirey, 1977); Mark Warren, *Nietzsche and Political Thought* (Cambridge, MA, and London: MIT Press, 1988); Bruce Detwiler, *Nietzsche and the Politics of Aristocratic Radicalism* (Chicago and London: University of Chicago Press, 1990); Paul Patton (ed.), *Nietzsche, Feminism and Political Theory* (London and New York: Routledge, 1993); Keith Ansell-Pearson, *An Introduction to Nietzsche as a Political Thinker* (Cambridge: Cambridge University Press, 1994); David Owen, *Nietzsche, Politics, Modernity* (London: Sage, 1995); Christian J. Emden, *Friedrich Nietzsche and the Politics of History* (Cambridge: Cambridge University Press, 2008); and Hugo Drochon, *Nietzsche's Great Politics* (Princeton, NJ and Oxford: Princeton University Press, 2016).
5. See Richard Wolin, *The Seduction of Unreason: The Intellectual Romance with Fascism from Nietzsche to Postmodernism* (Princeton, NJ and London: Princeton University Press, 2004).
6. For a left-wing/libertarian reading of Nietzsche, see Michel Onfray, *La Sagesse tragique: Du bon usage de Nietzsche* (Paris: Le Livre de poche, 2006); and *La Construction du surhomme [Contre-histoire de la philosophie, vol. 7]* (Paris: Grasset, 2011), 175–338; for the case against, see Aymeric Monville, *Misère du «nietzschéisme de gauche»: De Georges Bataille à Michel Onfray* (Brussels: Aden, 2007).
7. Geoff Waite, *Nietzsche's Corps/e: Aesthetics, Politics, Prophecy, or: The Spectacular Technoculture of Everyday Life* (Durham, NC and London: Duke University Press, 1996).
8. Bernhard H.F. Taureck, *Nietzsche und der Faschismus: Ein Politikum* (Leipzig: Reclam, 2000).

9. See "Aus meinem Leben" [1863], in Friedrich Nietzsche, *Werke in drei Bänden*, ed. Karl Schlechta (Munich: Hanser, 1966), vol. 3, 107–110 (107).

10. For a beautifully illustrated account of Nietzsche's travels, see David Farrell Krell and Donald L. Bates, *The Good European: Nietzsche's Work Sites in Word and Image* (Chicago and London: Chicago University Press, 1997).

11. *The Anti-Christ*, "Foreword," in Nietzsche, *Twilight of the Idols and The Anti-Christ*, trans. R.J. Hollingdale (Harmondsworth: Penguin, 1968), 114.

12. *The Anti-Christ*, §2; trans. Hollingdale, 116.

13. Alexandre Lacroix, "Phrase choc," *Philosophie Magazine* 1 (avril-mai 2006), 61.

14. Nietzsche, "The Greek State," in Nietzsche, *On the Genealogy of Morality*, ed. Keith Ansell-Pearson, trans. Carol Diethe (Cambridge: Cambridge University Press, 2007), 164–173 (166).

15. Nietzsche, *The Gay Science*, §377, "We Who Are Homeless," in Nietzsche, *The Gay Science*, trans. Walter Kaufmann (New York: Random House, 1974), 338. One might compare Nietzsche's thinking with the principle enunciated in Friedrich Theodor Vischer's satirical novel, *Auch Einer* (1879): "Service, sir, service! That's it! The moral principle should be: 'Thou shalt serve!' But who can understand that, if you only see individual beings and, behind them, Nothing? If you do not notice that the deeds and actions of the many have carved out something that stands over and above them — an upper storey, lasting ordinances, eternal laws, to serve which is pure pleasure, because this service elevates the servant into timelessness?" (F.T. Vischer, *Auch Einer: Eine Reisebekanntschaft* (Stuttgart and Leipzig: Deutsche Verlags-Anstalt, 1900), 32–33).

16. Nietzsche, "The Greek State," in Nietzsche, *On the Genealogy of Morality*, 172.

17. For discussion of Plato's thinking about war, see Henrik Syse, "Plato: The Necessity of War, the Quest for Peace," *Journal of Military Ethics* 1, no. 1 (2002), 36–44.

18. Diels-Kranz 22 B 53; cf. *Early Greek Philosophy*, trans. Jonathan Barnes (Harmondsworth: Penguin, 1987), 102.

19. Diels-Kranz 22 B 51; *Early Greek Philosophy*, 102.

20. Nietzsche, *Thus Spoke Zarathustra*, trans. R.J. Hollingdale (Harmondsworth: Penguin, 1969), "Of War and Warriors," 74.

21. "Conversation with the Kings," §2; *Thus Spoke Zarathustra*, trans. Hollingdale, 260.

22. "Of War and Warriors", *Thus Spoke Zarathustra*, trans. Hollingdale, 74; cf. "Conversation with the Kings," §2; *Thus Spoke Zarathustra*, 260.

23. "Of War and Warriors"; *Thus Spoke Zarathustra*, trans. Hollingdale, 74. Cf. *Beyond Good and Evil*, §229: "Almost everything we call 'higher culture' is based on the spiritualization of *cruelty*, on its becoming more profound: this is my proposition. That 'savage animal' has not really been 'mortified'; it lives and flourishes, it has merely become — divine" (*Basic Writings of Nietzsche*, ed. and trans. Walter Kaufmann (New York: The Modern Library, 1968), 348).

24. Cf. "Of War and Warriors"; *Thus Spoke Zarathustra*, trans. Hollingdale, 74.

25. "Morality as Anti-Nature," §3; *Twilight of the Idols*, trans. Hollingdale, 44.

26. "Morality as Anti-Nature," §3; *Twilight of the Idols*, trans. Hollingdale, 44.

27. "Expeditions of an Untimely Man," §38; *Twilight of the Idols*, trans. Hollingdale, 92.

28. "Why I am so wise," §7; *Ecce Homo*, trans. Hollingdale, 16.

29. "Why I am a Destiny," §1; *Ecce Homo*, trans. Hollingdale, 96.

30. "Why I am a Destiny," §1; *Ecce Homo*, trans. Hollingdale, 97.

31. "Why I am a Destiny," §1; *Ecce Homo*, trans. Hollingdale, 97.

32. "Why I am a Destiny," §7; *Ecce Homo*, trans. Hollingdale, 102. According to Nietzsche, "*you were born and kept in the lies of the good*," but now, thanks to him, "everything hitherto called 'truth' is recognized as the most harmful, malicious, most subterranean form of the lie" (§4 and §8 [99 and 103]).

33. *The Birth of Tragedy*, §12; *Basic Writings*, 82.

34. *The Birth of Tragedy*, §13; *Basic Writings*, 89.

35. *The Birth of Tragedy*, §15; *Basic Writings*, 97.

36. *The Birth of Tragedy*, §15; *Basic Writings*, 98.

37. "When Zopyrus, who professed to know the character of every one from his person, had heaped a great many vices on him in a public assembly, he was laughed at by others, who could perceive no such vices in Socrates; but Socrates kept him in countenance by declaring that such vices were natural to him, but that he had got the better of them by his reason" (Cicero, *Tusculan Disputations*, trans. C.D. Yonge (New York: Harper, 1877), 161).

38. Plato, *The Collected Dialogues*, ed. Edith Hamilton and Huntington Cairns (Princeton, NJ: Princeton University Press, 1989), 98.

39. Plato, *Collected Dialogues*, 17.

40. For further discussion of Nietzsche's relation to Plato, see Jean-François Mattei, *L'ordre du monde: Platon, Nietzsche, Heidegger* (Paris: Presses universitaires de France, 1989); Thomas Brobjer, "Nietzsche's Wrestling with Plato and Platonism," in Paul Bishop (ed.), *Nietzsche and Antiquity: His Reaction and Response to the Classical Tradition* (Rochester, NY: Camden House, 2004), 241–259; John Sallis, *Platonic Legacies* (Albany, NY: State University of New York Press, 2004); Mark Anderson, *Plato and Nietzsche: Their Philosophical Art* (London: Bloomsbury, 2014); Monique Dixsaut, *Platon-Nietzsche: L'autre manière de philosopher* (Paris: Fayard, 2015); and Paul Bishop, "Free the Spirit! Kantian, Jungian and Neoplatonic Resonances in Nietzsche," in Rebecca Bamford (ed.), *Nietzsche's Free Spirit Philosophy* (London and New York: Rowman & Littlefield International, 2015), 207–232.

41. Letter to Lou von Salomé of 16 September 1882; in Nietzsche, *Sämtliche Briefe: Kritische Studienausgabe*, ed. Giorgio Colli and Mazzino Montinari, 8 vols (Munich, Berlin and New York: dtv; de Gruyter, 1986), vol. 6, 259.

42. Letter of Nietzsche to Franz Overbeck of 22 October 1883; Nietzsche, *Sämtliche Briefe*, vol. 6, 449.

43. Nietzsche's relation to the discourse of Platonism is ripe for reconsideration, just as his relation to German Idealism has recently been reappraised: see Katia Hay and Leonel R. dos Santos (eds), *Nietzsche, German Idealism and its Critics* (Berlin and Boston: de Gruyter, 2015).

44. Nietzsche, *Thus Spoke Zarathustra*, trans. Hollingdale, 39.

45. For the discussion in Plato of the ascent to the Beautiful and the Good, see *Symposium*, 210a–212c; *Phaedrus*, 243e–257b; and *Republic*, 514a–518b.

46. Plato, *Collected Dialogues*, 749.

47. Nietzsche, *Thus Spoke Zarathustra*, trans. Hollingdale, 45.

48. Plato, *Collected Dialogues*, 749.

49. Nietzsche, *Thus Spoke Zarathustra*, trans. Hollingdale, 47.

50. Sophocles, *Antigone*, l. 332–333: "Many the wonders but nothing walks stranger than man" (David Grene and Richmond Lattimore (eds), *Greek Tragedies*, vol. 1 (Chicago and London: University of Chicago Press, 1960), 192. This passage also caught the interest of

Heidegger; see the passage in his *An Introduction to Metaphysics*, also available as "The Ode on Man in Sophocles' *Antigone*," in Thomas Woodward (ed.), *Sophocles: A Collection of Critical Essays* (Eaglewood Cliffs: Prentice, 1966), 86–100. For further discussion, see Dennis J. Schmidt, *On Germans and Other Greeks: Tragedy and Ethical Life* (Bloomington and Indianapolis: Indiana University Press, 2001), chapter 6, "Heidegger," 225–270.

51. Nietzsche, *Thus Spoke Zarathustra*, trans. Hollingdale, 75.
52. Nietzsche, *Thus Spoke Zarathustra*, trans. Hollingdale, 77.
53. Nietzsche, *Thus Spoke Zarathustra*, trans. Hollingdale, 79.
54. Nietzsche, *Thus Spoke Zarathustra*, trans. Hollingdale, 336.
55. Nietzsche, letter to Jacob Burckhardt, 22 September 1886; *Sämtliche Briefe: Kritische Studienausgabe*, vol. 7, 254.
56. Nietzsche, *Basic Writings*, 476–477.
57. Nietzsche, *Basic Writings*, 522.
58. Nietzsche, *Basic Writings*, 521.
59. Nietzsche, *Human, All Too Human*, trans R.J. Hollingdale (Cambridge: Cambridge University Press, 1986), 343. For further discussion of the centrality of this idea to Locke, Hegel, and especially Nietzsche, see Joshua Foa Dienstag, *"Dancing in Chains": Narrative and Memory in Political Theory* (Stanford, CA: Stanford University Press, 1997), esp. Chapters 3 and 4, "The Reveries of the Solitary" and "The Future of Pain" (77–139).
60. Voltaire, *Lettres choisies*, ed. Louis Moland, 2 vols (Paris: Garnier, 1876), vol. 1, 426; in his copy of this work, Nietzsche marks this passage and underlines the word *chaînes* (Giorgio Colli and M. Montinari, *Kommentar zu den Bänden 1-13* [*KSA*, vol. 14] (Munich, Berlin, and New York: dtv; de Gruyter, 1988), 192–193).
61. See the poem "Nature and Art" (*Natur und Kunst*), written c. 1800 and published 1807; in Johann Wolfgang von Goethe, *Selected Poems*, ed. Christopher Middleton (Boston: Suhrkamp/Insel, 1983), 164–165, translated by Michael Hamburger.
62. See Walter Kaufmann's note in *The Portable Nietzsche*, ed. and trans. Walter Kaufmann (New York: Viking Penguin, 1968), 463.
63. Nietzsche, Foreword, *Twilight of the Idols*, trans. Hollingdale, 22.
64. *The New Organon*, book 1, "Aphorisms on the Interpretation of Nature and on the Kingdom of Man," §42; in Francis Bacon, *The New Organon*, ed. Lisa Jardine and Michael Silverthorne (Cambridge: Cambridge University Press, 2000), 41. See Heraclitus, DK 22 B 2:

"For that reason you must follow what is common [i.e., what is universal—for 'common' means 'universal']. But although the account [*logos*] is common, most men live as though they had an understanding of their own" (Jonathan Barnes, *Early Greek Philosophy* (Harmondsworth: Penguin, 1987), 101).

65. Compare with Socrates's exposition of the allegory of the cave in the *Republic*, where he talks about "the contemplation of essence and the brightest region of being" (*Republic* 518c; in Plato, *Collected Dialogues*, 751; translated by W.H.D. Rouse as "the sight of being and the most brilliant light of being," in *Great Dialogues of Plato*, ed. Eric H. Warmington and Philip G. Rouse (New York: Mentor, 1956), 317), or those passages in Plotinus where he talks about the experience of the One as pure light and divine radiance, for example, in "On the Good, or the One": "Then of it and of itself the soul has all the vision that may be — of itself luminous now, filled with intellectual light, become pure, subtle and weightless. It has become divine, is part of the eternal that is beyond becoming" (*Enneads*, 6.9.9; in *The Essential Plotinus*, ed. and trans. Elmer O'Brian (Indianapolis, IN: Hackett, 1964), 86); or in "On the Intellectual Beauty," when he writes of the gods in the realm of pure intellect (*nous*): "To 'live at ease' is There; and to these divine beings verity is mother and nurse, existence and sustenance; all that is not of process but of authentic being they see, and themselves in all: for all is transparent, nothing dark, nothing resistant; every being is lucid to every other, in breadth and depth; light runs through light" (*Enneads*, 5.8.4; in *The Enneads*, trans. Stephen MacKenna, abridged John Dillon (Harmondsworth: Penguin, 1991), 414).

66. "The study of virtue and vice must be accompanied by an inquiry into what is false and true of existence in general and must be carried on by constant practice throughout a long period [...]. Hardly after practising detailed comparisons of names and definitions and visual and other sense perceptions, after scrutinizing them in benevolent disputation by the use of question and answer without jealousy, at last in a flash understanding of each blazes up, and the mind, as it exerts all its powers to the limit of human capacity, is flooded with light" (*Letter VII*, 344b; in *Collected Dialogues*, 1591. See Monique Dixsaut, "Platon, Nietzsche et les images," in Jean-Claude Gens and Pierre Rodrigo (eds), *Puissances de l'image* (Dijon: Editions universitaires de Dijon, 2007), 11–24 (22).

67. Friedrich Nietzsche, *The Case of Wagner; Nietzsche Contra Wagner; The Twilight of the Idols; The Antichrist*, trans. Thomas Common (London: Unwin, 1899), 124–125. For Heidegger's reading of this passage, see "Nietzsche's Overturning of Platonism," in Martin Heidegger, *Nietzsche: Volumes 1 and 2*, trans. David Farrell Krell (New York: HarperCollins, 1991), vol. 1, *The Will to Power as Art*, 200–210.

68. Although a two-world view is conventionally ascribed to Plato, it would be incorrect to describe Plato's outlook as a dualism: rather, both the ideal realm and the sensory realm stand in a relationship to each other, and the idea of the Good serves as the ultimate ground of Being. Thus there is a relationship not simply of correspondence but also of imitation: the world of ideas and the sensory world relate to teach other as the original (*paradeigma*) does to the copy (see Henning Ottmann, *Geschichte des politischen Denkens*, vol. 1, *Die Griechen*, Part 2, *Von Platon bis zum Hellenismus* (Stuttgart and Weimar: Metzler, 2001), 7). Likewise, in her attempt, written some twenty years ago, to "rethink" Plato and Platonism, Cornelia J. de Vogel comes to the following conclusion about the role and place of the body in the philosophy of Plato: "Plato [...] was, in fact, not an over-spiritualist. He did not identify man with the thinking soul or *noûs*; he did hold that the thinking soul was by nature superior to the body and thus had to lead and govern it. But he thought the body an extremely important thing, since it had to serve the soul. Therefore, Plato's whole system of education was built on the principle of equal training of both body and soul, and this was for him the absolute condition to a harmonious life" (Cornelia J. de Vogel, *Rethinking Plato and Platonism* (Leiden: Brill, 1986), 230).

69. Gregory Nagy, *The Ancient Greek Hero in 24 hours* (Cambridge, MA; London: Belknap Press of Harvard University Press, 2013).

70. Robert Curry, *Genius: An Ideology in Literature* (London: Chatto & Windus, 1974).

71. Nietzsche, *Thus Spoke Zarathustra*, trans. Hollingdale, 168.

72. "The Convalescent," §2; *Thus Spoke Zarathustra*, trans. Hollingdale, 234 (translation modified).

73. *The Anti-Christ*, §62; trans. Hollingdale, 186.

74. Martin Heidegger, *What Is Called Thinking?* [1951/1952], trans. J. Glenn Gray (New York: Harper & Row, 1968), 48–49; cf. "The Desert Grows: Woe to Him, Who Harbours Deserts," in Friedrich Nietzsche, *Dithyrambs of Dionysus*, trans. R.J. Hollingdale (London: Anvil Press Poetry, 1984), 28–37.

75. "*Sophist culture*, by which I mean *realist culture*, attains in [Thucydides] its perfect expression — this invaluable movement in the midst of the morality-and-ideal swindle of the Socratic schools which was then breaking out everywhere. [...] *Courage* in face of reality ultimately distinguishes such natures as Thucydides and Plato: Plato is a coward in face of reality — consequently he flees into the ideal [folglich *flüchtet er in's Ideal*]; Thucydides has *himself* under control — consequently he retains control over things ..." (*Twilight of the Idols*, "What I Owe to the Greeks," §2; trans. Hollingdale, 107).

76. Thucydides, *The Peloponnesian War*, book 2, §49, in Robert B. Strassler, *The Landmark Thucydides: A Comprehensive Guide to the Peloponnesian War* (New York: Free Press, 1996), 119.

77. Michel Onfray, *Les Freudiens hérétiques* [*Contre-histoire de la philosophie*, vol. 8] (Paris: Grasset, 2013), 16–17.

78. Gil Elliot, *Twentieth Century Book of the Dead* (New York: Penguin, 1972).

79. In 2000, the libel case brought by the British historian David Irving against the American historian Deborah Lipstadt and Penguin Books led to a public examination of the arguments and evidence proposed by Holocaust deniers. See Deborah Lipstadt, *Denying the Holocaust: The Growing Assault on Truth and Memory* (New York: Penguin, 1994); and Richard J. Evans, *Lying About Hitler: History, Holocaust, and the David Irving Trial* (New York: Basic Books, 2002).

80. For further discussion, see Louis P. Blond, *Heidegger and Nietzsche: Overcoming Metaphysics* (London and New York: Continuum, 2010); Babette Babich, Alfred Denker, and Holger Zaborowski, *Heidegger & Nietzsche* (Amsterdam and New York: Rodopi, 2012). A useful guide around Heidgger's reception of Nietzsche is Stephan Günzel [et al.], "Nietzsche in Heideggers Texten: Eine Konkordanz," *Heidegger-Jahrbuch* 2 (2005), 45–92.

81. Cited in Blond, *Heidegger and Nietzsche*, 2.

82. Cited in Blond, *Heidegger and Nietzsche*, 4.

83. Martin Heidegger, *Nietzsche*, 2 vols (Pfullingen: Neske, 1961); *Nietzsche*, ed. David Farrell Krell, trans. David Farrell Krell et al., 4 vols (San Francisco: Harper & Row, 1979–1987). The lecture series in question are "The Will to Power as Art" (1936/1937), "The Eternal Recurrence of the Same" (1937), "The Will to Power as Knowledge" (1939), "The Eternal Recurrence of the Same and the Will to Power"

(1939), "European Nihilism" (1940), "Nietzsche's Metaphysics" (1940), "Nihilism as determined by the History of Being" (1944/1946), as well as (untranslated) "Metaphysics as the History of Being" (1941), "Drafts for a History of Being as Metaphysics" (1941), and "Recollection in Metaphysics" (1941).

84. Heidegger, *Nietzsche*, vol. 1, part 2, 199–200.

85. Heidegger, *Nietzsche*, vol. 1, part 2, 204.

86. Heidegger, *Nietzsche*, vol. 1, part 2, 205.

87. Heidegger, *Introduction to Metaphysics*, trans. Ralph Manheim (New Haven, CT: Yale University Press, 1959), 36.

88. For further discussion of Heidegger's relation to National Socialism, see Victor Farías, *Heidegger und der Nationalsozialismus* [1987] (Frankfurt am Main: Fischer, 1989); Julian Young, *Heidegger, Philosophy, Nazism* (Cambridge: Cambridge University Press, 1997); andCharles Bambach, *Heidegger's Roots: Nietzsche, National Socialism, and the Greeks* (Ithaca and London: Cornell University Press, 2003).

89. William Earle, "The Rupture Between Jaspers and Heidegger" [review of *The Philosophy of Karl Jaspers*, edited by Paul Arthur Schilpp], *Modern Age: A Quarterly Review* 26, no. 2 (Spring 1982), 197–199 (198).

90. Earle, "The Rupture Between Jaspers and Heidegger," 198. Cf. in a conversation with Jaspers on 30 June 1933, Heidegger is reported as replying to Jasper's objection about how such a man could govern Germany: *Bildung ist ganz gleichgültig [...] Sehen Sie nur seine wunderbaren Hände an!* (Farías, *Heidegger und der Nationalsozialismus*, 175).

91. Otto Pöggeler, "Den Führer führen? Heidegger und kein Ende"[1985], in *Neue Wege mit Heidegger* (Freiburg im Breisgau and Munich: Alber, 1991), 203–254 (248).

92. *Daybreak*, §60; in *Daybreak*, trans. R.J. Hollingdale (Cambridge: Cambridge University Press, 1982), 36.

93. Richard Wolin, *Heidegger's Children: Hannah Arendt, Karl Löwith, Hans Jonas, and Herbert Marcuse* (Princeton, NJ and Oxford: Princeton University Press, 2001); Tom Rockmore, *Heidegger and French Philosophy: Humanism, Antihumanism and Being* (London and New York: Routledge, 1995); and Ethan Kleinberg, *Generation Existential: Heidegger's Philosophy in France, 1927–1961* (Ithaca, NY: Cornell University Press, 2005).

94. Hannah Arendt, "Heidegger the Fox" [1953], in *Essays in Understanding, 1930–1954: Formation, Exile, and Totalitarianism*, ed. Jerome Kohn (New York: Harcourt Brace, 1994), 361–362 (361); cited in Jacques Taminiaux, "The Platonic Roots of Heidegger's Political Thought," *European Journal of Political Theory* 6, no. 1 (January 2007), 11–29.

95. Harriet Pass Freidenreich, *Female, Jewish, and Educated: The Lives of Central European University Women* (Bloomington: Indiana University Press, 2002).

96. Hans Gadamer, "Back from Syracuse?", trans. J. McCumber, *Critical Inquiry* 15 (1989), 427–430 (429).

97. Plato, *Collected Dialogues*, 1588–1589.

98. For further discussion, see Robert J. Dostal, "Beyond Being: Heidegger's Plato," *Journal of the History of Philosophy* 23, no. 1 (January 1985), 71–98; Julia A. Lamm, "Schleiermacher as Plato Scholar," *The Journal of Religion* 80, no. 2 (April 2000), 206–239; and Mark A. Ralkowski, *Heidegger's Platonism* (London and New York: Continuum, 2009), 8–13. For a critical discussion of Heidegger's relation to Plato, see Francisco Gonzalez, "History of an Embarrassment: Heidegger's Critique of Platonic Dialectic," *History of the Journal of Philosophy* 40, no. 3 (July 2002), 361–389; and Francisco J. Gonzalez, *Plato and Heidegger: A Question of Dialogue* (University Park, PA: Pennsylvania State University Press, 2009), esp. Chapter 1, "Dialectic, Ethics, and Dialogue" (8–69).

99. Schleiermacher, *Introduction to the Dialogues of Plato*, trans. William Dobson (Cambridge and London: Deighton and Parker, 1836; reprinted New York: Arno Press, 1973).

100. *Aus Schleiermachers Leben: In Briefen*, 4 vols (Berlin: Reimer, 1860–1861), vol. 3, 349; cited in Lamm, "Schleiermacher as Plato Scholar," 206.

101. Wilhelm Dilthey, *Leben Schleiermachers* [1870], in *Gesammelte Schriften*, vol. 13, Parts 1 & 2, ed. Martin Redeker (Göttingen: Vandenhoeck & Ruprecht, 1970), vol. 13/2, 37; cited in Lamm, "Schleiermacher as Plato Scholar," 206–207.

102. Schleiermacher, *Introduction to the Dialogues of Plato*, 8.

103. See Schleiermacher, *Introduction to the Dialogues of Plato*, 9–13.

104. Schleiermacher, *Introduction to the Dialogues of Plato*, 14.

105. Schleiermacher, *Introduction to the Dialogues of Plato*, 9–13, 14, 19, 43; see Ralkowski, *Heidegger's Platonism*, 9.

106. Schleiermacher, *Introduction to the Dialogues of Plato*, 3.
107. Lamm, "Schleiermacher as Plato Scholar," 219.
108. Victor Farías, *Heidegger and Nazism*, 7. For further discussion, see Glenn W. Most, "Heidegger's Greeks," *Arion: A Journal of the Humanities and the Classics* 1, no. 1 (2002), 83–98; and Barbara Cassin (ed.), *Dictionary of Untranslatables: A Philosophical Lexicon*, trans. Steven Randall, Christian Hubert, Jeffrey Mehlman, Nathanael Stein, Michael Syrotinski, trans. ed. Emily Apter, Jacques Lezra, and Michael Wood (Princeton, NJ and Oxford: Princeton University Press, 2014), 419.
109. Most, "Heidegger's Greeks," 95.
110. Martin Heidegger, *Grundbegriffe der aristotelischen Philosophie*, unpublished lectures SS 1924; cited in Bambach, *Heidegger's Roots*, 209.
111. Kant, *Critique of Pure Reason*, A 314 /B 370: "I note […] that when we compare the thoughts that an author expresses about a subject, in ordinary speech as well as in writings, it is not at all unusual to find that we understand him even better than he understood himself […]" (*Critique of Pure Reason*, ed. and trans. Paul Guyer and Allen W. Wood (Cambridge: Cambridge University Press, 1997), 396). Cited in María del Carmen Paredes, "*Amicus Plato magis amica veritas*: Reading Heidegger in Plato's Cave," in Catalin Partenie and Tom Rockmore (eds), *Heidegger and Plato: Toward Dialogue* (Evanston, IL: Northwestern University Press, 2005), 108–120 (108).
112. *Die Grundprobleme der Phänomenologie* [1927] [*Gesamtausgabe*, vol. 23], ed. Friedrich-Wilhelm von Herrmann (Frankfurt am Main: Klostermann, 1997), 157; translated by del Carmen Paredes, in Partenie and Rockmore (eds), *Heidegger and Plato*, 108.
113. Martin Heidegger, *The Essence of Human Freedom: An Introduction to Philosophy*, trans. Ted Sadler (London and New York: Continuum, 2002), 35–36; cf. Martin Heidegger, *Vom Wesen der menschlichen Freiheit: Einleitung in die Philosophie* [1930] [*Gesamtausgabe*, vol. 31], ed. Hartmut Tietjen (Frankfurt am Main: Klostermann, 1994), 50–51.
114. For further discussion, see S.J. McGrath, *The Early Heidegger and Medieval Philosophy: Phenomenology for the Godforsaken* (Washington, DC: Catholic University of America Press, 2006), Chapter 5, "Mysticism" (120–150).

115. Theodore Kisiel, "In the Middle of Heidegger's Three Concepts of the Political," in François Raffoul and David Pettigrew (eds), *Heidegger and Practical Philosophy* (Albany, NY: State University of New York Press, 2002), 135–157.

116. Kisiel, "On the Purported Platonism of Heidegger's Rectoral Address," in Partenie and Rockmore (eds), *Heidegger and Plato: Toward Dialogue*, 3–21 (19). For further discussion of the origins of Heidegger's thinking, see Theodore Kiesel and John van Buren (eds), *Reading Heidegger from the Start: Essays in His Earliest Thought* (Albany, NY: State University of New York Press, 1994).

117. Martin Heidegger and Karl Jaspers, *The Heidegger-Jaspers Correspondence (1920–1963)*, ed. W. Biemel and H. Saner, trans. G.E. Avlesworth (Amherst, NY: Humanity Books, 2003), 143; cited in Ralkowski, *Heidegger's Platonism*, 95.

118. From Rüdiger Safranksi, *Martin Heidegger: Between Good and Evil*, trans. Ewald Osers (Cambridge, MA: Harvard University Press, 1998), 215; cited in Ralkowski, *Heidegger's Platonism*, 62.

119. Martin Heidegger, *Briefe: 1925–1975*, ed. Ursula Ludz (Frankfurt am Main: Klostermann, 1999), 147–148.

120. Drew A. Hyland, *Questioning Platonism: Continental Interpretations of Plato* (Albany, New York: State University of New York Press, 2005), Chapter 1, "Heidegger's Plato," 17–83 (17–18).

121. Hyland, *Questioning Platonism*, 18.

122. Martin Heidegger, *Plato's "Sophist"*, trans. Richard Rojcewicz and André Schuwer (Bloomington and Indianapolis: Indiana University Press, 2003), 8; cited in Ralkowski, *Heidegger's Platonism*, 122–123.

123. Heidegger, *Plato's "Sophist"*, 8.

124. Heidegger, *Plato's "Sophist"*, 117.

125. See §15, "The Question Concerning the Essence of Truth as the Question Concerning the History of Man's Essence and His *paideía*," in Martin Heidegger, *The Essence of Truth: On Plato's Cave Allegory and "Theaetetus"*, trans. Ted Sadler (London and New York: Continuum, 2002; 2005), 81. For a brief discussion of the relation between the 1931/1932 course and the 1933/1934 course, see the "Editor's Afterword," 238–241.

126. Plato, *Collected Dialogues*, 1591.

127. *Nicomachean Ethics*, 1143b; in Aristotle, *Complete Works*, ed. Jonathan Barnes, 2 vols (Princeton, NJ: Princeton University Press, 1984), vol. 2, 1806.

128. Ralkowksi, *Heidegger's Platonism*, 123.
129. See "On the Essence of Truth" (translated by John Sallis) in Martin Heidegger, *Basic Writings*, ed. David Farrell Krell (London: Routledge, 1978), 115–138. An earlier translation of "On the Essence of Truth" (translated by R.F.C. Hull and Alan Crick) is in Heidegger, *Existence and Being*, ed. Werner Brock (London: Vision, 1949), 73–97.
130. See Heidegger, *Basic Writings*, 113.
131. Kisiel, "On the Purported Platonism of Heidegger's Rectoral Address," in Partenie and Rockmore (eds), *Heidegger and Plato: Toward Dialogue*, 9.
132. Fritz Stern, *The Politics of Cultural Despair: A Study in the Rise of the German Ideology* (Berkeley, Los Angeles, and London: University of California Press, 1961); Jeffrey Herf, *Reactionary Modernism: Technology, Culture, and Politics in Weimar and the Third Reich* (Cambridge: Cambridge University Press, 1984); and Armin Mohler, *Die Konservative Revolution in Deutschland 1918–1932: Ein Handbuch*, 3rd edn (Darmstadt: Wissenschaftliche Buchgesellschaft, 1989).
133. Thomas Mann, "Russische Anthologie," in *Schriften und Reden zur Literatur, Kunst und Philosophie*, vol. 1 [*Thomas Mann Werke: Das essayistische Werk*, vol. 1] (Frankfurt am Main: Fischer, 1968), 110–120 (116). For further discussion, see Stefan Breuer, "Between 'Conservative Revolution,' Aesthetic Fundamentalism and New Nationalism: Thomas Mann's Early Political Writings," *History of the Human Sciences* 11, no. 2 (1998), 1–23; and Paul Bishop, "Reaction and Revolution in Thomas Mann," *Oxford German Studies* 34 (2005), 158–172.
134. Martin Heidegger, *Platons Lehre von der Wahrheit: Mit einem Brief über den «Humanismus»* (Berne and Munich: Francke, 1947; 3rd edn, 1975).
135. Martin Heidegger, "The Self-Assertion of the German University: Address, Delivered on the Solemn Assumption of the Rectorate of the University Freiburg; The Rectorate 1933/34: Facts and Thoughts," trans. Karsten Harries, *Review of Metaphysics* 38, no. 3 (March 1985), 467–502. Subsequent references to this address are given in the text in parentheses.
136. Martin Heidegger, *Die Selbstbehauptung der deutschen Universität; Das Rektorat 1933/34: Tatsachen und Gedanken* (Frankfurt am Main: Klostermann, 1983; 2nd edn, 1990).

137. Martin Heidegger and Elisabeth Blochmann, *Brifewechsel 1918–1969*, ed. Joachim W. Storck (Marbach am Neckar: Deutsche Schillergesellschaft, 1989), 60; translated in Frank W.H. Edler, "Selected Letters from the Heidegger-Blochmann Correspondence," *Graduate Faculty Philosophical Journal* 14, nos. 2 and 15, no. 1 (1992), 557–577 (571–572); cited in Kisiel, "On the Purported Platonism of Heidegger's Rectoral Address," in Partenie and Rockmore (eds), *Heidegger and Plato: Toward Dialogue*, 7.

138. Heidegger and Blochmann, *Briefwechsel*, ed. Storck, 60–61.

139. Bambach, *Heidegger's Roots*, 70.

140. Safranski, *Martin Heidegger*, 233.

141. Plato, *Collected Dialogues*, 733.

142. Bambach, *Heidegger's Roots*, 105.

143. Martin Heidegger, *Vom Wesen der Wahrheit: Zu Platons Höhlengleichnis und Theätet* [1931–1932] [*Gesamtausgabe*, vol. 34], ed. Hermann Mörchen (Frankfurt am Main: Klostermann, 1988; 2nd edn, 1997); cf. *The Essence of Truth: On Plato's Cave Allegory and "Theaetetus"*, trans. Sadler.

144. Here we shall follow the text of the lecture series *On the Essence of Truth* as given at Freiburg in the winter semester of 1933 to 1934, which took place during Heidegger's year as rector; see Heidegger, *Being and Truth*, trans. Gregory Fried and Richard Polt (Bloomington and Indianapolis: Indiana University Press, 2010), 67–201; and Hartmut Tietjen, "Editor's Afterword," 225–230. References to this work are given in the text in parentheses.

145. See Mark Wrathall, "Heidegger on Plato, Truth, and Unconcealment: The 1931–32 Lecture on *The Essence of Truth*," *Inquiry: An Interdisciplinary Journal of Philosophy* 47, no. 5 (2004), 443–463.

146. See Mark A. Wrathall, "Unconcealment," in Hubert L. Dreyfus and Mark A. Wrathall (ed.), *A Companion to Heidegger* (Malden, MA: Blackwell, 2005), 337–357.

147. Ralkowski, *Heidegger's Platonism*, 63.

148. See §35, §36, §37, §40, and §41, in Heidegger, *Being and Time*, trans. John Macquarrie and Edward Robinson (Oxford: Blackwell, 1962), 211–224, 228–235, 235–241. For further discussion of *Gerede*, see Jesús Adrián Escudero, "Heidegger on Discourse and Idle Talk: The Role of Aristotelian Rhetoric," *Gatherings: The Heidegger Circle Annual* 3 (2013), 1–17.

149. Plato, *Collected Dialogues*, 999.
150. See Werner Jaeger, *Paideia: The Ideals of Greek Culture* [1933–1947], trans. Gilbert Highet [1939–1943], 3 vols (New York and Oxford: Oxford University Press, 1965–1986). For further discussion, see Katie Fleming, "Heidegger, Jaeger, Plato: The Politics of Humanism," *International Journal of the Classical Tradition* 19, no. 2 (June 2012), 82–106.
151. E.G. Kolbenheyer, *Gesammelte Werke*, 8 vols (Munich: Langen & Müller, 1939–1941), vol. 8, *Aufsätze, Vorträge und Reden*, 63–86. For further discussion, see Jeffrey Andrew Barash, "Heidegger et la question de la race," *Les Temps Modernes* 63, no. 650 (juillet-octobre 2008), 290–305.
152. Unpublished lecture, "The Enframing" (*Das Ge-Stell*), part of Heidegger's 1949 lecture series held at Bremen on which "The Question Concerning Technology" (1954) was based (see Heidegger, *Basic Writings*, 307–341). For further discussion, see John D. Caputo, *Demythologizing Heidegger* (Bloomington and Indianapolis: Indiana University Press, 1993), 132–137.
153. René Major, *De l'élection: Freud face aux idéologies américaine, allemande et soviétique* (Paris: Aubier, 1986), 7–8. Further references to this work are in the text in parentheses. For further discussion of Major's thinking, see René Desgroseilles, "En son nom propre: La carrière et l'œuvre de René Major," *Filigrane* 11, no. 2 (2002), 157–184.
154. "Another […] aspect of the forest is its multiple immovability. Every single trunk is rooted in the ground and no menace from outside can move it. Its resistance is absolute; it does not give an inch. It can be felled, but not shifted. And thus the forest has become the symbol of the *army*, an army which has taken up position, which does not flee in any circumstances, and which allows itself to be cut down to the last man before it gives a foot of ground" (Elias Canetti, *Crowds and Power*, trans. Carol Stewart (New York: Continuum, 1981), 84–85).
155. See Adam Shar, *Heidegger's Hut* (Boston, MA: MIT Press, 2006).
156. Thus the famous lines (here translated by Michael Hamburger) in Paul Celan's poem, "Todtnauberg," alluding to his entry in the visitor's book in Heidegger's hut when he visited on 25 July 1967. See J.D. Golb, "Celan and Heidegger: A Reading of 'Todtnauberg,'" *Seminar: A Journal of Germanic Studies* 24, no. 3 (1988), 255–268; James K. Lyon, *Paul Celan and Martin Heidegger: An Unresolved*

Conversation, 1951–1970 (Baltimore, ML: Johns Hopkins University Press, 2006), 187–191; and Pajari Räsänan, "'Undecidedly Equivocal': On 'Todtnauberg' and Forgiveness," in Kuisma Korhonen and Pajari Räsänan (eds), *The Event of Encounter in Art and Philosophy: Continental Perspectives* (Helsinki: Gaudeamus Helsinki University Press, 2010), 125–170.

157. Martin Heidegger, "'Only a God Can Save Us': The *Spiegel* Interview (1966)", in *Heidegger: The Man and the Thinker*, ed. Thomas Sheehan, trans. William J. Richardson (New Brunswick, NJ and London: Transaction Publishers, 2009), 45–67. Further references to this work are in the text in parentheses. For further discussion of this interview, see Lutz Hachmeister, *Heideggers Testament: Der Philosoph, der SPIEGEL und die SS* (Berlin: Propyläen, 2014).

158. See Eduard Spranger, "März 1933," *Die Erziehung: Monatsschrift für den Zusammenhang von Kultur und Erziehung* 8 (1932–1933), no. 7 (April 1933), 401–408.

159. On 23 August 1966 NASA had released photographs showing the view of earth taken from the vicinity of the moon by Lunar Orbiter 1. A similar sense of shock had been experienced by Heidegger's pupil, Hannah Arendt, when the first satellite, Sputnik 1, had been launched into orbit by the Soviet Union on 4 October 1957 (see her Prologue in Arendt, *The Human Condition* (Garden City, NY: Doubleday, 1959), 1).

160. Alan Cardew, "'Only a God Can Save Us': Crisis and Resolution," in Linda H. Woodward (ed.), *Selections from the Prometheus Trust Conferences 2006–2010* (Dilton Marsh, Westbury: Prometheus Trust, 2013), 171–190 (171).

9

The Frankfurt School—Adorno and Horkheimer

The Frankfurt School is the name given to a group of thinkers associated with the Institute for Social Research, founded at the Goethe University in Frankfurt am Main in 1923. The first generation of Frankfurt School thinkers included Theodor W. Adorno (1903–1969), Max Horkheimer (1895–1973), Siegfried Kracauer (1889–1966), and Walter Benjamin (1892–1940); to the second and third generations belong, among others, Erich Fromm (1900–1980), Herbert Marcuse (1898–1979), and Jürgen Habermas (born 1929). (Habermas will be considered in more detail in the following chapter.)

One way to think of the Frankfurt School is to see it as emerging from a confluence of three major traditions in German Political Thought, namely Marx, Nietzsche, and Freud. What these thinkers have in common is also a characteristic of the Frankfurt School: they believe that reality is usually in some way fundamentally misunderstood, and we must look "behind" the phenomena of society in order to understand what is "really" going on. To use the phrase of Paul Ricœur (1913–2005), Marx, Nietzsche, and Freud are "masters of suspicion,"[1] while for André Glucksmann (1937–2015) they belong to the "master

© The Author(s) 2019
P. Bishop, *German Political Thought and the Discourse of Platonism*,
https://doi.org/10.1007/978-3-030-04510-4_9

thinkers,"[2] and what they offer is something the Frankfurt School sought to make its own—a tradition and technique of *critique*.[3]

As we have seen, the term "*critique*" is strongly associated with the thought of Kant, the author of the three *Critiques* of pure reason (1781; [2]1787), practical reason (1788), and judgement (1790), and in a way the principle of critique forms part of the discourse of Platonism. After all, an important strand of the dialogues is a critique of Sophism, and at the heart of the allegory of the cave lies a huge suspicion about our ontological and existential delusions. So while, in varying degrees, Marx, Nietzsche, and Freud offer critiques of Platonism, there is good reason for arguing that the archetypal "master of suspicion" is Plato himself.

How is the work of these three thinkers taken up and developed by the members of the Frankfurt School? (Fig. 9.1).

Each of these thinkers in his own way thought that we fundamentally misunderstand reality, and each of them proposed a different answer for what reality is "really" about. In the case of Marx, as we have just seen, the nature of reality is ultimately political. Our culture, beliefs, and institutions disguise the fact that reality is about class struggle, and the role played by the economy in structuring our view of the world.

For Nietzsche, the world is really about power: power in the widest sense of the term, that is, not just in a political sense. In one of his works, *Beyond Good and Evil* (§36), Nietzsche writes that "the world seen from within, the world described and defined according to its 'intelligible character' — it would be will to power and nothing more."[4]

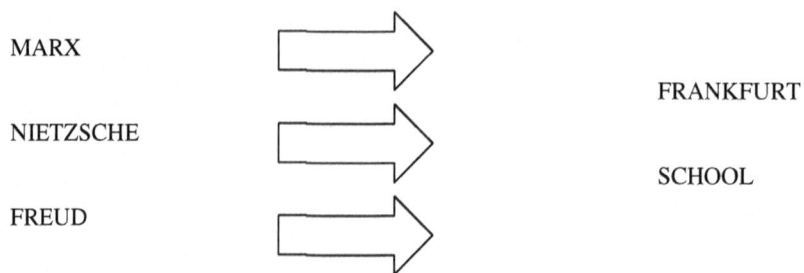

Fig. 9.1 Influences on the Frankfurt School

In the course of the twentieth history, Nietzsche's emphasis on power was (mis)used for political ends by the extreme Right; and this association has, unjustifiably, tarnished his reputation in the eyes of many (including many people who ought to know better…). Yet while the Communist Party is, in an obvious way, an embodiment of Marxist ideals, the link between the National Socialist Party and Nietzsche is, to say the least, pretty vague.

For Freud, the world is really about sex—or, to be more precise, about desire. In his writings, Freud tracks the paths of desire through the different forms of parapraxis (or "Freudian slip"), through the psychosexual development of the individual (the Oedipus complex), and through the institutions and practices of religions (in *Totem and Taboo*). In other words, of the three "masters of suspicion" Freud is the one who is closest to Plato, whose *Symposium* offers an account of the origin of male and female and foregrounds the daimonic power of Eros (202e–204a), and whose *Phaedrus* describes the power of Eros to lend us wings and raise us from the mortal to the immortal.[5]

What the thinkers of the Frankfurt School did, in varying degrees, was to draw on this complex tradition of political thought and apply it to the interpretation of contemporary culture and society; Marx, Nietzsche, and Freud, then, as the intellectual sources of *Kulturkritik*. As an example of this, consider the subtitle of Marcuse's *Eros and Civilization* (1955)—"A Philosophical Inquiry into Freud." In this work, Marcuse attempts a kind of synthesis of Marx and Freud; Marx, despite the absence of the dimension of desire in the Marxist emphasis on the material economy; Freud, despite the a-political, or arguably conservative, tendency of the Freudian approach.

Similarly, the three influences of Marx, Nietzsche, and Freud can be detected in a masterpiece of the Frankfurt School, the *Dialectic of Enlightenment* by Theodor W. Adorno and Max Horkheimer. This work was originally published in 1944 in New York under the title *Philosophical Fragments*; it was republished in a revised version in 1947 in Amsterdam. The fact that it originally appeared outside Germany reminds us of the historical and political conditions at the time: the rise of National Socialism, of Stalinism, and the fact of the Second World War. The rise of totalitarianism is a central theme of the work.

But so are the following features of the post-war settlement in the West: the organisational power of the state, the persistence of authoritarianism, and mass culture (or, as the Frankfurt School contemptuously referred to it, the "culture industry").

The very title of this work alerts us to how it can be read as responding to key elements in the history of German Political Thought—especially those that participate in the discourse of Platonism. First, it is a reaction and a response to the project of the Enlightenment, a project whose origins in the thought of Rousseau and its continuation in the thought of Kant we have already explored. "What is Enlightenment?" is, of course, the title of an essay written by Kant; the answer provided by Adorno and Horkeimer is, however, diametrically opposed to the answer given by Kant, i.e., "the emergence of a human being from his or her self-imposed tutelage." Rather than freeing us, they argue, Enlightenment only traps us in more subtle forms of bondage: it binds us, one might say, in invisible chains... Second, it draws on the notion of dialectic, a structure of thought found in Plato as well as in Hegel.

In Plato's *Republic*, the dialectic forms the sixth and final element in the philosophical training provided by a study of the arts (arithmetic, geometry, solid geometry; then astronomy, harmony, and dialectic) (522b–533d). For Plato, it is dialectic than proves the indispensable tool in finding our way out of the cave. In terms of this allegory, "sight at last tries to look at the animals themselves and at stars themselves and then finally at the sun itself" (532a). Correspondingly, "when a man"—or a woman—"tries by discussion"—by means of argument without the use of any of the senses—"to attain to each thing itself that *is* and doesn't give up before he"—or she—"grasps by intellection itself that which is good itself, he"—or she—"comes to the very end of the intelligible realm just as that other man"—i.e., in the allegory—"was then at the end of the visible" (532a–b). This is the journey Plato calls the dialectic.

In Hegel, the term *dialectic* is used in an analogous, if not identical, sense. While the model conventionally ascribed to Hegel was, in fact, formulated by Heinrich Moritz Chalybäus (1796–1862),[6] the three stages of thesis—antithesis—synthesis capture something of the dynamic of Hegel's thought. For Hegel is keenly alert to the way in which each and any historical stage or moment is related to the one preceding it, and paves the way for the one that will supersede it. The past, the present, and the future are inextricably linked together, just as, logically, one term can both preserve and negate another to produce a new, third term.

This dialectical dynamic is clear from the powerful opening words of the first chapter of *Dialectic of Enlightenment*: "Enlightenment," Horkheimer and Adorno declare, "understood in the widest sense as the advance of thought, has always aimed at liberating human beings from fear and installing them as masters. Yet"—and immediately this project is undermined in the most devastating way—"the wholly enlightened earth is radiant with triumphant calamity."[7] Understood in the widest sense, the project of Enlightenment antedates such figures as Francis Bacon (1561–1626), the "father of science," whom Adorno and Horkheimer explicitly mention. In fact, it goes right back to the earliest days of Western philosophy, to the Platonic and, before it, to the pre-Socratic tradition that sought to move away from a mythological to a conceptual understanding of the world.[8] The Enlightenment project in its eighteenth–century form is an extension and intensification of this project of "disenchantment" and the concomitant shift from myth to science: "Even the patriarchal gods of Olympus were finally assimilated by the philosophical *logos* as the Platonic forms," they write, but "the Enlightenment discerned the old powers in the Platonic and Aristotelian heritage of metaphysics and suppressed the universal categories' claims to truth as superstition." Ultimately, they declare, "for enlightenment, anything which does not conform to the standard of calculability and utility must be viewed with suspicion" (3).

As astute readers of Nietzsche, Adorno and Horkeimer are alert to the implications of this shift. As our understanding of, for example, the master category of "nature" changes, so does our sense of what "nature" actually represents—in this case, it becomes an object of domination: "Myth becomes enlightenment and nature mere objectivity. [...] In their transformation the essence of things is revealed as always the same, a substrate of domination" (6). Where Adorno and Horkheimer see the dialectic as entering the work of the enlightenment is the way in which mythology, far from being banished, enters the modern world, so to speak, through the back door. Or to put it another way: the scientific (or "enlightenment") world view "demystifies" or "desacralizes" the natural world, but the allure of mystification, sacralization, or mythology itself returns to "permeate the sphere of the profane." This is the "dialectic" of enlightenment: enlightenment drives out mythology, but mythology returns to drive out enlightenment:

> The countless agencies of mass production and its culture impress standardized behaviour on the individual as the only natural, decent, and rational one. Individuals define themselves now only as things, statistical elements, successes or failures. Their criterion is self-preservation, successful or unsuccessful adaptation to the objectivity of their function and the schemata assigned to it. [...] The noonday panic fear in which nature suddenly appeared to humans as an all-encompassing power has found its counterpart in the panic which is ready to break out at any moment today: human beings expect the world, which is without issue, to be set ablaze by a universal power which they themselves are and over which they are powerless. (21–22)

Thus far, Adorno and Horkheimer have presented their argument in largely abstract terms; this is a characteristic of their thinking, and one of the reasons for why it is usually regarded as difficult or challenging. In order to exemplify their argument, however, they turn to the example of Odysseus, basing themselves on the account of an episode in his adventures as found in the ancient Greek epic attributed to Homer.

The episode of the *Odyssey* to which they refer can be found in book 12 of this work, where we read how Odysseus, alerted by Circe to the danger of the Sirens, devises a strategem to hear their song yet avoid destruction:

> In mean time flew our ships, and straight we fetch'd
> The Sirens' isle; a spleenless wind so stretch'd
> Her wings to waft us, and so urged our keel.
> But having reach'd this isle, we could not feel
> The least gasp of it, it was stricken dead,
> And all the sea in prostrate slumber spread,
> The Sirens' devil charm'd all. Up then flew
> My friends to work, struck sail, together drew,

And under hatches stow'd them, sat, and plied
The polish'd oars, and did in curls divide
The white-head waters. My part then came on:
A mighty waxen cake I set upon,
Chopp'd it in fragments with my sword, and wrought
With strong hand every piece, till all were soft.
The great power of the sun, in such a beam
As then flew burning from his diadem,
To liquefaction help'd us. Orderly
I stopp'd their ears; and they as fair did ply
My feet and hands with cords, and to the mast
With other halsers made me soundly fast.
Then took they seat, and forth our passage strook,
The foamy sea beneath their labour shook.
Row'd on, in reach of an erected voice,
The Sirens soon took note, without our noise,
Tuned those sweet accents that made charms so strong,
And these learn'd numbers made the Sirens' song:
    [...]
This they gave accent in the sweetest strain
That ever open'd an enamour'd vein.
When my constrain'd heart needs would have mine ear
Yet more delighted, force way forth, and hear.
To which end I commanded with all sign
Stern looks could make (for not a joint of mine
Had power to stir) my friends to rise, and give
My limbs free way. They freely striv'd to drive
Their ship still on. When, far from will to loose,
Eurylochus and Perimedes rose
To wrap me surer, and oppress'd me more
With many a halser than had use before.
When, rowing on without the reach of sound,
My friends unstopp'd their ears, and me unbound,
And that isle quite we quitted.[9]

For Adorno and Horkheimer, this entire episode, especially the measures taken on Odysseus's ship in face of the sirens, are "a prescient allegory of the dialectic of enlightenment" (27). In line with this interpretation, Adorno and Horkeimer offer the following reading of Homer's text: Odysseus, they write, is "represented in the sphere of work," and "just as he cannot give way to the lure of self-abandonment, as owner he also forfeits participation in work and finally even control over it, while his companions, despite their closeness to things, cannot enjoy their work because it is performed under compulsion, in despair, with their senses forcibly stopped" (27). In short, "the servant is subjugated in body and soul, the master regresses," demonstrating how "the curse of irresistible progress is irresistible regression" (27–28). So what exactly are Adorno and Horkheimer arguing here? And what has an interpretation of Homer's *Odyssey* got to do with the tradition of German Political Thought?

First of all, Adorno's and Horkheimer's use of Homer is another example of the persistence of ancient Greek culture in modern German thought.[10] To be sure, it is no coincidence that Adorno and Horkheimer choose to anchor their argument in an interpretation of Homer; it is a way of signalling to the reader that they understand the importance of the ancient Greek and modern German periods of thought. Second, there is a long tradition of reading Homer in an allegorical way. For instance, the Neoplatonists—Plotinus, Porphyry, and in particular Proclus—all offered philosophical, even theological, readings of Homer.[11] The choice of allegory is itself significant; Plato, for example, makes extensive use in his writings of allegory, including (obviously) in the *Republic* the allegory of the cave. Third, one can read Homer's story of Odysseus as a parallel allegory to the allegory of the cave. Both allegories are concerned with the same fundamental themes: bondage, alienation, and liberation.

So how do Adorno and Horkheimer read book 12 of Homer's *Odyssey*, the story of Odysseus's encounter with the Sirens? On their account, Odysseus is a figure caught between the two worlds of mythology and enlightenment. The sirens themselves stand under the signs of both mythology and the enlightenment. They are mythological, insofar as they are creatures who belong to the canon of mythological figures— according to ancient sources, the sirens are two (Homer, Eustathius), three (Servius, Apollonius, Suidas), or four (Hyginus) in number—and for Adorno and Horkheimer they serve as a representation of nature.

For mythology and enlightenment alike, the sirens are something dangerous; to the extent that they represent forces of nature, they are read by Adorno and Horkheimer as an allegorical representation of nature as something that must be tricked, deceived, or dominated. Indeed, Odysseus dominates the nature of his men, when he orders their ears be stuffed with wax; he even dominates his own nature in the most palpably symbolic of ways, when he orders his men to tie him to the mask of the ship, in order to be able to resist the blandishments of the sirens, symbols of the nature from which he has become alienated and estranged.

In turn, the anecdote of Odysseus and the sirens serves as an allegory for modern life. The progress achieved under the influence of the enlightenment is subtly undermined by the progressive (and unacknowledged) return of myth. Like Odysseus, we as modern individuals are alienated and estranged, both economically and existentially in the market economy. We are forced to sell ourselves or our labour in return for money, just as Odysseus submits to being tied to the mast. We think of ourselves as "free" citizens of the "free" world, but are we really free? Free to be dominated, Adorno and Horkheimer seem to be saying, by the economic imperatives of the free market and by the blandishments, not of the sirens, but of the culture industry. Just as we have learned to dominate nature, so in turn we are dominated by the unfettered forces of the free (!) market and by the need to twist our individual natures to conform to the models society imposes on us.

Thus Adorno's and Horkheimer's reading of Homer segues seamlessly with their critique of the culture industry. As they write, "the regression of the masses today lies in their inability to hear with their own ears what has not already been heard, to touch with their hands what has not previously been grasped; it is the new form of blindness which supersedes that of vanquished myth," and consequently "the powerlessness of the workers is not merely a ruse of the rulers but the logical consequence of industrial society, into which the efforts to escape it have finally transformed the ancient concept of fate" (28–29). Before we turn to their critique of the culture industry, let us consider how Adorno and Horkheimer develop their allegorical reading of Homer in the first of two excurses in the *Dialectic of Enlightenment*, called "Odysseus or

Myth and Enlightenment." (The second excursus, called "Juliette or Enlightenment and Morality," offers a reading of Kant seen through an interpretative lens informed by the Marquis de Sade.)

Adorno and Horkheimer offer a reprise of their reading of Homer as revealing how myth becomes enlightenment, while in turn enlightenment becomes (again) myth. For them, just as the story of the Sirens "illustrates the intertwinement of myth and rational labour," the *Odyssey* as a whole "bears witness to the dialectic of enlightenment," and "as the Homeric spirit takes over and 'organizes' the myths, it comes into contradiction with them" (35). "The venerable cosmos of the Homeric world," they conclude, "a world charged with meaning, reveals itself as an achievement of classifying reason, which destroys myth by virtue of the same rational order which is used to reflect it" (35–36).

Adorno and Horkheimer explicitly align their interpretation of Homer with one of the great "masters of suspicion" discussed above, namely: Nietzsche. Citing directly from his unpublished writings or *Nachlass*, they maintain that Nietzsche "recognized the dialectic of enlightenment," and that he formulated "the ambivalent relationship of enlightenment to power" (36).[12] In other words, enlightenment has a "twofold character," something that "emerge[s] more clearly as a basic motif of history," just as its "concept," i.e., "that of advancing thought," was "traced back to the beginning of recorded history" (36). Surprisingly, perhaps, Adorno and Horkheimer identify enlightenment with Homer; yet, given their understanding of the dialectical relationship between enlightenment and myth as set out above, this identification should not cause us so much surprise. Examining Homer's work more closely helps us understand their thinking on this point (and why it is relevant for appreciating Adorno's and Horkheimer's contribution to German Political Thought).

For Adorno and Horkheimer, the epics of Homer can be read as depicting the shift from myth to science. Their very composition, the compiling of the epic narratives from existing oral sources, is a scientific gesture; or, as they put it, myths are "precipitated in the different strata of Homer's subject matter; but at the same time the reporting of them, the unity imposed on the diffuse legends, traces the path of the subject's flight from the mythical powers" (37). This view is illustrated with reference to the story of the *Iliad*, the epic poem which, against the backdrop of the Trojan War, relates the disputes and battles between King Agamemnon and Achilles. According to Adorno and Horkheimer: "The anger of the mythical son of a goddess"—i.e., Achilles—"against the rational warrior king and organizer; the hero's undisciplined inactivity; finally, the enlistment of the victorious, doomed hero in a cause which is national, Hellenic, and no longer tribal, an allegiance mediated by mythic loyalty to his dead comrade — all these reflect the intertwinement of history and prehistory" (37–38). Moreover, "the same development," they argue, is "even more vividly present in the *Odyssey*," the epic that narrates the ten years taken by Odysseus to complete the journey home after the fall of Troy—and that places great emphasis on the quality of *mētis*, of "cunning," that characterizes Odysseus (39).[13] They even diagnose this *mētis* as being at the very heart of religion itself, with its notion of sacrifice; "the sacrifice itself [...] appears as a human contrivance intended to control the gods, who are overthrown precisely by the system created to honour them" (40).[14] In their reading—admittedly, an idiosyncratic one—of Homer's *Odyssey*, Adorno and Horkheimer highlight a few key elements. To begin with, book 9 of the *Odyssey* tells the story of how Odysseus and his men are captured by the Cyclops, Polyphemus.

After landing on the island of the Cyclops, a primordial race of one-eyed giants, Odysseus and his men enter the cave of Polyphemus, and find it full of food and provisions. When Polyphemus returns home with his flocks, he blocks the entrance to the cave with a stone and eats two of Odysseus's men. The following morning, he eats two more, and after blocking up the cave with the stone he leaves to graze his sheep. In the evening, he returns again; two further men are eaten. So Odysseus offers Polyphemus some wine, and makes the giant drunk. In his inebriated state, Polyphemus asks Odysseus his name, and promises him a reward for his answer. Odysseus tells Polyphemus his name is "Outis" (i.e., No-one), and Polyphemus promises to eat him last of all. While Polyphemus slumbers in his drunken stupor, Odysseus fashions a wooden stake and drives it into the eye of the sleeping giant. Enraged, the giant awakes, and calls his fellow giants for help. When they ask him who has hurt him, Polyphemus replies, *No-one*, and so they turn back.

The next morning, the blinded Polyphemus takes out his sheep to graze, feeling their backs to ensure that Odysseus and his men are not escaping. But Odysseus has recourse to another ruse: he and his men tie themselves to the underbellies of the sheep, and so they are able to effect their escape.

This episode reveals a key quality of Odysseus, and Adorno and Horkheimer are again quick to point this aspect of Odysseus's character—his cunning, "the faculty by which the self survives adventures, throwing itself away in order to preserve itself" (39).[15] Again, this feature of the text is read in a primarily allegorical way, for "the seafarer Odysseus outwits the natural deities as the civilized traveller was later to swindle savages, offering them coloured beads for ivory" (39). The origin of this cunning is traced back by Adorno and Horkheimer to the primitive ritual act of sacrifice: the whole point of sacrifice is that something is offered to the gods, but this something can and could never be enough. It is all *cunning*: "The moment of fraud in sacrifice is the prototype of Odyssean cunning, just as many of Odysseus's ruses are wrapped up, as it were, in an offering to natural deities," they write; cunning "originates in the cult. Odysseus himself acts as both victim and priest"; and: cunning "is nothing other than the subjective continuation of the objective untruth of sacrifice, which it supersedes" (40–41). Even if the argumentation here is not exactly clear, the conclusion is: the process of enlightenment involves a training in cunning; the modern, capitalist world is free from demons and monsters—except those monsters which the capitalist system itself creates …

The second element highlighted by Adorno and Horkheimer is crucial to the ancient and the modern world alike: the contract. In his *On the Genealogy of Morals*, Nietzsche had traced the significance of the promise and the legally binding contract for the development of human consciousness and, above all, conscience; he points to the fact that, in German, the same word for "debt" (*Schuld*) also means "guilt."[16] For Adorno and Horkheimer, there is an important link between the kind of cunning embodied by Odysseus and the notion of the contract itself, for "the mythical monsters under whose power he falls represent, as it were, petrified contracts and legal claims dating from primeval times" (45); Odysseus "complies with the contract of his bondage and, bound to the mast, struggles to throw himself into the arms of the seductresses," but he finds "a loophole in the agreement, though which he eludes it while fulfilling its terms" (46); and so, "with the dissolution of the contract through its literal fulfilment," they argue, "a change occurs in the historical situation of language: it begins to pass over into designation" (47). Or as Adorno and Horkheimer tersely, and with characteristic abstraction, summarize their argument: "The lone voyager armed with cunning is already *homo oeconomicus*, whom all reasonable people will one day resemble" (48).

The third important element highlighted by Adorno and Horkheimer is connected with an issue about which, so far, we have had relatively little to say in our survey of German Political Thought—gender. This theme emerges in Adorno's and Horkheimer's discussion of Circe and the magical power she exercises. After visiting the Lotus-Eaters, after escaping Polyphemus, and after barely avoiding destruction in the harbour of the Laestrygonians, in book 10 of the *Odyssey*, Odysseus and men land on the island inhabited by Circe. Is she a goddess, an enchantress, a sorceress, or a nymph? In the Greek mythological tradition, her status is unclear, but in the *Odyssey* her powers are soon made evident. For she feeds half of Odysseus's men cheese and wine, turning them into swine. As Adorno and Horkheimer summarize this episode, Circe "seduces Odysseus's men into abandoning themselves to instinct, with which the animal form assumed by the victims has always been associated, while Circe has become the prototype of the courtesan" (54). To support their interpretation of Circe as a kind of courtesan, Adorno and Horkheimer point to the "erotic initiatives" which are "taken for granted" by these words of Hermes, "She will be afraid of you and ask you to go to bed. / And from that point on do not refuse the bed of the god."[17]

What, however, should we make of the transformation of Odysseus's men into swine? Adorno and Horkheimer recall that, in the chthonic cult of the goddess Demeter, the pig was sacred; they speculate that for the Ionians, as for the Jews, there was a taboo on mingling with the blood of a creature which, with its humanoid anatomy and nakedness, is so similar to human beings; and they recall the prohibition of cannibalism, since the taste of human flesh has, since as in Juvenal,[18] been compared to that of pigs (55–56). And they also propose that the image of the pig, snuffling around with its snout, is indexed to the sense of smell, a sense which has become "increasingly suppressed and repressed, and is closest not only to sex but to the remembrance of prehistory" (56). In so doing, Adorno and Horkheimer are in line with Freud's argument in *Civilization and its Discontents* (1930) that "the diminution of the olfactory stimuli seems itself to be a consequence of man's raising himself from the ground, of his assumption of an upright gait."[19] Hence when Circe transforms the men into swine, it is as if she, as a "sorceress-courtisan," is reenacting the same ritual to which, in patriarchal society, she herself is repeatedly subjected. In other words, "like her, women are predisposed, under the pressure of civilization, to adopt its judgment on women and to denigrate sex" (56).

What is the status in the modern world of the daimon Socrates called Eros? Or to put it another way, how does patriarchal society deal with the problem of sex? For Adorno and Horkheimer, the answer is clear— through marriage, Marriage is "society's middle way in dealing with this question", they explain, "woman remains powerless in that her power is mediated to her only through her husband" (56). And indeed "something of this," they add, "is reflected in the defeat of the courtesan-goddess of the *Odyssey*," i.e., Circe, while "the fully evolved marriage with Penelope, more recent in literary terms, represents a later stage in the objective structure of patriarchal arrangements" (56). So we have the two figures of Circe and Penelope, corresponding to the two types of the feminine identified by Freud,[20] the famous antithesis of the madonna and the whore. (What Freud originally proposed as a psychological structure to explain the phenomenon of intramarital psychic impotence is usually read today as a description of two different kinds of construction of sexual identity.) Or as Adorno and Horkheimer put it, "harlot and wife" are "complementary forms of female self-alienation in the patriarchal world: the wife betrays pleasure to the fixed order of life and property, while the harlot, as her secret accomplice, brings within the property relationship that which the wife's property rights do not include — pleasure — by selling it" (57–58).[21] Adorno and Horkheimer take a grim view of marriage, then; one wonders what their wives made of these pages in *Dialectic of Enlightenment* … For Adorno and Horkheimer, this fundamental fissure in the identity of woman is written into the structure of the *Odyssey*: Circe and Calypso, the "courtesans," are "introduced as diligent weavers," thus "resembling both mythical powers of fate and bourgeois housewives, while Penelope, like a harlot, mistrustfully scrutinizes the returning Odysseus to make sure he is not really just an old beggar or even a god trying his luck" (58)!

Already their analysis of the *Odyssey* highlights some of the themes taken up and developed in a later chapter of *Dialectic of Enlightenment*, entitled "The Culture Industry: Enlightenment as Mass Deception." In this chapter, Adorno and Horkheimer paint a grey, gloomy picture of the life in the modern (or, today, postmodern) world. Their entire outlook turns essentially on this thesis: that the free, Western world is, in reality, anything other than free. Like the prisoners in Plato's cave, the citizens of the so-called "free" West do not realized they are enslaved and in chains; indeed, like those prisoners, they have come to love their chains and their enslavement. The cave of the allegory has become a virtual world of radio, cinema, and TV: without much effort, one could easily update Adorno's and Horkheimer's critique to include such features of today's world as the internet and mobile phones, not to mention Facebook and Twitter, WhatsApp and Snapchat.

By the "culture industry" (or, in German, *Kulturindustrie*), Adorno and Horkheimer are referring to the influence exercised by mass media and popular culture on the citizens of Western societies. The backdrop to their account is their view of the ascendancy of what they term "aesthetic barbarism" (104). As they explain, the "general designation" *culture* already "contains, virtually, the process of identifying, cataloguing, and classifying which imports culture into the realm of administration," for "only what has been industrialized, rigorously subsumed, is fully adequate to this concept of culture" (104). Administration—for Adorno, this is the new tyranny that exercises power in the modern world. In fact, he coined the phrase "the totally administered society," to describe the bureaucratization of increasingly large numbers of aspects of everyday life.

Excursus: The Totally Administered Society

At this point, let us pause for a moment to consider in more detail how the critical theory of the Frankfurt School develops the notion of "the totally administered society" or *die verwaltete Welt*, as found in the writings of Adorno.[22] As he uses the term, the "administered world" refers to the society of late capitalism, in which a new form of Fascism has taken root in the form of administration—a self-legitimizing bureaucracy. Drawing on Horkheimer's study of class difference and organised criminality, in which a conspiratorial clique exercises control over the society around it,[23] and developing an analysis that is complementary to Weber's,[24] Adorno offered a chilling analysis of what one might call "structural" or "institutional evil." The phrase *verwaltete Welt* or "administered world" is first used in the subtitle to Adorno's 1956 study of music sociology, entitled *Dissonanzen: Musik in der verwalteten Welt*,[25] and it can also be found in his 1964 critique of existentialism in general and Heidegger in particular, published as *Jargon of Authenticity* (*Jargon der Eigentlichkeit*) (1964),[26] as well as in a short essay, "Marginalien zu Theorie und Praxis," published in *Stichworte. Kritische Modelle 2*.[27] The concept was given extensive treatment in a radio broadcast, transmitted from Frankfurt by Hessischer Rundfunk on 19 September 1959, of a discussion between Adorno, Horkheimer, and the historian and sociologist Eugen Kogon (1903–1987) under the title *Die verwaltete Welt*.[28]

In this broadcast Adorno argues that, as the Austrian writer Ferdinand Kürnberger (1821–1879) put it in his novel *Der Amerikamüde* (1855), "life no longer lives" (*das Leben lebt nicht*).[29] "There is," Adorno maintains, "no longer any life in the sense in which we all use the word life," because there has been "a transition of the entire world, of life as a whole, to a system of administration, to a particular kind of control from above." In particular, he emphasizes that, in its most recent forms, bureaucracy serves "to rationalize the irrational," whilst the system of planning conceals a complete lack of real planning.

Furthermore, for Adorno human beings are facing nothing less than the loss of "what was once called character [*Charakter*]," namely "the formative particularity of their ego, which they acquire from the past and preserve into the future"; indeed, they willingly participate in this loss, because the ego is gradually becoming "a burden that hinders their progress within the giant machinery of society." Developing this idea, Adorno goes on to argue that "human beings, who conform to everything, lose in this very process of conforming precisely this ego, this self [*dieses Selbst*], which they are seeking to preserve," and herein lies the "satanic dialectic" of this process of adaptation. Agreement with Adorno's view was expressed in this broadcast by Horkheimer, who added that "today human beings still make their own history, it's just that they don't know this"; they can "still make decisions, but they decide to go along with what is happening." For Horkheimer, the present age is the age of psychology and, in particular, psychoanalysis. But, on his account, the process of administration can now, thanks to psychoanalysis, be carried on within the individual. Human beings turn themselves into objects, and analysis, which used to offer a critical way out of this reified condition, remains very much part of the reified world.

In turn in agreement with Horkheimer's critique, Adorno argues that the development of the totally administered society can be seen at work within psychoanalysis, a discipline which "has seen better days." Originally, psychoanalysis sought to make repressed drives conscious, and thus liberate us, at least inwardly, but now this will-to-freedom within psychoanalysis itself appears as "unrealistic" or "neurotic," and instead psychoanalysis tends to help human beings to accommodate external pressures and to adapt themselves to them, so that those aspects of ourselves which cannot be smoothly adapted to societal demands are eradicated, and human beings, as subjects, are turned into what, as objects, they already are—into potential employees of a single, monstrous enterprise. Thus, psychoanalysis—which should be dedicated to the individual as something incommensurable, unconscious, and compelled by drives, and hence stand in opposition to the adminstered society—has become precisely the opposite, and seeks to manipulate the incommensurable, as Freud's programmatic statement, "where Id was, there shall Ego be," demonstrates. This duplicity (in all senses), whereby the individual is turned back onto himself in order to subordinate himself even more to the abstract, reified world, is expressed in the tendency to "pseudo-individualization" (*Pseudoindividualisierung*): a tendency which, Adorno concluded, is a swindle one should resist.[30]

For his part, Eugen Kogon put the view that human beings "still possess an inner freedom," but that our freedom to say yes or no to what is going on in the world around us is not followed by any consequences, which throws us back into our innermost self, so that the increasing administration of the external world is accompanied by a near total loss of what remains of our inner freedom. In *Dialectic of Enlightenment*, Adorno and Horkheimer describe the consequences of the subsumption of culture to the power of the economic.[31] As the old Hollywood song goes, "There's no business like show business," and for Adorno and Horkeimer, this line conceals or rather reveals an important truth: that entertainment has become, like everything else in capitalist society— think of the world of football, for instance—, just another example of big business.[32]

To even the most apparently innocent of mass cultural production, the Walt Disney cartoon, Adorno and Horkheimer bring a jaundiced, yet psychoanalytically informed, eye. What one finds precisely in Walt Disney films, as in so many other examples of popular "comedy," is a representation of the kind of sado-masochism that characterizes life in the capitalist world.[33] In particular, Adorno and Horkheimer argue, what the culture industry does is to interfere with the most intimate as well as the most primordial of our desires, the erotic. Although we might think that our most intimate of interpersonal relations are sacrosanct and private, Adorno and Horkheimer suggest that our desires are, unconscious to ourselves, preformatted in some way by the images of the culture industry.[34] But, rather than sublimating—that is, in psychoanalytic terms, turning an erotic or physiological drive into something intellectual, spiritual, or cerebral—, what the culture industry does is essentially repressive. While appearing to excite, instead it actually deadens.[35]

True, there is something a little prurient, censorious, or simply snobbish about these comments. One senses that Adorno and Horkheimer experienced the move from Germany to the US in the Forties as something of a culture shock. In the meantime, American culture has become so dominant that we have perhaps become insensitized to it; but Adorno's and Horkheimer's analysis of the prevalence of laughter is surely as relevant now as it was in the Forties. After all, "it's all a laugh, innit?"[36] For Adorno and Horkheimer, an analysis of culture is properly "dialectical"—a word of which they are, it must be confessed, inordinately fond—when it brings out the interrelationship between two apparently discrete or separate elements: in this case, culture on the other hand and industry (or big business) on the other. So Adorno and Horkheimer would not have been surprised by the existence of university courses on popular culture, on the pressure felt even by serious news organisations to "sex up" a story to find a bigger audience, or the presentation of classical artists as if they were rock stars.[37]

What is it about popular culture and the outputs of the culture industry that so annoys Adorno and Horkeimer? Could they not just relax a bit more, chill out, or if necessary simply go and lie down? Central to the disagreement between these two German sociologists and the modern Americanized world is the compulsion to participate and to conform. In this respect, they argue, popular culture is totalitarian.[38]

Or to put it another way, the products of the popular culture are deeply *ideological*. Now, for Marx, ideology is way of talking about how the superstructure of society is determined by its economic base. Ideology both reveals and conceals this fact: it can create false consciousness, which, if taken at face-value, is blind to economic and political truths, but which, when analysed, can show how intellectual and societal values are infused by the economic imperative. Subsequent Marxists emphasize the obscuring role of ideology; for instance, Louis Althusser (1918–1990) highlighted how an imaginary relationship of individuals in society to the realities experienced on the economic and political level is created and sustained.[39] As Adorno and Horkeimer put it, "ideology is split between the photographing of brute existence and the blatant lie about its meaning, a lie which is articulated directly but drummed in by suggestion" (118).[40]

What popular culture reveals, inasmuch as it try to conceals it, is, as Adorno and Horkheimer argue, "the irrationally systematic nature of this society" (120). To put it in terms of Plato's allegory of the cave, we are obsessed by the brand names of the objects carried behind us and casting an image on the wall, like so many items on a conveyor-belt of consumer commodities—rather than realizing that they are, after all, only shadows. In essence, we learn to love being prisoners in the Platonic cave …

Whereas it has always been a function of culture, Adorno and Horkheimer claim, to subdue barbaric and revolutionary instincts alike, what the culture industry does is something qualitatively new: it becomes part of the routine or the system that keeps us trapped in the cave, so to speak.[41] Drawing on the sociological category of the racket,[42] Adorno and Horkheimer argue that "society is made up of the desperate and thus falls prey to rackets" (123).[43] So whereas we are always told in the "free" West that this is a society in which individuality rules, in fact the opposite is the case: conformity rules, under the guise of what Adorno and Horkeimer call "pseudoindividuality".[44]

For Plato, we think we are free but in reality we are prisoners, stuck in a cave; we need a philosopher to find his or her way out, and then come back down to us again. For the Frankfurt School, we think we are individuals, but in reality we are just consumers of pseudoindividualistic consumerist junk; we need Adorno and Horkheimer to tell us where we are going wrong.[45] As thinkers working in the Marxist tradition, Adorno and Horkheimer are aware that there is nothing new about this state of affairs, rather it is the degree or concentration of the totalitarian reach of the system that makes it something qualitatively different from what has gone before. And there is another difference too.

In the past, on their Marxist account of art, a work of art, while being subject to the economic and ideological parameters of its creation, nevertheless had the potential to be a critical social voice. Precisely because it was art, such a work could indirectly, obliquely, subtly, hint at themes of social oppression and social injustice. (At least, this is how Adorno himself tended to read, or rather to listen to, works of classical music.) Yet now, even art itself is subsumed under the category of economic efficiency: classical music has its top 10 charts, museums and art galleries have to measure their foot-fall, and the "purposiveness without purpose" which has (since the time of Kant)[46] been understood to characterize the work of art has been forced to yield to the purposiveness of making a quick buck.[47]

Closely related to the culture industry—indeed, at times indistinguishable from it—is advertising. Adorno and Horkheimer describe advertising as culture's "elixir of life," but also as a "negative principle" or "a blocking device," inasmuch as "anything which does not bear its seal of approval is economically suspect" (131). Advertising works through images, but also through language: language which consciously (or, even more insidiously, unconsciously) consumers begin to make their own. In this respect, the use of language for commercial advertising begins to revert to its much earlier use in ritual magic.[48] In fact, the dialectic of enlightenment reveals itself to its full extent if we can realize how, in the modern (or postmodern) world, the archaic dimension of magic has once more begun to exert itself.[49]

In the grim conclusion to their chapter in *Dialectic of Enlightenment* on the culture industry, Adorno and Horkheimer present us with a depressing picture of a way of life that has become so alienated it doesn't even realize it *is* alienated; indeed, such is the exent of its alienation, it has probably lost all notion of what alienation is. To be sure, there is much that is out of date in Adorno and Horkheimer's account under the rule of the culture industry: nevertheless, there is equally much that is still true, if not even more true, today.[50] The tyranny, or even the totalitarianism of the totally administered society, pursues each and everyone of us into the most intimate parts of our being, shaping and determining our sexual preferences, our erotic fantasies, and even our personal hygiene.[51]

So now it becomes clear why Adorno and Horkheimer describe Enlightenment as nothing more than "mass deception." For their view of the modern world is, as we have suggested, entirely compatible with that set out by Plato when Socrates expounds the allegory of the cave. Only instead of the light from the flickering flames of the fire projecting shadowy images on the wall of the cave, we sit in comfortable chairs in our living rooms, gazing at the images on the television set, after a day spent at work staring at the screen of the desktop and, on the way to and from work, glancing at the information popping up on our mobile phone ….

Critique of the Critique

In the tradition of Kant and the critical philosophy, Adorno and Horkeimer offer us a critique. In return, let us offer a critique of their critique. First of all, Adorno and Horkheimer describe the relation between myth and science as dialectical, but is their understanding of myth correct? After all, as the anthropologist Bronisław Malinowski (1884–1942) argued, myth is not "an explanation put forward to satisfy curiosity," but rather "the rearising of a primordial [i.e., archetypal] reality in narrative form."[52] Yet it is precisely such a primordial or archetypal dimension (as found, for instance, in the works of Ludwig Klages or Carl Jung) that the Frankfurt School as a whole and Adorno in particular swiftly rejected.[53]

Second, the picture that Adorno and Horkheimer paint of society is one of it as completely suffused with ideology, completely in thrall to capitalist ideals, completely blinded by false consciousness. So the question surely arises: how is it that Adorno and Horkheimer themselves have escaped being blinded and have, so to speak, seen through it all? How have they managed, as it were, to find their critically conscious way out of the capitalist cave? After all, for them reason is not the solution, but part of the problem. Because they identify reason (*Vernunft*) with instrumental rationality (*instrumentelle Vernunft*), that is to say, with a form of reason that seeks less to understand and more to control the world around it. The problem here is that instrumental rationality can, as a form of technological fantasy, easily be harnessed or hijacked for militaristic or regressive ends. As Walter Benjamin, another prominent member of the Frankfurt School, memorably put it in his famous essay, "The Work of Art in the Age of Mechanical Reproduction" (1936): "Instead of draining rivers, society directs a human stream into a bed of trenches; instead of dropping seeds from airplanes, it drops incendiary bombs over cities; and through gas warfare the aura is abolished in a new way."[54] In this respect, the Frankfurt School has much in common—despite Adorno's savage critique of existentialism and the "jargon of authenticity"—[55] with Martin Heidegger's view of the dangers of technology.[56]

Hence, as a third and final point of critique, the Frankfurt School runs the risk of being critical in its methodology and radical in its outlook, but conservative in its conclusions. The preference for classical music over jazz, for austere works of contemporary modernism over popular music, and for intricate, labyrinthine sentences over transparent prose—is this ultimately a philosophical stance or an aesthetic one?

To put it bluntly, are the members of the Frankfurt School a bunch of snobs? And what price critical thinking, if the conclusion is that the system is so absolute, the administration so total, the consciousness so utterly false, that there is no chance of changing the model of society? There is surely little danger of a revolution taking place if the answer lies in reading James Joyce or Franz Kafka, or listening to late Beethoven quartets or Schoenberg (but not Stravinsky). In the place of active resistance, Adorno in particular seemed to prefer a stance of resigned melancholy. Again, as Walter Benjamin put it, "the concept of progress is to be grounded in the idea of catastrophe"—and "that things 'just go on' *is* the catastrophe."[57]

In this respect, perhaps there is something telling—allegorical, even—about the sad circumstances surrounding Adorno's demise and death. Towards the end of the 1960s, a number of European countries, including and especially Germany, witnessed a wave of student protests now referred to as the Sixties Revolution. After years of lecturing on the importance of critical thinking, it now turned out that Adorno was not so impressed by this particular form of political action. As Adorno wrote at the time, "barricades are ridiculous against those who administer the bomb."[58] In the summer semester of 1969, Adorno began a series of lectures entitled "An Introduction to Dialectical Thinking." But when, at the first lecture, three female students staged a protest by baring their breasts and scattering him with rose petals, he walked out of the lecture room and cancelled the rest of the lectures. (The incident informs the inspiration for an installation artwork by Hito Steyerl, *Adorno's Grey*, of 2012.) Nude protests were, it seems, insufficiently dialectical for him. On holiday in Switzerland in the summer of the same year, Adorno died of a heart attack. As the German philosopher Peter Sloterdijk describes and analyses this episode:

> [Adorno] was just about to begin his lecture when a group of demonstrators prevented him from mounting the podium [...] Among the disrupters were some female students who, in protest, attracted attention to themselves by exposing their breasts to the thinker. Here, on the one side, stood naked flesh, exercising "critique"; there, on the other side, stood the bitterly disappointed man without whom scarcely any of those present

would have known what critique meant. [...] It was not naked force that reduced the philosopher to muteness, but the force of the naked.[59]

For his part, in an interview with *Der Spiegel* given after this incident, Adorno remarked:

> I have always opposed all kinds of sex repression and taboos — and they did that for *my* benefit, of all people! Ridiculing me, and setting three hippy girls at me! I found them disgusting. The comic affect aimed at was basically the reaction of the philistine *Spießbürger* who giggles at the sight of a girl with bare breasts. The whole absurdity was of course calculated in advance.[60]

Both the passages discussed above in *Dialectic of the Enlightenment* and the seminar-room protest incident of 1969 stand in a relationship, and not simply an oblique one, to the discourse of Platonism. They do so, inasmuch as they raise the question of the status of the erotic, central to such dialogues as the *Phaedrus* and the *Symposium*. For Plato, Eros can serve as a means of moving, through the body, to the liberation of the mind; for Adorno and Horkheimer, Eros, desire, embodiment, touch, and pleasure are only possible today as fetishistic desire and onanistic tacticity. In the modern or postmodern world, Eros cannot lead us out of the cave, or even back to ourselves, but only round and round in permanently unsatisfied circles. No wonder Adorno's thought is so often described as one of melancholy.

Notes

1. "Three masters, seemingly mutually exclusive, dominate the school of suspicion: Marx, Nietzsche, and Freud" (Paul Ricoeur, *Freud and Philosophy: An Essay on Interpretation*, trans. Denis Savage (New Haven and London: Yale University Press, 1970), 32). A work by Vincent Descombes (born 1943), *Le même et l'autre: Quarante-cinq ans de philosophie française, 1933–1978* (1979), translated as *Modern French Philosophy* (1980), has been seen as central to French

intellectual history in introducing a shift in influence away from the "three H's", i.e., Hegel, Husserl, and Heidegger, and towards these "masters of suspicion"; or, more precisely, in operating "a deepening of issues first introduced by the 'three H's', now pursued under a different set of proper names" (Knox Peden, *Spinoza Contra Phenomenology: French Rationalism from Cavaillès to Deleuze* (Stanford, CA: Stanford University Press, 2014), 267).

2. André Glucksmann, *The Master Thinkers*, trans. Brian Pierce (New York: Harper & Row, 1980).
3. For an overview of different conceptions of critique, see Karin de Boer and Ruth Sonderegger (eds), *Conceptions of Critique in Modern and Contemporary Philosophy* (Basingstoke: Palgrave Macmillan, 2012).
4. Friedrich Nietzsche, *Basic Writings*, ed. and trans. Walter Kaufmann (New York: Basic Books, 1968), 238.
5. In his preface to the fourth edition (1920) of his *Three Essays on the History of Sexuality* (1905), Freud noted how "anyone who looks down with contempt upon psychoanalysis from a superior vantage-point should remember how closely the enlarged sexuality of psychoanalysis coincides with the Eros of the divine Plato" (Freud, *On Sexuality: Three Essays on the Theory of Sexuality and Other Works* [Pelican Freud Library, vol. 7], ed. Angela Richards, trans. James Strachey (Harmondsworth: Penguin, 1977), 43). In this context Freud refers to a paper by Max Nachmansohn, "Freuds Libidotheorie verglichen mit der Eroslehre Platons," *Internationale Zeitschrift der Psychoanalyse* 3 (1915), 65–83.
6. Heinrich Moritz Chalybäus, *Historical Development of Speculative Philosophy, from Kant to Hegel*, trans. Alfred Edersheim (Edinburgh: Clark, 1854).
7. Horkheimer and Adorno, *Dialectic of Enlightenment: Philosophical Fragments*, ed. Gunzelin Schmid Noerr, trans. Edmund Jephcott (Stanford, CA: Stanford University Press, 2002), 1. Further references to this work are included in the text in parentheses.
8. For Ernst Cassirer (1874–1945), mythology and science are two different forms of what he calls "symbolic knowledge"; see his *Philosophy of Symbolic Forms* [1923–1929], trans. Ralph Manheim, 3 vols (New Haven and London: Yale University Press, 1955–1957), esp. vol. 2, *Mythical Thought*, and vol. 3, *The Phenomenology of Knowledge*.
9. George Chapman, *Works, Homer's Iliad and Odyssey*, ed. Richard Herne Shepherd, vol. 3 (London: Chatto & Windus, 1924), 414.

10. The popularity of the figure of Odysseus in the post-War German context is examined in Jessica Resch, *Odysseus' Wandlung im Nachkriegsdeutschland: Die Figur des griechischen Helden in der deutschsprachigen Erzählprosa* (Marburg: Tectum, 2012).

11. See Robert Lamberton, *Homer the Theologian: Neoplatonist Allegorical Reading and the Growth of the Epic Tradition* (Berkeley, Los Angeles, and London: University of California Press, 1986); and David A. Beardsley, *The Journey Back To Where You Are: Homer's "Odyssey" as Spiritual Quest* (Highland Park, NJ: Ideograph Media, 2014).

12. The passages they cite are from Nietzsche, *Sämtliche Werke: Kritische Studienausgabe*, ed. Giorgio Colli and Mazzino Montinari, 15 vols (Munich; Berlin and New York: dtv and de Gruyter, 1988), vol. 11, 25 [294], 86, and 36 [48], 570.

13. For further discussion, which challenges Adorno's and Horkheimer's reading, see Jeffrey Barnouw, *Odysseus, Hero of Practical Intelligence: Deliberation and Signs in Homer's "Odyssey"* (Lanham, MD: University Press of America, 2004).

14. As Gunzelin Schmid Noerr points out, the materialistic interpretation of sacrifice embraced by Nietzsche stands in contrast to the interpretation of sacrifice and exchange in terms of *magic* proposed by Ludwig Klages (1872–1956); see his *Der Geist als Widersacher der Seele*, 6th edn (Bonn: Bouvier, 1981), 1401–1415 (cf. *Dialectic of Enlightenment*, 260, note 6). For an introduction to the curiously neglected figure of Klages, see Paul Bishop, *Ludwig Klages and the Philosophy of Life: A Vitalist Toolkit* (London and New York: Routledge, 2017); and for further discussion of various theories of sacrifice, see Dennis King Keenan, *The Question of Sacrifice* (Bloomington and Indianapolis: Indiana University Press, 2005).

15. For their extensive discussion of Polyphemus, see *Dialectic of Enlightenment*, 50–54. Although Homer presents Polyphemus as a savage, cannibalistic (i.e., man-eating) giant, other classical sources— such as a lost play by Philoxenus of Cythera, a lost idyll by Bion of Smyrna, and Theocritus (in his *Idyll*, XI)—cast him in a more positive light and associate him with the nymph Galatea. Similarly, Adorno and Horkheimer have some sympathy for Polyphemus, and in their excursus on the *Odyssey*, they write that he has "redeeming traits" (cf. 52).

16. See Nietzsche, *On the Genealogy of Morals*, II, "'Guilt,' 'Bad Conscience,' and the Like," §4–§6; in *Basic Writings*, 498–503.

This argument has recently been reproposed by Richard Seaford, who has argued that money provides the conditions in which the individual can be imagined; and that money provides a model for the construction of an inner self (see Richard Seaford, "Monetisation and the Genesis of the Western Subject," *Historical Materialism* 20, no. 1 (2012), 78–102; and *Money and the Early Greek Mind: Homer, Philosophy, Tragedy* (Cambridge: Cambridge University Press, 2004)).

17. *Odyssey*, book 10, ll. 296–297; trans. Albert Cook, 2nd edn (New York and London: Norton, 1993), 110.

18. Are Adorno and Horkheimer alluding here to Satire 14, ll. 96–106, which satirizes habits and beliefs which a Jewish father inculcates in his child: "And, since their father abstained from pork, they think it is just as sacred as human flesh" (Juvenal, *The Satires*, trans. Niall Rudd (Oxford and New York: Oxford University Press, 1992), 123)?

19. Freud, *Civilization and Its Discontents*, §4, fn. 1; Freud, *Civilization, Society and Religion* [Penguin Freud Library, vol. 12], ed. Albert Dickson, trans. James Strachey et al. (Harmondsworth: Penguin, 1985), 288–289.

20. See Freud, "A Special Type of Choice of Object Made by Men," and "On the Universal Tendency of Debasement in the Sphere of Love," in *The Standard Edition of the Complete Psychological Works*, vol. 11 (London: Hogarth Press, 1957), 165–175 and 179–190.

21. Compare with the remarks by Marx and Engels in the *Communist Manifesto*: "The bourgeois sees in his wife a mere instrument of production. He hears that the instruments of production are to be exploited in common, and, naturally, can come to no other conclusion than that the lot of being common to all will likewise fall to the women. He has not even a suspicion that the real point aimed at is to do away with the status of women as mere instruments of production" (in Eugen Kamenka (ed.), *The Portable Karl Marx* (New York: Viking Penguin, 1983), 224).

22. For further discussion, see Harvey C. Greisman and George Ritzer, "Max Weber, Critical Theory, and the Administered World," *Qualitative Sociology* 4, no. 1 (Spring 1981), 34–55.

23. Max Horkheimer, "On the Sociology of Class Relations" (*Zur Soziologie der Klassenverhältnisse*) [1943], in *Gesammelte Schriften*, ed. Alfred Schmidt, vol. 12 (Frankfurt am Main: Suhrkamp, 1985), 75–104. For further discussion, see Alfried Schulte-Bockholt, "A Neo-Marxist Explanation of Organized Crime," *Critical Criminology* 10

(2001), 225–242; and James Schmidt, "The *Eclipse of Reason* and the End of the Frankfurt School in America," *New German Critique* 34 (2007), 47–76.

24. See H.C. Greisman, "'Disenchantment of the World': Romanticism, Aesthetics and Sociological Theory," *The British Journal of Sociology* 27 (1976), 495–507.

25. Adorno, *Dissonanzen: Musik in der verwalteten Welt* [1956], 3rd edn, in *Gesammelte Schriften*, ed. Rolf Tiedemann, 20 vols (Frankfurt am Main: Suhrkamp, 1997), vol. 14, 7–167.

26. Adorno, *Jargon der Eigentlichkeit: Zur deutschen Ideologie* (1964), in *Gesammelte Schriften*, vol. 6, 413–526 (436 and 466).

27. Adorno, "Marginalien zu Theorie und Praxis," in *Stichworte: Kritische Modelle 2* (1969), in *Gesammelte Schriften*, vol. 10.2, 759–782 (see §4 and §8, 767 and 772).

28. "Die verwaltete Welt," Hessischer Rundfunk, 19 September 1959; rebroadcast by ORF, Ö1, "Im Gespräch," 14 October 2010.

29. For Adorno's use of this expression in another context, see Theodor W. Adorno, *Minima Moralia: Reflections on a Damaged Life*, trans. E.F.N. Jephcott (London and New York: Verso, 2005), 19.

30. Compare with Klages's critique of America and his notion of *Schablonisierung* ("becoming stereotyped"), in *Die Grundlagen der Charakterkunde* (4th edn, 1926; 10th edn, 1947), in Ludwig Klages, *Charakterkunde I* [*Sämtliche Werke*, vol. 4], ed. Heinz Alfred Müller (Bonn: Bouvier, 1983), 191–428 (408).

31. Adorno and Horkheimer, *Dialectic of Enlightenment*, 104.

32. Adorno and Horkheimer, *Dialectic of Enlightenment*, 108.

33. Adorno and Horkheimer, *Dialectic of Enlightenment*, 110.

34. Adorno and Horkheimer, *Dialectic of Enlightenment*, 111.

35. Adorno and Horkheimer, *Dialectic of Enlightenment*, 111–112.

36. Adorno and Horkheimer, *Dialectic of Enlightenment*, 112.

37. Adorno and Horkheimer, *Dialectic of Enlightenment*, 114–115.

38. Adorno and Horkheimer, *Dialectic of Enlightenment*, 115–116.

39. "Ideology represents the imaginary relationship of individuals to their real conditions of existence" ("Lenin and Philosophy," in Louis Althusser, *Lenin and Philosophy and Other Essays*, trans. Ben Brewster (New York: Monthly Review Press, 2001), 11–44 (109)). In other words, whereas Marx saw ideology as *concealing* the real world, for Althusser ideology *represents* individuals' "imaginary relationship" to it;

in effect, Althusser is mixing Marx and Lacan, just as Marcuse in *Eros and Civilization* (1956) fuses Marx and Freud.

40. Adorno and Horkheimer, *Dialectic of Enlightenment*, 119.

41. Adorno and Horkheimer, *Dialectic of Enlightenment*, 123.

42. The concept of the "racket" is associated with organised crime, and "racketeering" is defined as "coercion or extortion of individuals or businesses for personal profit; the running of any illegal business; a criminal career; the unlawful acts and businesses in organized crime" (Jay Robert Nash, *Dictionary of Crime, Criminal Justice, Criminology, & Law Enforcement* (Lanham, ML: Rowman & Littlefield, 1992), 303).

43. Adorno and Horkheimer, *Dialectic of Enlightenment*, 123–124.

44. Adorno and Horkheimer, *Dialectic of Enlightenment*, 124–125.

45. Adorno and Horkheimer, *Dialectic of Enlightenment*, 125–126.

46. See Kant, *Critique of Judgement*, Part 1, §17: "*Beauty* is an object's form of *purposiveness* insofar as it is perceived in the object *without the presentation of a purpose*"; in Kant, *Critique of Judgment*, trans. Werner S. Pluhar (Indianapolis, IN: Hackett, 1987), 84, cf. §10, §15, and §22 (65, 73, and 92).

47. Adorno and Horkheimer, *Dialectic of Enlightenment*, 127–128.

48. Adorno and Horkheimer, *Dialectic of Enlightenment*, 133.

49. Adorno and Horkheimer, *Dialectic of Enlightenment*, 134.

50. Adorno and Horkheimer, *Dialectic of Enlightenment*, 135–136.

51. Adorno and Horkheimer, *Dialectic of Enlightenment*, 136.

52. See Karl Kerényi, "Prolegomena," in C.G. Jung and Karl Kerényi, *Essays on a Science of Mythology*, trans R.F.C. Hull (New York: Princeton University Press, 1969), 1–24 (6), citing Malinowski, "Myth in Primitive Psychology" [1926], in *Magic, Science and Religion and other Essays* (Garden City, NY: Doubleday, 1948), 72–123.

53. For an account of how the second chapter of *Dialectic of the Enlightenment*, the famous "excursus" on Homer's *Odyssey*, owes much to Adorno's "productive confrontation" with the neo-Romantic *Kulturkritik* and *Zivilisationskritik* of such German conservative intellectuals as Ludwig Klages (1872–1956) and the poet Rudolf Borchardt (1877–1945), see Vicenzo Martella, *Dialectics of Cultural Criticism: Adorno's Confrontation with Rudolf Borchardt and Ludwig Klages in the "Odyssey" Chapter of "Dialektik der Aufklärung"*, Ph.D. dissertation, Justus-Liebig-Universität Gießen, 2012 (I am grateful to Christian Kerslake for this reference). For a perceptive description

of Klages as a patchwork combination of a Frankfurt School account of Enlightenment, as well as a Derridean critique of logocentrism, a Heideggerian interrogation of technology, a Deleuzian (and Guattarian) celebration of productive desire, and a Cixousian challenge to patriarchy, see Jason Ā. Josephson-Storm, *The Myth of Disenchantment: Magic, Modernity, and the Birth of the Human Sciences* (Chicago and London: University of Chicago Press, 2017), 214. (I am grateful to Roderick Main for this reference.)

54. Walter Benjamin, "The Work of Art in the Age of Mechanical Reproduction," in *Illuminations*, trans. Harry Zorn (London: Cape, 1970), 211–244 (235).

55. See Adorno, *The Jargon of Authenticity* [1964], trans. Knut Tarnowski and Frederic Will (Evanston: Northwestern University Press, 1973).

56. See Martin Heidegger, "The Question Concerning Technology," in David Farrell Krell (ed.), *Basic Writings* (London: Routledge and Kegan Paul, 1978), 307–341.

57. Walter Benjamin, "Central Park," trans. Lloyd Spencer and Mark Harrington, *New German Critique* 34 (Winter 1985), 32–58 (50). Indeed, according to Benjamin, "hell [...] is not something that lies before us, but *this life here*."

58. Theodor W. Adorno, "Marginalia to Theory and Praxis" [1969], in *Critical Models: Interventions and Catchwords*, trans. Henry W. Pickford (New York: Columbia University Press, 2005), 259–278 (269).

59. Peter Sloterdijk, *Critique of Cynical Reason*, trans. Michael Eldred (Minneapolis: University of Minnesota Press, 1987), xxxvii.

60. Theodor W. Adorno, "Of Barricades and Ivory Towers: Interview with T.W. Adorno," *Encounter* 33, no. 3 (September 1969), 63–69 (67); this interview was originally published in *Der Spiegel*.

10

Habermas and Communicative Action

As we saw at the end of the previous chapter, Peter Sloterdijk seems to take great pleasure in relating the tale of the female students' naked protest in one of Adorno's lectures, and he enjoys the joke at the expense of Adorno's discomfiture. Whether even today, despite the press coverage of the famous protest made in February 2012 in Moscow's Cathedral of Christ the Saviour by members of the female band, Pussy Riot, any of us would be able to remain sanguine in such circumstances is another matter. In a sense, too, Adorno was surely right: students displaying their naked breasts to him was not going to lead to the abolition of nuclear weapons.

If it has any significance at all, the female students' protest points to a turning-point in the tradition of German Political Thought. Further on in his *Critique of Cynical Reason*, Sloterdijk asks whether the reader remembers "the episode in the lecture hall" described in the preface, "the disturbance of the lecture and the female students' naked breasts?" And he remarks that "their baring was no run-of-the-mill erotic-cheeky argument with female skin," but "they were, almost in the ancient sense, cynically bared bodies, bodies as arguments, bodies as weapons."[1] By *cynical*, Sloterdijk is using the word, not in its modern sense,

© The Author(s) 2019
P. Bishop, *German Political Thought and the Discourse of Platonism*,
https://doi.org/10.1007/978-3-030-04510-4_10

but referring back to the ancient Greek school of philosophy associated with Antisthenes of Athens, a former pupil of Socrates, and Diogenes of Sinope, known as the philosopher of the tub because of the barrel he used as his home.[2] This is pre-eminently a philosophy of the body, carrying on its work as much through the physical gesture as through anything else: in the case of Diogenes, for example, urinating on people who insulted him, defecating in the theatre, and masturbating in public in the marketplace.[3] (When chided for pleasuring himself in the sight of others, Diogenes is said to have replied: "If only it were as easy to banish hunger by rubbing my belly.")[4]

Nothing could be further removed from the tradition of German Political Thought, particularly in its most recent manifestation in the work of the contemporary German philosopher, Jürgen Habermas, who was born in Düsseldorf in 1929. At the time of writing, Habermas is still alive: he stands as a symbol of continuity through the various generations of the Frankfurt School, first (Adorno, Benjamin, Horkheimer), second (Fromm, Marcuse), and third (Habermas). But he also stands as a symbol of continuity with precisely the philosophical tradition which Cynicism opposes, the Platonic. For how does the Platonic tradition operate? Through the dialogue: through the dialogues conducted by Socrates with his interlocutors in the marketplace, on the agora, at the symposium or drinking-party; subsequently, through the imaginary reconstructions of these dialogues in written form by Socrates's pupil, Plato. (Hence the fascination in parts of Plato's dialogues with the relationship of the written to the spoken word; an aspect famously problematized and turned into the notion of "deconstruction" by the French philosopher, Jacques Derrida.)[5] Precisely the importance of conversation, of exchange, of dialogue is emphasized by Jürgen Habermas, who envisages as central to the philosophical activity a setting he calls the "ideal speech situation."

There is continuity in another respect, too. As we saw when we looked at the contributions of such figures as Kant and Hegel, the tradition of German Political Thought becomes largely something carried on by academics. (In ancient Greece, of course, the Academy referred to something quite specific—and very different.)[6] True, neither Marx nor Engels had academic jobs, but their influence was continued by such figures as Adorno and Horkheimer, who cultivated an abstract, intellectual, academic discourse. (In some ways, this style of discourse has been the downfall of the Western Marxist tradition they represent: no one is able to understand what they are saying any more!) So, too, with Habermas, who has enjoyed a distinguished academic career in Germany and in the US, and who has continued to intervene on the subject of contemporary political events, such as German re-unification, the aftermath to the terrorist attacks of 9/11 and the "War on Terror" (including the invasion of Iraq), the handling by the German government of the euro-crisis and the question of Greek debt; and, most recently, the recent UK referendum decision to leave the EU. For non-native-speakers of German who want to follow what he is saying in German, there is a cruel irony in the fact that his lectures, addresses, and interviews can sometimes be difficult to understand because of a speech impediment caused by a cleft palate (hair-lip).

After studying in Göttingen, Zurich, and Bonn, Habermas completed his doctorate in philosophy in Bonn in 1954, writing a study on the absolute and history in the thought of the German Romantic philosopher, F.W.J. Schelling (1775–1854). He went on to write his *Habilitation* under the supervision of Horkheimer and Adorno, subsequently published in 1962 under the title *The Structural Transformation of the Public Sphere: An Inquiry into a Category of Bourgeois Society*. The title betrays the academic tone of Habermas's writings in general, but they address a current, and pressing, question: what are the conditions required for a discourse leading to genuine social change? Among Habermas's early works one can also include such titles as *Knowledge and Human Interests* (1968), *On the Logic of the Social Sciences* (1967), and *Legitimation Crisis in Late Capitalism* (1975), while his *magnum opus*, *Theory of Communicative Action* appeared in two volumes in 1981. Subsequent publications include *The Philosophical Discourse of Modernity* (1985), *Between Facts and Norms: Contributions to a Discourse Theory of Law and Democracy* (1992), and *The Inclusion of the Other* (1996).

To this short list of Habermas's earlier publications one could also add *Theory and Practice* (1963), on which we shall focus here.[7] In this work, Habermas notes, against the background of his analysis of "the historical interconnection between the development of capitalism and the rise and dissolution of the liberal public," how there has been a game-changing moment in the development of modern society—the rise of the notion of the public sphere, and the way in which "the ever more densely strung communications network of the electronic mass media today is organized in such a manner that it controls the loyalty of a depoliticized population, rather than serving to make the social and state controls in turn subject to a decentralized and uninhibited discursive formation of the public will, channeled in such a way as to be of consequence — and this in spite of the technical potential for liberation which this technology represents".[8]

Already, in the thought of Marx and Engels, we saw the realization that political philosophy had to take account of the changes in technology. Thanks to the Industrial Revolution, the very nature of work changed: from the agricultural to the industrial. It would be fair to say that the materialist tradition of thought, to which Marxism belongs, is more alert to the influence of technology on human society than is its counterpart, the Idealist tradition. (This tradition, founded in the thought of Plato, nevertheless saw something of a renaissance in the late nineteenth century, for instance in the work of the British Idealists, inspired by the thought of Kant, Fichte, Schelling, and, above all, Hegel.)[9]

For the Frankfurt School, the development of technology in general and electronic communications in particular had been not so much influential, as catastrophic. (To this extent Adorno and Horkheimer shared the analysis of technology offered from a very different philosophical tradition, the phenomenological one, by Heidegger.) For Habermas, however, modern communications technology offered an opportunity as well. It opened up the public sphere to new opportunities for political discourse. To participate in democracy, one did not have to go to the market-square or town hall to listen to a speaker, participate in a debate, or simply heckle. Now political talk shows on television and radio phone-ins offered fresh new ways to have a participative democracy. At the same time, this opportunity could turn into a threat. It could encourage a passivity on the part of its audience, the general public, and indeed there is a sense in which democracy itself was entering a period of crisis. Put simply, in the modern world, everything is becoming more complex. As a result, Habermas discerned a crisis of legitimation: by what right does society organise itself in the way it does? Against the background of "two tendencies of development which are characteristic of advanced capitalism [...] with a view to the depoliticization of the public"—i.e., first, "the cumulative growth, on the part of the state, of interventionist activity which is designed to secure the stability and growth of the economic system"; and second, "the growing interdependence of research, technology, and governmental administration, which has converted the system of the sciences into a primary force of production"—"a chronic need for legitimation is developing today."[10]

To take a concrete example, consider the way in which, in traditional working-class communities, the consumption of alcohol was strictly regulated. When the factories closed, the men would leave and go to the pub: the older ones could keep an eye on the younger ones, and discourage inebriation or drunken behaviour. With the demise of manufacturing, this kind of social or cultural control has disappeared. On the one hand, alcohol consumption is no longer the preserve of men in their male-dominated pubs; on the other, both men and women can get drunk, with alcohol more readily available, a leisure culture that tolerates (or, in some cases, actually encourages) inebriation or drunken behaviour, and so the health problems, let alone the social ones, caused by alcohol abuse are on the increase. How do we decide what is a socially acceptable norm and what is not? In other words, what is and what is not *legitimate*?

For Habermas, however, the question is far more fundamental. As he argues above, capitalism in its advanced form unleashes two lines of development: on the one hand, increasingly governmental intervention in economic activity; on the other, a growing nexus of interdependence between research, technology, and government. What emerges, says Habermas, is something called technocracy, a form of government where the power of special or technical expertise comes to replace the exercise of democratic authority by elected representatives. This technocratic shift has the effect of depoliticizing the general public; or, to put it another way, what arises is a crisis of legitimacy.

Habermas tracks the development of this crisis and looks to provide a solution to it through a close (and extremely detailed) analysis of what he calls *discourse*, a key term in Habermasian vocabulary. Here lies one of Habermas's chief political theoretical innovations: paying attention not just to political *institutions*, but to the *language* of politics. In his major work of 1975, *Legimitation Crisis*, Habermas defines discourse as "that form of communication that is removed from contexts of experience and action and whose structure assures us" of three things: first, that "the bracketed validity claims of assertions, recommendations, or warnings are the exclusive object of discussion"; second, that "participants, themes and contributions are not restricted except with reference to the goal of testing the validity claims in questions; that no force except that of the better argument is exercised"; and third, that "all motives except that of the cooperative search for truth are excluded." [11] Under these conditions, the consensus that arises can be said to express a "rational will."

For Marx and for Engels, political analysis required an understanding of powers of production and relations of production. The workers supplied the labour, but not the factories; the workers produced the products, but after they had added value to them, these goods were taken away and sold for a profit; thanks to modern industrial production techniques, most workers simply performed the same repetitive tasks, losing all sense of a meaningful connection to their work (i.e., becoming alienated). But in the era of late capitalism, Habermas argued, capitalism was no longer unfettered but increasingly bound up with systems of adminstration and government, to the extent that the political and economic have become ever more difficult to separate.[12]

In other words, what Habermas is trying to address, and from a critical, theoretically-informed perspective, is a set of social conditions which has become far more complex than Marx and Engels could ever have dreamed of. When government operations, such as providing passports or building roads, are handed over to private companies to provide, then where do the state and private commerce begin and end? When a state government funds a broadcaster such as the BBC, which has to follow the logic of the market in order to ensure its programmes reach a sufficiently wide audience, where do the state and the market begin and end? As Habermas sets out in *Theory and Practice* at some length,[13] technocratic ideology becomes the meeting-point of governmental and societal interests.

So while Habermas borrows from Marxism the distinction between theory and practice, he follows the practice of the earlier members of the Frankfurt School in resisting the temptation to close the process of dialectic too soon, and he goes beyond them in arguing that social theory was always to interrogate the ground of its own enquiry. "A theory," he argues, "can only be formulated under the precondition that those engaged in scientific work have the freedom to conduct theoretical discourse"; in short, "there is no privileged access to truth."[14] Compared with some of the thinkers we have examined in this survey of German Political Thought and its use of the discourse of Platonism, Habermas can appear unexciting. There is no great revolutionary rhetoric, no central allegory, and no simple political slogan that can be taken from his work. And yet, in his quietly methodical way, Habermas returns us to some of the central issues with which we began—and which refer us back precisely to Platonism.

In the debate between Foucault and Habermas that took place in the 1970 and 1980s (a debate that was conducted in some ways as much by their followers as by the two thinkers themselves), certain important contours can be seen beginning to take shape.[15] For the French sociologist Michel Foucault (1926–1984), the master concept in his analysis of society is one that resonates with Nietzschean overtones—*power*. Foucault invites us to try and track how power informs all our relations, political and personal (particularly sexual), and he was closely associated with the Sixties Revolution, one of whose expressions proved to be so fatal to Adorno. Yet Foucault's notion of power is notoriously vague and tricky to define; although this could, of course, be the source of its attraction to so many.

By contrast, Habermas proposes the notion of "communicative rationality." This is his answer to the problem of "instrumental rationality," highlighted as something fundamentally aggressive, regressive, and dangerous by Adorno and Horkheimer in their *Dialectic of Enlightenment*. On this account, rationality is only truly rational when it emerges from and contributes to successful communication.

Thus communicative rationality serves as a reaction, a response and a resolution to the reduction of reason to three kinds of "formal" reason: (1) cognitive-instrumental; (2) moral-practical; and (3) aesthetic-expressive. Communicative rationality involves a notion that could be described as the master concept in Habermas's thought, the "ideal speech situation." In such a situation, the assertions of the participants are evaluated on the basis of reason alone. Free from all kinds of coercion, the interlocutors in the ideal speech situation seek to find a rational consensus on the basis of rational discussion. Habermas sets out the following five conditions.[16]

First, participation in the ideal speech situation is open to each and every speaking actor who is competent to speak and to conform to these rules. Second, anyone is allowed to question any assertion that anyone else makes. Third, anyone may make any assertion that he or she chooses, although of course he or she must also allow it to be submitted to rational interrogation by other interlocutors. Fourth, this right to assertion of one's own views holds good for any and all of them: freedom of expression is paramount. Fifth, no one should be coerced in any way whatsoever, implicitly or explicitly, from making use of rules 1, 2, 3 or 4. The exercise of communicative rationality under these conditions allows for the ethical conduct of discourse; in fact, *discourse ethics* is precisely the name Habermas gives to these "presuppositions of argumentation."

Well, one can see why Habermas describes this situation as ideal! Such a situation can, if ever, only rarely be encountered in the workplace, in the office, or even (or especially) in the university... Yet in a way, this is the point: and closer examination of the idea of communicative rationality and the ideal speech situation reveals the extent to which Habermas brings us back to the central motif of this survey of German Political Thought, its relation to the discourse of Platonism and the allegory of the cave. And it does so in at least four respects.

First, it returns us to the importance of speech, dialogue, and discourse. Speech is the central item in Socrates's philosophical toolkit, and the *Republic* begins and ends with a speech-act: Socrates recalling his journey down to the Piraeus with Glaucon, son of Ariston, to pray to the goddess, at the festival of the moon goddess Bendis, and the ensuing conversation with Glaucon, Polemarchus, Adeimantus, and others; and, at the end, Socrates recounting to Glaucon the myth of Er, son of Armenius—the story of how a soldier is killed on the battlefield, but comes back to life just as he is about to be buried and himself recounts what he had seen in the other world. Speech within speech within speech: Plato's entire approach is eminently one focused on dialogue.

Second, the ideal speech situation is, as we have said, ideal: and yet without it, Habermas believes, we cannot be truly rational. (We can never be rational entirely on our own: that way, madness lies.) Similarly, for Plato, behind the concrete reality of individual objects, there lies the ideal; more important, behind each specific individuation of justice, there lies the ideal of Justice. And behind everything, so we learn from the allegories of the cave, the line, and the sun, can be found the idea of the Good.

Third, while Plato is clearly interested in questions of ontology (the science of what is) and epistemology (the science of how we know things), he is also interested in questions of ethics (the science of how we should act). For this reason, his dialogue *The Republic* is given by later editors the subtitle, "On the Just." And what constitutes justice is a central question in the *Republic*: as Socrates remarks to Thrasymachus, "the argument is not about just any question, but about the way one should live" (352d). In book 1 of the *Republic*, we find exactly what Habermas describes as an ideal speech situation: Cephalus, Polemarchus, Thrasymachus—each is free to propose his own definition of justice; each of them is free to scrutinize the statements made by the others; and there is no coercion to accept one definition over another. Step by step, in an exercise of communicative rationality, Socrates leads Thrasymachus to a rational conclusion: "Didn't we agree that justice is virtue of soul, and injustice vice?" …. "Then the just soul and the just man will have a good life, and the unjust man a bad one" … "And the man who lives well is blessed and happy, and the man who does not is the opposite" … "Then the just man is happy and the unjust man wretched" … "But it is not profitable to be wretched, rather it is profitable to be happy" … "Then, my blessed Thrasymachus, injustice is never more profitable than justice" (353e–354b). It looks as if Socrates has won; but when Glaucon, and then Adeimantus, in turn question

Socrates's account, then Socrates invites them to consider the relation between the "justice of one man" and the "justice of a whole city", and on the premise that "if we should watch a city coming into being, *in speech* [...], we would also see its justice coming into being, and its injustice," the rest of the argumentation of the remaining eight books of the *Republic* is born (368e and 369b; my emphasis).

Finally, as the references at the outset to the festival of the moon goddess, Bendis, explicitly remind us, and as the allegory of the cave can be read to imply, there is a religious backdrop, maybe even a religious dimension, to the argument of the *Republic*. (Indeed, a good deal of the Neoplatonic tradition subsequent to Plato involves reading his work in an esoteric or spiritual sense.) Now the conditions for the ideal speech situation raise the question: what happens if one of the interlocutors doesn't accept one or any or all of these rules? What happens, for example, if an interlocutor claims religious privilege and argues that an assertion he or she is making is non-negotiable, because it is not a matter of rationality, but a matter of revelation? In short, what is the public role of religion?

This brings us to another famous debate between Habermas and a leading intellectual figure, this time Cardinal Joseph Ratzinger, at the time Prefect of the Congregation for the Doctrine of the Faith (an office previously known as the Inquisition ...), and subsequently Pope Benedict XVI. On January 14 2004, the Catholic Academy of Bavaria in Munich invited Habermas and Ratzinger to a debate before a limited audience, and the discussion was later published under the title *The Dialectic of Secularization*.[17] At the heart of their discussion lies the status of reason, and what provides the ultimate grounding of reason. As Ratzinger argues, there is something circular about grounding reason on reason itself; already, he suggests, in submitting to reason, we are making an act of faith. Significantly, Habermas conceded that Ratzinger has a point, and he has gone on to argue for a role for Judeo-Christian ethics in informing our society's culture, and to accept that the exclusion of religious voices from the public sphere is essentially "illiberal." One cannot help but be reminded that Socrates tells Glaucon how the allegory of the cave recounts "the soul's journey up to the intelligible good," and his statement that "in the knowable the last thing to be seen, and that with considerable effort, is the *idea* of the good" (517b-c).

From its beginning to its end, and in its continuation in the present day, the tradition of German Political Thought—in line with *all* political thought, to be sure—is concerned with the question of what the ancients called "the good life." Originally associated with Aristotle's teaching on ethics and with the ancient Greek notion of *eudaimonia*, this notion, far from being simplistic or banal, involves some of the most fundamental questions one can ask about how one should live one's life. Necessarily, because human beings are, as Aristotle observed, political animals, this involves the question of how one should lead one's life with the other people around one. Unsurprisingly for a category that is over two millennia old, the notion of the good life remains as relevant and as timely as it has always been. For as Socrates argues in the *Crito*, the question of justice is one of both political and personal urgency:

SOCRATES: And is life worth living for us with that part of us corrupted that unjust action harms and just action benefits? Or do we think that part of us, whatever it is, that is concerned with justice and injustice, is inferior to the body?
CRITO: Not at all.
SOCRATES: It is more valuable?
CRITO: Much more.
SOCRATES: We should not then think so much of what the majority will say about us, but what he will say who understands justice and injustice, the one, that is, and the truth itself.[18]

Notes

1. Peter Sloterdijk, *Critique of Cynical Reason*, trans. Michael Eldred (Minneapolis: University of Minnesota Press, 1987), 109.
2. For further discussion, see R. Bracht Branham and Marie-Odile Goulet-Cazé, *The Cynics: The Cynic Movement in Antiquity and Its Legacy* (Berkeley, Los Angeles, and London: University of California Press, 1996).
3. See Michel Onfray, *Cynismes: Portrait du philosophe en chien* (Paris: Grasset, 1990), 43–52; *Les Sagesses antiques* [*Contre-histoire de la*

philosophie, vol. 1] (Paris: Grasset, 2006), 64, 136–137. Likewise, see Sloterdijk, *Critique of Cynical Reason*, 101–106, where Diogenes's masturbation in public is described as a "model situation" (106).

4. See Diogenes Laërtius, *Lives and Opinions of Eminent Philosophers*, trans. C.D. Yonge (London: Bell, 1895), book 6, §46, §49 (233, 243).

5. See Derrida's three works, *Writing and Difference* (1967), *Speech and Phenomena* (1967), and *Of Grammatology* (1967).

6. The Academy, centered around a sacred grove of olive trees dedicated to Athena (the goddess of wisdom) and located just outside the city walls of Athens, was founded by Plato in c. 387 BCE. It persisted through the Hellenistic period, came to an end in 83 BC, was revived in 410 CE as centre for Neoplatonism, until it was finally closed by Emperor Justinian I in 529 CE. For further discussion, see Harold Cherniss, *The Riddle of the Early Academy* (Berkeley and Los Angeles: University of California Press, 1945); John Dillon, *The Heirs of Plato: A Study of the Old Academy (347–274 BC)* (Oxford: Clarendon Press, 2003).

7. See Eberhard Braun, Felix Heine, and Uwe Opolka (eds), *Politische Philosophie: Ein Lesebuch: Texte, Analysen, Kommentare* (Reinbek bei Hamburg: Rowohlt, 2008), 477–496.

8. Jürgen Habermas, *Theory and Practice*, trans. John Viertel (Cambridge and Malden, MA: Polity Press, 1988), 4.

9. For an overview of this tradition, to which such thinkers as, in its first generation, T.H. Green (1836–1882), F.H. Bradley (1846–1924), and Bernard Bosanquet (1848–1923), and, in its second, J.M.E. McTaggart (1866–1925), H.H. Joachim (1868–1938), John Henry Muirhead (1855–1940), and R.G. Collingwood (1889–1943) belonged, see David Boucher (ed.), *The British Idealists* (Cambridge: Cambridge University Press, 1997).

10. Habermas, *Theory and Practice*, trans. Viertel, 4–5.

11. Jürgen Habermas, *Legitimation Crisis*, trans. Thomas McCarthy (Cambridge and Malden, MA: Polity Press, 1988), 107–108.

12. Jürgen Habermas, *Legitimation Crisis*, 54–55.

13. Habermas, *Theorie und Praxis: Sozialphilosophische Studien*, 3rd edn (Frankfurt am Main: Suhrkamp, 1996), 352–357.

14. Habermas, *Theory and Practice*, 32–34.

15. See Michael Kelly (ed.), *Critique and Power: Recasting the Foucault/ Habermas Debate* (Cambridge, MA: MIT Press, 1994), for some of the major interventions in this debate; and, for further discussion, see

David Ingram, "Foucault and Habermas on the Subject of Reason," in Gary Gutting (ed.), *The Cambridge Companion to Foucault* (Cambridge: Cambridge University Press, 1994), 215–261; Samantha Ashenden and David Owen (eds), *Foucault Contra Habermas: Recasting the Dialogue between Genealogy and Critical Theory* (London: Sage, 1999).

16. Jürgen Habermas, "Discourse Ethics: Notes on a Program of Philosophical Justification," in *Moral Consciousness and Communicative Action*, trans. Christian Lenhart and Shierry Weber Nicholson (Cambridge, MA: MIT Press, 1990), 43–115.

17. Jürgen Habermas and Joseph Ratzinger, *The Dialectics of Secularization: On Reason and Religion* [2005], trans. Brian McNeil (San Francisco: Ignatius Press, 2006); translated from *Dialektik der Säkularisierung: Über Vernunft und Religion* (Freiburg im Breisgau, Basel, Vienna: Herder, 2005).

18. *Crito*, 47e–48a; translated by G.M.A. Grube in Peter J. Steinberger (ed.), *Readings in Classical Political Thought* (Indianapolis, IN: Hackett, 2000), 162.

11

By Way of Conclusion

Those who do not move do not notice their chains.
(Rosa Luxemburg, attrib.)[1]

It is hard to write a conclusion to this book, because the narrative it has related is an example, if ever there was one, of a never-ending story. So perhaps the best way of bringing our discussion to a close is to return to its starting-point and to ask a question about Plato's *Republic*: Where did Plato find his cave?[2]

Or to put this question in another way: Is there a source for his image of the cave? (In answering this question, we must for reasons of space leave aside the question of actual, physical caves in the ancient Greek world, where their function was a threefold one, as Yulia Ustinova has shown. First, descent into the darkness of a cave was a way to enlightenment and a sojourn in a cave was a means of acquiring ultimate or divine knowledge. Second, passage through a cave served as a mental image of the road to divine truth. And third, the cosmos itself was mystically envisioned as a cave.[3] Caves were often the location for a kind of incubation experience, stimulating altered states of consciousness through sensory deprivation or allowing narcotic gases to be inhaled.)[4]

© The Author(s) 2019
P. Bishop, *German Political Thought and the Discourse of Platonism*,
https://doi.org/10.1007/978-3-030-04510-4_11

One place to look for prototypes of the cave in Plato's *Republic* are the thinkers called the pre-Socratics, that is, the thinkers that preceded the figure of Socrates (c. 469–c. 399 BCE) (even if some of them, chronologically speaking, were contemporaries of Socrates). In this respect the figure of Empedocles (c. 490–c. 430 BCE) comes to mind. Very little of his work is extant, the exceptions being fragments from two poems (which may, in fact, be part of a single poem) known as "On Nature" and "Purifications." One such fragment is, however, particularly suggestive for our present endeavour.

Now in his treatise or essay "On the Cave of the Nymphs," the Neoplatonic thinker Porphyry takes as his starting-point the description given by Homer in book 13 of the *Odyssey* of the cave in the harbour of Ithaca where Odysseus hides the gifts from King Alcinoos of the Phaeacians.[5] This cave is precisely the cave of the nymphs of which Porphyry's treatise goes on to speak at some length. Later on, Porphyry cites the opening of the allegory of the cave from book 7 of the *Republic*, but before doing so he cites a fragment from Empedocles, "We have come to this roofed cave."[6] (In turn, Empedocles may be drawing on Pythagorean tradition.)[7]

Porphyry attributes this remark to "the powers that guide souls," and he believes that Homer's description of the cave is "where the Pythagoreans and Plato after them got the idea of calling the cosmos a cave or grotto."[8] In support of this interpretation that the cave symbolizes the world, Porphyry cites Plato's account of the "subterranean cave" from the *Republic*,[9] and in his *Ennead* entitled "On the Descent of the Soul into Bodies" Plotinus confirms this reading:

> The godlike Plato [...] said many fine things about the soul and about its coming [into this world] in his writings [...]. [He] says that "the esoteric saying is a great one", which asserts that the soul is "in custody"; and his cave, like the den of Empedocles, means, I think, this universe, where he says that the soul's journey to the intelligible world is a "release from fetters" and an "ascent from the cave."[10]

But could there have been an actual cave? In an earlier dialogue, the *Phaedo*, Socrates describes in considerable detail the geography of the underworld; to be sure, in part following such predecessors as Homer and Pindar.

As Socrates explains to Simmias, we assume that we are living "on the earth's surface," but in reality we are living "in the hollow places of the earth" (109c). "We live," he says, "round the sea like ants or frogs round a pond — and there are many other peoples inhabiting similar regions" (109b). He goes on to present a description of the world that demonstrates significant parallels to the predicament of the prisoners in the allegory of the cave:

> Imagine someone living in the depths of the sea. He might think that he was living on the surface, and seeing the sun and the other heavenly bodies through the water; he might think that the sea was the sky. He might be so sluggish and feeble that he had never reached the top of the sea, never emerged and raised his head from the sea into this world of ours, and seen for himself — or even heard from someone who had seen it — how much purer and more beautiful it really is than the one in which his people lives. *Now we are in just the same position.* (109c–d; my emphasis)[11]

As in the allegory of the cave, Socrates emphasizes the difficulty and struggle involved in making one's way from the hollow of the earth (or from the interior of the cave) up to the surface:

> Although we live in a hollow of the earth, we assume that we are living on the surface, and we call the air heaven, as though it were the heaven through which the stars move. And this point too is the same, that we are too feeble and sluggish to make our way out to the upper limits of the air. If someone could reach to the summit, or put on wings and fly aloft, when he put up his head he would see the world above, just as fishes see our world when they put up their heads out of the sea. And if his nature were able to bear the sight, he would recognize that that is the true heaven and the true light and the true earth. (109e–110a)[12]

And as in allegory of the cave, Socrates is confident in his discussion with Simmias about what life on the true earth (or outside the cave) looks like:

> There are [...] human beings [...] [and] their climate is so temperate that they are free from disease and live much longer than people do here, and in sight and hearing and understanding and all other faculties they are as far superior to us as air is to water or aether to air in clarity. They also have sanctuaries and temples which are truly inhabited by gods, and oracles and prophecies and visions and all other kinds of communion with the gods occur there face to face. They see the sun and moon and stars as they really are, and the rest of their happiness is after the same manner. (111b–c)[13]

In short, this description of life on the true earth or outside the cave sounds like exactly what Socrates had described earlier in the *Phaedo* to Cebes as the life of the soul and the attainment of wisdom:

> When [the soul] investigates itself, it passes into the realm of the pure and everlasting and immortal and changeless, and being of a kindred nature, when it is once independent and free from interference, consorts with it always and strays no longer, but remains, in that realm of the absolute, constant and invariable, through contact with beings of a similar nature. And this condition of the soul we call wisdom. (79d)[14]

Even more starkly, in the *Gorgias*, in which another myth is related, Socrates wonders whether Euripides did not have it right when he asked, "Who knows whether being alive is being dead, and being dead is being alive?",[15] adding: "And perhaps we are actually dead, and [...] our body is a tomb, and [...] that part of the soul in which dwell the desires is of a nature to be swayed and to shift to and fro" (492e–493a). On this account, life on earth is really living in the underworld.[16]

It has been argued that the details of Socrates's description of the underworld in the *Phaedo* suggest that the location of Tartarus, the deep abyss that serves as a place of punishment for wicked souls, is beneath Mount Etna. Does this meaning that the opening of the underworld could (or can) be found in Sicily? Yet even to pose the question in such terms is, as Peter Kingsley has argued, futile. (While it has become commonplace to approach ancient culture in terms of a distinction between *mythos* and *logos*,[17] the Danish philosopher Johannes Sløk (1916–2001) has used the philosophy of language to problematize this simple (and simplistic) opposition.[18] As we have seen, the question of the relation between *mythos* and *logos*, or "irrationality" and "rationality," recurs in the work of the Frankfurt School.) On a number of occasions in Plato's dialogues, the distinction is explicitly refused. In the *Gorgias*, Socrates invites Callicles to listen to "a very fine story, which you, I suppose, will consider fiction, but I consider fact, for what I am going to tell you I shall recount as the actual truth" (523a); while in the *Phaedrus*, in his discourse on the different kinds of madness, Socrates remarks that his proof "assuredly will prevail with the wise, though not with the learned" (245c). As Kingsley points out, Plato not only refuses the distinction between *mythos* and *logos* but goes further, insisting that what is a "myth" to someone superficial may well constitute a *logos* to someone with deeper perception.[19]

Applied to the myth in the *Phaedo*, where Socrates sets about describing "the real earth" (110b), this means (in Kingsley's words) that analysing it into its component levels "puts an end once and for all to [...] the debate as to whether the 'earth' referred to in the myth is to be understood literally as a reference to our own familiar earth, or metaphorically as an allusion to something else."[20] On one level, the narrative of the myth in the *Phaedrus* describes the shape of the earth in terms compatible with the geography of Sicily. On another level, this narrative can be applied allegorically to philosophical—even mystical—ends.[21]

So how would this apply to the allegory of the cave in the *Republic*, a work where Plato repeatedly suggests he is presenting "mythologizing in a *logos*," as when Socrates encourages Adeimantus, "Come, then, like men telling tales in a tale and at their leisure, let's educate the men in speech" (376d); or when he prophesies, "Before the philosophic class becomes master of a city, there will be no rest from ills either for city or citizens nor will the regime about which we tell tales in speech gets its completion in deed" (501e)? This is a question we have borne in mind throughout the preceding chapters and to which we shall now return: how are we to understand the allegory of the cave?

As we have seen, within the Pythagorean tradition before Plato the cave played an important role in philosophical thought. On the island of Samos there still exists a system of caves said to have been used by Pythagoras as a classroom where he delivered his teachings to his disciples. It was here, on Mount Kerkis, that Pythagoras went into hiding when Polycrates, the tyrant of Samos, was trying to hunt him down. Yet there is an important symbolic dimension to the image of the cave within the discourse of Platonism as well.

In one of the early dialogues, the *Cratylus*, which focuses on the origins of language, Socrates remarks that, according to some, "the body is the grave [*soma*] of the soul which may be thought to be buried in our present life" (400c). This play on words (*soma* = body; *sema* = grave), is attributed by Socrates to the Orphics, the followers of the cult of the god and the participants in the Orphic Mysteries named after him,[22] ascribing to them the view that "the body is an enclosure or prison in which the soul is incarcerated, kept safe, [...] until the penalty is paid."[23] (Elsewhere, in the *Phaedrus*, Socrates speaks of the body as a "prison house," something in which we are "fast bound" as "an oyster in its shell"[24]; and in the *Phaedo*, he explains that "despising the body and avoiding it, and endeavouring to become independent" constitutes the task of the philosopher.)[25] Does this mean that Plato is a dualist?

As R.T. Wallis has argued, Plato's attitude toward the sensible world might more accurately be described as an *equivocal* one. After all, in the *Timaeus* the soul is regarded as an *intermediary* between the sensible and the intelligible worlds (and, by that token, as responsible for the organisation of the former).[26] And in the first of his two tractates on "Difficulties about the Soul," Plotinus insists on the *reciprocal relationship* between the soul and the material world, explaining the relationship between soul and cosmos by using the image of a net in the sea. "The universe lies in soul which bears it up, and nothing is without a share of soul," he says, explaining that "it is as if a net immersed in the waters was alive, but unable to make its own that in which it is," for "the sea is already spread out and the net spreads with it, as far as it can"; in other words, "soul's nature is so great, just because it has no size, as to contain the whole of body in one and the same grasp," allowing Plotinus to come to the aphoristic conclusion that "wherever body extends, there soul is."[27] How could the body be something bad, bathing as it does in an ocean of soul?

Here we must leave aside the complicated question of the Platonic view of the body, but we should note Cornelia J. de Vogel's conclusion about the role and place of the body in the philosophy of Plato, namely that Plato "was, in fact, not an over-spiritualist," for although he "did not identify man with the thinking soul or *noûs*," he "did hold that the thinking soul was by nature superior to the body and thus had to lead and govern it," and so he "thought the body an extremely important thing, since it had to serve the soul"; accordingly, Plato's entire system of education is "built on the principle of equal training of both body and soul, and this was for him the absolute condition to a harmonious life."[28]

If the body is a prison, then the only way out of it is death: hence the emphasis in Plato's early dialogues on the relationship between philosophy and death. In the *Phaedo*, Socrates describes the philosopher as "practising death" (65; 67e); as a consequence, philosophy offers a liberation from the prison of the body (82d–84b). Yet is death the only way to be released from this corporeal incarceration? It would not have been for those in the ancient world who had been initiated into the Mysteries: be it the Orphic ones, to which Plato alluded above, or any of the other mystery cults of the ancient world (the Bacchic Mysteries, the Dionysian Mysteries, or the Eleusinian Mysteries in the form of its Lesser or its Greater Rites). Did Plato, who alludes to the Bacchic Mysteries in the *Phaedo* when Socrates says, "many bear the thyrsus, but the devotees are few" (69c), know of the Mysteries? Within the discourse of Platonism, there has always been a tension between, on the one hand, those who read Plato as participating in or systematizing philosophy as an exercise in logic, and, on the other, those who read him in an "esoteric" sense.

On this account, Plato himself—the "divine Plato," as the Renaissance humanist scholar and translator Marsilio Ficino (1433–1499), called him—[29] had visited Egypt and, at the age of 49, had been initiated into the "Greater Mysteries" in a subterranean chamber beneath the Great Pyramid of Giza over a period of three months. Thus initiated, Plato was then sent out into the world "to do the work of the Great Order, as Pythagoras and Orpheus had been before him." Or such is the view attributed in the early twentieth century by the Canadian-born historian of occultism, Manly P. Hall (1901–1990), to the nineteenth-century English translator and latter-day Neoplatonist, Thomas

Taylor (1758–1835).[30] According to the founder of anthroposophy, Rudolf Steiner (1861–1925), there is "only one way of making Plato fully intelligible," and this is to place him "in the light that streams from the Mysteries."[31] And this view has been restated by such more recent commentators as Jeremy Naydler, who regards Plato as a kind of shaman figure, arguing that the kind of knowledge into which Plato would have been initiated might have included a technique for separating his soul (or consciousness) from his body,[32] or the anthroposophist Carol Dunn, who claims that the dialogues as a whole constitute "a complete course of spiritual/religious study" and that the *Symposium* and the *Republic* in particular demonstrate "the goal of all seeking" to be "a sudden and direct experience of the Good that would engulf the soul in what is termed a state of illumination or enlightenment."[33] Indeed, Michael L. Morgan has argued that Plato's dialogues constitute a transposition of "ecstatic" Mystery rituals into rational discursive form, pointing to an Orphic-Pythagorean influence on Plato.[34]

While such claims often leave behind many of the conventional assumptions of academic "evidence," they too form part of the ongoing discourse of Platonism in its popular forms. Moreover, they illustrate the continuity between the *Oedipus Aegyptiacus* (3 vols, 1652–1654) of the seventeenth-century German Jesuit priest and scholar, Athanasius Kircher (1602–1680), and the more recent work that has been undertaken by Peter Kingsley on the shamanic roots of early Greek philosophy.[35] (Maybe this gap between the academic and the esoteric, between working within the framework of convention and questioning those assumptions, can be bridged by discourse analysis—or even by the aesthetic?)[36] And they raise the question of how, within the discourse of Platonism, the political intersects with the spiritual—and the spiritual with the political.

Equally, maybe we should also interrogate the implications of Plato's choice to locate his allegory inside (and outside) a cave, and the impact this may have had on its reception in the German tradition? After all, as Gary Lachman (among other commentators) has noted, there is a long German tradition about "the secrets and magic of caves."[37] This is particularly true of German Romanticism with its fascination for caves, mountains, and mining. One thinks of the early short story

"The Rune Mountain" (*Der Runenberg*) (1802) and the late novella "The Old Man of the Mountain" (*Der Alte vom Berge*) (1828) by Ludwig Tieck (1773–1853); the short story "The Mines of Falun" (*Die Bergwerke zu Falun*) (1819) by E.T.A. Hoffmann (1776–1822); and *Heinrich of Ofterdingen* (1802) by Novalis (1772–1801). One might well ask, with Theodore Ziolkowski, why the image of mining "appealed so strongly" to young writers in Germany between 1790 and 1820. As Ziolkowski notes, some of them actually had training as mining engineers: Goethe, for instance, was responsible as an administrator in Saxe-Weimar with the reopening of the silver mines at Ilmenau; Novalis served as an administrator in the royal saltworks in Saxony; and Clemens Brentano, Joseph von Eichendorff, Heinrich Steffens, Theodor Körner, Alexander von Humboldt, Franz von Baader, and Gotthilf Heinrich Schubert all had interest in, experience of, or connections to mining in one way or another.[38] Mining and caves participate in what has been described as a "liminal semiotics," and Melanie Lörke has explored in her study of "boundary phenomena" in Romanticism how an "idealized perception" of mining—"mysterious caves, wise miners, hidden secrets and ancient knowledge symbolized by precious minerals"—arose in German Romanticism.[39]

Now if mining encourages a particular way of thinking, which could be described as a "bonanza psychology," this is even more true of investigating caves: what treasure might they possibly contain? Moreover, there is clearly a psychological dimension to mines and to caves, as Ziolkowski emphasizes: for German Romanticism, a mine is "not simply a cold dark hole in the ground," but rather "a vital, pulsing place into which man descends as into his own soul for the encounter with three dimensions of human experience: history, religion, and sexuality."[40] Indeed, it is hard not to exclude a psychoanalytic dimension: the cave as a mysterious location of origin, of renewal, of rebirth.[41] In German Romanticism, some paintings seem positively to insist on the visual and symbolic proximity of the cave to female genitalia. (One thinks, for example, of certain works by Caspar David Friedrich or Karl Friedrich Schinkel …) But if, read in Freudian terms, the cave is a symbol of the vagina, it is, in Jungian terms, a symbol of the collective unconscious; and, read in Lacanian terms, leaving the cave represents the rejection of the symbolic order of the Other and the traumatic access to the Real. Once again, the image of the cave serves to bridge the literal dimensions of the geological, the archaeological, and the sphere of economics, and the more intimate symbolic dimensions of the personal, the sexual, and the spiritual.

The argument of the previous pages has been that Plato's allegory of the cave provides us with a useful conceptual framework in which to approach the major texts of German Political Thought. Or to put it another way, the tradition of German Political Thought is informed at a deep level by the discourse of Platonism, and the later European thinkers in this tradition can be read as a reaction and a response to the key elements of Plato's allegory by being sensitive to the discourse of enchainment and liberation it proposes and with which they operate.

Not all of them explicitly engage with Plato in the same way, it is true. Yet Kant engages with Plato on several occasions in, for example, the *Critique of Pure Reason* (1781; [2]1787), contrasting him (as a philosopher of intellect) with Epicurus (as a philosopher of sensibility), and again (as a noologist) with Aristotle (as an empiricist)[42]; Hegel has, inevitably, much to say about Plato in his lectures on the history of philosophy[43]; and Marx knew well two figures surrounding the Platonic tradition in chronological terms, although both opposed to it, in varying ways: Democritus and Epicurus.[44] And it seems safe to say that Nietzsche and Heidegger were well aware of their respective relationships, as complicated and ambiguous as they were, to Plato.

Equally, there are other figures, peripheral to (but still significant for) the tradition of German Political Thought, whom we could have included in this book: for instance, we might have mentioned St Augustine of Hippo (354–430), a thinker on whom the influence of Platonism (and of Neoplatonism) was so strong.[45] This influence makes itself felt in his theology and in his political theory alike, especially in his huge reckoning with pagan thought in *The City of God*— or to give it its full title, *De Civitate Dei contra Paganos*, or *The City of God Against the Pagans*. Then again, we could have mentioned the Italian Renaissance thinker Niccolò Machiavelli (1469–1527), a figure who fascinated (among others) the German Idealist philosopher Johann Gottlieb Fichte (1762–1814).[46] In fact, in the seventeenth century, an

English politician and satirist, Henry Nevill (1620–1694), had, in a dialogue entitled *Plato Redivivus* (1681), hailed "the divine Machiavel" as "the best and most honest of all the modern politicians," someone who sought, as had Plato—"the greatest Philosopher, the greatest Politician (I had almost said the greatest Divine too) that ever lived"—before him, to treat the moral and political diseases of humankind.[47] In *The Prince* (1513), Machiavelli takes cunning, a characteristic associated with Odysseus (see below), to new levels, and at the same time rehearses the fundamental issue which lies at the outset of the *Republic*: Glaucon's challenge to Socrates in the form of the contrast between the seemingly just (but, in fact, unjust) man and the seemingly unjust (but, in fact, truly just) man. This challenge leads Socrates to propose the strategy of comparing "justice of a whole city" with "justice of one man" (368e) and to compare the city with the individual, on the basis that "if we should watch a city coming into being, in speech, […] [we would] also see its justice coming into being, and its injustice" (369a).[48] In turn, this leads him to consider the question of justice as one, not of *seeming*, but of *being*—an argument of which the allegory of the cave is subsequently part.

Then again, we could have investigated the role of Plato in the development of the political thought of the English philosopher Thomas Hobbes (1588–1679), even if his *Leviathan* (1651), a major contribution to the notion of the social contract, is usually seen as opposed in epistemology and in politics alike to Plato's *Republic*.[49] Rousseau and Kant, among others, explicitly position themselves as opponents of Hobbes. (Needless to say, all these figures and others are featured in Norbert Hoerster's *Klassische Texte der Staatsphilosophie*, and could easily be included in a study extending the scope of the present one.) In his *Pensées*, Blaise Pascal (1623–1662) cast a sceptical, not to say—jaundiced—, glance at Plato and Aristotle in their "long academic gowns," imagining them to be "ordinary decent people like anyone else" who "enjoyed a laugh with their friends." Pascal pictured them composing their *Laws* and *Politics* "for fun," as "the least philosophical and least serious part of their lives," since "if they wrote about politics it was as if to lay down rules for a madhouse"…[50] And if we wanted to correct the gender bias not so much in Hoerster's selection as in the history of philosophy itself, then there could be no better figure to consider than Hannah Arendt (1906–1975), a German-born, Jewish political theorist who emigrated to America, following her arrest and imprisonment by the Gestapo in 1931 for her research into antisemitism. We have already encountered Arendt in the context of her lectures on Kant's political philosophy and her relationship to Heidegger; and it is worth noting the role played by Plato in one of her key works, *The Human Condition* (1958).

In its first chapter, Arendt notes that it is of little importance whether Socrates or Plato "discovered the eternal as the true center of strictly metaphysical thought," although she goes on to contrast Socrates's lack of interest in writing with Plato, for whom "concern with the eternal and the life of the philosopher are seen as inherently contradictory and in conflict with the striving for immortality, the way of life of the citizen, the *bios politikos*."[51] This conflict arises because, on Arendt's reading of the allegory of the cave, "the philosopher's experience of the eternal"—i.e., what Plato calls *arrhēton* (unsayable), Aristotle calls *aneu logon* (without word), and the Scholastic tradition the *nunc stans* (the standing now)—"can occur only outside the realm of human affairs and outside the plurality of men." In that allegory, the philosopher, liberated from his shackles, leaves the cave "in perfect 'singularity' [...] neither accompanied nor followed by others." (If we look closely at Plato's text, that is, of course, not quite true ...) In political terms, "if to die is the same as 'to cease to be among men,' experience of the eternal is a kind of death"—and yet, precisely this experience separates the *vita contemplativa* (contemplation or *theōria*) from the *vita activa* (labour, work, action) in the medieval tradition. For *theōria* or contemplation is "the word given to the experience of the eternal, as distinguished from all other attitudes, which at most may pertain to immortality."[52] Arendt's emphasis on its metaphysical dimension confirms the validity of some the alternative approaches outlined in this conclusion.

Strikingly, two of the more recent figures examined in our discussion, T.W. Adorno (1903–1969) and Max Horkheimer (1895–1973), go back beyond the Platonic tradition to the very sources of Western culture itself—that is, to Homer and to the tradition of epic. As we saw, the figure of Odysseus constitutes a kind of *Schlüsselfigur* or "key figure" in their analysis of the "dialectic of Enlightenment." Yet perhaps this should not surprise us; after all, the US classicist and philosopher Seth Benardete (1930–2001) once wrote that "the archaeology of the human spirit is one of the characteristics of ancient poetry."[53] For Benardete, essential insights into the nature of the human spirit or soul are revealed by the image of the sea, particularly as it is used in Sophocles' *Antigone*[54]:

> The sea has both a surface and a depth. It thus lends itself to be the paradigm for the human soul, which, as the Chorus of Sophocles' *Antigone* says, when stirred brings to the surface the blackness within. The soul retains the very nature of historical time, in whose sediment are stored the experiences of an original terror. Aulus Gellius remarks that the sons of Zeus are outstanding in virtue, prudence, and strength, but the sons of Poseidon are monstrous, cruel, and alien from any hint of humanity. The archaeology of the human spirit is one of the characteristics of ancient poetry. It consists in the attempt to consider the origins of things in light of the current experience of those things. This juxtaposition of the beginning with the present, of the roots with the flowering, tends to expose the criminality of the presumably lawful, whether it be that the fraternity at which the city aims is built on the incest of Oedipus and the fratricide of his sons, or that the name of Oedipus himself, which like all proper names designates but does not mean, expresses the truth of the crimes he cannot will in retrospect but nonetheless cannot deny to be his very nature.[55]

In Benardete's view, Homer revealed nothing less than "the uncanniness — the *deinótes* — of man" in "the nonexistence of any limits to man," symbolized by, first, sailing (followed by agriculture, hunting birds and mammals, fishing, domestication of animals, language, and the construction of shelters).[56] On this account, Odysseus's "search for wisdom" is a search to "see things as they are," and as such necessarily violates "the prohibition not to look beyond one's own" laid down by the law[57]; for Benardete, the essential "transgressiveness of knowledge" reaches its culmination—symbolized by the tragic figure of Oedipus— in philosophy and its "desacralization of everything in the element of self-ignorance."[58]

This urge, desire, and project to go beyond informs Plato's allegory of the cave as well. As we mentioned in the introduction, the motif of the cave in book 7 of the *Republic* was complicated in the twentieth century by Leo Strauss (1899–1973) (as it happens, one of Benardete's teachers).[59] The importance of the allegory of the cave for Strauss was acutely realized by Benardete, who wrote in his memorial speech for Leo Strauss in 1974:

> He realized that a special effort had to be made by us in order to attain to the distinction, which is at the heart of philosophy, between those things which are first for us and those things which are first by nature. His was an ascent from the cave beneath the cave for the sake of ascending from the cave.[60]

Now Strauss is a good example of an inheritor of the Western European intellectual tradition (and, as a Jew who left Europe to go to America, an embodiment of the persistence of the discourse of Platonism in German Political Thought). To understand what he meant by the second cave or "the cave beneath the cave," we have to go back to some of Strauss's early writings from his time in Germany in the 1930s. In a lecture prepared for the federal camp of *Kadimah* held in Brieselang, near Berlin, in December 1930, entitled "Religious Situation of the Present," Strauss explicitly drew a link between the situation of the modern world and the situation depicted in Plato's allegory of the cave:

> In [the *Republic*], in order to illustrate the difficulty of truthful knowing, Plato compares the situation of the human being with the situation of cave dwellers [...]. — Thus, then, Plato presents the difficulties of doing philosophy, the *natural* difficulties. If they are so extraordinary, no wonder that there are so many contradictory opinions. Mindful of the Platonic parable, we shall not be deterred by the anarchy of opinions, but we will have to try as hard as we can to leave the cave.[61]

Yet precisely this possibility of leaving the cave appears to be put in doubt by another text written by Strauss at about the same time (1931), his review of a study entitled *On the Progress of Metaphysics* (1931) by

Julius Ebbinghaus (1885–1981), a philosopher who was close to the Heidelberg school of Neo-Kantianism. In his review of this work, published in the *Deutsche Literaturzeitung* in December 1931, Strauss explained that the modern world was confronted with even more problems than the ancient world had been, for we moderns find ourselves in a "second cave":

> To use the classical presentation of the natural difficulties of philosophizing, namely Plato's parable of the cave, one may say that today we find ourselves in a second, much deeper cave than the lucky ignorant ones Socrates dealt with; we need history first of all in order to *ascend* to the cave from which Socrates can lead us to light; we need a propaedeutic, which the Greeks did not need, namely, learning through reading.[62]

As Michael Zank, the editor of Strauss's early writings, has pointed out, the reason why we moderns find ourselves in a "second cave" has been given by the medieval Saphardic philosopher, Moses Maimonides (1135/38–1204) in his *Guide for the Perplexed*.[63] In addition to the three causes adduced by Alexander of Aphrodisias for why human beings are prevented from discovering the truth—first, "arrogance and vainglory"; second, "the subtlety, depth, and difficulty of any subject which is being examined"; and third, "ignorance and want of capacity to comprehend what might be comprehended"—there was, Maimonides argued, now a fourth: "namely, habit and training."[64] As an example, Maimonides cited "the vulgar notions with respect to the corporeality of God, and many other metaphysical questions," and he claimed that such individuals were mistaken in clinging to "passages of the Bible [...], the literal sense of which implies the corporeality of God and other false notions," insisting instead that "these words were employed as figures and metaphors."[65] Or as Strauss interpreted this passage from Maimonides, "the difficulty of doing philosophy is fundamentally increased, and the *freedom* of doing philosophy is fundamentally reduced, by the fact that a revelation-based tradition has stepped into the world of philosophy."[66]

If Strauss regards revealed religion as the creator of a "second cave," an artificial cave beneath the natural cave of Plato's allegory, then, as

David Janssens has argued, one might regard Christianity, an opponent as well as an inheritor of the pagan (ancient Greek) and the Jewish
belief systems alike, as bringing into existence yet a further cave: so to
speak, a cave beneath the cave beneath the cave.[67] (Alternatively, Greg
Andonian has sketched out how European identity has evolved around
three different "cave" scenarios, moving from "reflective and critical
thinking" via "imaginative and projective spirituality" to "innovative
and creative vision," or from the "perfect intellectual" human via the
"perfect spiritual" human to the "perfect hi-tech" human. The first
"cave," located in the first millennium, i.e., fifth century BCE to fifth
century CE, is Plato's: its dwellers—particularly the escaped prisoner—
embodied the Platonic pursuit of universal truth, advanced Socratic
reflection on human morality, and anticipated the Aristotelian ethical
mission for realistic goals and objectives. The second "cave" is the Holy
Sepulchre, representing the existential narratives, individual spirituality, and metaphysical aspirations of Christianity. "Visitors" to this
"cave" included St. Augustine, the Armenian monk and philosopher St.
Gregory of Narek, and Dante, while Luther's translation of the Bible
and Gutenberg's invention of the printing-press heralded the opening
of the third "cave." This "third cave" is science and technology, a world
of cybernetic control and AI that puts us in control of our environment yet entraps and enslaves us in ways hitherto unimaginable. In
effect, the tools of our advancement risk becoming "tools of utter dis-
integation, subjugation and manipulation," prompting us to reflect on
whether we have ever learned anything from our experiences of these
three "caves.")[68]

Ultimately these arguments about caves beneath caves beneath caves
or "first, "second," "third," or—why not?—"fourth" and "fifth" caves
result in the sort of *mise en abyme* envisaged by French postmodernists,
such as Gilles Deleuze (1925–1995) in his discussion of Nietzsche's
doctrine of eternal return as kind of "*ungrounding*," understood as
"the freedom of the non-mediated ground, the discovery of a ground
behind every other ground, the relation between the groundless and the
ungrounded, the immediate reflection of the formless and the superior
form which constitutes the eternal return":

Every thing, animal or being assumes the status of a simulacrum; so that the thinker of eternal return — who indeed refuses to be drawn out of the cave, finding instead another cave beyond, always another in which to hide — can rightly say that he is himself burdened with the superior form of everything that is, like the poet "burdened with humanity, even that of the animals."[69] These words themselves have their echo in the superposed caves.[70]

Not surprisingly, Deleuze describes his philosophy, with a nod in the direction of Nietzsche, as the "overturning" of Platonism.[71] This "overturning" has been explained by one commentator in terms of a contrast between the orthodox or "upright" Platonist who "proceeds out of the cave, out of the world of appearances," and the "overturned" Platonist as "a diver" who "plunges into the depths of the cave itself, into the uncanny world of difference and repetition."[72]

Where does this leave us today, with the sound of Rimbaud's words echoing through the cave(s) and in our ears? It leaves us with the end of Idealism (or maybe its only vestigial survival)[73]; with the collapse of Marxism—whatever Yanis Varoufakis might tell us—,[74] at least in its Leninist-Stalinist form; and with Jürgen Habermas as the last surviving member of the Third Generation of the Frankfurt School, whose critical theory has largely been surpassed by the postmodernism of Jean Baudrillard (1929–2007) or Jean-François Lyotard (1924–1998) or by the biopolitics of Giorgio Agamben (b. 1942). Does this mean that the discourse of Platonism, whose subterranean influence on the German Political Tradition we have been tracing, has lost its relevance as well?

For some, this may well seem to be the case; even though such edited volumes (arising from conferences held under the auspices of the Dublin Centre for the Study of the Platonic Tradition) as *Platonism and the World Crisis* (2010) and *Towards the Noosphere* (2012) present powerful arguments for the relevance of Platonism as a tool for understanding a world crisis—[75] a crisis which has, by common consent, grown larger over recent years, thanks to the continuing consequences of the global financial crash of 2007–2008 and the increase in global terrorism following the September 11 attacks on the World Trade Towers in New York of

2001, the ensuing wars in Afghanistan and Iraq, the civil war in Syria, and the rise of the militant Islamic group, ISIS, in the Middle East.

And even an out-and-out opponent of Plato, such as the contemporary French philosopher Michel Onfray, can still find it useful to have recourse to him as a reference-point. In *Cosmos* (2015), the first volume of his planned trilogy (or possibly even pentalogy) entitled *Brief Encyclopedia of the World* (*Brève encyclopédie du monde*), this promoter of a "hedonist materialism" declares that, in the modern (or postmodern) world, we have all became Platonists:

> Our age lives according to the Platonic order: it is well-known that, in the allegory of the cave, Plato condemns those deceived people who believe in the truth of shadows and do not know that these arise from the truth of real objects. Chained up, in other words shackled by their ignorance of the mechanism which produces simulacra, the slaves are mistaken in interpreting the virtual for the real. The television viewer, too, is equally a shackled slave who takes for real the construction of a fiction and mis-recognizes the truth of reality which is the reality of truth. Numerous listeners and viewers, while not exactly devotees of the screen, believe more in the illusion than they do in the materiality of the world.[76]

In Onfray's view, the time of the cosmos, thousands of years old, has disappeared and been replaced by a "time of machines that produce virtuality." In our nihilistic age, the status of the virtual and the real has become confused and inverted. Thanks to television, we inhabit a virtual reality which means we are surprised when, on the street, we see people we usually see on television: the remarkable thing is not being seen on a screen, but the materiality which is usually erased. Or in other words, what is really and empirically true is dead, and a false transcendental reality has taken its place. No wonder Onfray exclaims, "We have never been so Platonic!"[77] Or as the American writer Philip K. Dick (1928–1982) put it many years earlier in 1974, "UBIK is true and we're in a sort of cave, like Plato said, and they're showing us endless funky films."[78]

This sense that the world in which we now all live is a modern or postmodern version of the allegory of the cave is beautifully captured in a painting by the Canadian artist, Lalita Hamill. Entitled "Plato's Cave," this work subtly but powerfully reimagines the world of the cave in its full primordial nature, with a technological twist. To the left of the painting, a group of young people are sitting on or in front of a (stone) sofa, staring—one presumes—at the shadows on the wall, as if they were enjoying an evening's entertainment on their favourite television station. A woman looks utterly bored, staring to the side and clasping her face in a gesture of despair; a man is laughing and pointing (to the screen?) with his finger, glancing at a woman beside him, whom he is embracing; leaning forward, she is looking away to the scene in the centre of the painting. Sitting on the floor in an athletic pose, another man is looking straight ahead—and hence out of the painting, at us. Rather than a panoply of individuals carrying objects along a pathway in front of a huge fire, these projections are achieved by a single woman holding a child's toy, a plastic spinning windmill, while to the right the blaze of a fire can be seen, although partially occluded. On the other side of the painting, two even younger people are absorbed in the glow coming from the screen of a handheld device, maybe an iPhone or some other portable communication device. In the centre of the painting, a man in a white shirt and white shorts—a returning philosopher?—is pointing with his right hand to the exit from the cave, while his left hand is stretched out—in a gesture of support? or despair?—toward a woman who is lying in the floor. Is she blinded by the light from the entrance to the cave? Or is she staggered by what the man in white is saying, and has fallen to the floor in surprise, raising her arm in a defensive gesture of rejection?

Hamill's painting, apart from being a work of great beauty, raises all kinds of questions about how we are to understand the allegory of the cave today in the tradition of German Political Thought. If we find ourselves, as Strauss suggests, in a cave beneath the cave—or, as Janssens extends this analysis, in a cave beneath the cave beneath the cave—then how are we ever going to get out? For that matter: Do we still believe that there is anywhere out to which we can get? If, as Jacques Derrida (1930–2004) famously argued, *il n'y a pas de hors-texte*—usually translated as "there is nothing outside the text,"[79] but more accurately rendered as "there is no outside-text"—,[80] is it not so much a question of whether we believe in inside or outside as a question of whether, in our image-saturated world, we believe in any kind of text—or even *logos*—at all?

The great strength of Plato's allegory of the cave lies not simply in the immense power and suggestiveness of its images, and its narrative of imprisonment, liberation, and then return, but in the fact that it is an allegory. If we are to learn anything from Maimonides and, by the same token, from Strauss, it is the importance—and the persistence—of allegory as a mode of thought. It is not for nothing that, in his *Guide to the Perplexed*, Maimonides tried to harmonize the Old Testament with Aristotelian thought, subsequently influencing not just Jewish, Christian, and Islamic, but also Enlightenment thought. Nor is it for nothing that, in his political writings, Strauss kept recurring to the problem for philosophy of revelation.

So it is telling that, in January 2004, at an event organised by the Bavarian Catholic Academy in Munich, Jürgen Habermas engaged in a debate with Joseph Ratzinger, then a cardinal, and shortly to become pope, taking the name Benedict XVI. This debate, subsequently published as *The Dialectics of Secularization*, showed not only how seriously the cardinal took philosophy, but how seriously the philosopher took religion.[81] And it points to a question left largely undiscussed until now: the question of the role that religion should play in the state.

For as greatly as such New Atheists as Richard Dawkins and Christopher Hitchens might deplore it, a "religious turn" is discernible in numerous contemporary thinkers, be it in Derrida and deconstruction,[82] in phenomenology,[83] or in Habermas, who has argued for a role for religion in the public sphere.[84] (Perhaps that debate with Ratzinger had some effect, after all ...) For Habermas, religious traditions have "a special power to articulate moral intuitions, especially with regard to vulnerable forms of communal life." As a consequence, this potential "makes religious speech a serious candidate to transporting possible truth contents, which can then be translated from the vocabulary of a particular religious community into generally accessible language." Indeed, Habermas argues that "the ostensibly critical overcoming of [...] a narrow secularist consciousness is itself an essentially contested issue — at least to the same extent as the demythologizing response to the cognitive challenges of Modernity."[85]

Perhaps this "religious turn" should not come as a surprise. After all, the allegory of the cave positively invites not just a political, but a religious, spiritual, or mystical reading. As Tim Addey has pointed out, there is a direct route from the caveman to the contemplative, and this road—in contrast to the road less travelled, as the title of a popular New Age book calls it[86]—was extremely *well* travelled by such later Neoplatonists as Proclus.[87] Later thinkers have travelled the same road, too. For instance, in December 1964 to February 1965 and then again in December 1965 to January 1966, the South African philosopher J.N. Findlay (1903–1987) delivered the prestigious Gifford Lectures at the University of St Andrews in Scotland. While his first set of lectures was entitled *The Discipline of the Cave*, the second set was called *The Transcendence of the Cave*, moving from chapters on the "furnishings of the cave," phenomenological and dialectical "methods of cave-exploration," the "cave foreground" in terms of the "resting" and the "moving" face of bodies, the "dissolution" of bodies and the "dissolution" of the realm of minds to the "foundations of the realm of reason and spirit," the realms of "notions and meaning" and "values and disvalues," the "collapse" of the realm of reason and spirit, "otherworldy geography," the "noetic cosmos," the life of the soul, the life of God, and the "return to the cave."

From the outset, however, Findlay distanced himself from the great British discussions of the allegory of the cave in the wake of the translations of Plato by Benjamin Jowett (1817–1893), reflected in the expositions of James Adam (1860–1907), H.A. Prichard (1871–1947), John Ferguson (1921–1989), Richard Lewis Nettleship (1846–1892), Bernard Bosanquet (1848–1923), and other commentators. Rather, Findlay regarded the allegory of the cave as "one of the greatest, the most telling images of philosophy — a study in which, it may be held, one always operates with images and diagrams, though one does not usually have the frankness to draw them clearly [...]."[88] Rejecting the notion that the image of the cave was intended to illustrate "every winding of some complicated doctrine," however the Pythagoreans or their

Orphic predecessors may have used it, Findlay argued that it represents "'the human condition' in a true and poignant manner," inasmuch as "we do all feel somehow, whether with justification or not, that we are fixed in a situation involving many strange restrictions: there are features in our life as immovable, as fixedly presented, and also as deeply as astonishing and absurd as are the wall, the parapet, the fire, the chains, the social games and the speaking shadows of Plato."[89] However strange the allegory of the cave may seem, Findlay suggests, perhaps the strangest aspect of it is precisely its familiarity. Findlay's reading of the cave was, as he freely admitted, "inspired by certain strands in Plato, by some condemned as mythical or mystical," citing as examples of such strands the *Phaedo*, the *Republic*, the *Symposium*, the *Timaeus*, the *Phaedrus*, and the second part of the *Parmenides*. On Findlay's account, Plato was never "weaned away from the ideas that these works represent into a pure passion for logical analysis," and consequently "logical analysis in the middle ranges flanked by mystical ultimates are at *all* times characteristic of his work and thought."[90]

In 1971, the French Traditionalist thinker René Guénon (1886–1951) argued that there is a close symbolic relationship between the cave and the heart, conceived ("from the initiatic point of view") as representing a "spiritual centre."[91] In the context of the tradition of German Political Thought, these kinds of considerations might be more at home than one might suspect, German culture being more comfortable than many outside the country realize with "alternative" therapies, homeopathy, or even the occult.[92] Ultimately the cave allegory explores the relation between the rational and the irrational, and as such it informs the German Political Tradition and its attempt to find a balance between the rational and the irrational (or, as Weimar Classicism would have it, between the body and the mind, or the flesh and the soul, or the senses and the intellect).[93]

Some two decades or so before René Guénon, the Prussian-born philosopher and Hispanist linguist Jean Gebser (1905–1973) published a major study of human culture, *The Ever-Present Origin* (*Ursprung und Gegenwart*, vol. 1, 1949; vol. 2, 1953).[94] In this work, Gebser uses linguistic evidence as a central part of his method of analysis (1–2, 123), drawing on the work of the German comparative philogist Karl Abel

(1837–1906) into what he called "antithetical meanings of primal words" (see *Über den Gegensinn der Urworte*, 1884), a work which attracted the interest of Sigmund Freud and, subsequently, Jacques Derrida. For Gebser, one example of such a word pair evincing this polarity or ambivalence (and hence expressing a unity)—here, the relation of consciousness to the unconscious—is the pair *Höhle*, i.e., "cavern," and *Helle*, i.e. "brightness." Both words are said to derive from the Indo-Germanic root *kel*, to which (among others) the Latin words *clam*, i.e., "secretly," and *clamare*, "to scream," as well as the German words *hehlen*, i.e., "to conceal," *Halle*, i.e., "hall," *hohl*, i.e., "hollow," *Hülle*, i.e., "cloak, shell," and *Hülse*, i.e., "hull, husk," are in turn related (126). In a footnote, Gebser draws on Kluge-Götze's *Etymologisches Wörterbuch der deutschen Sprache* to draw attention to further borrowings that can all be traced to the root word, *kel*: from the Latin—cell from *cella*, i.e., "chamber," related to *celare*, i.e., "to conceal, disguise"; cloister, from *claustrum*, i.e., "closure"; from the Greek—chalice, from *kalyx*, via Latin *calyx*; as well as "cellar";—in Sanskrit *Kali*, an Indian goddess venerated for her dark aspect; and *Kalypso*, a Greek nymph (156, n. 7).

From these and other linguistic considerations, Gebser draws the following remarkable conclusions about human "mystery" and "destiny." But what do these words, mystery and destiny, actually mean? For Gebser, these words have a psychological and an existential sense, but one can also see they have a political sense as well—mystery "denotes non-freedom," while destiny "denotes an absence or lack of freedom," suggesting these words "actually belong to two different structures of consciousness":

Mystery is an outgrowth of the magic realm; it is the indissoluble relation to the concealment and shelter of the dark cavern-world — the covert world that is displaced by the inscrutable world of destiny. Destiny in turn is associated with the mythical structure, for it has nothing covert or secret in its nature; characteristic of destiny is the expulsion from, not the shelter of[,] the cavern world. Destiny is the inscrutable fulfillment of events that seems irrevocable since mythical man has no will of his own and is consequently bound to the fateful course of events which relentlessly presses toward fulfillment. (136)

On this account, the cave or cavern represents the magic "spacelessness" of the magic structure of consciousness (48–49), as well as the magic structure of the auditory organ, the ear (144). Exiting the cavern represents a crucial stage on our journey from (1) an archaic structure of consciousness, via the (2) magic, (3) mythical, and (4) mental structures, to (5) an integral structure of consciousness.

In 1956, Gebser followed up his discussion in *The Ever-Present Origin* with a short paper on the cave and the labyrinth.[95] In it he explored the contrast between the cave as a "primal phenomenon" that fulfils the "primal yearning" for sheltered security (*Geborgenheit*) and the labyrinth, whose "primal formal is the spiral," as an indication of "a different, more wakeful aspect of the world." In doing so, Gebser explored a polarity within the phenomenon of the cave, its "fascination and enchantment." For if, on the one hand, the image of the cave offers "an optimal place of refuge," on the other, what is "mysterious" can switch into the "uncanny," in which case "the cave or hollow [*Höhle*] is turned into hell [*Hölle*]"—the close relationship between these words is "not accidental." On this account, if the labyrinth represents a chance—"that other primal yearning for greater awareness," "an expression of the possibility of advancing"—then the cave constitutes a danger, for "to go back to the cave, even only in thought, is regression from life into the state of being unborn, into unconsciousness or timelessness," and hence its apparent offer of security is deceptive, inasmuch as it "removes us from the demands of being born, of consciousness, and of time."

No wonder, then, Gebser associated the cave with the maternal, matriarchal aspect of the world: evidenced symbolically by the fact that three world-renowned crypts (the cathedral of Chartres, the monastery church at Montserrat, and the church of Saintes-Maries-de-la-Mer) all harbour a black Madonna, representing "the primal fact of the maternal aspect of the cave." This observation underscores again the important psychoanalytic, or archetypal, dimension to the image of the cave, of the kind explored by C.G. Jung (1875–1961).[96] Consistent with Jung's analysis is Gebser's conclusion that the cave guards a "hidden secret," which is in turn made transparent by a "greater secret," i.e., "the manifest secret of transfiguration"—a highly Platonic theme, bearing in mind that "the soul's journey up to the intelligible place" (517b) involves "the turning around of a soul from a day that is like night to the true day" (521c).

But if Guénon is right about the heart being "essentially a symbol of the centre," whether it be "the centre of a being or, analogously, the centre of the world"—and "the same significance thus naturally comes to be attached to the cave also, in virtue of its relationship with the heart"—then maybe we can, precisely for this reason, read the message of the allegory of the cave in Plato's *Republic* as an eminently political one? For in this sense it encourages the listener or the reader to go out into the world and to discover whether it is, in the Greek sense of the word, a *kosmos* or not; and, if it is not, to try and turn what is outside into a *kosmos*. Whether this *kosmos* involves a model of an Ideal kind, as Plato would argue, or remodelling or reshaping the world from within the individual, as the modern world has (at least since Romanticism) believed, is possibly the biggest political decision facing us in the future.

Notes

1. I have been unable to identify the source of this quotation attributed to the revolutionary socialist Rosa Luxemburg (1871–1919); but cf. her speech "Our Program and the Political Situation" of December 1918, where she declares: "Where the chains of capitalism are forged, there they must be broken" (Rosa Luxemburg, *Politische Schriften*, vol. 2 (Frankfurt: Europäische Verlagsanstalt, 1966), 171–201; translated in Rosa Luxemburg, *Selected Political Writings*, ed. Dick Howard (New York and London: Monthly Review Press, 1971), 377–403 (397)).
2. See John Henry Wright, "The Origin of Plato's Cave," *Harvard Studies in Classical Philology* 17 (1906), 131–142.
3. Yulia Ustinova, *Caves and the Ancient Greek Mind: Descending Underground in the Search for Ultimate Truth* (Oxford and New York: Oxford University Press, 2009), 2. See also David Lewis-Williams, *The Mind in the Cave: Consciousness and the Origins of Art* (London: Thames & Hudson, 2002).
4. Ustinova, *Caves and the Ancient Greek Mind*, 259. For further discussion, see C.A. Meier, *Antike Inkubation and moderne Psychotherapie*

(Zurich: Rascher, 1949), translated as *Ancient Incubation and Modern Psychotherapy* (Evanston, IL: Northwestern University Press, 1967); and *Der Traum als Medizin* (Einsiedeln: Daimon, 1985), translated as *Healing Dream and Ritual: Ancient Incubation and Modern Psychotherapy*, 4th edn (Einsiedeln: Daimon, 2012).

5. See the *Odyssey*, book 13, ll. 102–112; Homer, *The Odyssey*, ed. and trans. Albert Cook, 2nd edn (New York and London: Norton, 1993), 143. For further discussion of the crucial analysis by Porphyry of this passage, see Robert Lamberton, *Homer the Theologian: Neoplatonist Allegorical Reading and the Growth of the Epic Tradition* (Berkeley, Los Angeles and London: University of California Press, 1986), 108–133 and 318–324; and Porphyre [Porphyry], *L'antre des nymphes dans l'Odyssée*, trans. Yann Le Lay (Lagrasse: Verdier, 1989), which contains Guy Lardreau's essay, "La philosophie de Porphyre et la question de l'interprétation" (7–47).

6. Empedocles, DK B 120; in Jonathan Barnes, *Early Greek Philosophy* (Harmondsworth: Penguin, 1987), 197; cf. Jean-Paul Dumont (ed.), *Les Présocratiques* (Paris: Gallimard, 1988), 424.

7. According to the fifth-century historian Herodotus, Salmoxis (a follower of Pythagoras) "prepared a banqueting-hall where he entertained and feasted the leading citizens. And he taught them that neither he nor his fellow-drinkers nor any of their descendents would die but would come to a country where they would live for ever in possession of all good things. In the place where he had done and said what I have reported he built an underground chamber. When the chamber was completed he vanished from among the Thracians, descending into the underground chamber and staying there for three years. They missed him and mourned for him as though he were dead. But in the fourth year he appeared to the Thracians — and in this way what Salmoxis had said appeared plausible to them" (Barnes, *Early Greek Philosophy*, 83–84).

8. Porphyry, *On the Cave of the Nymphs*, trans. Robert Lamberton (Barrytown, NY: Station Hill Press, 1983), 26. Compare with Peter Kingsley's remark to the effect that "the 'covered-over cave' which Empedocles describes fallen souls as descending into is not a literal cave but a symbol of the world we live in" (*Ancient Philosophy, Mystery, and Magic: Empedocles and Pythagorean Tradition* (Oxford: Clarendon Press, 1995), 36).

9. See Kingsley, *Ancient Philosophy, Mystery, and Magic*, 38.

10. Plotinus, *Enneads*, IV.8.§1, in Plotinus, *Ennead IV*, trans. A.H. Armstrong (Cambridge, MA and London: Harvard University Press, 1984), 399; cf. Kingsley, *Ancient Philosophy, Mystery, and Magic*, 38.

11. Plato, *Collected Dialogues*, ed. Edith Hamilton and Huntington Cairns (Princeton, NJ: Princeton University Press, 1989), 90–91.

12. Plato, *Collected Dialogues*, 91.

13. Plato, *Collected Dialogues*, 92.

14. *Phaedo*, 79d; in Plato, *Collected Dialogues*, 62–63.

15. Euripides, *Polyidus* (fragment 638); cf. *Georgias*, 493a; in *Collected Dialogues*, 275. The story of how Polyeidos, a seer from Corinth, saved the life of a young child, Glaucus, after he had fallen into a cask of honey, by resurrecting him from the dead, was the subject of a play, now lost, by the classical Greek tragedian, Euripides.

16. Kingsley, *Ancient Philosophy, Mystery, and Magic*, 105.

17. See Richard Buxton (ed.), *From Myth to Reason? Studies in the Development of Greek Thought* (Oxford: Oxford University Press, 1999); and Walter A. Shelburne, *Mythos and Logos in the Thought of Carl Jung* (Albany, NY: State University of New York Press, 1988).

18. Johannes Sløk, *Devotional Language*, trans. Henrik Mossin (Berlin and New York: de Gruyter, 1996).

19. Kingsley, *Ancient Philosophy, Mystery, and Magic*, 80.

20. Kingsley, *Ancient Philosophy, Mystery, and Magic*, 106.

21. Kingsley, *Ancient Philosophy, Mystery, and Magic*, 107–108.

22. Gary Lachman, *The Secret Teachers of the Western World* (New York: Tarcher/Penguin, 2015), 82.

23. *Cratylus*, 400c; in Plato, *Collected Dialogues*, 437–438.

24. *Phaedrus*, 250c; in Plato, *Collected Dialogues*, 497.

25. *Phaedo*, 65c–d; in Plato, *Collected Dialogues*, 48.

26. R.T. Wallis, *Neoplatonism*, 2nd edn (London: Bristol Classical Press, 1995), 111.

27. Plotinus, Ennead IV.3.9; in Plotinus, *Ennead IV*, trans. Armstrong, 65.

28. Cornelia J. de Vogel, *Rethinking Plato and Platonism* (Leiden: Brill, 1986), 230.

29. Ficino's Preface to his Latin translation of the *Corpus Hermeticum* in *Opera Omnia* (Basel, 1576); cited in Brian P. Copenhaver and Charles B. Schmitt, *Renaissance Philosophy* [*A History of Western Philosophy*, vol. 3] (Oxford: Oxford University Press, 1992), 147.

30. Manly P. Hall, *The Secret Teachings of All Ages: An Encyclopedic Outline of Masonic, Hermetic, Qabbalistic and Rosicrucian Symbolical Philosophy* [1928] (New York: Tarcher/Penguin, 2003), 162. Aside from the question of the source of this "manuscript" by Taylor, there is the question

of the evidence for his reconstruction of the ceremony which took place—or for the fact of it having taken place at all.

31. Rudolf Steiner, *Christianity as Mystical Fact* [1902; revised 1910], trans. Andrew Welburn (Hudson, NY: Anthroposophic Press, 1997), 40.

32. Jeremy Naydler, *Plato, Shamanism, and Ancient Egypt* (Oxford: Abzu Press, 2005).

33. Carol Dunn, *Plato's Dialogues: Path to Initiation* (Great Barrington, MA: Portal Books, 2012), xviii.

34. Michael L. Morgan, *Platonic Piety: Philosophy and Ritual in Fourth-Century Athens* (New Haven and London: Yale University Press, 1990).

35. Peter Kingsley, *In the Dark Places of Wisdom* (Inverness, CA: Golden Sufi Center, 1999).

36. See Robert McGahey, *The Orphic Moment: Shaman to Poet-Thinker in Plato, Nietzsche, and Mallarmé* (Albany, NY: State University of New York Press, 1994).

37. Lachman, *The Secret Teachers of the Western World*, 274.

38. Theodore Ziolkowski, *German Romanticism and Its Institutions* (Princeton, NJ: Princeton University Press, 1990), 19–20.

39. Melanie Maria Lörke, *Liminal Semiotics: Boundary Phenomena in Romanticism* (Berlin: Akademie-Verlag, 2013), 200.

40. Ziolkowski, *German Romanticism and Its Institutions*, 32–33.

41. Harold P. Blum, "The Psychological Birth of Art: A Psychoanalytic Approach to Prehistoric Cave Art," *International Forum of Psychoanalysis* 20 (2011), 196–204.

42. *Critique of Pure Reason*, A 864/B 881, in Immanuel Kant, *Critique of Pure Reason*, ed. and trans. Paul Guyer and Allen W. Wood (Cambridge: Cambridge University Press, 1997), 702–703.

43. See G.W.F. Hegel, *Lectures on the History of Philosophy*, vol. 1, *Greek Philosophy to Plato*, trans. E.S. Haldane, and vol. 2, *Plato and the Platonists*, trans. Frances H. Simson and E.S. Haldane (Lincoln, NE: University of Nebraska Press, 1995).

44. See Marx's doctoral dissertation, *The Difference Between the Democritean and Epicurean Philosophy of Nature* [1841], in Marx/Engels, *Collected Works*, vol. 1 (Moscow: Progress Publishers, 1975), 25–107.

45. For further discussion, see Gerard O'Daly, *Platonism Pagan and Christian: Studies in Plotinus and Augustine* (Aldershot and Burlington, VT: Ashgate, 2001).

46. See his *On Machiavelli, as a Writer, and Passages from his Writing* (1807), available as "Ueber Machiavelli, als Schriftsteller, und Stellen

aus seinen Schriften," in Johann Gottlieb Fichte, *Werke 1806–1807*, ed. Reinhard Lauth and Hans Gliwitzky [*Gesamtausgabe*, vol. I/9] (Stuttgart-Bad Cannstatt: Frommann (Holzboog), 1995), 213–275.

47. Henry Neville, *Plato redivivus: Or, A Dialogue concerning Government*, 4th edn (London: A. Millar, 1763), Second Dialogue, 24, 47 and 121; and Third Dialogue, 213; cf. "The Publisher to the Reader," viii. For further discussion of the vexed question of Machiavelli's relation to Plato and to Platonism, see Erica Brenner, *Machiavelli's Ethics* (Princeton, NJ: Princeton University Press, 2009), esp. "Preface" (10–11), "The Socratic tradition of philosophical politics" (49–53), and "The Socratic metaphor of hunting" (116–123).

48. *The Republic of Plato*, trans. Allen Bloom (New York: Basic Books, 1991), 45.

49. See Karl Schumann, "Hobbes and the Political Thought of Plato and Aristotle," in Karl Schumann, *Selected Papers on Renaissance Philosophy and on Thomas Hobbes*, ed. Piet Steenbakkers and Cees Leijenhorst (Dordrecht: Springer, 2004), 191–218.

50. *Pensées*, §533 (=Brunschvicg, §331), in Pascal, *Pensées*, trans. A.J. Krailsheimer (Harmondsworth: Penguin, 1966), 216–217.

51. Hannah Arendt, *The Human Condition: A Study of the Central Dilemmas Facing Modern Man* (Garden City, NY: Doubleday, 1959), 20.

52. Hannah Arendt, *The Human Condition*, 20–21. For further discussion, see Miguel Abensour, "Against the Sovereignty of Philosophy Over Politics: Arendt's Reading of Plato's Cave Allegory," *Social Research* 74, no. 4 (Winter 2007), 955–982.

53. "The Poet-Merchant and the Stranger from the Sea" [1993], in Seth Benardete, *Archaeology of the Soul: Platonic Readings of Ancient Poetry and Philosophy*, ed. Ronna Burger and Michael Davis (South Bend, IN: St. Augustine's Press, 2012), 1–6 (1).

54. See Sophocles, *Antigone*, ll. 586–593 and 929–930, in David Grene and Richard Lattimore (eds), *Greek Tragedies*, vol. 1 (Chicago and London: University of Chicago Press, 1960), 202 and 212; cf. Herodotus, 7.16α: "The sea can be the most beneficial thing of all to mortals, but the force of the winds that fall upon it prevent it from being true to its nature" (*The Landmark Herodotus: The Histories*, ed. Robert B. Strassler (London: Quercus, 2008), 503).

55. Benardete, "The Poet-Merchant and the Stranger from the Sea," *Archaeology of the Soul*, 1.

56. Benardete, "The Poet-Merchant and the Stranger from the Sea," *Archaeology of the Soul*, 1. For further discussion, see Seth Benardete, *The Bow and the Lyre: A Platonic Reading of the Odyssey* (Lanham: Rowman & Littlefield, 1997).

57. Benardete, "The Poet-Merchant and the Stranger from the Sea," *Archaeology of the Soul*, 6.

58. Benardete, "The Poet-Merchant and the Stranger from the Sea," *Archaeology of the Soul*, 2; and "Socrates and Plato: The Dialectics of Erōs," in *Archaeology of the Soul*, 112–140 (249).

59. For further discussion, see Laurence Lampert, *Leo Strauss and Nietzsche* (Chicago and London: University of Chicago Press, 1996); and *The Enduring Importance of Leo Strauss* (Chicago and London: University of Chicago Press, 2013).

60. "Memorial Speech for Leo Strauss" [1974], in *The Archaeology of the Soul*, 375–377.

61. Strauss, "Die religiöse Lage der Gegenwart," in *Gesammelte Schriften*, vol. 2, *Philosophie und Gesetz: Frühe Schriften*, ed. Heinrich Meier (Stuttgart: Metzler, 1997), 377–391 (385–386); translated in Michael Zank, "Introduction," in Leo Strauss, *The Early Writings (1921–1932)*, ed. and trans. Michael Zank (Albany, NY: State University of New York Press, 2002), 29–30.

62. Strauss, "Review of Julius Ebbinghaus, *On the Progress of Metaphysics* (1931)," in *Early Writings*, 214–215 (215).

63. See "Introduction," in Strauss, *The Early Writings (1921–1932)*, 30–31. For further discussion of this "second cave" which appears in "Religious Situation of the Present" (1930) and returns in "The Spiritual Situation of the Present" (1932), see Heinrich Meier, *Die Denkbewegung von Leo Strauss: Die Geschichte der Philosophie und die Intention des Philosophen* (Stuttgart and Weimar: Metzler, 1996), 21–28 and 42–43. For an alternative reading, see William H.F. Altman, "Altruism and the Art of Writing: Plato, Cicero, and Leo Strauss," *Humanitas* 22, nos. 1–2 (2009), 69–98 (74–77).

64. Moses Maimonides, *The Guide for the Perplexed*, trans. M. Friedländer, 2nd edn (New York: Dover, 1956), 41.

65. Maimonides, *Guide for the Perplexed*, 41–42.

66. Strauss, "Religious Situation of the Present," cited in Zank, "Introduction," in Strauss, *Early Writings*, 31.

67. David Janssens, *Between Athens and Jerusalem: Philosophy, Prophecy, and Politics in Leo Strauss's Early Thought* (Albany, NY: State University of New York Press, 2008), Chapter 3, "The Second Cave," 77–108.

68. Greg Andonian, "The Three Caves of European Identity: From Critical to Creative Thinking," *Consciousness, Literature and the Arts 2*, no. 1 (April 2001); available http://www.dmd27.org/andonian.html. Accessed 09.01.2018.

69. Deleuze alludes here to the letter—one of those known as the *Lettres du voyant* (i.e., the "letters of the visionary")—sent by the French Symbolist poet, Arthur Rimbaud (1854–1891), to Paul Demeny on 15 May 1871, where Rimbaud describes the poet as *chargé de l'humanité, des animaux même* (Rimbaud, *Œuvres*, ed. Suzanne Bernard (Paris: Garnier, 1960), 347). Note the alternative translation of this line as "he is responsible for humanity, even for the *animals*" (Rimbaud, *Complete Works; Selected Letters*, ed. and trans. Wallace Fowlie (Chicago and London: University of Chicago Press, 1966), 309).

70. Gilles Deleuze, *Difference and Repetition* [1968], trans. Paul Patton (London: Athlone Press, 1994), 67.

71. "The task of modern philosophy has been defined: to overturn Platonism" (Deleuze, *Difference and Repetition*, 59); cf. "My philosophy, *inverted Platonism*: the further away from true bring, the more pure, more beautiful, better it is. The life of appearance as goal" (Nietzsche, *Sämtliche Werke: Kritische Studienausgabe*, ed. Giorgio Colli and Mazzino Montinari, 14 vols (Munich; Berlin and New York: dtv; de Gruyter, 1999), vol. 7, *Nachgelassene Fragmente 1869–1874*, 7[156], 199. See Heidegger's discussion of this statement in *The Will to Power as Art*, in *Nietzsche*, vols 1 and 2, trans. David Farrell Krell (San Francisco: Harper & Row, 1979–1987), "Truth in Platonism and Positivism: Nietzsche's Attempt to Overturn Platonism on the Basis of the Fundamental Experience of Nihilism," 151–161. For further discussion, see Joshua Ramey, *The Hermetic Deleuze: Philosophy and Spiritual Ordeal* (Durham and London: Duke University Press, 2012), Chapter 4, "The Overturning of Platonism," 112–147.

72. Ramey, *The Hermetic Deleuze*, 127.

73. Jeremy Dunham, Iain Hamilton Grant, and Sean Watson, *Idealism: The History of a Philosophy* [2011] (Abingdon and New York: Routledge, 2014).

74. See Yanis Varoufakis, "Confessions of an Erratic Marxist in the Midst of a Repugnant European Crisis" (talk to the 6th Subversive Festival in Zagreb, May 2013); available http://yanisvaroufakis.eu/2013/12/10/confessions-of-an-erratic-marxist-in-the-midst-of-a-repugnant-european-crisis/.

75. John M. Dillon, Brendan O'Byrne, and Tim Addey, *Platonism and the World Crisis*, 2nd edn (Westbury: Prometheus Trust, 2010); and John M. Dillon and Stephen R.L. Clark, *Towards the Noosphere* (Westbury: Prometheus Trust, 2012).

76. Michel Onfray, *Cosmos: Une ontologie matérialiste* (Paris: Flammarion, 2015), 114.

77. Onfray, *Cosmos*, 114–115.

78. *The Selected Letters of Philip K. Dick: 1974* (Novato, CA, and Lancaster, PN: Underwood-Miller, 1974), 260: "Did you know that UBIK is true and we're in a sort of cave, like Plato said, and they're showing us endless funky films? And now and then reality breaks through, as in UBIK, from our friend who was here once and then dies, but has turned back?" See also the motif of the Black Iron Prison, known as the Cave of Treasures, in his novel *The Divine Invasion* [1981] (Boston and New York: Mariner Books, 2011), 128 and 223; cf. Dick's remarks in conversation with Paul Williams on 31 October 1974 (see Paul Williams, *Only Apparently Real: The World of Philip K. Dick* (New York: Arbor House, 1986), 72).

79. Derrida, *De la grammatologie* (Paris: Minuit, 1967), 227; *Of Grammatology*, trans. Gayatri Chakravorty Spivak (Baltimore: Johns Hopkins University Press, 1975), 158–159.

80. See J.G. Merquior, *From Paris to Prague: A Critique of Structuralist and Poststructuralist Thought* (London: Verso, 1986), 220.

81. Jürgen Habermas and Joseph Ratzinger, *The Dialectics of Secularization: On Reason and Religion* [2005] (San Francisco: Ignatius Press, 2006); translated from *Dialektik der Säkularisierung: Über Vernunft und Religion* (Freiburg im Breisgau, Basel and Vienna: Herder, 2005).

82. Arthur Bradley, "Derrida's God: A Genealogy of the Theological Turn," *Paragraph* 29, no. 3 (November 2006), 21–42.

83. Michel Henry, *C'est moi la Vérité: Pour une philosophie du christianisme* (Paris: Seuil, 1996).

84. See Jürgen Habermas, "Religion in the Public Sphere," *European Journal of Philosophy* 14, no. 1 (2006), 1–25; and *Between Naturalism and Religion*, trans. C. Cronin (Cambridge: Polity Press, 2008).

85. Habermas, "Religion in the Public Sphere," 10 and 16.

86. N. Scott Peck, *The Road Less Travelled: A New Psychology of Love, Traditional Values and Spiritual Growth* [1978] (London: Arrow, 1990).

87. Tim Addey, "From Caveman to Contemplative," *The Aquarian Theosophist* 3, no. 4 (February 17, 2003), 1–7. At the same time, one might note there is something of a contrast in degree of complexity

between, on the one hand, Socrates's division in the *Republic* of society into three classes (guardians, i.e., leaders or philosophers; auxiliaries, i.e., soldiers or defenders of the state; and producers, i.e., workers or labourers), of the human soul into reason, spiritedness, and appetite, and Glaucon's division of good things into three classes (good in themselves, good both in themselves and for their consequences, and good only for their consequences; 357b–d), and, on the other, Proclus's division in his *Platonic Theology* (book 3, Chapter 2, i.e., 20.3–23.14 and Chapter 1, i.e., 13.4–23) of being into six orders, described variously as (1) the intelligible order, (2) the intelligible and at the same time intellectual, (3) the intellectual, (4) the supermundane, (5) the liberated, and (6) the mundane, or as (1) being, (2) life, (3) intellect, (4) soul, (5) nature, and (6) body (see Proclus, *The Theology of Plato*, trans. Thomas Taylor [TTS, vol. 8] (Westbury: Prometheus Trust, 1995), 183–184 and 177–178; and see Lucas Siorvantes, *Proclus: Neo-Platonic Philosophy and Science* (New Haven and London: Yale University Press, 1996), 56 and 114–206), or his division in his *Commentary on the First Alcibiades* (71.1–72.12) of six orders of spirits or daimons into (1) divine daimons, through (2) the noetic, (3) psychic, (4) physical, and (5) corporeal levels, down to (6) material daimons (see Proclus, *Commentary on the First Alcibiades*, ed. L.G. Westerink and trans. William O'Neill (Westbury: Prometheus Trust, 2011), 94–96; and see Crystal Addey, "The Daimonion of Socrates: Daimones and Divination in Neoplatonism," in Danielle A. Layne and Harold Tarrant (eds), *The Neoplatonic Socrates* (Philadelphia: University of Pennsylvania Press, 2014), 51–72 (61–62)).

88. J.N. Findlay, *The Discipline of the Cave* (London and New York: Allen and Unwin and Humanities Press, 1966), 22–23.
89. Findlay, *The Discipline of the Cave*, 23.
90. Findlay, *The Discipline of the Cave*, 39.
91. René Guénon, "The Heart and the Cave," *Studies in Comparative Religion* 4, no. 1 (Spring 1971), 69–72; reprinted in *Symbols of Sacred Science*, ed. Samuel D. Fohr and trans. Henry D. Fohr (Hillsdale, NY: Sophia Perennis, 2004), 202–206; and in John Herlihy (ed.), *The Essential René Guénon: Metaphysics, Tradition, and the Crisis of Modernity* (Bloomington, IN: World Wisdom, 2009), 243–247.
92. The dangers of this intertwining of politics and the occult is well illustrated by the rise of National Socialism, as analysed by Nicholas Goodrick-Clarke, *The Occult Roots of Nazism: Secret Aryan Cults and Their Influence on Nazi Ideology: The Ariosophists of Austria and*

Germany, 1890–1935 (Wellingborough: Aquarian Press, 1985); and *Black Sun: Aryan Cults, Esoteric Nazism and the Politics of Identity* (New York: New York University Press, 2002). For a critique of this account, see Julian Strube, "Die Erfindung des esoterischen Nationalsozialismus im Zeichen der Schwarzen Sonne," *Zeitschrift für Religionswissenschaft* 30, no. 2 (2012), 223–268.

93. See R.H. Stephenson, "The Aesthetic Theory of Weimar Classicism," in *Studies in Weimar Classicism: Writing as Symbolic Form* (Oxford, Bern and Berlin: Lang, 2010), 89–154.

94. Jean Gebser, *The Ever-Present Origin*, trans. Noel Barstad and Algis Mickunas (Athens: Ohio University Press, 1985). References to this work are in the text in parentheses.

95. Jean Gebser, "Cave and Labyrinth," trans. Georg Feuerstein, *Integrative Explorations: Journal of Culture and Consciousness* 4, no. 1 (January 1997), 42–43. The original text is in Gebser, *Gesamtausgabe*, vol. 6, *Asien lächelt anders; Kleine Schriften* (Schaffhausen: Novalis Verlag, 1977), 298–301.

96. On the cave as a place of "death and rebirth" and as a "maternal womb," see C.G. Jung, *Symbols of Transformation* [*Collected Works*, vol. 5], trans. R.F.C. Hull (Princeton: Princeton University Press, 1967), §576 and §659.

Bibliography

Primary Authors

Adorno, Theodor W., *Critical Models: Interventions and Catchwords*, trans. Henry W. Pickford (New York: Columbia University Press, 2005).

Adorno, Theodor W., *Gesammelte Schriften*, ed. Rolf Tiedemann, 20 vols (Frankfurt am Main: Suhrkamp, 1997).

Adorno, Theodor W., *Minima Moralia: Reflections on a Damaged Life*, trans. E.F.N. Jephcott (London and New York: Verso, 2005).

Adorno, Theodor W., *Negative Dialectics*, trans. E.B. Ashton (New York and London: Continuum, 1973).

Adorno, Theodor W., "Of Barricades and Ivory Towers: Interview with T.W. Adorno," *Encounter* 33, no. 3 (September 1969), 63–69.

Adorno, Theodor W., *The Jargon of Authenticity*, trans. Knut Tarnowski and Frederic Will (Evanston: Northwestern University Press, 1973).

Ansell-Pearson, Keith, *An Introduction to Nietzsche as a Political Thinker* (Cambridge: Cambridge University Press, 1994).

Aristotle, *Basic Works*, ed. Richard McKeon (New York: Random House, 1941).

Aristotle, *Complete Works*, ed. Jonathan Barnes, 2 vols (Princeton, NJ: Princeton University Press, 1984).

© The Editor(s) (if applicable) and The Author(s) 2019
P. Bishop, *German Political Thought and the Discourse of Platonism*,
https://doi.org/10.1007/978-3-030-04510-4

Aristotle, *Politics*, trans. H. Rackham (Cambridge, MA; London: Harvard University Press; Heinemann, 1944).

Aristotle, *The Politics of Aristotle*, trans. Ernest Barker (Oxford: Clarendon Press, 1952).

Bloom, Allan, *The Republic of Plato: Translated with Notes and an Interpretive Essay* (New York: Basic Books, 1991).

Engels, Friedrich, *Feuerbach: The Roots of the Socialist Philosophy*, trans. Austin Lewis (Chicago: Kerr, 1906).

Engels, Friedrich, *Socialism: Utopian and Scientific*, trans. Edward Aveling (New York: International Publishers, 1935).

Engels, Friedrich, "Socialism: Utopian and Scientific" (1880), in Marx/Engels, *Selected Works*, vol. 3 (Moscow: Progress Publishers, 1970), 95–151.

Habermas, Jürgen, "Religion in the Public Sphere," *European Journal of Philosophy*, vol. 14, no. 1 (2006), 1–25.

Habermas, Jürgen, *Between Naturalism and Religion*, trans. C. Cronin (Cambridge: Polity Press, 2008).

Habermas, Jürgen, *Legitimation Crisis*, trans. Thomas McCarthy (Cambridge and Malden, MA: Polity Press, 1988).

Habermas, Jürgen, *Moral Consciousness and Communicative Action*, trans. Christian Lenhart and Shierry Weber Nicholson (Cambridge, MA: MIT Press, 1990).

Habermas, Jürgen, *Theory and Practice*, trans. John Viertel (Cambridge and Malden, MA: Polity Press, 1988).

Habermas, Jürgen, *Theorie und Praxis: Sozialphilosophische Studien*, 3rd edn (Frankfurt am Main: Suhrkamp, 1996).

Habermas, Jürgen and Joseph Ratzinger, *Dialektik der Säkularisierung: Über Vernunft und Religion* (Freiburg im Breisgau, Basel, and Vienna: Herder, 2005).

Habermas, Jürgen and Joseph Ratzinger, *The Dialectics of Secularization: On Reason and Religion*, trans. Brian McNeil (San Francisco: Ignatius Press, 2006).

Hegel, G.W.F., *Elements of the Philosophy of Right*, ed. Allen W. Wood, trans. H.B. Nisbet (Cambridge: Cambridge University Press, 1991).

Hegel, G.W.F., *Hegel's Philosophy of Right*, trans. Samuel Walters Dyde (London: Bell, 1896).

Hegel, G.W.F., *Hegel's Philosophy of Right*, trans. T.M. Knox (London, Oxford, and New York: Oxford University Press, 1976).

Hegel, G.W.F., *Lectures on the History of Philosophy, 1825–6*, vol. 2 *Greek Philosophy*, ed. Robert F. Brown, trans. R.F. Brown and J.M. Stewart (Oxford: Clarendon Press, 2006).

Hegel, G.W.F., *Lectures on the History of Philosophy*, trans. E.S. Haldane, 3 vols (London: Kegan Paul, Trench, Tübner, 1892).

Hegel, G.W.F., *Lectures on the History of Philosophy*, vol. 1, *Greek Philosophy to Plato*, trans. E.S. Haldane and vol. 2, *Plato and the Platonists*, trans. Frances H. Simson and E.S. Haldane (Lincoln, NE: University of Nebraska Press, 1995).

Hegel, G.W.F., *Lectures on the Philosophy of World History*, trans. from the third German edition by John Sibree (London: Bohn, 1861).

Hegel, G.W.F., *Lectures on the Philosophy of World History: Introduction: Reason in History*, trans. H.B. Nisbet (Cambridge: Cambridge University Press, 1980).

Hegel, G.W.F., *Phenomenology of Spirit*, trans. A.V. Miller (Oxford: Oxford University Press, 1979).

Hegel, G.W.F., *Reason in History: A General Introduction to the Philosophy of History*, trans. Robert S. Hartman (Indianapolis and New York: Bobbs-Merrill, 1953).

Hegel, G.W.F., *The Encyclopedia Logic: Part I of the Encyclopedia of Philosophical Sciences with the Zusätze*, trans. Théodore F. Geraets, W.A. Suchting, and H.S. Harris (Indianapolis, IN: Hackett, 1991).

Hegel, G.W.F., *The Letters*, trans. Clark Butler and Christine Seiler (Bloomington, IN: University of Indiana Press, 1984).

Hegel, G.W.F., *The Philosophy of History* (Mineola, NY: Dover, 1956).

Heidegger, Martin, *An Introduction to Metaphysics*, trans. Ralph Manheim (New Haven and London: Yale University Press, 1959).

Heidegger, Martin, *Basic Writings*, ed. David Farrell Krell (London: Routledge, 1978).

Heidegger, Martin, *Being and Time*, trans. John Macquarrie and Edward Robinson (Oxford: Blackwell, 1962).

Heidegger, Martin, *Being and Truth*, trans. Gregory Fried and Richard Polt (Bloomington and Indianapolis: Indiana University Press, 2010).

Heidegger, Martin, *Briefe: 1925–1975*, ed. Ursula Ludz (Frankfurt am Main: Klostermann, 1999).

Heidegger, Martin, *Die Grundprobleme der Phänomenologie* [*Gesamtausgabe*, vol. 23], ed. Friedrich-Wilhelm von Herrmann (Frankfurt am Main: Klostermann, 1997).

Heidegger, Martin, *Die Selbstbehauptung der deutschen Universität; Das Rektorat 1933/34: Tatsachen und Gedanken* (Frankfurt am Main: Klostermann, 1983; 2nd edn, 1990).

Heidegger, Martin, *Early Greek Thinking*, trans. David Farrell Krell and Frank A. Capuzzi (New York: HarperSanFrancisco, 1984).

Heidegger, Martin, *Existence and Being*, ed. Werner Brock (London: Vision, 1949).

Heidegger, Martin, *Identity and Difference*, trans. Joan Stambaugh (New York: Harper & Row, 1969).

Heidegger, Martin, *Introduction to Metaphysics*, trans. Ralph Manheim (New Haven, CT: Yale University Press, 1959).

Heidegger, Martin, *Nietzsche*, 2 vols (Pfullingen: Neske, 1961).

Heidegger, Martin, *Nietzsche*, ed. David Farrell Krell, trans. David Farrell Krell et al., 4 vols (San Francisco: Harper & Row, 1979–1987).

Heidegger, Martin, *Plato's "Sophist"*, trans. Richard Rojcewicz and André Schuwer (Bloomington and Indianapolis: Indiana University Press, 2003).

Heidegger, Martin, *Platons Lehre von der Wahrheit: Mit einem Brief über den «Humanismus»* (Berne and Munich: Francke, 1947; 3rd edn, 1975).

Heidegger, Martin, *The Essence of Human Freedom: An Introduction to Philosophy*, trans. Ted Sadler (London and New York: Continuum, 2002).

Heidegger, Martin, *The Essence of Truth: On Plato's Cave Allegory and Theaetetus*, trans. Ted Sadler (London and New York: Continuum, 2002).

Heidegger, Martin, "The Self-Assertion of the German University: Address, Delivered on the Solemn Assumption of the Rectorate of the University Freiburg; The Rectorate 1933/34: Facts and Thoughts," trans. Karsten Harries, *Review of Metaphysics* 38, no. 3 (March 1985), 467–502.

Heidegger, Martin, *Vom Wesen der menschlichen Freiheit: Einleitung in die Philosophie* [*Gesamtausgabe*, vol. 31], ed. Hartmut Tietjen (Frankfurt am Main: Klostermann, 1994).

Heidegger, Martin, *Vom Wesen der Wahrheit: Zu Platons Höhlengleichnis und Theätet* [*Gesamtausgabe*, vol. 34], ed. Hermann Mörchen (Frankfurt am Main: Klostermann, 1988; 2nd edn, 1997).

Heidegger, Martin, *What Is Called Thinking?* trans. J. Glenn Gray (New York: Harper & Row, 1968).

Heidegger, Martin and Elisabeth Blochmann, *Brifewechsel 1918–1969*, ed. Joachim W. Storck (Marbach am Neckar: Deutsche Schillergesellschaft, 1989).

Heidegger, Martin and Eugen Fink, *Heraclitus Seminar 1966/67*, trans. Charles H. Seibert (University, AL: University of Alabama Press, 1979).

Heidegger, Martin and Karl Jaspers, *The Heidegger-Jaspers Correspondence (1920–1963)*, ed. W. Biemel and H. Saner, trans. G.E. Avlesworth (Amherst, NY: Humanity Books, 2003).

Horkheimer, Max, *Gesammelte Schriften*, ed. Alfred Schmidt, 19 vols (Frankfurt am Main: Suhrkamp, 1985–1996).

Horkheimer, Max and Theodor W. Adorno, *Dialectic of Enlightenment: Philosophical Fragments*, ed. Gunzelin Schmid Noerr, trans. Edmund Jephcott (Stanford, CA: Stanford University Press, 2002).

Kant, Immanuel, *Critique of Judgment*, trans. Werner S. Pluhar (Indianapolis, IN: Hackett, 1987).

Kant, Immanuel, *Critique of Pure Reason*, ed. and trans. Paul Guyer and Allen W. Wood (Cambridge: Cambridge University Press, 1997).

Kant, Immanuel, *Grounding for the Metaphysics of Morals* [1785], trans. James W. Ellington, 3rd edn (Indianapolis: Hackett, 1993).

Kant, Imannuel, *Political Writings*, ed. Hans Reiss, trans. H.B. Nisbet (Cambridge and New York: Cambridge University Press, 1970; 2nd edn, 1991).

Kant, Immanuel, *Practical Philosophy*, ed. and trans. Mary J. Gregor (Cambridge: Cambridge University Press, 1996).

Kant, Immanuel, *The Philosophy of Law: An Exposition of the Fundamental Principles of Jurisprudence and the Science of Right*, trans. William Hastie (Edinburgh: T. & T. Clark, 1887).

Marx, Karl, *A Contribution to the Critique of Political Economy*, in Marx/Engels, *Collected Works*, vol. 29 (Moscow: Progress Publishers, 1987), 257–417.

Marx, Karl, *Capital: A Critique of Political Economy*, vol. 1, *The Process of Production of Capital*, in Marx/Engels, *Collected Works*, vol. 34 (London: Lawrence & Wishart, 2010).

Marx, Karl, *The Difference Between the Democritean and Epicurean Philosophy of Nature*, in Marx/Engels, *Collected Works*, vol. 1 (Moscow: Progress Publishers, 1975), 25–107.

Marx, Karl, *Value, Price and Profit*, in Marx/Engels, *Collected Works*, vol. 20 (Moscow: Progress Publishers, 1985), 101–149.

Marx, Karl and Friedrich Engels, *Correspondence*, trans. Donna Torr (New York: International Publishers, 1968).

Marx, Karl and Friedrich Engels, *The German Ideology*, in Marx/Engels, *Collected Works*, vol. 5 (Moscow: Progress Publishers, 1976), 19–539.

Nietzsche, Friedrich, *Basic Writings*, ed. and trans. Walter Kaufmann (New York: Basic Books, 1968).

Nietzsche, Friedrich, *Daybreak*, trans. R.J. Hollingdale (Cambridge: Cambridge University Press, 1982).

Nietzsche, Friedrich, *Dithyrambs of Dionysus*, trans. R.J. Hollingdale (London: Anvil Press Poetry, 1984).

Nietzsche, Friedrich, *Ecce Homo*, trans. R.J. Hollingdale (Penguin: Harmondsworth, 1992).

Nietzsche, Friedrich, *Human, All Too Human*, trans R.J. Hollingdale (Cambridge: Cambridge University Press, 1986).

Nietzsche, Friedrich, *On the Genealogy of Morality*, ed. Keith Ansell-Pearson, trans. Carol Diethe (Cambridge: Cambridge University Press, 2007).

Nietzsche, Friedrich, *Sämtliche Briefe: Kritische Studienausgabe*, ed. Giorgio Colli and Mazzino Montinari, 8 vols (Munich; Berlin and New York: dtv; de Gruyter, 1986).

Nietzsche, Friedrich, *Sämtliche Werke: Kritische Studienausgabe*, ed. Giorgio Colli and Mazzino Montinari, 15 vols (Munich; Berlin and New York: dtv; de Gruyter, 1988).

Nietzsche, Friedrich, *The Case of Wagner; Nietzsche Contra Wagner; The Twilight of the Idols; The Antichrist*, trans. Thomas Common (London: Unwin, 1899), 124–125.

Nietzsche, Friedrich, *The Gay Science*, trans. Walter Kaufmann (New York: Random House, 1974).

Nietzsche, Friedrich, *The Portable Nietzsche*, ed. and trans. Walter Kaufmann (New York: Viking Penguin, 1968).

Nietzsche, Friedrich, *The Pre-Platonic Philosophers*, ed. and trans. Greg Whitlock (Urbana and Chicago: University of Illinois Press, 1995).

Nietzsche, Friedrich, *The Will to Power*, ed. Walter Kaufmann, trans. Walter Kaufmann and R.J. Hollingdale (New York: Vintage, 1968).

Nietzsche, Friedrich, *Thus Spoke Zarathustra*, trans. R.J. Hollingdale (Harmondsworth: Penguin, 1969).

Nietzsche, Friedrich, *Twilight of the Idols; the Anti-Christ*, trans. R.J. Hollingdale (Harmondsworth: Penguin, 1968).

Nietzsche, Friedrich, *Untimely Meditations*, trans. R.J. Hollingdale (Cambridge: Cambridge University Press, 1983).

Nietzsche, Friedrich, *Werke in drei Bänden*, ed. Karl Schlechta, 3 vols (Munich: Hanser, 1966).

Plato, *Apology; Crito; Phaedo; Symposium; Republic*, ed. Louise Ropes Loomis, trans. Benjamin Jowett (Toronto, New York, and London: Van Nostrand, 1942).

Plato, *Collected Dialogues*, ed. Edith Hamilton and Huntington Cairns (Princeton, NJ: Princeton University Press, 1989).

Plato, *Gorgias: A Revised Text with Introduction and Commentary*, ed. E.R. Dodds (Cambridge: Cambridge University Press, 1959).

Plato, *Great Dialogues of Plato*, ed. Eric H. Warmington and Philip G. Rouse (New York: Mentor, 1956).

Plato, *Phaedrus,* trans. R. Hackforth (Cambridge: Cambridge University Press, 1952).

Plato, *Selected Myths*, ed. Catalin Partenie (New York: Oxford University Press, 2004).

Plato, *The Laws of Plato*, trans. Thomas Pangle (Chicago and London: University of Chicago Press, 1980).

Plato, *The Republic of Plato*, ed. and trans. Allan Bloom (New York: Basic Books, 991).

Plotinus, *Porphyry on Plotinus; Ennead I*, trans. A.H. Armstrong, vol. 1 (Cambridge, MA and London: Harvard University Press, 1966).

Rousseau, Jean-Jacques, *Confessions*, trans. Angela Scholar, ed. Patrick Coleman (Oxford: Oxford University Press, 2000).

Rousseau, Jean-Jacques, *Emile, or on Education*, trans. Allan Bloom (New York: Basic Books, 1979).

Rousseau, Jean-Jacques, *Rêveries of the Solitary Walker*, trans. Russell Goulbourne (Oxford and New York: Oxford University Press, 2011).

Rousseau, Jean-Jacques, *The Confessions*, trans. J.M. Cohen (Harmondsworth: Penguin, 1953).

Rousseau, Jean-Jacques, *The Social Contract and Discourses*, trans. G.D.H. Cole (London: Dent, 1973), 76.

Rousseau, Jean-Jacques, *The Social Contract & Discourses*, trans. G.D.H. Cole (London and Toronto; New York: Dent; Dutton, 1913).

Further and Secondary Reading

Abensour, Miguel, "Against the Sovereignty of Philosophy Over Politics: Arendt's Reading of Plato's Cave Allegory," *Social Research* 74, no. 4 (Winter 2007), 955–982.

Ackrill, J.L., "Aristotle on *eudaimonia*," *Proceedings of the British Academy* 60 (1974), 339–359.

Addey, Tim, "From Caveman to Contemplative," *The Aquarian Theosophist* 3, no. 4 (February 17, 2003), 1–7.

Ajavon, François-Xavier, "L'étrange et inquiétant Platon de Hans F.K. Günther: Un exemple d'appropriation idéologique de la pensée grecque," *Laval théologique et philosophique* 62, no. 2 (2006), 267–284.

Althusser, Louis, *Lenin and Philosophy and Other Essays*, trans. Ben Brewster (New York: Monthly Review Press, 2001).

Altman, Matthew C., *The Palgrave Handbook of German Idealism* (Houndmills, Basingstoke, and New York: Palgrave Macmillan, 2014).

Altman, William H.F., "Altruism and the Art of Writing: Plato, Cicero, and Leo Strauss," *Humanitas* 22, nos. 1–2 (2009), 69–98.

Altman, William H.F., *The Revival of Platonism in Cicero's Late Philosophy: Platonis aemulus and the Invention of Cicero* (Lanham, ML: Lexington Books, 2016).

Ameriks, Karl (ed.), *The Cambridge Companion to German Idealism* (Cambridge and New York: Cambridge University Press, 2000).

Anderson, Mark, *Plato and Nietzsche: Their Philosophical Art* (London: Bloomsbury, 2014).

Andonian, Greg, "The Three Caves of European Identity: From Critical to Creative Thinking," *Consciousness, Literature and the Arts* 2, no. 1 (April 2001), available HTTP: http://www.dmd27.org/andonian.html. Accessed 09.01.2018.

Andriopoulos, Stefan, "Occult Conspiracies: Spirits and Secret Societies in Schiller's 'Ghost Seer,'" *New German Critique* 103 (2008), 65–81.

Appleby, David, and Teresa Olsen Pierre (eds), *On the Shoulders of Giants: Essays in Honor of Glenn W. Olsen* (Toronto: Pontifical Institute of Medieval Studies, 2015).

Arendt, Hannah, *Eichmann in Jerusalem: A Report on the Banality of Evil* (New York: Penguin, 2006), 135–136.

Arendt, Hannah, *Essays in Understanding, 1930–1954: Formation, Exile, and Totalitarianism*, ed. Jerome Kohn (New York: Harcourt Brace, 1994).

Arendt, Hannah, *Lectures in Kant's Political Philosophy*, ed. by Ronald Beiner (Chicago and London: University of Chicago Press, 1992).

Arendt, Hannah, *The Human Condition: A Study of the Central Dilemmas Facing Modern Man* (Garden City, NY: Doubleday, 1959).

Ashenden, Samantha, and David Owen (eds), *Foucault Contra Habermas: Recasting the Dialogue Between Genealogy and Critical Theory* (London: Sage, 1999).

Ayers, Michael (ed.), *Rationalism, Platonism, and God: A Symposium on Early Modern Philosophy* (Oxford: Oxford University Press, 2007), 15–44.

Babich, Babette, Alfred Denker, and Holger Zaborowski, *Heidegger & Nietzsche* (Amsterdam and New York: Rodopi, 2012).

Bacon, Francis, *The New Organon*, ed. Lisa Jardine and Michael Silverthorne (Cambridge: Cambridge University Press, 2000).

Baldwin, Anna, and Sarah Hutton (eds), *Platonism and the English Imagination* (Cambridge: Cambridge University Press, 2005).

Bambach, Charles, *Heidegger's Roots: Nietzsche, National Socialism, and the Greeks* (Ithaca and London: Cornell University Press, 2003).

Bambrough, Renford (ed.), *Plato, Popper and Politics: Some Contributions to a Modern Controversy* (Cambridge; New York: Heffer; Barnes & Noble, 1967).

Bamford, Rebecca (ed.), *Nietzsche's Free Spirit Philosophy* (London and New York: Rowman & Littlefield International, 2015).

Barash, Jeffrey Andrew, "Heidegger et la question de la race," *Les Temps Modernes* 63, no. 650 (juillet–octobre 2008), 290–305.

Barnes, Jonathan, *Aristotle: A Very Short Introduction* (Oxford: Oxford University Press, 2000).

Barnes, Jonathan (ed.), *Early Greek Philosophy* (Harmondsworth: Penguin, 1987).

Barnouw, Jeffrey, *Odysseus, Hero of Practical Intelligence: Deliberation and Signs in Homer's "Odyssey"* (Lanham, MD: University Press of America, 2004).

Behler, Ernst (ed.), *Philosophy of German Idealism* (New York: Continuum, 1987).

Beiser, Frederick, *Hegel* (New York and Abingdon: Routledge, 2005).

Beiser, Frederick, *Schiller as Philosopher: A Re-Examination* (Oxford: Clarendon Press, 2005).

Beiser, Frederick C. (ed.), *The Cambridge Companion to Hegel* (Cambridge: Cambridge University Press, 1993).

Beiser, Frederick C. (ed.), *The Cambridge Companion to Hegel and Nineteenth-Century Philosophy* (Cambridge: Cambridge University Press, 2008).

Beiser, Frederick C. (ed. and trans.), *The Early Political Writings of the German Romantics* (Cambridge: Cambridge University Press, 1996).

Benardete, Seth, *Archaeology of the Soul: Platonic Readings of Ancient Poetry and Philosophy*, ed. Ronna Burger and Michael Davis (South Bend, IN: St. Augustine's Press, 2012).

Benhabib, Seyla, "Carl Schmitt's Critique of Kant: Sovereignty and International Law," *Political Theory* 40, no. 6 (December 2012): 688–713.

Benjamin, Walter, "Central Park," trans. Lloyd Spencer and Mark Harrington, *New German Critique* 34 (Winter 1985), 32–58.

Benjamin, Walter, *Illuminations*, trans. Harry Zorn (London: Cape, 1970).

Benn, Gottfried, *Gesammelte Werke*, ed. Dieter Wellershoff (Wiesbaden: Limes, 1968).

Bernal, Martin, *Black Athena: The Afroasiatic Roots of Classical Civilization*, 3 vols (New Brunswick, NJ: Rutgers University Press, 1991–2006).

Bernard of Clairvaux, *Monastic Sermons*, trans. Daniel Griggs (Collegeville, MN: Liturgical Press, 2016).

Billig, Michael, *Freudian Repression: Conversation Creating the Unconscious* (Cambridge: Cambridge University Press, 1999).

Bishop, Paul (ed.), *A Companion to Friedrich Nietzsche: Life and Works* (Rochester, NY: Camden House, 2012).

Bishop, Paul, *Ludwig Klages and the Philosophy of Life: A Vitalist Toolkit* (London and New York: Routledge, 2017).

Bishop, Paul (ed.), *Nietzsche and Antiquity: His Reaction and Response to the Classical Tradition* (Rochester, NY: Camden House, 2004).

Bishop, Paul, "Reaction and Revolution in Thomas Mann," *Oxford German Studies* 34 (2005), 158–172.

Bloch, Ernst, *The Principle of Hope*, trans. Neville Plaice, Stephen Plaice, and Paul Knight, 3 vols (Cambridge, MA: MIT Press, 1986).

Bloch, Ernst, *The Spirit of Utopia*, trans. Anthony A. Nassar (Stanford, CA: Stanford University Press, 2000).

Blond, Louis P., *Heidegger and Nietzsche: Overcoming Metaphysics* (London and New York: Continuum, 2010).

Bloom, Allan, *The Closing of the American Mind* (New York: Simon & Schuster, 1988).

Blum, Harold P., "The Psychological Birth of Art: A Psychoanalytic Approach to Prehistoric Cave Art," *International Forum of Psychoanalysis* 20 (2011), 196–204.

Boer, Karin de and Ruth Sonderegger (eds), *Conceptions of Critique in Modern and Contemporary Philosophy* (Basingstoke: Palgrave Macmillan, 2012).

Boucher, David (ed.), *The British Idealists* (Cambridge: Cambridge University Press, 1997).

Boucher, David (ed.), *The Scottish Idealists: Selected Philosophical Writings* (Exeter and Charlottesville, VA: Imprint Academic, 2004).

Bradley, Arthur, "Derrida's God: A Genealogy of the Theological Turn," *Paragraph* 29, no. 3 (November 2006), 21–42.

Branham, R. Bracht and Marie-Odile Goulet-Cazé, *The Cynics: The Cynic Movement in Antiquity and Its Legacy* (Berkeley, Los Angeles, and London: University of California Press, 1996).

Braun, Eberhard, Felix Heine, and Uwe Opolka (eds), *Politische Philosophie: Ein Lesebuch: Texte, Analysen, Kommentare* (Reinbek bei Hamburg: Rowohlt, 2008).

Brecht, Bertolt, *Poems 1913–1956*, ed. John Willett and Ralph Manheim (London: Methuen, 1987), 185–186.

Brecht, Franz Josef, *Platon und der George-Kreis* (Leipzig: Dieterich, 1929).

Brenner, Erica, *Machiavelli's Ethics* (Princeton, NJ: Princeton University Press, 2009).

Breuer, Stefan, "Between 'Conservative Revolution,' Aesthetic Fundamentalism and New Nationalism: Thomas Mann's Early Political Writings," *History of the Human Sciences* 11, no. 2 (1998), 1–23.

Brisson, Luc, *Introduction à la philosophie du mythe*, vol. 1, *Sauver les mythes* (Paris: Vrin, 1996), translated as *How Philosophers Saved Myths: Allegorical Interpretation and Classical Mythology*, trans. Catherine Tihanyi (Chicago and London: University of Chicago Press, 2004).

Brisson, Luc, *Platon, les mots et les mythes: Comment et pourquoi Platon nomma le mythe?* (Paris: Maspero, 1982; 2nd edn, Paris: Éditions La Découverte, 1994), translated as *Plato the Myth Maker*, ed. and trans. Gerard Naddaf (Chicago and London: University of Chicago Press, 1998).

Browning, Gary K., *Plato and Hegel: Two Modes of Philosophizing About Politics* (London and New York: Routledge, 2013).

Buber, Rüdiger, *Deutscher Idealismus* [*Geschichte der Philosophie in Text und Darstellung*, vol. 6] (Stuttgart: Reclam, 1978).

Bubner, Rüdiger, *German Idealist Philosophy* (Harmondsworth: Penguin, 1997).

Burnyeat, M.F., "Socratic Midwifery, Platonic Inspiration," *Bulletin of the Institute of Classical Studies* 24 (1977), 7–16.

Bussanich, John and Nicholas D. Smith (eds), *The Bloomsburg Companion to Socrates* (London and New York: Bloomsbury Academic, 2013).

Buxton, Richard (ed.), *From Myth to Reason? Studies in the Development of Greek Thought* (Oxford: Oxford University Press, 1999).

Cahn, Steven M., *Political Philosophy: The Essential Texts* (New York and Oxford: Oxford University Press, 2015).

Cairns, Douglas, *Sophocles: "Antigone"* (London and New York: Bloomsbury, 2016).

Cairns, Huntington, *Legal Philosophy from Plato to Hegel* (Baltimore: Johns Hopkins Press, 1949).

Canetti, Elias, *Crowds and Power*, trans. Carol Stewart (New York: Continuum, 1981).

Caputo, John D., *Demythologizing Heidegger* (Bloomington and Indianapolis: Indiana University Press, 1993).

Cassin, Barbara (ed.), *Dictionary of Untranslatables: A Philosophical Lexicon*, trans. Steven Randall, Christian Hubert, Jeffrey Mehlman, Nathanael Stein, and Michael Syrotinski, trans. ed. Emily Apter, Jacques Lezra, and Michael Wood (Princeton, NJ and Oxford: Princeton University Press, 2014).

Cassirer, Ernst, *An Essay on Man: An Introduction to the Philosophy of Culture* (New Haven and London: Yale University Press, 1972).

Cassirer, Ernst, *Language and Myth*, trans. Susanne K. Langer (New York: Dover, 1953).

Cassirer, Ernst, *Philosophy of Symbolic Forms*, trans. Ralph Manheim, 3 vols (New Haven and London: Yale University Press, 1955–1957).

Cassirer, Ernst, *The Myth of the State* (New Haven and London: Yale University Press, 1974).

Cassirer, Ernst, *Wesen und Wirkung des Symbolbegriffs* (Darmstadt: Wissenschaftliche Buchgesellschaft, 1969), 169–200 (175).

Chalybäus, Heinrich Moritz, *Historical Development of Speculative Philosophy, from Kant to Hegel*, trans. Alfred Edersheim (Edinburgh: Clark, 1854).

Chapman, George Chapman, *Works*, vol. 3, *Homer's Iliad and Odyssey*, ed. Richard Herne Shepherd (London: Chatto & Windus, 1924).

Chattopadhyay, Paresh, *Marx's Associated Means of Production: A Critique of Marxism* (New York: Palgrave Macmillan, 2016).

Cherniss, Harold, *Aristotle's Criticism of Plato and the Academy* (Baltimore: Johns Hopkins Press, 1944).

Cherniss, Harold, *Aristotle's Criticism of Presocratic Philosophy* (Baltimore: Johns Hopkins Press, 1935; reprinted New York: Octagon Books, 1964).

Cherniss, Harold, *The Riddle of the Early Academy* (Berkeley and Los Angeles: University of California Press, 1945).

Cherniss, Harold, "The Sources of Evil According to Plato," *Proceedings of the American Philosophical Society* 98, no. 1 (February 1954), 23–30.

Cicero, *Tusculan Disputations*, trans. C.D. Yonge (New York: Harper, 1877).

Collingwood, R.G., *The Idea of History: Revised Edition* (Oxford and New York: Oxford University Press, 1993).

Cooper, Laurence D., *Eros in Plato, Rousseau, and Nietzsche: The Politics of Infinity* (University Park, PA: Penn State University Press, 2008).

Cooper, Laurence D., "Human Nature and the Love of Wisdom: Rousseau's Hidden (and Modified) Platonism," *The Journal of Politics* 64, no. 1 (February 2002), 108–125.

Copenhaver, Brian P. and Charles B. Schmitt, *Renaissance Philosophy* [*A History of Western Philosophy*, vol. 3] (Oxford: Oxford University Press, 1992).

Coskun, Deniz, *Law as Symbolic Form: Ernst Cassirer and the Anthropocentric View of Law* (Dordrecht: Springer, 2007).

Cottingham, John, *Philosophy and the Good Life: Reason and the Passions in Greek, Cartesian and Psychoanalytic Ethics* (Cambridge: Cambridge University Press, 1998).

Cudworth, Ralph, *The True Intellectual System of the Universe: Wherein All the Reason and Philosophy of Atheism Is Confuted, and Its Impossibility Demonstrated, with a Treatise Concerning Eternal and Immutable Morality*, 3 vols (London: Thomas Tegg, 1845).

Curd, Patricia and Daniel W. Graham (eds), *The Oxford Handbook of Presocratic Philosophy* (New York: Oxford University Press, 2008).

Curran, Jane V. and Christophe Fricker (eds), *Schiller's "On Grace and Dignity" in Its Cultural Context* (Rochester, NY: Camden House, 2005).

Curry, Robert, *Genius: An Ideology in Literature* (London: Chatto & Windus, 1974).

D'Onofrio, Andrea, "Die Antike im Spiegel der Blut-und-Boden Ideologie: Odal und die Deutung des Klassischen Altertums im Dritten Reich," *Storia della Storiografia* 42 (2002), 74–102.

Deleuze, Gilles, *Difference and Repetition* [1968], trans. Paul Patton (London: Athlone Press, 1994).

Demetriou, Kyriakos N., "A 'Legend' in Crisis: The Debate Over Plato's Politics, 1930–1960," *Polis* 19, nos. 1–2 (2002), 61–91.

Demos, Marian, "Callicles' Quotation from Pindar in the *Gorgias*," *Harvard Studies in Classical Philology* 96 (1994), 85–107.

Derrida, Jacques, *De la grammatologie* (Paris: Minuit, 1967).

Derrida, Jacques, *Of Grammatology*, trans. Gayatri Chakravorty Spivak (Baltimore: Johns Hopkins University Press, 1975).

Descombes, Vincent, *Modern French Philosophy*, trans. L. Scott-Fox and J.M. Harding (Cambridge: Cambridge University Press, 1980).

Desgroseilles, René, "En son nom propre: La carrière et l'œuvre de René Major," *Filigrane* 11, no. 2 (2002), 157–184.

Detwiler, Bruce, *Nietzsche and the Politics of Aristocratic Radicalism* (Chicago and London: University of Chicago Press, 1990).

Dick, Philip K., *The Selected Letters of Philip K. Dick 1974* (Novato, CA and Lancaster, PN: Underwood-Miller, 1974).

Dienstag, Joshua Foa, *"Dancing in Chains": Narrative and Memory in Political Theory* (Stanford, CA: Stanford University Press, 1997).

Dillon, John, *The Heirs of Plato: A Study of the Old Academy (347–274 BC)* (Oxford: Clarendon Press, 2003).

Dillon, John M. and Stephen R.L. Clark, *Towards the Noosphere* (Westbury: Prometheus Trust, 2012).

Dillon, John M., Brendan O'Byrne and Tim Addey, *Platonism and the World Crisis*, 2nd edn (Westbury: Prometheus Trust, 2010).

Dilthey, Wilhelm, *Leben Schleiermachers*, in *Gesammelte Schriften*, ed. Martin Redeker, vol. 13, parts 1 and 2 (Göttingen: Vandenhoeck & Ruprecht, 1970), vol. 13/2.

Diogenes Laërtius, *Lives and Opinions of Eminent Philosophers*, trans. C.D. Yonge (London: Bell, 1895).

Dixsaut, Monique, *Platon-Nietzsche: L'autre manière de philosopher* (Paris: Fayard, 2015).

Dostal, Robert J., "Beyond Being: Heidegger's Plato," *Journal of the History of Philosophy* 23, no. 1 (January 1985), 71–98.

Draper, Hal, *The "Dictatorship of the Proletariat" from Marx to Lenin* (New York: Monthly Review Press, 1987).

Dreyfus, Hubert L. and Mark A. Wrathall, *A Companion to Heidegger* (Malden, MA: Blackwell, 2005).

Drochon, Hugo, *Nietzsche's Great Politics* (Princeton, NJ and Oxford: Princeton University Press, 2016).

Dumont, Jean-Paul (ed.), *Les Présocratiques* (Paris: Gallimard, 1988).

Dumont, Jean-Paul and Jean Monod, *Le fœtus astral: Essai d'analyse structurale d'un mythe cinématographique* (Paris: Bourgeois, 1970).

Dunham, Jeremy, Iain Hamilton Grant, and Sean Watson, *Idealism: The History of a Philosophy* (Abingdon and New York: Routledge, 2014).

Dunn, Carol, *Plato's Dialogues: Path to Initiation* (Great Barrington, MA: Portal Books, 2012).

Dynes, Russell R., "The Dialogue Between Voltaire and Rousseau on the Lisbon Earthquake: The Emergence of a Social Science View," *International Journal of Mass Emergencies and Disasters* 18, no. 1 (March 2000), 97–115.

Earle, William, "The Rupture Between Jaspers and Heidegger," *Modern Age: A Quarterly Review* 26, no. 2 (Spring 1982), 197–199.

Edler, Frank W.H., "Selected Letters from the Heidegger-Blochmann Correspondence," *Graduate Faculty Philosophical Journal* 14, nos. 2 and 15, no. 1 (1992), 557–577.

Edmonds III, Radcliffe G., "Socrates the Beautiful: Role Reversal and Midwifery in Plato's *Symposium*," *Transactions of the American Philological Association* 130 (2000), 261–285.

Eisler, Robert, *Man into Wolf: An Anthropological Interpretation of Sadism, Masochism, and Lycanthropy* (London: Spring Books, 1951).

Elliot, Gil, *Twentieth Century Book of the Dead* (New York: Penguin, 1972).

Emden, Christian J., *Friedrich Nietzsche and the Politics of History* (Cambridge: Cambridge University Press, 2008).

Escudero, Jesús Adrián, "Heidegger on Discourse and Idle Talk: The Role of Aristotelian Rhetoric," *Gatherings: The Heidegger Circle Annual* 3 (2013), 1–17.

Evans, Richard J., *Lying About Hitler: History, Holocaust, and the David Irving Trial* (New York: Basic Books, 2002).

Farías, Victor, *Heidegger und der Nationalsozialismus* (Frankfurt am Main: Fischer, 1989).

Fichte, Johann Gottlieb, *Addresses to the German Nation*, trans. Gregory Moore (Cambridge and New York: Cambridge University Press, 2008).

Fichte, Johann Gottlieb, *Early Philosophical Writings*, ed. and trans. Daniel Breazeale (Ithaca and London: Cornell University Press, 1988).

Fichte, Johann Gottlieb, *Foundations of Natural Right*, ed. Frederick Neuhouser, trans. Michael Baur (Cambridge: Cambridge University Press, 2000).

Fichte, Johann Gottlieb, *Werke 1806–1807* [*Gesamtausgabe*, vol. I/9], ed. Reinhard Lauth and Hans Gliwitzky (Stuttgart-Bad Cannstatt: Frommann (Holzboog), 1995).

Findlay, J.N., *The Discipline of the Cave* (London; New York: Allen and Unwin; Humanities Press, 1966).

Fleming, Katie, "Heidegger, Jaeger, Plato: The Politics of Humanism," *International Journal of the Classical Tradition* 19, no. 2 (June 2012), 82–106.

Fogelin, Robert J., "Three Platonic Analogies," *The Philosophical Review* 80, no. 3 (July 1971), 371–382.

Foster, M.B., *The Political Philosophies of Plato and Hegel* (Oxford: Clarendon Press, 1935).

Freeman, Kathleen, *Ancilla to The Pre-Socratic Philosophers: A Complete Translation of the Fragments in Diels, "Fragmente der Vorsokratiker"* (Cambridge, MA: Harvard University Press, 1983).

Freidenreich, Harriet Pass, *Female, Jewish, and Educated: The Lives of Central European University Women* (Bloomington: Indiana University Press, 2002).

Freud, Sigmund, *Civilization, Society and Religion* [Penguin Freud Library, vol. 12], ed. Albert Dickson, trans. James Strachey et al. (Harmondsworth: Penguin, 1985).

Freud, Sigmund, *On Sexuality: Three Essays on the Theory of Sexuality and Other Works* [Pelican Freud Library, vol. 7], ed. Angela Richards, trans. James Strachey (Harmondsworth: Penguin, 1977).

Freud, Sigmund, *Standard Edition of the Collected Works of Sigmund Freud*, ed. James Strachey and Anna Freud, 24 vols (London: Hogarth Press, 1957–1974).

Freud, Sigmund, *Totem and Taboo: Some Points of Agreement Between the Mental Lives of Savages and Neurotics*, trans. James Strachey (London: Routledge & Kegan Paul, 1960).

Furness, Raymond, *Zarathustra's Children: A Study of a Lost Generation of German Writers* (Rochester, NY and Woodbridge: Camden House, 2000).

Gadamer, Hans, "Back from Syracuse?" trans. J. McCumber, *Critical Inquiry* 15 (1989), 427–430.

Galton, David J., "Greek Theories on Eugenics," *Journal of Medical Ethics* 24 (1998), 263–267.

Gebser, Jean, "Cave and Labyrinth," trans. Georg Feuerstein, *Integrative Explorations: Journal of Culture and Consciousness* 4, no. 1 (January 1997), 42–43.

Gebser, Jean, *Gesamtausgabe*, vol. 6, *Asien lächelt anders; Kleine Schriften* (Schaffhausen: Novalis Verlag, 1977).

Gebser, Jean, *The Ever-Present Origin*, trans. Noel Barstad and Algis Mickunas (Athens: Ohio University Press, 1985).

Gens, Jean-Claude and Pierre Rodrigo (eds), *Puissances de l'image* (Dijon: Editions universitaires de Dijon, 2007).

Gerth, H.H. and C. Wright Mills (eds and trans.), *From Max Weber: Essays in Sociology* (New York: Oxford University Press, 1946; revised edn, London and New York: Routledge, 2009).

Giglioni, Guido and Anna Corrias (eds), *Brill's Companion to Medieval and Early Modern Platonism* (Leiden and Boston: Brill, forthcoming).

Gilbert, Francis, *Yob Nation: The Truth About Britain's Yob Culture* (London: Portrait, 2007).

Gleichen-Rußwurm, Alexander von, *Philosophische Profile: Erinnerungen und Wertungen* (Stuttgart: Strecker und Schröder, 1922).

Glucksmann, André, *The Master Thinkers*, trans. Brian Pierce (New York: Harper & Row, 1980).

Goethe, Johann Wolfgang von, *Selected Poems*, ed. Christopher Middleton (Boston: Suhrkamp/Insel, 1983).

Golb, J.D., "Celan and Heidegger: A Reading of 'Todtnauberg,'" *Seminar: A Journal of Germanic Studies* 24, no. 3 (1988), 255–268.

Gonzalez, Francisco, "History of an Embarrassment: Heidegger's Critique of Platonic Dialectic," *History of the Journal of Philosophy* 40, no. 3 (July 2002), 361–389.

Gonzalez, Francisco J., *Plato and Heidegger: A Question of Dialogue* (University Park, PA: Pennsylvania State University Press, 2009).

Goodrick-Clarke, Nicholas, *Black Sun: Aryan Cults, Esoteric Nazism and the Politics of Identity* (New York: New York University Press, 2002).

Goodrick-Clarke, Nicholas, *The Occult Roots of Nazism: Secret Aryan Cults and Their Influence on Nazi Ideology: The Ariosophists of Austria and Germany, 1890–1935* (Wellingborough: Aquarian Press, 1985).

Goyard-Fabre, Simone, *Nietzsche et la question politique* (Paris: Éditions Sirey, 1977).

Graham, Gordon (ed.), *Scottish Philosophy in the Nineteenth and Twentieth Centuries* (Oxford: Oxford University Press, 2015).

Greisman, H.C., "'Disenchantment of the World': Romanticism, Aesthetics and Sociological Theory," *The British Journal of Sociology* 27 (1976), 495–507.

Greisman, Harvey C. and George Ritzer, "Max Weber, Critical Theory, and the Administered World," *Qualitative Sociology* 4, no. 1 (Spring 1981), 34–55.

Grene, David and Richmond Lattimore (eds), *Greek Tragedies*, vol. 1 (Chicago and London: University of Chicago Press, 1960).

Grimes, Pierre and Regina L. Uliana, *Philosophical Midwifery: A New Paradigm for Understanding Human Problems, With Its Validation* (Costa Mesa, CA: Hyparxis Press, 1998).

Grote, Dale, "Callicles' Use of Pindar's NOMOS BASILEUS: *Gorgias* 484B," *The Classical World* 90 (1994), 21–31.

Guénon, René, *Symbols of Sacred Science*, ed. Samuel D. Fohr, trans. Henry D. Fohr (Hillsdale, NY: Sophia Perennis, 2004).

Guéroult, Martial [et al.], *Studien zu Kants philosophischer Entwicklung* (Hildesheim: Olms, 1967).

Günther, Hans F.J., *Platon als Hüter des Lebens: Platons Zucht- und Erziehungsgedanken und deren Bedeutung für die Gegenwart* (Munich: Lehmanns, 1928; 2nd edn, 1936; 3rd edn, Pähl: von Bebenburg, 1966).

Günzel, Stephan [et al.], "Nietzsche in Heideggers Texten: Eine Konkordanz," *Heidegger-Jahrbuch* 2 (2005), 45–92.

Guthrie, Kenneth Sylvan (ed. and trans.), *The Pythagorean Sourcebook and Library: An Anthology of Ancient Writings Which Relate to Pythagoras and Pythagorean Philosophy*, ed. David R. Fideler (Grand Rapids, MI: Phanes Press, 1987).

Guthrie, W.K.C., *The Sophists* (Cambridge: Cambridge University Press, 1971).

Gutting, Gary (ed.), *The Cambridge Companion to Foucault* (Cambridge: Cambridge University Press, 1994).

Hachmeister, Lutz, *Heideggers Testament: Der Philosoph, der SPIEGEL und die SS* (Berlin: Propyläen, 2014).

Hadot, Pierre, *Philosophy as a Way of Life: Spiritual Exercises from Socrates to Foucault*, ed. Arnold Davidson, trans. Michael Chase (Malden, MA and Oxford: Blackwell, 1995).

Hadot, Pierre, *What Is Ancient Philosophy?* trans. Michael Chase (Cambridge, MA and London: Belknap Press of Harvard University Press, 2002; revised edn, 2004).

Hall, Manly P., *The Secret Teachings of All Ages: An Encyclopedic Outline of Masonic, Hermetic, Qabbalistic and Rosicrucian Symbolical Philosophy* (New York: Tarcher/Penguin, 2003).

Havelock, Eric A., *Preface to Plato* (Cambridge, MA and London: Belknap Press of Harvard University Press, 1963).

Hay, Katia and Leonel R. dos Santos (eds), *Nietzsche, German Idealism and Its Critics* (Berlin and Boston: de Gruyter, 2015).

Haym, Rudolf, *Hegel und seine Zeit* (Hildesheim: Olms, 1962).

Hazareesingh, Sudhir, *How the French Think: An Affectionate Portrait of an Intellectual People*, London: Allen Lane, 2015.

Hedly, Douglas and Sarah Hutton (eds), *Platonism at the Origins of Modernity: Studies on Platonism and Early Modern Philosophy* (Dordrecht: Springer, 2008).

Heftrich, Eckhard, Paul Gerhard Klussmann, and Hans Joachim Schrimpf (eds), *Stefan George-Kolloquium* (Cologne: Wienand, 1971).

Heimsoeth, Heinz, "Kant and Plato," *Kant-Studien* 56 (1965), 349–372.

Helvétius, C.A., *De l'esprit, or, Essays on the Mind and Its Several Faculties* (London: Albion, 1810).

Herf, Jeffrey, *Reactionary Modernism: Technology, Culture, and Politics in Weimar and the Third Reich* (Cambridge: Cambridge University Press, 1984).

Herlihy, John (ed.), *The Essential René Guénon: Metaphysics, Tradition, and the Crisis of Modernity* (Bloomington, IN: World Wisdom, 2009).

Herman, Arthur, *The Cave and the Light: Plato versus Aristotle, and the Struggle for the Soul of Western Civilization* (New York: Random House, 2013).

Hesiod, *The Homeric Hymns and Homerica*, trans. Hugh G. Evelyn-White (Cambridge, MA; London: Harvard University Press; Heinemann, 1982).

Hippolyte, Jean, *Genesis and Structure of the "Phenomenology of Spirit"*, trans. Samuel Cherniak and John Heckman (Evanston: Northwestern University Press, 1974).

Hobbes, Thomas, *Leviathan: Revised Student Edition*, ed. Richard Tuck (Cambridge: Cambridge University Press, 1996).

Hobbes, Thomas, *Man and Citizen* (Indianapolis, IN: Hackett, 1998).

Hoerster, Norbert (ed.), *Klassische Texte der Staatsphilosophie* (Munich: dtv, 2011).

Holbach, Baron d', *The System of Nature: Or, the Law of the Moral and Physical World* [1770], trans. H.D. Robinson, 2 vols (New York: Matsell, 1835).

Homer, *The Odyssey*, ed. and trans. Albert Cook, 2nd edn (New York and London: Norton, 1993).

Horn, Christoph and James Wilberding (eds), *Neoplatonism and the Philosophy of Nature* (Oxford: Oxford University Press, 2012).

Houlgate, Stephen, *Hegel's "Phenomenology of Spirit": A Reader's Guide* (London and New York: Bloomsbury Academic, 2012).

Houlgate, Stephen and Michael Baur (eds), *A Companion to Hegel* (Malden, MA and Oxford: Wiley Blackwell, 2011).

Hughes, Bettany, *The Hemlock Cup: Socrates, Athens and the Search for the Good Life* (London: Jonathan Cape, 2010).

Hyland, Drew A., *Questioning Platonism: Continental Interpretations of Plato* (Albany, NY: State University of New York Press, 2005).

Irvine, William B., *A Guide to the Good Life: The Ancient Art of Stoic Joy* (Oxford and New York: Oxford University Press, 2009).

Jacobs, David C., *The Presocratics After Heidegger* (Albany, NY: State University of New York Press, 1999).

Jaeger, Werner, *Humanistische Reden und Vorträge*, 2nd edn (Berlin: de Gruyter, 1960).

Jaeger, Werner, *Paideia: The Ideals of Greek Culture*, trans. Gilbert Highet, 3 vols (New York and Oxford: Oxford University Press, 1965–1986).

James, David, *Rousseau and German Idealism: Freedom, Dependence and Necessity* (Cambridge: Cambridge University Press, 2013).

Janssens, David, *Between Athens and Jerusalem: Philosophy, Prophecy, and Politics in Leo Strauss's Early Thought* (Albany, NY: State University of New York Press, 2008).

Jordan, Rudolf, *Homo Sapiens Socialis: Principles of the Philosophy of Responsibility* (South Africa: Central News Agency, 1944).

Josephson-Storm, Jason Ā., *The Myth of Disenchantment: Magic, Modernit, and the Birth of the Human Sciences* (Chicago and London: University of Chicago Press, 2017).

Jowett, Benjamin, *The Republic of Plato: Translated into English with Introduction, Analysis, Marginal Analysis and Index*, 3rd edn (Oxford: Clarendon Press, 1888).

Jung, C.G., *Symbols of Transformation* [*Collected Works*, vol. 5], trans. R.F.C. Hull (Princeton: Princeton University Press, 1967).

Jung, C.G. and Karl Kerényi, *Essays on a Science of Mythology*, trans. R.F.C. Hull (New York: Princeton University Press, 1969).

Kalkavage, Peter, *The Logic of Desire: An Introduction to Hegel's "Phenomenology of Spirit"* (Philadelphia: Paul Dry Books, 2007).

Kamenka, Eugene (ed.), *The Portable Marx* (New York: Viking Penguin, 1983).

Karlauf, Thomas, *Stefan George: Die Entdeckung des Charisma* (Munich: Pantheon, 2008).

Kaufmann, Walter, *Hegel: A Reinterpretation* (Notre Dame, IN: University of Notre Dame Press, 1978).

Kelly, George Armstrong, *Idealism, Politics and History: Sources of Hegelian Thought* (Cambridge: Cambridge University Press, 1969).

Kelly, Michael (ed.), *Critique and Power: Recasting the Foucault/Habermas Debate* (Cambridge, MA: MIT Press, 1994).

Kennen, Dennis King, *The Question of Sacrifice* (Bloomington and Indianapolis: Indiana University Press, 2005).

Kiesel, Theodore and John van Buren (eds), *Reading Heidegger from the Start: Essays in His Earliest Thought* (Albany, NY: State University of New York Press, 1994).

Kim, Alan (ed.), *Brill's Companion to German Platonism* (Leiden and Boston: Brill, forthcoming).

Kim, Alan, *Plato in Germany: Kant—Natorp—Heidegger* (Sankt Augustin: Academia-Verlag, 2010).

Kingsley, Peter, *Ancient Philosophy, Mystery, and Magic: Empedocles and Pythagorean Tradition* (Oxford: Clarendon Press, 1995).

Kingsley, Peter, *In the Dark Places of Wisdom* (Inverness, CA: Golden Sufi Center, 1999).

Klages, Ludwig, *Charakterkunde I* [*Sämtliche Werke*, vol. 4], ed. Heinz Alfred Müller (Bonn: Bouvier, 1983).

Kleinberg, Ethan, *Generation Existential: Heidegger's Philosophy in France, 1927–1961* (Ithaca, NY: Cornell University Press, 2005).

Klosko, George, *History of Political Theory: An Introduction*, vol. 1, *Ancient and Medieval*, vol. 2, *Modern*, 2nd edn (Oxford: Oxford University Press, 2012–2013).

Klosko, George, "The 'Straussian' Interpretation of Plato's *Republic*," *History of Political Thought* 7, no. 2 (Summer 1986), 275–293.

Knowles, Dudley, *Hegel and the "Philosophy of Right"* (London: Routledge, 2002).

Kolbenheyer, E.G., *Gesammelte Werke*, 8 vols (Munich: Langen & Müller, 1939–1941).

Korhonen, Kuisma and Pajari Räsänan (eds), *The Event of Encounter in Art and Philosophy: Continental Perspectives* (Helsinki: Gaudeamus Helsinki University Press, 2010).

Korotin, Ilse (ed.), *"Die besten Geister der Nation": Philosophie und Nationalsozialismus* (Vienna: Pictus, 1994).

Kozljanič, Robert Josef, *Lebensphilosophie: Eine Einführung* (Stuttgart: Kohlhammer, 2004).

Krell, David Farrell and Donald L. Bates, *The Good European: Nietzsche's Work Sites in Word and Image* (Chicago and London: Chicago University Press, 1997).

Kristeller, Paul, *Eight Philosophers of the Italian Renaissance* (Stanford: Stanford University Press, 1964).

Krois, John Michael, *Cassirer: Symbolic Forms and History* (New Haven and London: Yale University Press, 1987).

Lachman, Gary, *The Secret Teachers of the Western World* (New York: Tarcher/Penguin, 2015), 82.

Lactantius, *The Works of Lactantius*, trans. William Fletcher (Edinburgh: T. & T. Clark, 1871).

Lamberton, Robert, *Homer the Theologian: Neoplatonist Allegorical Reading and the Growth of the Epic Tradition* (Berkeley, Los Angeles, and London: University of California Press, 1986).

Lamm, Julia A., "Schleiermacher as Plato Scholar," *The Journal of Religion* 80, no. 2 (April 2000), 206–239.

Lampert, Laurence, *Leo Strauss and Nietzsche* (Chicago and London: University of Chicago Press, 1996).

Lampert, Laurence, *The Enduring Importance of Leo Strauss* (Chicago and London: University of Chicago Press, 2013).

Lane, Melissa S. and Martin A. Ruehl (eds), *A Poet's Reich: Politics and Culture in the George Circle* (Rochester, NY: Camden House, 2011).

Laplanche, Jean and Jean-Bertrand Pontalis, *The Language of Psychoanalysis*, trans. Donald Nicholson-Smith (London: Karnac, 1998).

Layne, Danielle A. and Harold Tarrant (eds), *The Neoplatonic Socrates* (Philadelphia: University of Pennsylvania Press, 2014).

Lefkowitz, Mary, *Not Out of Africa: How Afrocentrism Became an Excuse to Teach Myth as History* (New York: Basic Books, 1996; revised 1997).

Lefkowitz, Mary and Guy MacLean Rogers (eds), *Black Athena Revisited* (Chapel Hill, NC: University of North Carolina Press, 1996).

Leibniz, G.W., *Political Writings*, ed. Patrick Riley, 2nd edn (Cambridge: Cambridge University Press, 1988).

Leibniz, G.W., *Theodicy: Essays on the Goodness of God, the Freedom of Man and the Origin of Evil*, trans. E.M. Huggard (La Salle, IL: Open Court, 1985).

Lewis, H.D, "Plato and the Social Contract", *Mind* [NS] 48, no. 189 (January 1939), 78–81.

Lewis-Williams, David, *The Mind in the Cave: Consciousness and the Origins of Art* (London: Thames & Hudson, 2002).

Lewkowicz, Sergio and Thierry Bolkanowski with Georges Pragier (eds), *On Freud's "Constructions in Analysis"* (London: Karnac, 2011).

Lipstadt, Deborah, *Denying the Holocaust: The Growing Assault on Truth and Memory* (New York: Penguin, 1994).

Locke, Grahame, *Political Philosophy: An Audio Course on Western Political Theory* (Gouderak: Home Academy, 2016).

Lörke, Melanie Maria, *Liminal Semiotics: Boundary Phenomena in Romanticism* (Berlin: Akademie-Verlag, 2013).

Losin, Peter, "Education and Plato's Parable of the Cave," *Journal of Education* 178, no. 3 (1996), 48–65.

Ludwig, Bernd, *Die Wiederentdeckung des Epikureischen Naturrechts: Zu Thomas Hobbes' philosophischer Entwicklung von „De Cive" zum „Leviathan" im Pariser Exil 1640–1651* (Frankfurt am Main: Klostermann, 1998).

Lukács, Georg, *Der junge Hegel: Über die Beziehungen von Dialektik und Ökonomie*, 2 vols (Frankfurt am Main: Suhrkamp, 1973).

Lukács, Georg, *History and Class Consciousness: Studies in Marxist Dialectics* [1920], trans. Rodney Livingstone (Cambridge, MA: MIT Press, 1971).

Luxemburg, Rosa, *Politische Schriften*, vol. 2 (Frankfurt: Europäische Verlagsanstalt, 1966).

Luxemburg, Rosa, *Selected Political Writings*, ed. Dick Howard (New York and London: Monthly Review Press, 1971).

Lyon, James K., *Paul Celan and Martin Heidegger: An Unresolved Conversation, 1951–1970* (Baltimore, ML: Johns Hopkins University Press, 2006).

Macrobius, *Commentary on the Dream of Scipio*, trans. William Harris Stahl (New York: Columbia University Press, 1990).

Magee, Glenn Alexander, *Hegel and the Hermetic Tradition* (Ithaca and London: Cornell University Press, 2001).

Mahon, Michael, *Foucault's Nietzschean Genealogy: Truth, Power, and the Subject* (Albany, NY: State University of New York Press, 1992).

Maier, Hans and Horst Denzer (eds), *Klassiker des politischen Denkens*, vol. 1, *Von Plato bis Hobbes*, and vol. 2, *Von Locke bis Max Weber*, 3rd edn (Munich: Beck, 2007).

Maimonides, Moses, *The Guide for the Perplexed*, trans. M. Friedländer, 2nd edn (New York: Dover, 1956).

Maitland, Sara, *A Book of Silence* (London: Granta, 2008).

Major, René, *De l'élection: Freud face aux idéologies américaine, allemande et soviétique* (Paris: Aubier, 1986).

Malcolm, John, "The Cave Revisited," *Classical Quarterly* 31, no. 1 (1981), 60–68.

Malcolm, John, "The Line and the Cave," *Phronesis* 7, no. 1 (1962), 38–45.

Malebranche, Nicolas, *The Search After Truth*, ed. Thomas M. Lennon and Paul J. Olscamp (Cambridge: Cambridge University Press, 1997).

Malebranche, Nicolas, *Trois Lettres de l'auteur de la Recherche de la Vérité* (Rotterdam: Leers, 1685).

Malinowski, Bronisław, *Magic, Science and Religion and Other Essays* (Garden City, NY: Doubleday, 1948).

Mann, Thomas, *Schriften und Reden zur Literatur, Kunst und Philosophie*, vol. 1 [*Thomas Mann Werke: Das essayistische Werk*, vol. 1] (Frankfurt am Main: Fischer, 1968).

Marcuse, Herbert, *Eros and Civilization: A Philosophical Inquiry into Freud* (London: Ark, 1987).

Marcuse, Herbert, *Hegel's Ontology and the Theory of Historicity*, trans. Seyla Benhabib (Cambridge, MA and London: MIT Press, 1987).

Marcuse, Herbert, *One-Dimensional Man: Studies in the Ideology of Advanced Industrial Society* (London: Ark, 1986).

Marcuse, Herbert, *Reason and Revolution: Hegel and the Rise of Social Theory* (London: Routledge & Kegan Paul, 1986).

Martella, Martella, *Dialectics of Cultural Criticism: Adorno;s Confrontation with Rudolf Borchardt and Ludwig Klages in the "Odyssey" Chapter of "Dialektik der Aufklärung"*, D. Phil. Thesis, Justus-Liebig-Universität Gießen, 2012.

Mattei, Jean-François, *L'ordre du monde: Platon, Nietzsche, Heidegger* (Paris: Presses universitaires de France, 1989).

McCoy, Marina, *Plato on the Rhetoric of Philosophers and Sophists* (New York: Cambridge University Press, 2008).

McGahey, Robert, *The Orphic Moment: Shaman to Poet-Thinker in Plato, Nietzsche, and Mallarmé* (Albany, NY: State University of New York Press, 1994).

McEvoy, James, "Plato and the Wisdom of Egypt," *Irish Philosophical Journal* 1 (1984), 1–24.

McGrath, S.J., *The Early Heidegger and Medieval Philosophy: Phenomenology for the Godforsaken* (Washington, DC: Catholic University of America Press, 2006).

McTaggart, John McTaggart Ellis, *Studies in the Hegelian Dialectic*, 2nd edn (Cambridge: Cambridge University Press, 1922).

Meckler, Michael, *Classical Antiquity and the Politics of America: From George Washington to George W. Bush* (Waco, TX: Baylor University Press, 2006).

Meier, Heinrich, *Carl Schmitt, Leo Strauss und "Der Begriff des Politischen": Zu einem Dialog unter Abwesenden*, 3rd edn (Stuttgart: Metzler, 2013).

Meier, Heinrich, *Das theologisch-politische Problem: Zum Thema von Leo Strauss* (Stuttgart: Metzler and Poeschel, 2003).

Meier, Heinrich, *Die Denkbewegung von Leo Strauss: Die Geschichte der Philosophie und die Intention des Philosophen* (Stuttgart and Weimar: Metzler, 1996).

Mendham, Matthew D., "Rousseau's Discarded Children: The Panoply of Excuses and the Question of Hypocrisy," *History of European Ideas* 41, no. 1 (January 2015), 131–152.

Merquior, J.G., *From Paris to Prague: A Critique of Structuralist and Poststructuralist Thought* (London: Verso, 1986).

Michael Casey, "*In communi vita fratrum:* St Bernard's Teachings on Cenobitic Solitude," *Analecta Sacri Ordinis Cisterciensis* 46 (1990), 243–261.

Miller, Paul Allen, "Lacan's *Antigone*: The Sublime Object and the Ethics of Interpretation," *Phoenix* 61/1–2 (Spring–Summer 2007), 1–14.

Mohler, Armin, *Die Konservative Revolution in Deutschland 1918–1932: Ein Handbuch*, 3rd edn (Darmstadt: Wissenschaftliche Buchgesellschaft, 1989).

Mojvisch, Burkhard and Orrin F. Summerell (eds), *Platonismus im Idealismus: Die platonische Tradition in der klassischen deutschen Philosophie* (Munich and Leipzig: Saur, 2003).

Monville, Aymeric, *Misère du «nietzschéisme de gauche»: De Georges Bataille à Michel Onfray* (Brussels: Aden, 2007).

Morgan, Michael L., *Platonic Piety: Philosophy and Ritual in Fourth-Century Athens* (New Haven and London: Yale University Press, 1990).

Most, Glenn W., "Heidegger's Greeks," *Arion: A Journal of the Humanities and the Classics* 1, no. 1 (2002), 83–98.

Mothe-Fénelon, Salignac de la, *The Adventures of Telemachus, the Son of Ulysses*, trans. John Hawkesworth (Manchester: Thomas Johnson, 1847), 71.

Mueller, Gustav E., "The Hegel Legend of 'Thesis-Antithesis-Synthesis,'" *Journal of the History of Ideas* 19, no. 3 (June 1958), 411–414.

Muirhead, John H., *The Platonic Tradition in Anglo-Saxon Philosophy: Studies in the History of Idealism in England and America* (London; New York: Allen & Unwin; Macmillan, 1931).

Mulgan, R.G., *Aristotle's Political Theory: An Introduction for Students of Political Theory* (Oxford: Clarendon Press, 1977).

Nadler, Steven (ed.), *A Companion to Early Modern Philosophy* (Madden, MA and Oxford: Blackwell, 2002).

Nagy, Gregory, *The Ancient Greek Hero in 24 hours* (Cambridge, MA and London: Belknap Press of Harvard University Press, 2013).

Nash, Jay Robert, *Dictionary of Crime, Criminal Justice, Criminology, & Law Enforcement* (Lanham, ML: Rowman & Littlefield, 1992).

Naydler, Jeremy, *Plato, Shamanism, and Ancient Egypt* (Oxford: Abzu Press, 2005).

Neville, Henry, *Plato Redivivus: Or, a Dialogue Concerning Government*, 4th edn (London: A. Millar, 1763).

Nightingale, Andrea Wilson, "Plato's 'Gorgias' and Euripides' 'Antiope': A Study in Generic Transformation," *Classical Antiquity* 11, no. 1 (April 1992), 121–141.

Nisbet, Robert A., "Rousseau and Totalitarianism," *The Journal of Politics* 5, no. 2 (May 1943), 93–114.

Norton, Robert E., *The Beautiful Soul: Aesthetic Morality in the Eighteenth Century* (Ithaca, NY and London: Cornell University Press, 1995).

O'Connor, Brian and Georg Mohr, *German Idealism: An Anthology and Guide* (Chicago: University of Chicago Press, 2006).

O'Daly, Gerard, *Platonism Pagan and Christian: Studies in Plotinus and Augustine* (Aldershot and Burlington, VT: Ashgate, 2001).

O'Meara, Dominic J., *Pythagoras Revived: Mathematics and Philosophy in Late Antiquity* (Oxford: Clarendon Press, 1989).

O'Regan, Cyril, *The Heterodox Hegel* (Albany, NY: State University of New York Press, 1994).

Onfray, Michel, *Cosmos: Une ontologie matérialiste* [*Brève encyclopédie du monde*, vol. 1] (Paris: Flammarion, 2015).

Onfray, Michel, *Cynismes: Portrait du philosophe en chien* (Paris: Grasset, 1990).

Onfray, Michel, *Journal hédoniste*, 1–4 vols (Paris: Grasset, 1996–2007); vol. 5 (Paris: Flammarion, 2013).

Onfray, Michel, *La Construction du surhomme* [*Contre-histoire de la philosophie*, vol. 7] (Paris: Grasset, 2011).

Onfray, Michel, *La Puissance d'exister: Manifeste hédoniste* (Paris: Grasset, 2006).

Onfray, Michel, *La Sagesse tragique: Du bon usage de Nietzsche* (Paris: Le Livre de poche, 2006).

Onfray, Michel, *La Sculpture de soi: La morale esthétique* (Paris: Grasset, 1993).

Onfray, Michel, *L'Eudémonisme social* [*Contre-histoire de la philosophie*, vol. 5] (Paris: Grasset, 2008).

Onfray, Michel, *Les Freudiens hérétiques* [*Contre-histoire de la philosophie*, vol. 8] (Paris: Grasset, 2013).

Onfray, Michel, *Le Songe d'Eichmann* (Paris: Galilée, 2008).

Onfray, Michel, *Les sagesses antiques: De Leucippe à Diogène d'Oenanda* [*Contre-histoire de la philosophie*, vol. 1] (Paris: Grasset, 2006).

Onfray, Michel, *Les ultras des Lumières* [*Contre-histoire de la philosophie*, vol. 4] (Paris: Grasset, 2007).

Onfray, Michel, *Manifeste hédoniste* (Paris: Éditions Autrement, 2011).

Ottmann, Henning, *Geschichte des politischen Denkens*, vol. 1, *Die Griechen*, part 2, *Von Platon bis zum Hellenismus* (Stuttgart and Weimar: Metzler, 2001).

Owen, David, *Nietzsche, Politics, Modernity* (London: Sage, 1995).

Partenie, Catalin and Tom Rockmore (eds), *Heidegger and Plato: Toward Dialogue* (Evanston, IL: Northwestern University Press, 2005).

Pascal, Blaise, *Pensées*, trans. A.J. Krailsheimer (Harmondsworth: Penguin, 1966).

Patrides, C.A. (ed.), *The Cambridge Platonists* (Cambridge: Cambridge University Press, 1980).

Patton, Paul (ed.), *Nietzsche, Feminism and Political Theory* (London and New York: Routledge, 1993).

Pausanias, *Description of Greece*, Books I–II, trans. W.H.S. Jones (Cambridge, MA and London: Harvard University Press, 1918).

Peden, Knox, *Spinoza Contra Phenomenology: French Rationalism from Cavaillès to Deleuze* (Stanford, CA: Stanford University Press, 2014)

Pindar, *The Odes, Including the Principal Fragments*, trans. John Sandys (London; New York: Heinemann; Putnam, 1927).

Pinkard, Terry, *German Philosophy 1760–1860: The Legacy of Idealism* (Cambridge: Cambridge University Press, 2002).

Plotinus, *Ennead IV*, trans. A.H. Armstrong (Cambridge, MA; London: Harvard University Press, 1984).

Plotinus, *The Enneads*, trans. Stephen MacKenna, 4th edn, rev. B.S. Page (London: Faber and Faber, 1969).

Plotinus, *The Enneads*, trans. Stephen MacKenna, abridged John Dillon (Harmondsworth: Penguin, 1991).

Plotinus, *The Essential Plotinus*, ed. and trans. Elmer O'Brian (Indianapolis, IN: Hackett, 1964).

Pöggeler, Otto, *Neue Wege mit Heidegger* (Freiburg im Breisgau and Munich: Alber, 1991).

Popper, Karl, *Conjectures and Refutations: The Growth of Scientific Knowledge* [1963] (London and New York: Routledge, 2002).

Popper, Karl, *The Open Society and Its Enemies*, 2 vols (London: Routledge, 1945).

Popper, Karl, *The Open Society and Its Enemies* (Princeton, NJ and Oxford: Princeton University Press, 2013).

Popper, Karl R., *The Open Society and Its Enemies*, vol. 1, *The Spell of Plato*, vol. 2, *The High Tide of Prophecy: Hegel, Marx, and the Aftermath* (London: Routledge, 1945).

Porphyre [Porphyry], *L'antre des nymphes dans l'Odyssée*, trans. Yann Le Lay (Lagrasse: Verdier, 1989).

Porphyry, *On the Cave of the Nymphs*, trans. Robert Lamberton (Barrytown, NY: Station Hill Press, 1983).

Proclus, *Commentary on the First Alcibiades*, ed. L.G. Westerink, trans. William O'Neill (Westbury: Prometheus Trust, 2011).

Proclus, *The Theology of Plato*, trans. Thomas Taylor [TTS, vol. 8] (Westbury: Prometheus Trust, 1995).

Rabinow, Paul (ed.), *The Foucault Reader* (Harmondsworth: Penguin, 1984).

Radcliffe G. Edmonds III, *Myths of the Underworld Journey: Plato, Aristophanes, and the "Orphic" Gold Tablets* (New York: Cambridge University Press, 2004).

Raffoul, François and David Pettigrew (eds), *Heidegger and Practical Philosophy* (Albany, NY: State University of New York Press, 2002).

Ralkowski, Mark A., *Heidegger's Platonism* (London and New York: Continuum, 2009).

Ramey, Joshua, *The Hermetic Deleuze: Philosophy and Spiritual Ordeal* (Durham and London: Duke University Press, 2012).

Raulff, Ulrich, *Kreis ohne Meister: Stefan Georges Nachleben* (Munich: dtv, 2012).

Rebenich, Stefan, "'Dass ein strahl von Hellas auf uns fiel': Platon im George-Kreis," *George-Jahrbuch* 7 (2008–2009), 115–141.

Reed, T.J., *Thomas Mann: The Uses of Tradition* (Oxford: Clarendon Press, 1974).

Resch, Jessica, *Odysseus' Wandlung im Nachkriegsdeutschland: Die Figur des griechischen Helden in der deutschsprachigen Erzählprosa* (Marburg: Tectum, 2012).

Ricoeur, Paul, *Freud and Philosophy: An Essay on Interpretation*, trans. Denis Savage (New Haven and London: Yale University Press, 1970).

Rippere, Vickey, *Schiller and "Alienation"* (Berne: Lang, 1981).

Robert, Peri and Peter Sutch, *An Introduction to Political Thought: A Conceptual Toolkit*, 2nd edn (Edinburgh: Edinburgh University Press, 2012).

Rockmore, Tom, *Cognition: An Introduction to Hegel's "Phenomenology of Spirit"* (Berkeley, Los Angeles, and London: University of California Press, 1997).

Rockmore, Tom, *Heidegger and French Philosophy: Humanism, Antihumanism and Being* (London and New York: Routledge, 1995).

Rosen, Allen D., *Kant's Theory of Justice* (Ithaca and London: Cornell University Press, 1993).

Rosen, Michael and Jonathan Wolff, *Political Thought* (Oxford: Oxford University Press, 1999).

Rosenblatt, Helena, "On the 'Misogyny' of Jean-Jacques Rousseau: The Letter to d'Alembert in Historical Context," *French Historical Studies* 25, no. 1 (Winter 2002), 91–114.

Russell, Bertrand, *A History of Western Philosophy* (London: Unwin, 1985).

Safranksi, Rüdiger, *Martin Heidegger: Between Good and Evil*, trans. Ewald Osers (Cambridge, MA: Harvard University Press, 1998).

Sallis, John, *Platonic Legacies* (Albany, NY: State University of New York Press, 2004).

Sartre, Jean-Paul, "Paris Under the Occupation", *Sartre Studies International* 4, no. 2 (1998), 1–15 (2–3).

Sasaki, Takeshi, "Plato and *Politeia* in Twentieth-Century Politics," *Études platoniciennes* 9 (2012), 147–160.

Schiller, Friedrich, *On the Aesthetic Education of Man in a Series of Letters*, ed. and trans. Elizabeth M. Wilkinson and L.A. Willoughby, 2nd edn (Oxford: Clarendon Press, 1982).

Schleiermacher, Friedrich, *Aus Schleiermachers Leben: In Briefen*, 4 vols (Berlin: Reimer, 1860–1861)

Schleiermacher, Friedrich, *Introduction to the Dialogues of Plato*, trans. William Dobson (Cambridge; London: Deighton; Parker, 1836; reprinted New York: Arno Press, 1973).

Schmidt, Dennis J., *On Germans and Other Greeks: Tragedy and Ethical Life* (Bloomington and Indianapolis: Indiana University Press, 2001).

Schmidt, James, "The *Eclipse of Reason* and the End of the Frankfurt School in America," *New German Critique* 34 (2007), 47–76.

Schönhart, Korinna, *Wissen und Visionen: Theorie und Politik der Ökonomen im Stefan George-Kreis* (Berlin: Akademie-Verlag, 2009).

Schulman, Alex, *The Secular Contract: The Politics of Enlightenment* (New York, NY: Continuum, 2011).

Schulte-Bockholt, Alfried, "A Neo-Marxist Explanation of Organized Crime," *Critical Criminology* 10 (2001), 225–242.

Schumann, Karl, *Selected Papers on Renaissance Philosophy and on Thomas Hobbes*, ed. Piet Steenbakkers and Cees Leijenhorst (Dordrecht: Springer, 2004).

Schwabe, Christian, *Politische Theorie 1: Von Platon bis Locke*, 2nd edn (Paderborn: Fink, 2010).

Schwabe, Christian, *Politische Theorie 2: Von Rousseau bis Rawls*, 3rd edn (Paderborn: Fink, 2013).

Seaford, Richard, "Monetisation and the Genesis of the Western Subject," *Historical Materialism* 20, no. 1 (2012), 78–102.

Seaford, Richard, *Money and the Early Greek Mind: Homer, Philosophy, Tragedy* (Cambridge: Cambridge University Press, 2004).

Seidel, George Joseph, *Martin Heidegger and the Pre-Socratics: An Introduction to His Thought* (Lincoln, NE: University of Nebraska Press, 1984).

Seneca, *Moral Essays*, trans. John W. Basore (London: Heinemann, 1928–1935).

Shapiro, Gary, "Peirce's Critique of Hegel's Phenomenology and Dialectic," *Transactions of the Charles S. Peirce Society* 17, no. 3 (Summer, 1981), 269–275.

Shar, Adam, *Heidegger's Hut* (Boston, MA: MIT Press, 2006).

Sheehan, Thomas (ed.), *Heidegger: The Man and the Thinker* (New Brunswick, NJ and London: Transaction Publishers, 2009).

Shelburne, Walter A., *Mythos and Logos in the Thought of Carl Jung* (Albany, NY: State University of New York Press, 1988).

Shield, Christopher (ed.), *The Oxford Handbook of Aristotle* (Oxford and New York: Oxford University Press, 2012).

Silver, Jeffrey H., "Wrongdoing and Ignorance: Socrates Defended," *Philosophy Today* 40, no. 4 (Winter 1996), 496–503.

Siorvantes, Lucas, *Proclus: Neo-Platonic Philosophy and Science* (New Haven and London: Yale University Press, 1996).

Skoll, Geoffrey L., *Dialectics in Social Thought: The Present Crisis* (New York: Palgrave Macmillan, 2014).

Sløk, Johannes, *Devotional Language*, trans. Henrik Mossin (Berlin and New York: de Gruyter, 1996).

Sloterdijk, Peter, *Critique of Cynical Reason*, trans. Michael Eldred (Minneapolis: University of Minnesota Press, 1987).

Solomon, Robert C. and Kathleen M. Higgins (eds), *The Age of German Idealism* [*Routledge History of Philosophy*, vol. 6] (London and New York: Routledge, 1993).

Spengler, Oswald, *The Decline of the West*, trans. Charles Francis Atkinson (New York: Knopf, 1926 and 1928).

Spinoza, *Selections*, ed. J. Wild (London: Scribner, 1928).

Spranger, Eduard, "März 1933," *Die Erziehung: Monatsschrift für den Zusammenhang von Kultur und Erziehung* 8 (1932–1933), no. 7 (April 1933), 401–408.

Steinberger, Peter J. (ed.), *Readings in Classical Political Thought* (Indianapolis, IN: Hackett, 2000).

Steiner, Rudolf, *Christianity as Mystical Fact*, trans. Andrew Welburn (Hudson, NY: Anthroposophic Press, 1997).

Stepelevich, Lawrence S. (ed.). *The Young Hegelians: An Anthology* (Cambridge: Cambridge University Press, 1983).

Stephenson, R.H., *Studies in Weimar Classicism: Writing as Symbolic Form* (Oxford, Bern, and Berlin: Lang, 2010).

Stern, Fritz, *The Politics of Cultural Despair: A Study in the Rise of the German Ideology* (Berkeley, Los Angeles, and London: University of California Press, 1961).

Stern, Paul, *Knowledge and Politics in Plato's "Theaetetus"* (Cambridge: Cambridge University Press, 2007).

Stern, Robert, *Hegel and the "Phenomenology of Spirit"* (London and New York: Routledge, 2002).

Sternberger, Dolf, *Drei Wurzeln der Politik*, 2 vols (Frankfurt am Main: Insel, 1978).

Stewart, John Alexander (trans.), *Myths of Plato* (London: Macmillan, 1905).

Stewart, Jon (ed.), *The Hegel Myths and Legends* (Evanston, IL: Northwestern University Press, 1996).

Stirling, James Hutchison, *The Secret of Hegel: Being the Hegelian System in Origin, Principle, Form and Matter* (London: Longman, Green, Longman, Roberts, & Green, 1865).

Strassler, Robert B. (ed.), *The Landmark Herodotus: The Histories* (London: Quercus, 2008), 503).

Strassler, Robert B. (ed.), *The Landmark Thucydides: A Comprehensive Guide to the Peloponnesian War* (New York: Free Press, 1996).

Strauss, Leo, *Gesammelte Schriften*, vol. 2, *Philosophie und Gesetz: Frühe Schriften*, ed. Heinrich Meier (Stuttgart: Metzler, 1997).

Strauss, Leo, *Persecution and the Art of Writing* [1952] (Chicago and London: University of Chicago Press, 1988),

Strauss, Leo, *The City and Man* (Chicago and London: University of Chicago Press, 1964), 19–20.

Strauss, Leo, *The Early Writings (1921–1932)*, ed. and trans. Michael Zank (Albany, NY: State University of New York Press, 2002).

Strauss, Leo, *What Is Political Philosophy? And Other Studies* (Chicago: University of Chicago Press, 2001).

Strube, Julian, "Die Erfindung des esoterischen Nationalsozialismus im Zeichen der Schwarzen Sonne," *Zeitschrift für Religionswissenschaft* 30, no. 2 (2012), 223–268.

Syse, Henrik, "Plato: The Necessity of War, the Quest for Peace," *Journal of Military Ethics* 1, no. 1 (2002), 36–44.

Taminiaux, Jacques, "The Platonic Roots of Heidegger's Political Thought," *European Journal of Political Theory* 6, no. 1 (January 2007), 11–29.

Tanner, R.G., "ΔΙΑΝΟΙΑ and Plato's Cave," *Classical Quarterly* 20, no. 1 (1970), 81–91.

Taureck, Bernhard H.F., *Nietzsche und der Faschismus: Ein Politikum* (Leipzig: Reclam, 2000).

Thomas Aquinas, *Questiones Disputatae de Veritate: Questions 10–20*, trans. James V. McGlynn (Chicago: Henry Regnery, 1953).

Thucydides, *The Peloponnesian War*, ed. Walter Blanco and Jennifer Tolbert Roberts, trans. Walter Blanco (New York and London: Norton, 1998).

Tomin, Julius, "Socratic Midwifery," *The Classical Quarterly* [NS] 37, no. 1, 1987, 97–102.

Ustinova, Yulia, *Caves and the Ancient Greek Mind: Descending Underground in the Search for Ultimate Truth* (Oxford and New York: Oxford University Press, 2009).

Vallentin, Berthold, *Gespräche mit Stefan George 1902–1931* (Amsterdam: Castrum Peregrini, 1967).

Verene, Donald Phillip, *Hegel's Absolute: An Introduction to Reading the "Phenomenology of Spirit"* (Albany, NY: State University of New York Press, 2007).

Vergely, Bertrand, *Cassirer: La Politique du juste* (Paris: Michalon, 1998).

Vierecke, Andreas, Bernd Mayerhofer and Franz Kohut, *dtv-Atlas Politik*, illus. Werner Wildermuth, 2nd edn (Munich: dtv, 2011).

Vischer, F.T., *Auch Einer: Eine Reisebekanntschaft* (Stuttgart and Leipzig: Deutsche Verlags-Anstalt, 1900).

Vogel, Cornelia J. de, *Rethinking Plato and Platonism* (Leiden: Brill, 1986).

Waite, Geoff, *Nietzsche's Corps/e: Aesthetics, Politics, Prophecy, or: The Spectacular Technoculture of Everyday Life* (Durham, NC and London: Duke University Press, 1996).

Walbridge, John, *The Leaven of the Ancients: Suhrawardi and the Heritage of the Greeks* (Albany, NY: State University of New York Press, 1999).

Wallis, R.T., *Neoplatonism*, 2nd edn (London: Bristol Classical Press, 1995), 111.

Ware, Robert Bruce, "Freedom as Justice: Hegel's Interpretation of Plato's *Republic*," *Metaphilosophy* 31, no. 3 (April 2000), 287–310.

Warren, Mark, *Nietzsche and Political Thought* (Cambridge, MA and London: MIT Press, 1988).

Weber, Max, *Gesammelte Aufsätze zur Wissenschaftslehre* (Tübingen: Mohr (Siebeck), 1988).

Weber, Max, *On the Methodology of the Social Sciences*, ed. and trans. Edward A. Shils and Henry A. Finch (Glencoe, IL: Free Press, 1949).

Westphal, Kenneth, "Hegel on Political Representation: Laborers, Corporations, and the Monarch," *The Owl of Minerva* 25, no. 1 (1993), 111–116.

Westphal, Kenneth R. (ed.), *The Blackwell Guide to Hegel's "Phenomenology of Spirit"* (Malden, MA and Oxford: Wiley-Blackwell, 2009).

Whittaker, Thomas, *The Neo-Platonists: A Study in the History of Hellenism*, 2nd edn (Cambridge: Cambridge University Press, 1918).

Wiedmann, Franz, *Hegel: An Illustrated Biography*, trans. Joachim Neugroschel (New York: Pegasus, 1968).

Wild, John D., *Plato's Modern Enemies and the Theory of Natural Law* (Chicago: University of Chicago Press, 1953).

Wild, John D., *Plato's Theory of Man: An Introduction to the Realistic Philosophy of Culture* (Cambridge, MA: Harvard University Press, 1946).

Williams, David Lay, *Rousseau's Platonic Enlightenment* (University Park, PA: Pennsylvania State University Press, 2007).

Williams, James D. (ed.), *An Introduction to Classical Rhetoric: Essential Readings* (Chichester, West Sussex: Wiley-Blackwell, 2009).

Williams, Paul, *Only Apparently Real: The World of Philip K. Dick* (New York: Arbor House, 1986).

Williamson, Elizabeth, Anne Riches and Malcolm Higgs, *Glasgow* [*The Buildings of Scotland*] (London: Penguin, 1990).

Wolin, Richard, *Heidegger's Children: Hannah Arendt, Karl Löwith, Hans Jonas, and Herbert Marcuse* (Princeton, NJ and Oxford: Princeton University Press, 2001).

Wolin, Richard, *The Seduction of Unreason: The Intellectual Romance with Fascism from Nietzsche to Postmodernism* (Princeton, NJ and London: Princeton University Press, 2004).

Woodward, Linda H. (ed.), *Selections from the Prometheus Trust Conferences 2006–2010* (Dilton Marsh, Westbury: Prometheus Trust, 2013).

Wrathall, Mark, "Heidegger on Plato, Truth, and Unconcealment: The 1931–32 Lecture on *The Essence of Truth*," *Inquiry: An Interdisciplinary Journal of Philosophy* 47, no. 5 (2004), 443–463.

Wright, John Henry, "The Origin of Plato's Cave," *Harvard Studies in Classical Philology* 17 (1906), 131–142.

Young, Julian, *Heidegger, Philosophy, Nazism* (Cambridge: Cambridge University Press, 1997).

Zajonc, Arthur, *Catching the Light: The Entwined History of Light and Mind* (New York and Oxford: Oxford University Press, 1993).

Ziolkowski, Theodore, *German Romanticism and Its Institutions* (Princeton, NJ: Princeton University Press, 1990).

Index

© The Editor(s) (if applicable) and The Author(s) 2019
P. Bishop, *German Political Thought and the Discourse of Platonism*,
https://doi.org/10.1007/978-3-030-04510-4

Printed by Printforce, the Netherlands